From Goodwill to Grunge

STUDIES IN UNITED STATES CULTURE

Grace Elizabeth Hale, *series editor*

Series Editorial Board
Sara Blair, University of Michigan
Janet Davis, University of Texas at Austin
Matthew Guterl, Brown University
Franny Nudelman, Carleton University
Leigh Raiford, University of California, Berkeley
Bryant Simon, Temple University

Studies in United States Culture publishes provocative books that explore U.S. culture in its many forms and spheres of influence. Bringing together big ideas, brisk prose, bold storytelling, and sophisticated analysis, books published in the series serve as an intellectual meeting ground where scholars from different disciplinary and methodological perspectives can build common lines of inquiry around matters such as race, ethnicity, gender, sexuality, power, and empire in an American context.

JENNIFER LE ZOTTE

From Goodwill to Grunge
A History of Secondhand Styles and
Alternative Economies

The University of North Carolina Press *Chapel Hill*

This book was published with the assistance of the Authors Fund of the University of North Carolina Press.

© 2017 Jennifer Le Zotte
All rights reserved
Set in Arno Pro by Westchester Publishing Services
Manufactured in the United States of America

The University of North Carolina Press has been a member of the Green Press Initiative since 2003.

Library of Congress Cataloging-in-Publication Data

Names: Le Zotte, Jennifer, author.
Title: From Goodwill to grunge : a history of secondhand styles and alternative economies / Jennifer Le Zotte.
Other titles: Studies in United States culture.
Description: Chapel Hill : University of North Carolina Press, [2017] | Series: Studies in United States culture | Includes bibliographical references and index.
Identifiers: LCCN 2016024923 | ISBN 9781469631899 (cloth : alk. paper) | ISBN 9781469631905 (pbk : alk. paper) | ISBN 9781469631912 (ebook)
Subjects: LCSH: Secondhand trade—Social aspects—United States. | Vintage Clothing—Social aspects—United States. | Thrift shops—Social Aspects—United States. | Used clothing industry—Social aspects—United States.
Classification: LCC HF5482 .L42 2017 | DDC 381/.190973—dc23 LC record available at https://lccn.loc.gov/2016024923

Cover illustrations: top, © Shutterstock/hifashion; bottom, © Shutterstock/Anthony Hall.

For Melita and Bud Gardner, my mom and dad

Contents

Acknowledgments xi

Introduction 1

CHAPTER ONE
Thrift Stores and the Gilded Age Shopper 17

CHAPTER TWO
Dressing Dada and the Rise of Flea Markets 52

CHAPTER THREE
Garage Sales and Suburban Subversiveness 92

CHAPTER FOUR
The Invention of Vintage Clothing 122

CHAPTER FIVE
Elective Poverty and Postwar Politics 153

CHAPTER SIX
Genderfuck and the Boyfriend Look 183

CHAPTER SEVEN
Connoisseurs of Trash in a World Full of It 214

EPILOGUE
Popping Tags in the Twenty-First Century 239

Notes 245
Index 317

Figures

1.1 Salvation Army Industrial Homes pushcart, New York City, circa 1900 30
1.2 Cover of *The Goodwill Magazine*, Milwaukee edition, 1924 35
1.3 Major Emma Bown with tenement child and a fellow "slum sister," circa 1890 41
1.4 Evangeline Booth posing in rags with a pedal harp, circa 1910 44
1.5 Promotional pamphlet, circa 1920 50
2.1 Baroness Elsa Von Freytag-Loringhoven working as a model, 1915 64
2.2 Merchants and shoppers along Maxwell Street, Chicago, 1917 72
2.3 Daddy Stovepipe on Maxwell Street, Chicago, November 1959 73
2.4 Man Ray, "Marcel Duchamp as Rrose Sélavy" 88
3.1 The Ericksons' garage sale, *Life* magazine, 18 August 1972 93
3.2 "Use It Up—Wear It Out—Make It Do!" poster 1941–45 99
4.1 Sue Salzman posing for "Raccoon Swoon," *Life* magazine, 9 September 1957 129
4.2 Reprints of various vintage raccoon coat ads, *Life* magazine, 9 September 1957 130
4.3 "Jane Ormsby-Gore: Fashion Original," *Vogue* (U.K.), January 1966 146
4.4 The Charlatans, 1964 150
5.1 Advertisement for Truth and Soul Fashion, *Rags*, February 1971 180
6.1 José Sarria performing at the Black Cat, circa 1963 187
6.2 José Sarria dressed "straight" on a promotional flyer when running for city and county supervisor, 7 November 1961 190
6.3 Jack Smith, *Untitled*, circa 1958–62 195
6.4 The Cockettes, circa 1970 201

6.5   Sylvester James, circa 1970   204
6.6   Patti Smith as Bob Dylan, 1970   209
6.7   Jean Genet, 1948   212
7.1   Kurt Cobain on the cover of *Request* magazine, November 1993   217

Acknowledgments

I was just ten years old when my goth-punk older sister introduced me to my first thrift store. Tucked among live oaks in my small north Florida hometown, the musty, cramped rooms of the shotgun shack that housed the Methodist Church Bargain Box became one of my favorite places. Prices matched those of Salvation Army stores from a century before, and the variety of its contents afforded me endless hours of delight, inspiring an early interest in material culture, history, and fashion. My sister, whose style I desperately admired, relied on such venues. She wore faded band T-shirts, secondhand dresses and skirts (preferably black or 1930s-style floral printed), pet-rat-nibbled stockings, Army-Navy surplus boots, and jewelry crafted from long lengths of the stainless steel chain ball strings liberated from the tanks of public restroom toilets.

As for me, I was born too late—as the Violent Femmes song goes—for such extravagances, and often mourned my near-miss of post-punk fashion. I entered high school the month Nirvana released *Nevermind*. Kurt Cobain killed himself on the eve of my sixteenth birthday. In between those events, I spent most Wednesday and Saturday mornings—the Bargain Box's only operating hours—scouring its oddball offerings. I collected flannels, drab-colored air force T-shirts, men's suit vests, babydoll dresses, and newsboy caps one year, and long polyester paisley gowns and ugly platform boots the next. At first, I was sometimes the only one there, but that changed; throughout much of the 1990s, Saturday mornings found a queue of young, Manic-Panicked shoppers crowding the Box's slant-floored front stoop. Watching the elderly Methodist volunteers sweetly pack the selections of the motley teenaged crew into recycled Piggly-Wiggly grocery bags struck me as a pleasant but curious disjuncture.

An abiding interest in the value of secondhand clothing and my own awareness of the cultural meaning of dress began at the Bargain Box, and so did this book. Its final fruition, however, owes to the generosity and support of too many people to possibly count. Early in my academic career, Brian Ward's enthusiasm, Jack Davis's friendly encouragement, and Jeffrey Adler's formidable critiques provided me with the variety of support needed to begin the endeavor. Allan Megill, Cindy Aron, Eric Lott, Alon Confino, and Peter Onuf read my work, inspired my research, and helped shape my philosophical approach to academia. Grace Elizabeth Hale has been one the greatest advocates of my postdoctoral work; our mutual intellectual and personal respect has only grown since my graduation from the University of Virginia.

For invigorating conference experiences, and for thoughtful encouragement and critique of material appearing in this book, I would like to thank Alison Isenberg, Wendy Woloson, Susan Strasser, Larry Glickman, Diane Winston, Helen Sheumaker, Jonathan Z. S. Pollack, Ted Ownby, and Tara Saunders. I am especially grateful to Bryant Simon and Deirdre Clemente, whose clarifying advice on this entire manuscript helped shape the final product. Deirdre has offered me much more than her inestimable insight into fashion history (and some really cool sources); I've relied on her level-headed advice and infectious energy and confidence through numerous crises. The generous and prolific Daniel Horowitz not only provided me with some of the most valuable feedback on my writing but also gave me an example of unparalleled collegial kindness by broadening his concern for my success to include every aspect of my life. Quite simply, he is the model of a scholar and a mentor to which I aspire.

Secondhand commerce has no central archive or easily accessible records, so my research required the patient expertise of many archivists, including those at the Metropolitan Museum of Art, the Fashion Institute of Technology, the New York City Municipal Archives, and the San Francisco GLBT Historical Society. Scott Bedio, Susan Mitchem, and Tyler Boenecke at The Salvation Army National Archives welcomed several return visits and innumerable follow-up e-mails. I am also grateful to Jerry Stokes and Gail Barron from the National Flea Market Association, as well as former Cockettes Fayette Hauser and Rumi Missabu for sharing their knowledge, memories, and photos of secondhand commerce and culture, and Gregory Pickup for sending me a copy of his unreleased film, featuring members of the Cockettes and Allen Ginsberg, among others. I would also like to thank all who helped me acquire the images in this book, including Tyler Boenecke at the Salvation Army, Joanna Black with the San Francisco GLBT History Society, and Laurel Baker with the Mathewson-IGT Knowledge Center at the University of Nevada, Reno. Some material from chapters 1 and 2 first appeared in *Winterthur Portfolios* and *New England Journal*, and those journals' incisive editors helped me to understand and better articulate the historical importance of my ideas. Mark Simpson-Vos with the University of North Carolina Press has demonstrated his patient conviction in the contents of this book for years now and has made the publication process a pleasure. Without him, his colleagues

Lucas Church and Jessica Newman, and a host of copy editors, this book clearly would not be possible.

Looking back at the process of becoming a historian, I would never have survived the rarefied world of doctoral work at Mr. Jefferson's school without heated arguments, cold drinks, and spontaneous wrestling matches with my grad school colleagues Jon Grinspan, Michael Caires, and Kobi Kabalek. Hamutal Jackobson Girshengorn and Oscar Ax helped me develop my ideas—and vent my frustrations—at critical times. Amidst the beautiful seasons and delicious restaurants of Charlottesville, Virginia, Erin O'Donnell, Rachel Bennett, Eglantine Morvant, Wes King, and Laura Newberry sustained me by talking about things other than work. For providing necessary balance to academic life at just the right time, the Charlottesville Derby Dames will always have a special place in my heart—and other muscles. Thanks also to Erich Nunn and Shaun Cullen, whose academic discourse and friendship at and since UVa have been a source of inspiration.

I am very grateful to the colleagues who have made my peripatetic academic path enjoyable and edifying. Without Bryce and Margo Beemer, Holly Karibo, Michael and Whitney Landis, Chris Drohan, and Chris Hickman, I would have passed a couple of lonely years; instead, I was able to grow as a scholar and have some fun while weathering April snowstorms and ducking May tornadoes. Chris Hickman, who offered some very thorough and helpful edits on chapter 1, joins the many other friends and colleagues who have helped steer the course of this book, including most recently, Emily Hobson. Though my time at the University of Nevada, Reno, has been short, I feel at home thanks to the support and friendship of Emilie Meyer, James Mardock, Rachel Van Pelt, Justin Lewis, Katherine Fusco, Angie Bennett, Casey Bell, Dan Morse, Ned Schoolman, and Erica Westhoff. Mixing motherhood with intellectual, creative pursuits is no mean task, and for solidarity, practical help, and everyday wisdom, I would also like to thank Courtney Cole, Stacey "Constance" Peters, Michal Shuldman, and Gwynne Johnson.

For any accomplishments in life, I owe fortitude and self-confidence to that amazing group of women I've been privileged to know since girlhood. Among other things, Andrea Fehl, Lisa Donovan, Erin O'Donnell, Glory Anna Dole, and Anne Philip thoroughly abetted my teenaged obsession with discarded clothing. Since then, I've watched them leave our little Bayou town and become amazing people—innovative, compassionate, motivated, and ever-original in their goals. Knowing they have my back has emboldened me to make important mistakes and set unrealistic goals. Sharing in Lisa's ambition (and unparalleled baked goods), Erin's unswerving friendship, and Glory's self-acknowledgment has been one of the deepest pleasures of my adult life.

Long before adolescence, my parents, to whom I wholeheartedly dedicate this book, provoked and encouraged my lifelong goal of writing. Teachers and scholars themselves, they encouraged a healthy love of (sometimes contentious) conversation and, especially, of the written word. They also provided me with a joyous, messy wealth of brilliant, loving siblings. Sasha Von Dassow, Sumi Von Dassow, Antonia Gardner, Chris Gardner, and Paul Gardner formed the inspirational and competitive environment of my childhood and have each, in various ways, offered me support and encouragement in my intellectual pursuits (as well as comfort and razzing during less lofty ordeals). Doctors, musicians, potters, and engineers, my brothers and sisters showed me that there is nothing members of this family can't do, and do well. Antonia has been my best friend and most reliable confidante—and if she had not introduced ten-year-old me to the Bargain Box, and taught me the fine art of cultivating personal style on a shoestring budget, I may never have been fascinated by this topic in the first place. My brother Paul's financial generosity and facilitation of at-least annual family reunions has served as the most consistent fellowship throughout the long writing of this book. I am beyond fortunate to have the confidence borne of being surrounded by people who steadfastly believe in my abilities and my vision. Also, if the reader finds buried in these pages the remnants of terrible, irresistible puns, they get some of the blame, too.

My family doesn't end there. Everybody who knows me agrees I've won the in-law lottery. The love and support of Ron, Lynn, Jen, Philip, Charlie, and Will Ragain have added stability and hilarity—as well as great food and drink—to my life in the years I've been lucky enough to know them. And finally, this accomplishment owes most of all to the best life partner I could possibly have. Nathan Ragain's scholarly integrity, intellectual devotion, and passion for teaching humbles me, inspiring me to try harder at my craft every day. At the same time, his love, compassion, sacrifice, and domestic care makes it logistically possible for me to push myself. His delicious cooking, reliable parenting, enduring sense of humor, and even temper have sustained me through the hardest and best years of my life, through yearly cross-country moves, personal disappointments, those horrendous bed bugs, and our usually sweet and hilarious son's recent temperamental months. Tantrums notwithstanding, Theodore Givens Ragain has given everything a fresh and better context these past four years. As of this writing, our second son urges me (with powerful rib kicks and cervix punches) to finish this book so he can join in the mayhem.

From Goodwill to Grunge

Introduction

Modern consumer society is symbolized at least as much by the mountains of rubbish, the garage and jumble sales, the columns of advertisements of second-hand goods for sale and the second-hand car lots, as it is by the ubiquitous propaganda on behalf of new goods.
—Colin Campbell, *The Romantic Ethic and the Spirit of Modern Consumerism*

In 1906, the wistful-eyed, auburn-haired commander of the United States Salvation Army took center stage at Carnegie Hall. Flanked by a troop of "slum sisters" wearing the torn gingham dresses of tenement wives, Evangeline Booth regaled wealthy theatergoers with tales of the charitable organization's work among the poor, especially her own time spent living in tenements, proselytizing to the unfortunate. Booth glamorized the labor in song and sensationalized the clothing with her demeanor.[1] The *New York Times* described her outfit and bearing as though she were famed Broadway dancer and actor Irene Castle: the diminutive Commander Booth wore "a tartan shawl, a tattered print skirt, and broken-heeled shoes laced with string."[2]

Booth, the wealthy youngest daughter of the founder of the Salvation Army, frequently used cross-class dress to publicize the Christian humility of the group's evangelical "soldiers," as well as to satisfy a personal desire for drama.[3] In the musical display at Carnegie Hall, theatrical ragwear made manifest the Salvation Army soldiers' sacrifice of worldly pleasures—including fashion, which was an increasingly important part of Gilded Age life. By the end of the nineteenth century, all of the Salvation Army's soldiers were required to wear a uniform, a practice intended to announce separation from secular life, distinction from conventional Protestantism, and unity within the organization. Before the Army itself produced and sold standard uniform garments, Salvationists patched together uniforms from anything that "suggested the soldier": hussars' coats, artillery regiment garb, helmets from the Household Troop Bands, or even just yachting caps. In other words, the first Salvation Army uniforms also used secondhand items.[4]

Conveniently for early Salvationists, the Carnegie Hall performers, and real-life slum workers, the Salvation Army had easy access to enormous stores of old clothes. In 1906, both the Salvation Army and Boston's Goodwill Industries were building charitable salvaging businesses reliant on the acquisition, repair, and resale of secondhand household goods and clothing. Those first "thrift" stores would permanently alter the dynamics between charity, labor, and profit—and become a central part of a vast resource for generations of sartorial experimentalists.[5]

Fast-forward nearly ninety years to another New York City stage. At Sony Music Studios in November 1993, Nirvana's lead singer, Kurt Cobain, slouched in the seat of a cheap-looking office swivel chair, strumming his guitar to some of the band's lesser-known songs and Lead Belly and David Bowie covers. Cobain's unwashed blond hair skimmed a stubbled chin, his light-colored jeans bore visible stains, and the floppy laces of his classic black Converses looked gray. Over a screen-printed T-shirt from a feminist punk band called Frightwig, Cobain wore a pastel-striped, button-down shirt from the perfectly outdated mid-1980s, rumpled and undone.[6] A beige-colored cardigan—lumpy, stretched-out, pilled and fuzzy—topped off the "grunge" look emulated by the thousands of enamored viewers of MTV's *Unplugged*, which first aired in December 1993.[7]

For Cobain, grunge—the music and the style—both referenced his origins from an impoverished rural Washington town and presented a cultivated cynicism about self-image and artistic identity.[8] Secondhand clothing was so essential to the oft-copied style that some Salvation Army stores advertised themselves as "grunge headquarters."[9] In the 1992 film *Singles*, which depicts the Seattle-born grunge music scene, the establishing shot zooms past the iconic Space Needle and focuses in on a sidewalk view of an Army-Navy surplus store.[10] The original adherents of grunge style self-consciously emphasized secondhand dress, as did the eager, adolescent fans tuning into representative music videos and crowding concert venues.[11]

Both Booth and Cobain used secondhand clothing to showcase their public positions—as a philanthropic business leader and as a wildly influential rock musician. The motives of the wearers and the perception of the viewing public differed from across the decades, but both performers understood and leveraged the powerful meanings of pre-owned goods, meanings that changed along with the growth of secondhand economies. The "branding" of certain used clothing as fashionable and valuable—a slow and lengthy process—must be understood through an exploration of both supply and demand. Over the course of the century, the sale of used goods in the United States grew from a series of suspiciously regarded professions on the economic margins of society to include multimillion-dollar businesses such as Goodwill Industries thrift stores, Buffalo Exchange consignment shops, and enormous, circus-like flea markets.[12] Similarly, pre-owned cloth materials went from heralding disease and poverty to signifying cultivated cynicism and rebellious creativity for white, middle-class Nirvana fans. Alterations in the meanings of pre-owned materials highlighted anxieties surrounding class status, an erratic economy, and the growth in the importance of carefully curated identities.

In studying the growth of secondhand markets and styles, this work expands the commonly understood roles of women, immigrants, and minorities in establishing the economic and cultural landscape of modernizing America; tracks the sentimentalization of poverty; examines the apparent contradictions and persisting legacies of postwar social movements; and charts the rise of a queer style sensibility in twentieth-century musical performances. A simple narrative of appropriation does not explain the ascent of secondhand styles or the increase in monetary exchange related to secondhand materials. Drag queens, titled nobility, musicians, poor immigrants, corporate moguls, displaced black southerners, filmmakers, housewives, Ivy League students, and social activists all participated in the long-term project of elevating the value of certain discarded materials in a clothing-centered society. The destitute and the rich, the liberal and the conservative, all at various points helped promote the value of used materials. The cultural capital of the secondhand sector rose alongside its monetary gains and industry standardization, attendant to changes in the commercial meaning of "novelty" amidst expanding firsthand production. Thus, grunge dress with its widespread accessibility, gender-role deviance, cross-class identification, and ironic inflections, referenced a century of secondhand exchange.

Relating that history counters a decades-long scholarly privileging of firsthand markets and consumption, and established scholarly habits of separating supply from demand, and commerce from culture. Ever since economist and social critic Thorstein Veblen coined "conspicuous consumption" to apply to the spending habits of the new leisure class at the end of the nineteenth century, consumer scholars from various disciplines have focused on the seemingly never-ending proliferation of new commercial goods.[13] They have examined changes in the "national character," the psychological impetus to buy, the fantasy-building role of advertisers, the physical spaces of commerce, and the political machinations of the economy and its participants—all in relation to the production or consumption of *new* goods.[14] Aside from a handful of sociologists and anthropologists looking at contemporary examples of flea markets or garage sales, little scholarship focusing on these venues exists. Only recently have scholars such as Susan Strasser, Alison Isenberg, and Wendy Woloson offered more than fleeting glimpses into the ineluctable historical forces of secondhand exchange.[15] *From Goodwill to Grunge* adds to this nascent body of work by exploring multiple niche markets of secondhand items in the context of modern corporatizing capitalism. In doing so, this book offers a corrective to historians' previous concentration on firsthand markets.

Focusing solely on the effects and influences of firsthand goods exchange creates a skewed perspective of American commercial engagement. Indeed, when only firsthand goods and mainstream fashions are considered, thrift appears as a severely diminishing if not absent attribute of consumer culture.[16] Ideals of frugality and personal stewardship have, to some degree, taken refuge in the unprepossessing rows of flea-market stalls, on the neatly mown lawns at Saturday morning garage sales, and in the heavy-laden shelves of thrift stores. Secondhand commerce, however, was not without serious concession to the increasingly high standard of living in the United States, to a time and place where the line between want and need was broad and blurred. Luxury and thrift are not mutually exclusive; the exaggerated stylization of both punk and grunge acknowledges the potential extravagance of secondhand consumerism, as do the time and knowledge required to replicate such specialized looks.

The specific workings and diverse motives of secondhand commerce participation often vary considerably from the operative reasonings of primary economies. The disjunction—intentional and otherwise—between first- and secondhand markets forces the acknowledgment of not just one cohesive capitalism, but the simultaneous persistence of multiple, sometimes intersecting, capitalisms, of which these are just two examples. In keeping with the mission of new histories of capitalism, *From Goodwill to Grunge* dissolves constricting disciplinary barriers by engaging economic history in a study centered on cultural performativity—both that of consumers and of businesses, the shifting ideologies of which easily demonstrate the fungibility of capitalism's premises.[17]

The fluid and previously uncharted relationships between democracy and capitalism, between producers and consumers, and between markets and rhetoric have similarly claimed the attention of historians such as Sven Beckert, Bethany Moreton, and Jonathan Levy in various contexts and on diverse topics.[18] Considering businesses in the context of the motivations of employers, the social and cultural lives of workers, and the global predilections of buyers and demand creates a fuller understanding of economic trends, labor practices, and consumer responses. A coordinated look at both use and provision is vital to this study because within secondhand markets, the roles of consumer, producer, and supplier were rarely discrete. Thrift-store workers gleaned, repaired, sold, and bought resale goods. Antique collectors—and vintage clothiers—frequently became dealers to better indulge their passion. Gay rights activists used pre-owned clothing both for political fund-raising and personal cross-dressing.

Secondhand exchange was riddled with bold acclaims and embarrassing contradictions. The various markets brought with them opposing advantages and costs. Certainly, twentieth-century used goods capitalism was not free of the moral ambiguities frequently attributed to the corporate capitalism of the same era. As thrift stores boasted, secondhand buying enabled consumers to acquire daily necessities when their incomes could not accommodate first-hand prices, and yet according to postwar analysts such as Michael Harrington, it also helped mask the true costs of poverty and growing disparities in wealth.[19] Used goods commerce gave people who wanted to resist middle-class culture or corporate capitalism the apparent means to participate in crafting individual identities based on consumer choices—arguably, by substituting superficial cultural solutions for genuine political action. Yet again, sometimes secondhand dress was itself political action—of a performative and staged sort but not without real effect. Though occasionally promoted as an anticapitalist pursuit, secondhand commerce justified accelerated buying for many participants. Through donations, civically responsible citizens rationalized *new* purchases based on their forfeiture of used items—after all, last season's discarded shoes were not crowding landfills or taxing municipal incinerators. They were, presumably, going to someone who needed those shoes. The persistence of this perception has global economic, political, and environmental repercussions. In reality, cast-off materials in the United States reached a monumental tonnage by the last quarter of the twentieth century, and only major exportation of secondhand goods could accommodate America's consumer discards.[20] As Elizabeth L. Cline's recent book *Overdressed: The Shockingly High Cost of Cheap Fashion* acknowledges, secondhand exchange has become an intrinsic and lucrative part of the controversial global economies of fast fashion. Decades before the end of the twentieth century, discarded clothing, much of it donated with charitable intent, far outpaced domestic need. Profit-oriented trade organizations such as Secondary Materials and Recycled Textiles (SMART) systematized the sorting and redistribution of millions of tons of clothing rejected annually by American thrift-store shoppers.[21] Secondhand clothing exports and profits grew steadily throughout the second half of the twentieth century.[22]

What began in the late nineteenth century as spaces of Progressive-Era philanthropic capitalism working to Christianize historically Jewish businesses and Americanize immigrants turned into variously priced repositories for the accessories of middle-class rebellions. When Reverend Edgar J. Helms set out to establish Goodwill Industries, he saw the resale of secondhand clothing as a particular impediment. "We have been taught to look askance on discarded clothing," Helms bemoaned. "'It's junk,' some have said. They have taught us to abhor it."[23] Yet in the 1990s, thrift stores were crowded with throngs of fashionable youth, their pockets filled with disposable income. Secondhand clothing went from Goodwill to grunge in less than a century—and not only because middle-class white people appropriated marginalized cultures. This book offers a fuller picture of the complicated socioeconomic structure of commercial growth by exploring the political, demographic, and cultural contexts of previously unexamined economic developments.

Elective secondhand consumption and philanthropic capitalist aims grew together in close quarters, nourished by the same aspects of a rapidly industrializing nation, and brought to maturity through the same social disruptions and economic expansions. Supply and demand were, are, and will continue to be inextricable from each other, a message central to the simplest high school economics lesson. Yet historians have often separated the two, considering businesses in relative isolation from their products' consumers. This book assumes that "Where did those clothes come from?" and "Why did people wear them?" are equally important and mutually constitutive questions. Secondhand exchange in the twentieth-century United States was not simply a throwback to preindustrial systems or an outgrowth of long-standing humanitarian practices but the direct result of expanding capitalism. True, the sale of secondhand goods was no invention of the twentieth century; its history charts in part a course of alienation from and prejudice against a Jewish diaspora in Europe as well as the United States. At the turn of the twentieth century, junk shops, pushcarts, and pawnshops were largely the province of Jewish immigrants, a group that was often barred from professional opportunities both in the United States and Europe and therefore relegated to marginal economies. But throughout the twentieth century United States, used goods markets were central to the infrastructure of a rapidly expanding industrial economy. The philanthropic capitalism of thrift stores, the publicly conducted entrepreneurialism of flea markets, and the semi-private intimacy of garage sales permanently altered the commercial landscape of the United States. At the same time, they provided pathways apart from aggressive marketing schemes such as planned obsolescence and etched-out avenues of both conservative social maintenance and radical opposition.

With adept plasticity, secondary economies offered financial opportunities for marginalized groups such as African Americans, Jews, women, and gender nonconformists; preserved a waning element of civic interaction within monetary exchange; and supplied the raw materials for alternative political and cultural expression. As secondhand commodities grew in value alongside demand, secondhand sales became an area of potentially high profits, and thus an arena for big business as well as charitable reformers. Throughout the twentieth century, and especially after the end of World War II, so-called shadow economies gained a substantial voluntary consumer following. First, nostalgia and elitist sentiments elevated certain secondhand materials above common, mass-produced, affordable items, including at first few wearables but an increasing number of durable goods and decorative items. Starting as early as World War I, an identifiable attraction to marginality and exoticism—whether through self-conscious bohemian identification or the "radical chic" of the 1960s and 1970s—expanded and altered the meanings of voluntary secondhand dress, eventually making it acceptable and accessible to many white, middle-class youth. In the process, secondhand markets became an important resource for the public articulation of minority opinions, including on the one hand, those of social elitists and nostalgic conservatives, and on the other hand, of anticapitalists, war protesters, advocates of gender and sexuality equality, and environmentalists. Participants in secondhand commerce worked with and against evolving ideals of fashion, fueled by the growing importance of individual identity and notions of celebrity, to disrupt existing categories of sexuality and gender and to oppose the political status quo. Using consumerism to illuminate and combat social problems stemming from a commodity culture produced contradictory results, however, which in part led to the sartorial irony intrinsic to later secondhand styles, such as punk and grunge.

Among secondhand objects, clothing had special potential for social symbolism. Increasingly in the twentieth century, clothing became directly associated with the personality, beliefs, and status of its wearer. Because of long-standing stigmas attached to pre-owned apparel, the acceptance of secondhand clothing as a respectable commodity lagged behind the approved collectability of nonantique, secondhand household goods. However, it was precisely those persistent qualms about wearing pre-owned garments that encouraged oppositional meanings, spurring the voluntary adoption of secondhand styles as expressions of both rebellion and of elitism. Because it had already cycled through at least one series of personal associations and because of its economic and social liminality, secondhand clothing played a unique (and thus far unexamined) role in crafting the complex cultures of capitalist societies. Exploring that role helps us understand the motivations behind material acquisition and personal adornment. Elizabeth Wilson describes fashion as an aesthetic enterprise that, like many other artistic forms, performs an ideological task: "to resolve formally, at the imaginary level, social contradictions that cannot be resolved."[24] Voluntary secondhand dressers sought (unsuccessfully) to resolve the contradictions of social and economic inequality in the twentieth-century United States.

Clothing is perhaps the most intimate of publicly displayed commodities, the items physically closest to our flesh and most immediately associated with our personalities. Over the course of the twentieth century, the social anxieties and superstitions surrounding used clothing changed, but novelists, screenwriters, poets, musicians, and even comic book creators continued to represent a popular belief in the almost mystical powers of transference from one clothing owner to the next. In the nineteenth century, Charles Dickens and Henry James declared unambiguously that secondhand spoils maintained the flaws, weaknesses, and cruelties of their previous owners and were adopted at serious peril. Turn-of-the-century journalists warned of the joint risks of disease and disrepute associated with pre-owned cloth materials. Anti-Semitism further discouraged "proper" consumers from considering secondhand options dominated by Jewish salespeople.

Slowly over the course of the century, superstitions about prior sartorial associations evolved to include neutral or positive associations. In 1923, Fanny Brice's hit song "Second Hand Rose" connected Greenwich Village bohemia with the historically Jewish trade in secondhand items and also humorously tempered perennial public disdain of used materials. After the end of World War II, the positive associations with secondhand materials mounted. Drag queens sometimes imagined absorbing the glamour and elegance with which they guessed secondhand gowns must be drenched. By the time punk rock star (and fashion icon) Patti Smith became a public figure in the 1970s, her poetic suggestions that thrift-store clothing linked her with creative artists of the past, even inspiring her own artistic growth, showed both a continuation of the popular belief in used clothing as vector, and the changed tenor of that belief.

Julien Devivier's 1942 film *Tales of Manhattan*, which was produced during the middle of this shift, demonstrated ambivalence about the character of secondhand clothing's influence on its possessor. A star-studded cast including Rita Hayworth, Paul Robeson, Edward G. Robinson, and Henry Fonda accompanied a man's formal tailcoat through no fewer than six reincarnations, which saw the coat's worth fluctuate wildly, in ways only indirectly connected to its exchange value.[25] The coat, cursed by a vengeful tailor, first causes the downfall of two wealthy wearers, complicating their relationships and compromising their physical health. Once taken to a thrift shop, the coat's curse morphs into a tool of uplift, helping to raise a talented composer to renown and earning a reformed drunk a second chance. Throughout the film, the secondhand material blesses and curses successive wearers with reversals of fortune—but never leaves its owners unaffected, signifying the continued belief in secondhand clothing's mystical prowess.

To unravel the complex and vacillating roles of used goods exchange in U.S. commerce and culture, I look at the origins, growth, and persistence of the three major innovations in twentieth-century secondhand trade—thrift stores, garage sales, and flea markets—alongside the use of pre-owned products, especially clothing, by an increasingly diverse body of consumers. For much of the century, many networks of secondhand distribution were untaxed or unmeasured and therefore offer no large, central archives or easily tracked statistics. The inventive source-finding skills of cultural historians who study marginal lives—perhaps best represented in George Chauncey's work on early twentieth-century gay male urban culture—emboldened me to undertake a historical project with elusive sources. I created my own library of primary sources on secondhand exchange and came to rely on a large variety of materials, including documents from archives such as those of the Salvation Army and various public libraries from San Francisco to New York City, interviews, sales catalogues, song lyrics, personal receipts, memoirs, diaries, photographs, newspapers, magazines, released and unreleased films, music videos, pamphlets, business accounts, novels, legislative records, sociological studies, and poetry. Apropos of my topic, I gleaned references to used commerce from surprising sources. In some cases, blind casting was best rewarded. For example, when poking through San Francisco GLBT Historical Society's archives, I had no idea that the personal papers of early gay rights leader and cross-dresser José Sarria would include stacks of flea-market and thrift-store receipts.[26]

Early in the century, the commercial success of the secondhand sector relied on a broad need for used, less expensive goods, as well as the manipulation of xenophobic fears, reformist impulses, and shifts in urban regulations. The emergence of unevenly codified and regulated used goods sales undoubtedly relied in part on growing disparities of wealth, most apparent in crowded urban areas. The changing demographics, politics, and social opportunities in cities, along with advances in technology and goods production, similarly encouraged new variabilities in expressive dress. When public presentation no longer clearly broadcast obvious social and financial status, the categorizations of styles multiplied *and* individualized across class spectrums.

From Goodwill to Grunge analyzes these origins and transitions through seven chapters that move across time, place, and topic. Chapter 1, "Thrift Stores and the Gilded Age Shopper," enunciates the social, moral, and hygienic anxieties plaguing popular perceptions of secondhand trade and the steps taken to placate such concerns. As everyday goods increased in availability and decreased in cost, more still-viable discarded goods made secondhand economies attractive to a broader range of entrepreneurs. Protestant-run salvage businesses, known as "thrift stores" by the 1920s, used contemporary marketing tools to advertise Christianized, sanitized, and Americanized venues for secondhand products. In linking charity to capitalist profit amidst the urban goals of the Progressive Era, the Salvation Army and Goodwill Industries established two of the earliest, still-existing American chain businesses. From the start, clientele included voluntary shoppers who used secondhand venues to expand their sartorial options.

In chapter 2, "Dressing Dada and the Rise of Flea Markets," which describes the economic, cultural, and demographic supports for the rise of flea markets during the interwar period, I introduce the duality of secondhand consumer motivations, as well as the contradictions of a recurrent avant-garde adoration of used materials. The reframing of novelty to include the not-new was connected to, on the one hand, transnational art movements tinged with political radicalism, and on the other, nostalgic sentimentalism forged by conservative patriotism. After the end of World War I, modernist artists spurred an enamorment with flea markets that spread from Europe to the United States. French surrealist luminary André Breton preached the mystical properties of objects at a distance from originally intended use, and Dadaist Marcel Duchamp introduced the art world to the concept of "readymades," that is, found objects removed from their productive context. The little-known but influential Greenwich Village "mother of Dada," the German-born baroness Elsa von Freytag-Loringhoven, intermixed Dadaist artistic aims, including the incorporation of discarded objects, and the contemporary theatricality of dress and public appearance; as publisher Jane Heap remarked, she was the only New York artist who "dresse[d] Dada."[27] At the same time, wealthy, conservative collectors such as automobile mogul Henry Ford helped encourage the popularity of quotidian collectibles in a bid to romanticize preindustrial labor and life.

While the growth of flea markets did rely on a broadening consumer market for secondhand goods, the forms and locations of the outdoor venues demonstrated the independent determination and entrepreneurialism of marginalized classes, especially immigrants and black southern migrants. As chain grocery stores such as the Great Atlantic & Pacific Tea Company (the A&P) replaced direct-to-consumer food distribution via farmer's markets in rural regions and city-sanctioned public markets in urban areas, secondhand commodities filled in the gap, sustaining preexisting open-air venues. Then, throughout the Great Depression and World War II, demand for practical secondhand items soared, while supplies plummeted. Even as some thrift stores and flea markets had a difficult time maintaining profits, the secondhand market extended to global distribution, especially at the conclusion of the war as Americans helped rebuild devastated European nations in need of basic supplies and clothing.

The 1950s brought the unquestionable arrival of the voluntary consumer of secondhand clothing. After the war, all established forms of consumption, of both new and used goods, rapidly accelerated in the United States. Leagues of Americans rushed to spend cashed-in war bonds on new consumer items, and the stores of abandoned secondhand goods grew accordingly—much as they had during the advent of the large-scale production of clothing. During the 1950s, Goodwill Industries tripled their number of stores. Flea markets expanded as well, many following the decline of drive-in movie theaters, with owners converting or supplementing the suddenly unprofitable tracts of land into open-air markets of mostly used goods. The consignment model of used clothing exchange also grew, enabling patrons to consign their lightly worn items to the store proprietor in return for a cut of the profit or store credit, helping consumers—mostly women—meet demanding wardrobe needs while maintaining modest budgets.

Chapter 3, "Garage Sales and Suburban Subversiveness," focuses on the origins and rise of another new form of secondhand exchange: the garage sale. Hosted and attended mostly by women, garage sales emerged in 1950s suburbs as a way for newly isolated housewives to earn intermittent income, participate in politics, and build community networks. From huge Barry Goldwater campaign fund-raisers to small family sales to bring in "pin money," these intimate events both adapted to and defied the spatial limitations of suburban domesticity and postwar gender expectations. Moreover, garage sales introduced a new, larger-than-ever generation of middle-class youth to secondhand goods and clothing—providing provocative glimpses of the tools that could be used to reject class status, sexual normativity, and political consensus.

The year 1957, especially, was a banner year for secondhand commerce. Jack Kerouac published *On the Road*, espousing the Beat philosophy of material disengagement and describing ramshackle clothes and Beat appearances as emblematic of freedom from middle-class constrictions. That same year, Vance Packard warned Americans that business advertisers were manipulating Americans into the "kind of catatonic dough that will buy, give or vote at their command." His best-seller *The Hidden Persuaders* boosted the growing popularity of outré forms of consumption, now assumedly evidence of strong-mindedness, nonconformity, and individuality.[28] Also in 1957, major department stores such as Macy's and Lord & Taylor sold eager collegians moth-eaten raccoon fur coats from the 1920s, marking the first major trend in which clothing was formally tagged as "vintage."

Chapters 4 and 5 examine two distinct but entwined routes by which secondhand clothing became covetable in the 1950s and 1960s. Chapter 4, "The Invention of Vintage Clothing," recounts a process of upgrading certain older apparel, a transnational process led by the wealthy and famous, including rich collegians, titled nobility, and rock stars such as Jimi Hendrix and Janis Joplin. Celebrations of affluence, elitism, individuality, and fame framed this path. The invention of "vintage" owes to a desire for visible distinction—one almost classically linked to affluence and in keeping with the 1899 thesis of economist Thorstein Veblen. For example, the 1956–57 college fad for old raccoon-fur coats from the 1920s was emblematic of a rising class of wealthy youth to whom chain department stores such as Lord & Taylor eagerly appealed. The process involved individual innovation, market approval, and finally, product exhaustion. After the coats were gone, the concept of vintage clothing remained.

Vintage exhibitionism usually disavowed political affiliations while reveling in bucking convention. Chapter 5, "Elective Poverty and Postwar Politics," tracks the rise of voluntary poor dress and its links to a middle-class rejection of inherited class positions often rooted in political protest—against widespread poverty, the Vietnam War, gender inequality, and environmental destruction. The exhibitionism of vintage dress certainly overlapped with the social and political protests of cross-class identification, but the initial motives and the style details of the prime participants often differed. However, one commonality attends almost all the wide array of secondhand dressers in the postwar years: they expressed a disaffiliation with the middle class and its connotations of homogeneity, conformity, and bland plasticity.

Historian Thomas Frank argues in *The Conquest of Cool* that the admen and fashion designers of the 1950s and 1960s were active participants of that era's "counterculture"—an ill-defined subset of American youth that historical memory tends to either demonize or sanctify.[29] Recently, the final scene in the final episode of the wildly popular HBO series *Mad Men* (2007–15) reflected Frank's formulation by summarizing claims of marketing's revolutionary complicity in the transformations of the late 1960s, using the multicultural 1971 Coca-Cola commercial that was a real-life success, "I'd Like to Buy the World a Coke." The ad represented the cumulative dissatisfactions, reluctant revelations, and innate creativity of *Mad Men*'s central character, advertising maverick Don Draper, a "man in the gray flannel suit" gone rogue.

As *Mad Men* reflects, the old "binary narrative" of the 1960s has given way to a new mythology of the decade. The old account described the co-optation of anticommercial youth-driven styles by profit-minded businesses and offered evidence of the predatory nature of all corporate systems, supposedly reigning over the mindless operations of suburbanite minions and their dropped-out offspring. In the new narrative, both the counterculture and big business are monolithic and primary, and if anyone, it is the corporate mavericks working within the system themselves who have nuance and variation. Frank directs attention to "hip" innovators within the "straight" corporate world who responded to the same societal frustrations as hippies and created sales pitches that appealed to a generation of nonconformists. Yet in seeking to correct an omission in academic analysis, the hip-business, auto-co-optation narrative overcorrects: not *everyone* was a Don Draper.

My argument does not absolutely counter Thomas Frank's model of gentle co-optation; rather, I contend that co-optation in this situation worked *more* than "both" ways. Indeed, it worked back and forth, up and down, and across race, gender, and class lines—nearly whichever way you can imagine. Capitalism, if considered in the singular, is messy. This book sometimes describes a capitalism that was mean-spirited and racist, and that alienated women and sought to invalidate sexual unconventionality. More optimistically, it also tells of a side of American capitalism that was chaotic and innovative, and that was utopic and joyously irreverent. Sometimes secondhand commerce provided real, measurable opportunities for oppressed classes, beyond just providing an economic stopgap for people barred from genuine social mobility.

The opportunities secondhand exchange provided could be material, political, or personal. In chapter 6, "Genderfuck and the Boyfriend Look," I describe the many ways in which secondhand exchange became a tool in the gay liberation movement. At a time when deviance from normative gender appearance was an arrestable offense, secondhand shops' comparative leniency offered opportunities for experimentation denied by firsthand venues. More broadly, secondhand commerce aided in the political and cultural advancement of gay rights and in helping to create a broader scope of sexual identities and related imagery through not only political activism but also cultural routes such as glam rock, punk, underground art and film, and avant-garde performance art. During the 1960s and 1970s, secondhand dressers such as activist José Sarria used secondhand exchange to both financially support gay rights and to oppose homophobic public perceptions. Others, such as underground filmmaker Jack Smith and Hibiscus of the psychedelic drag troupe the Cockettes, cited anticommercial motives for seeking alternative economies and for presenting "queer" appearances. Both men and women—such as the Bowery-browsing punk icon Patti Smith—displayed cross-gendered appearances, yet public reception of "genderfuck" suggested that men in women's clothing were assumed to be more politically radical than women in men's attire. Descriptions of cross-dressing women as trying on "the boyfriend look" worked to discredit feminist motivations or interpretations as well as gender-transgressive possibilities. Regardless of these inconsistencies, by the end of the 1970s, a queer, "trash" self-presentation had entered the country's visual lexicon and was specifically associated with popular musicians and artists.

The final chapter, "Connoisseurs of Trash in a World Full of It," examines the links between trash aesthetics, secondhand dress, and pop iconography, focusing on the myths and dismissals of the short-lived but massively popular music and fashion fad grunge. Whether dubbed retro, kitsch, camp, or trash, borrowing from the ideas and images of the past was an intrinsic part of the postmodern artistic landscape, and debates about the worth of such reflexive borrowing raged. During the 1990s, grunge style was often dismissed as an adolescent form of slumming—perhaps as a reaction to the profligacy of the Reagan years. But viewing grunge styles as simply reactive loses the social meaning embodied in the specific ironic posturing of 1990s dress and music, views that preserved and sustained foregoing models of creativity and style at least as much as they upset them. Grunge was not just "the way we dress when we have no money," as designer Jean-Paul Gaultier sniffed disdainfully, but an elaboration on what secondhand aficionados had cultivated for almost a century.

In 1962, Claude Lévi-Strauss introduced the concept of the "bricoleur," someone who rearranged existing elements for new purposes—often ones assumed to be destructive of the original thought, image, or device.[30] Bricolage has since (and indeed, had before) been associated with avant-garde film, assemblage art, popular music, and secondhand styles. In the 1980s, theorists such as Jean Baudrillard concluded that postmodern aesthetes patching together historical elements in "retro" representations contributed to the "death pangs of the real and the rational" from which much of culture suffered.[31] But in 1996, British historian Raphael Samuel admitted that retro was "a way of constructing knowledge," and not just a lazy reach into a grab bag of historical flotsam.[32] Grunge combined elective poverty, cross-gender dress, and vintage exhibitionism, highlighting a strong vein of cynicism based on the knowledge of the contradictions plaguing any consumer rebellion reliant on specified codes of buying. Still, for all the apparent apathy and pessimism pundits ascribed to "Generation X," grunge also signaled hope for a way outside "the system." Though Kurt Cobain proposed the futility of such goals by appearing on the cover of *Rolling Stone* magazine wearing a hand-penned T-shirt that sneered "corporate magazines still suck," his fans' deep mourning at his suicide indicated their belief in alternative futures, invested in the emblematic rock star.

In a consumerist sphere obsessed with novelty and shaped by planned obsolescence, a thriving secondhand commercial realm seems illogical. Yet in the postwar United States, this phenomenon extended from the lowest registers of commerce to the loftiest ranks of artistic production. As did Gaultier, many young grunge adherents reviled high-end fashion's quick appropriation of their street-born style. The viscerally negative reactions to couture grunge reflected in part a long-standing assumption that secondhand goods embodied a kind of consumer "authenticity"—that thrift-store shopping, the anti-consumption consumerism, was exactly the opposite of exorbitantly priced runway fashion.[33] This belief downplayed the fact that many secondhand distribution networks, including thrift stores and flea markets, were, in fact, highly profitable businesses that played an intrinsic part in the development of twentieth-century American corporate capitalism. In popular and academic accounts, the supply of secondhand goods is mystified, shrouded by simultaneous assumptions of economic insignificance and moral superiority.[34] This approach ignores the actual political, economic, and cultural effects of the recirculation of goods.

Secondhand consumerism is exempt from neither the restrictions nor the opportunities of primary-goods capitalism. As a cheap and plentiful commercial resource, used goods have encouraged cultural innovation, supported social reform, and supplied marginalized Americans with work and clothing.

At the same time, easy systems of disposal for barely worn and low-quality clothing validated ever-quickening rotations of style and increased the expectations of cheap fashion, produced by underpaid global workers. The persistent myths that used goods exchange is either too inconsiderable to study or morally excepted from the contradictions of corporate capitalism place a limit on understanding not only the history of American styles and markets but global processes of trade, employment, fashion, and cultural exchange. Indeed, to understand the embedded significance of secondhand economies, we need to understand the context of their emergence.

CHAPTER ONE

Thrift Stores and the Gilded Age Shopper

On 3 May 1884, the *Saturday Evening Post* carried a short story titled "The Blue Silk" that underscored the public's fears about buying secondhand clothing in the late nineteenth century. The tale's protagonist—the comely, young Louisa—yearns to accept an invitation to a grand party, but her cantankerous father refuses to pay for her "ball frippery." Against the advice of her cousin, who argues that only "second-hand gentility" would resort to such means, Louisa gathers together what little money she has and buys a beautiful, pale blue gown from "the Jewess behind the counter" of a resale shop.[1] At the party, the gown's train, presumably strained from prior use, tears; just then, an already abject Louisa overhears the hostess wondering aloud how it is that Louisa would be wearing Emily Lourele's dress. Her secondhand transgression is found out.

Evidently, the author thought public humiliation an insufficient lesson, for Louisa later learns that the store where she had purchased the gown has since closed, all of its workers having been stricken with smallpox, initially brought in with the stock now carted away for disposal. Louisa's household soon succumbs to the illness, and her own case is the most severe. In the course of its ravages, Louisa loses, along with her social reputation, her fine looks. "The Blue Silk" warned readers not only of the dangers of vanity and filial disregard but also of the contempt to which status dissemblers were vulnerable. As one midcentury etiquette manual (directed at young women "who are dependent on their own exertion") primly warned: "We never love to see people strutting in a borrowed dress."[2] At a time when Jewish immigration was on the rise, the story also registers Jewish domination of secondhand trades—and native-born Americans' distrust of those dealers. And the central role of the dress itself, carrier of dangerous contagions, reflects a long-standing belief in the uncanny, supernatural, and even vengeful potentials of pre-owned clothing, one with literary precedents. In his 1848 "Meditations on Monmouth Street," Charles Dickens attributed old clothes trapped in limbo at a secondhand clothing market with the indulgences, sadnesses, recriminations, and even the violence of the articles' dead owners.[3] In an early Henry James ghost story evocatively titled "The Romance of Certain Old Clothes" (1868), a similarly stagnating wardrobe went so far as to enact its dead owner's murderous revenge.[4] The dread of used clothing was less pragmatic than assiduous hygiene standards could account for—especially when considering that Dickens's and James's musings predate the common acceptance of the germ theory, which gave scientific legitimation to such horrors as those expressed in *The Post*.

But around the turn of the twentieth century—despite these long-standing social, moral, and hygienic trepidations—used goods' disrepute faded just a bit in the face of widespread necessity, a rise in recreational shopping, and the marketing efforts of Christian-run salvage businesses. Soon, efficiently organized, purportedly sanitized, and increasingly standardized sites of secondhand shopping helped temper prohibitions against buying used things. By the 1920s, these innovations would be known as "thrift stores." The leaders of Protestant mission groups promoting thrift stores were savvy advocates who accessed a hugely profitable market niche by revolutionizing secondhand sales. Industrial capitalism, large-scale production, mass immigration (along with reactionary xenophobia), and urbanization set the stage for success. However, these salvage businesses were not just offshoots of primary commercial endeavors. Rather than drifting in the wake of department stores, salvage sales constituted a deliberate and profitable sea change in religious organizations' particular brand of social welfare. By adapting Progressive-Era reforms to a workable business model attuned to a consumer society, thrift-store organizers linked charity to capitalism decades before the "nonprofit sector" had been so designated. Thrift stores thrived in part because of their perceived exception from, on the one hand, the more casual and condemned methods of used goods sales—such as Jewish-run pushcart peddling and pawnshops—and on the other, the transparent profit motives and corporate organization of firsthand endeavors—exemplified by new department stores. In the course of crafting a new "philanthropic capitalism,"[5] the Salvation Army and Goodwill Industries established one of the earliest and longest-running chain businesses in the United States.[6]

Thrift-store businesses succeeded because they conformed conventional charity and civic responsibility to the conditions of modern consumerism. One aspect of those conditions was a rising demand for alternatives to modern shopping experiences and to new, mass-produced items, a demand that coincided with supply, as more affordable, new goods soon meant more discarded but usable goods. As the average standard of living increased, desires for satisfying consumer experiences and for expressive personal dress eluded easy categorization. For some immigrants and working-class women, colloquial modes of shopping, including reuse, held personal value and even represented a means of retaining ethnic identification. During the early years of modern consumerism, what it meant to dress "American" was a matter of multiparty negotiation, despite reformist urgings for immigrant assimilation. Eager consumers across class boundaries, from diverse locations, and with assorted ambitions required multiple options. As capacious as it was, firsthand consumerism created new demands as quickly as it satisfied them.

This chapter explores the roots of American thrift stores in the context of the industrializing United States. Journalistic, literary, and theatrical evidence of popular opinions on dress and secondhand commerce help reveal the fluidity of entrepreneurial aims, reformist notions, and consumer agency. Thrift-store innovators conformed widespread and persistent ideals of thrift and stewardship to the changing political economy of Gilded Age America.[7] Progressive Christians such as Goodwill Industries' founder Reverend Edgar J. Helms gave equivalent weight to both the social gospel and the Gospel of Wealth, valuing business growth as part of projects intended to Americanize and Christianize the foreign-born. However, Jewish immigrant Anzia Yezierska's writings show the layers of personal interrogation and reflection that comprised secondhand buyers' motives and belie facile interpretations of assimilatory ambitions. Variable motives for adopting secondhand dress were not limited to the targeted shoppers. Evangeline Booth, the commander of the United States Salvation Army, used secondhand materials and clothing to lead members of her organization and to satisfy her personal expressive desires, demonstrating the mutual embeddedness of supply and demand, categories that overlap and intertwine at all levels of capital exchange, but perhaps especially in secondhand trade. At the turn of the century, participants in secondhand exchange reflected and affected evolving notions of charity, religion, and profit as well as changing expectations of class, race, and gender—identities increasingly expressed through dress and style.

The Salvation Army's salvage efforts began in the United States in 1897; Goodwill Industries followed suit in 1902. Both organizations had their share of critics, stemming in part from perennial misgivings regarding the sale of used materials.[8] Anti-resale prejudices, rooted in superstition, magnified by anti-Semitism, and heightened by growing population densities and the acceptance of the germ theory, both challenged and supported the creation of thrift stores, which used up-to-date public relation methods to reassure wary consumers of their products' cleanliness and moral worth. Like department store moguls, large-scale salvage business entrepreneurs benefitted from the growing societal emphasis on consumer satisfaction and desire. Writing in 1901, sociologist Emily Fogg Mead declared that a steady stream of advertisements and novelty goods served to awaken in Americans "the ability to want and choose." But according to Mead, deprived of the variety that the modern consumer culture afforded, the "lower class [wa]s still the slave of simple and undiversified habits."[9] As department stores gained urban prominence, the definition of necessity expanded to include a consumers' right to choose, attendant to an "ethic of consumption" largely generated by producers in an appeal to their clientele.[10] Contrary to what secondhand venues' muted presence in most historical accounts (and Mead's own contemporary considerations) suggests, places like thrift stores were paramount to the creation of a varied modern consumer landscape and key to understanding the role that immigrants, women, and racial minorities played in shaping the consumer economy of the United States. Thrift stores were both deviations from and adaptations to the new capitalist rhetoric of obsolescence and choice, befitting an increasingly diverse population.

Urban Dress and Scientific Giving

When Reverend Edgar J. Helms, founder of what would become Goodwill Industries, first set out to collect used goods from Boston's wealthier residents and redistribute them to the city's more needy inhabitants, he recognized the difficulty of overcoming the public's concerns about selling and buying discarded materials, particularly wearables. "We have been taught to look askance on discarded clothing," Helms bemoaned. "'It's junk,' some have said. They have taught us to abhor it."[11] Given that large-scale manufacturing produced relatively affordable new goods, abundantly available through catalogues, specialty shops, and department stores, many citizens thought potentially unhygienic secondhand clothing was suitable for donating to the poorest of the poor but was hardly fit for public sale. On top of that, religious critics saw the Salvation Army's and Goodwill Industries' profitable trade in used goods as evidence of the organizations' materialist priorities and spiritual duplicity.

Despite such apparent resistance, by 1935 Goodwill Industries had established ninety-six newly dubbed "thrift stores" in U.S. cities as well as a dozen abroad. Salvation Army salvage stores expanded throughout the first part of the century as well, especially during the affluent 1920s, revealing that the commercial viability of the secondhand trade did not rely on recessions. At the time of the 1929 stock market crash, thrift-store income provided approximately half the annual budget for the eastern Men's Social Service, the large shelter and jobs program under which the Salvation Army's nationwide thrift-store chain operated.[12] Secondhand business was booming.

As a business open to the public, the Salvation Army and Goodwill Industries quickly eliminated any litmus test of need, envisioning their salvage sales instead to be venues of profit—profit that would then finance global outreach and aid missions. Reverend Helms's earlier salvaging initiatives, like those of many settlement homes, usually limited distribution to the "deserving" or "worthy" poor and often adopted a cooperative model. The new chains of secondhand stores were corporate capitalist endeavors whose wares were available to anyone willing to pay the nominal prices.[13] And unlike pawnshops or junk stores, thrift stores soon had the persuasive power of standardization, including well-advertised criteria of cleanliness, careful product organization, and relatively uniform pricing. Ultimately, though, the consumer appeal of thrift stores came from more than an imperfect resemblance to department stores; their deviance from the limited offerings of firsthand venues and their maintenance of the apparently dissipating value of thrift also appealed. Thrift stores not only provided economical alternatives for impoverished and provident shoppers; they also functioned as supplementary tools for the inventive dresser. Looking at thrift stores themselves, the organizations responsible, and consumer reception reveals an increasingly intricate relationship between industrial capitalism, social welfare, and mass culture, one that was responsive to changes in the meaning of public appearance.

As urban populations quintupled during the last third of the nineteenth century, the unswept streets of the industrializing United States became stages. Style's role shifted without diminishing; it grew in general economic, personal aesthetic, and political expressive value while declining as a clear indication of luxury and exclusivity.[14] More and more people lived in close proximity to an increasing number of strangers. Women were less confined than before to domestic realms—especially working-class women, whose public presence grew as the century closed. Often, impressions of others relied on fleeting glimpses of color and rustles of material. Costuming was essential. The potential for anonymity in city life encouraged a direct imaginative link between the way one looked and the deepest aspects of personality.[15] Accordingly, the possibilities for sartorial expression multiplied in the last decades of the nineteenth century. No simple top-down formula of technological or industrial advances, marketing schemes, or reformist impulses accounts for the manifold looks and styles of the time. Neither does economist and curmudgeon Thorstein Veblen's 1899 thesis on the poor emulating the "conspicuous consumption" of the rich quite explain the variety.[16]

Historians Nan Enstad and Kathy Peiss underscore the ambiguous value of ready-made dress in the social and political lives of not just middle- and upper-middle-class women, but also of the young working women laboring in cities' multiplying factories, many of whom were immigrants or first-generation Americans. Peiss describes a reciprocal relationship, one that recounts mass culture's responsiveness to working women's role as wage earners and consumers.[17] Enstad broadens the story of fashion and labor to include the creation of political subjectivities supported and reified by interactions with popular culture. The styles adopted by garment workers expressed their status as laborers, as "ladies," and as thorough participants in mass culture. Working women did not simply follow the aesthetic lead of wealthier patrons; rather, they appropriated and reconfigured elements of high fashion, while also incorporating "low" sartorial expressions, such as the layered lace flourishes and bright colors enabled by new synthetic dyes, favored by prostitutes. The important distinction of color is dimmed in popular memory by the paucity of its visual reproduction. Since many working women not only consumed but also helped produce clothing, their choices had professional weight in their own neighborhoods. Undeniably, the working-class urban immigrant was a fashionable subject—and one who at least occasionally shopped secondhand.[18]

A 1902 *New York Times* article, "See New York's Cheapest Department Store," described an average day's patrons at the Salvation Army's Brooklyn salvage store, and illustrated the roles of recreational shopping and working-class styles in remaking perceptions of secondhand materials. Initially, however, the article supported common beliefs about used clothing's dichotomized social role as either a safety net for the very poor or a derelict market for the dishonest. Early in the morning, a mother of nine shed tears of gratitude over her purchases. Her ability to afford an updated wardrobe for her large family highlighted the philanthropic mission of these shops, which often were referred to at that time as "family service" or "social service" stores. Arriving on her worn heels, though, a shifty-eyed huckster hoping to turn a profit validated suspicions of resale's crooked affiliates. This buyer's supposed plans to cash out on his purchases upheld some native-born Americans' dim view of junk stores, pushcart businesses, and pawnshops run by Jewish immigrants.[19]

However, the article's author then confessed surprise in witnessing another kind of secondhand shopper: the recreational one. The midday clamor of women trying on shirtwaists over their dresses took on a celebratory air. The author acknowledges that "[s]ome, strange to say, have no intention of buying, but are enjoying a daily excitement which serves them in place of a matinee."[20] Or perhaps some were coming *from* the theater—where fashion played a growing role in the early part of the century—to seek out affordable alternatives to the showcased styles.[21] Later in the day, the store became a place of leisure and enjoyment, far from the staid site of practical exchange marked by the wistful embarrassment that middle-class sensibilities expected. Different dialects and accents added auditory texture to the visual diversity provided by the patchwork of discarded material goods.

The last shopper of the working hours got the closest editorial attention. Described as a "straight, red-lipped young girl with a cool, steady, black eye, who saunters in and leans against the counter, chewing gum and surveying the stock with careful indifference," she chose a cute pair of bronze slippers to impress the "cream of the ward" at the last Navy Street dance of the season, languidly ordering the stiff German proprietor to "Hump them slippers down here."[22] This shopper's desires did not match any strict definition of need or an underhanded intent to profit economically. Rather, she used the inexpensive stock in a precociously modern, unabashedly frivolous manner. As though to underscore her impulsiveness, she casually ditched the perfectly serviceable shoes in which she arrived. The final buyer's carefree attitude foreshadowed the creative abandonment with which silent star Clara Bow (another Brooklynite) would play a young, desirable department store clerk preparing to dine at the Ritz in the hit film *It*—a full quarter of a century later.[23] In the 1927 film, dissatisfied with her plain white-collared dress, Bow shrugs and takes a pair of scissors directly to the material while wearing it, creating an all-black, low-cut, sleeveless gown, embellished with cheap crepe and fake flowers lying around the apartment she shares with a single mother. By applying knowledge gained working with fashionable clothing—clothing she clearly cannot afford—Bow's character is able to improvise a cutting-edge style suitable for catching her love interest's eye and befitting the Ritz, which was pretty much the poshest possible establishment.[24] For her efforts at crossing class boundaries, the screenplay writers do not give her yellow fever or publicly shame her; instead, she snags a rich mate. This chapter and the next describe some of the economic, social, and sartorial changes that made it possible for the consummate *It* girl to emerge as a plucky, upwardly mobile heroine rather than a fraud humbled by misfortune.

In 1902, the *New York Times* conveyed the changing societal role of secondhand clothing sales in turn-of-the-century American cities. First, the writer satisfied long-standing public expectations about secondhand exchange as the realm of the desperate and the deviant, but the playful motives of some consumers showed that the new recreational appeal of shopping extended to used goods, a twist at which the article's title hints, with its reference to still-novel department stores. In the beginning of the century, women workers in New York City often had fraught relationships with fashion and firsthand dress since many toiled sweatily to create styles they could not buy. Navy Street in 1902 Brooklyn, where the salvage-shopping proto-Clara Bow was headed with new-to-her bronze shoes, ran straight through the burrough's largest Italian community.[25] Many young immigrant women living there held jobs in the flourishing garment factories just over the bridge on the Lower East Side of Manhattan, and attended dances in their own communities after work or on rare days off.[26] By 1890, 44 percent of all ready-made clothes in the United States originated in New York City factories, with the bulk of that total focused on women's clothing and high-end pieces.[27] Those factories' employees, a majority of whom were women, did not get paid enough to buy the products they helped create but they did receive an education in style, one that informed their cheaper, sometimes secondhand, choices. Some garment workers supplemented their wardrobes with select used materials and embellished bland ready-made outfits by sewing on interesting secondhand elements, practices that dignified their own undervalued labor and creatively expressed their reciprocal relationship with mass culture.[28]

Whether or not the Navy Street dancer worked in a garment factory, the goals of that secondhand consumer veered decisively from the instructive meaning of *The Post*'s scolding moral tale. The benefits of buying used were clear for desperately poor consumers who might have preferred to shop at Macy's or Wanamaker's, but also applied to those who could and did shop at least in the bargain bins of major stores, for it would be shortsighted to assume no one did both. The fluxed state of pre-owned goods—not defined by department store categorization but up for sale nevertheless—inspired creative adaptations of style, not only for impoverished individuals but also for those who tapped into secondhand sources more out of desire than any easily definable physical need.

The Salvation Army as Secondhand Consumer

Before young partygoers benefitted from the expanded choices thrift stores provided, the imaginative power of secondhand was already at work on the organizing members of secondhand businesses themselves. Pre-owned materials were central to crafting the public image of the Gilded Age Salvation Army, the pioneers of the large-scale philanthropic salvage goods system. The Salvation Army's relationship with used apparel was multifaceted and wide spanning. Their direct use of secondhand materials demonstrates the inherent instability of the categories "consumer" and "producer," as well as used goods' interclass significance.

Founded in 1865 by former Methodist minister William Booth as the East London Christian Mission, the organization originally provided food, shelter, and work for indigents who, in turn, repaired donated materials at large factory workhouses. Sober and diligent individuals were sent to rural "colonies," where they were groomed to spread the Christian message abroad. Profits from workers' renovated products helped fund these worldwide missionary pursuits.[29] The arrangement soon grew to include retail stores, usually situated in urban areas. In England, the earlier industrial production of new goods alongside informal modes of secondhand exchange—much of which was sold by members of the Jewish diaspora—readied the way for the thrift-store system decades ahead of the United States.[30]

Leaders of the English Salvation Army were attuned to the value of sartorial display from the start. Historian Diane Winston acknowledges Salvationists' intentional manipulation of an urban public's perception of style, noting their willingness to "play into society's own uncertainties about the relationship between clothes and costumes, personhood and role."[31] William Booth and his wife Catherine formed their evangelical group with the revivalist intent associated with the Holiness movement, which emphasized Methodist founder John Wesley's doctrine of Christian perfection. Progress toward perfection was expressed in all areas of adherents' lives, including dress. Salvationists, perhaps "the quintessential expression" of the Holiness movement, indicted popular, conformist dress as evidence of a complacent Christianity.[32] From the outset, the Booths fashioned visual manifestations of their group's collective identity as soldiers of God.

Even before the group name reflected a paramilitary identification, East London Christian Mission members tinkered with group uniforms that relied directly on secondhand materials—specifically, anything that "suggested the soldier," including hussars' coats, helmets from the Household Troop Bands, elements of artillery regiment, or even just yachting caps.[33] Booth's followers used clothing separated by disuse from their original purpose to craft an elaborate spectacle of religious defiance and public evangelism. Conversely similar to how garment workers supplemented their cheaply fashionable apparel with informed secondhand choices, these suppliers drew on their own commercial stock of pre-owned clothing for institutional dress.

In 1878, "General" Booth formalized the paramilitary guise, renaming the group the Salvation Army and assigning ranks to its "soldiers." By the time Salvationists arrived in the United States two years later, a uniform was common but not yet mandatory. Within a decade, Salvation officers always had to wear specified elements of the uniform when in public; other soldiers encountered soft commands to don the garb at least fifteen times a week, a directive that imagines several daily costume changes. By the time salvage brigades were canvassing New York City at the century's end, the Army had formed its own U.S. factory for clothing production, ensuring regularity in design and securing additional profits.[34] While the initial uniforms emerged from the group's vast repository of used materials, it did not take long for the consumer of old goods to become the producer of new ones, an example of the common slippage between supply and demand, and firsthand and secondhand sales.

By the time the Salvation Army began establishing salvage systems in the United States, the organization had swelling ranks of adherents to commend their efforts as well as vocal teams of critics to denounce them. Within ten years of its arrival in the United States, the Salvation Army had 410 corps in 35 states. Despite this rapid growth—or because of it—much public response remained critical of members' appearances, which, after all, was implicitly critical of the public, particularly conformist Christians. Disapproval of the Army's reliance on public spectacle informed media censure; in a nod toward the Salvationists' reliance on self-consciously performative appearances, the *New York Times* decreed in 1892 that "who ever joins the Salvation Army bids good-bye to respectability as much as if he went upon the stage of a variety show."[35]

Women wearing the quasi-military uniform attracted extra reproval. Such criticism arose from the display of a sartorial standard historically associated with men, albeit adapted to a skirted structure. Also, Army leaders, many of whom were women, bid female members, often called "Hallelujah lassies," to use the uniform to gain safe entry into the public sphere, a still-masculine realm. In her role as co-commander of the American Salvation Army (1887–1896), Maud Ballington Booth urged women to wear the uniform precisely so that they might publicly evangelize with greater assurance of safety. Dressed as such, Salvationists would be protected from the usual risks of their urban environment as "a distinctive dress throws around a woman a shield which says to everyone: 'My business is salvation.'"[36] To detractors such as Rev. R. Heber Newton in 1886, however, the "gaily dressed 'salvation lassies' swinging tambourines" showed disdain for religious propriety.[37] During the decades straddling the new century, more and more women frequented urban streets, but the assumption remained that such gadabouts were of less-than-soaring social or moral reputation.

The Salvationists' junk salvaging efforts further provoked critics. In 1909, a Catholic priest—perhaps venting denominational enmities through disapproval of reform tactics—condemned the Salvation Army's outreach operations. "From a religious organization they have developed into a bunch of junk dealers," he opined.[38] For many, trafficking in used goods was plainly incompatible with religious goals. Methodists—the Protestant denomination with which both the Salvation Army and Goodwill Industries were at least loosely affiliated—were prohibited from profiting not just from taverns and theaters but also from pawnshops.[39] Pawnshops, a hybrid of lending and secondhand trade that matured alongside the formalizing of taxed and measured commerce in the nineteenth century, were strongly associated with vice and profligacy.[40] Ethnic prejudice (many pawnbrokers were Jewish) and geographic affiliation (pawnshops were usually relegated to the same urban areas as prostitutes and gamblers) secured the venues' disrepute, further stigmatizing secondhand sales generally.

Pawnbroking, though generally looked down upon by native-born, middle-class Americans, grew together with and directly supported the development of firsthand consumer culture in the nineteenth century. By the end of the century, some consumers regularly levied their nicer wares against immediate needs. Urban women, particularly, used pawnshops to supplement insufficient wages, which allowed them to participate in the broader capitalist market.[41] The lending-store amalgams offered a necessary service to the working poor as well as an unsteady crutch for the blankly profligate. This alliance with respectable commerce notwithstanding, the negative reputation of pawnshops, and by extension, nascent thrift stores, persisted. Despite the fact that providing the poor with clothing and other necessities had long been the purview of religious charity, many still saw *selling* used goods to the public as a shady business.

Sanitizing, Christianizing, and Americanizing Used Commerce

Salvage entrepreneurs clearly had to boost the public image of both the supply and demand sides of secondhand exchange. Nonetheless, for reform-minded businesses such as Goodwill Industries and the Salvation Army, secondhand sales made good economic sense—if only the public's wariness could be allayed. At the turn of the twentieth century, city denizens were throwing away more things than ever before. The large-scale commercial production of items previously made at home changed people's relationship with material goods; the easier it was to purchase something, the more people thought of it as a temporary acquisition. As urban populations swelled, the size of residential living quarters shrank for many residents, and so did convenient storage for unused goods. But even though Gilded Age Americans abandoned some personal practices of stewardship, I argue that these practices did not simply die.[42] Rather, industrial corporations and government entities began to absorb some of the responsibilities (and the profits). Salvage stores were a part of that adaptation.

Concerns over sanitation and proper hygiene reinforced the phasing out of domestic reuse. A woman of middling means in the 1880s was likely to have repurposed cloth materials several times over. She mended her husband's shirts, remade them into her children's pinafores, and, finally, used the worn out, unwearable fabric to clean house or to stuff furniture.[43] In the early twentieth century, the popular acceptance of the germ theory—which described how illnesses could be transferred by invisible substances that clung to and bred on materials, especially cloth—expanded American women's responsibilities in the home to include a much stricter definition of good hygiene for their families.[44] The affordability of new materials made rampant disposal possible, but the middle-class imperative of domestic cleanliness made it requisite.

Alongside the trash of individuals, growing industrial activity itself generated more salvageable waste. In response to the increased supply of consumer and industrial waste, pawnshops, pushcarts, and junk stores multiplied. The number of scrap businesses, whose purpose was to glean domestic and industrial flotsam, grew steadily between 1865 and the end of World War I. Jewish entrepreneurs disproportionately operated such businesses, as they did other secondhand professions in the United States and much of Europe. The mass media's common portrayal of Jewish sellers as dishonest and greedy applied doubly to junk dealers, who were viewed as a public sanitation hazard, and even a moral menace. In 1919, one writer for a trade journal described scrap dealers as a group comprised of "foreigners, and classes of collectors who [were] constantly going beyond the limit of the law" and who were "low on the scale of ethics and intelligence."[45]

The disproportionate presence of Jews in secondhand trade had roots in the economic persecution of the Jewish diaspora. In the United States as well as in Europe, Jews were often barred from professional vocations and forced into low-status jobs at the margins of the economy. European Jews were especially central to the old clothes trade (or "old clo,'" as the peddler's call had it). Early in the nineteenth century, an enormous proportion of the world's increasingly international trade in used clothing cycled through East London's Old Clothes Exchange, a sophisticated system of secondhand trade. By the end of the century, Chatham Street in New York City was a similar harlequin collage of used-clothes dealers, mostly suiting the working class—an increasing percentage of which worked in the production of new apparel and were foreign born.[46]

Between 1880 and 1920, the secondhand trade in the United States grew along with the unprecedented influx of immigrants. At the same time that the absolute number of immigrants rose, the composition of their national origins shifted. Before the 1880s, the majority of America's newcomers were from Germany, Ireland, and Great Britain, but afterward, the numbers of incoming Irish and Germans fell, while Italians, Russians, Poles, Greeks, Austro-Hungarians, and Jews of various nationalities dominated the statistics. By 1910, almost 15 percent of all Americans were foreign born, with immigrants and their children comprising approximately three-quarters of the populations of Boston, New York, Chicago, and Detroit.[47] And according to an 1890 survey of Jewish families in several Manhattan wards, peddling (an informal mode of sales that frequently included pre-owned goods) was the second largest occupation among that demographic, behind another clothing-oriented vocation, tailoring.[48]

At the end of the nineteenth century, overtly anti-Semitic prejudices allied with concerns over sanitation and complaints of theft and fire hazard (in New York City, fires in rag shops frequently threatened nearby businesses and residents) to create new rag sales regulations. In many major cities, "nuisance laws"—common law torts that gave the public recourse for noises, smells, or anything deemed a public nuisance, and often used to target minorities' activities—were passed, usually resulting in more rigorous or costly licensing procedures for small-scale or traveling sellers of secondhand materials.[49] In addition to xenophobic constraints, after a devastating yellow fever epidemic struck the Mississippi Valley in the 1870s and 1880s, many cities turned their attention to preventing water contamination and thus more closely adjudicating waste disposal. In 1895, George E. Waring Jr., a former Civil War colonel and the "greatest apostle of cleanliness," was appointed commissioner of street cleaning in New York City. Waring launched an informational campaign to help residents understand the need for sanitary practices. Among the useful advice he circulated was an organized plan for profiting from efficient refuse sales rather than consigning unwanted objects to overtaxed city dumps and incinerators.[50] Such plans may have seemed to validate small-scale junk dealers, but in reality, new regulations limited the ways in which detritus might be gleaned.

Protestant social activists pioneering salvage sales enjoyed a distinct advantage over independent Jewish entrepreneurs as they appealed to like-minded

FIGURE 1.1 Salvation Army Industrial Homes pushcart, New York City, circa 1900. Courtesy of The Salvation Army National Archives.

secular reformers and at least some fellow Christians. The first Salvation Army basement-run salvage brigade consisted of twenty shelter residents with four pushcarts among them, roaming through local neighborhoods asking for scrap paper—which accounted for the bulk of the early profits—as well as cast-off household goods and clothing, which they sold to salvage yards or directly to industries (see figure 1.1).[51] At this point, the U.S. Salvation Army's salvage operation differed little from Jewish-run scrap metal and junk dealerships.

New York City's Salvationists piggy-backed their own promotional drive on Commissioner Waring's crusade for citizen-based initiatives to enhance municipal cleanliness. As officials in New York, Chicago, and Boston sought to curb the activities of urban scrap dealers, salvage ventures like those of the Salvation Army relied on donations and sold from established storefronts, and so were exempt from restrictions on street gleaning and pushcart perambulating. In response to concerns about potential contagions, the Salvationists published pamphlets explaining their salvaging businesses' ultrahygienic processes for preparing goods for public sale, processes that included "huge laundries working constantly," which thoroughly sanitized donated cloth materials.[52]

Instructions for cleanliness were key elements of the social reform programs associated with many salvage stores. In the 1890s, a new social department—which would conduct the Salvation Army's salvage program—adopted as its motto, "Soup, Soap, and Salvation!"[53] The same emphasis on hygiene that limited economic possibilities for some immigrants also applied to efforts to assimilate the same groups, efforts often referred to as "Americanization." Strategies for Americanization ranged along a spectrum from multicultural acceptance to strict, xenophobic demands of absolute assimilation. At settlement homes and churches, programs abounded for acclimating immigrants to American ways of cooking, cleaning, speaking, and yes, dressing.[54]

Assimilationist rhetoric of cleanliness and American habits of shopping and dress provided a script for the incorporation of secondhand sales into a variety of social reform programs, many less grandiose than those of Goodwill Industries or the Salvation Army. When well-to-do, native-born, Protestant women volunteered time and donated funds to form California's West Oakland Settlement in the 1890s, their original aim was to offset the ill effects of an area sporting more dirty factories and saloons than playgrounds and reading rooms. "[A]n unsavory spot in moral and material aspects," its inhabitants, mostly immigrants, reportedly lacked the positive attributes of "industry, perseverance, patience, dexterity, economy, cleanliness and thrift."[55] Although household studies often revealed the exact opposite—newer immigrants showed stolid habits of frugality and held to old patterns of diligent work that native-born, middle-class Americans were beginning to abandon—Progressive reformers repeatedly reported similar impressions and sought to remedy the newcomers' perceived flaws.[56] From gardening to children's games, the West Oakland volunteers organized activities and programs in pretty, well-ordered settings that were designed to instill white, American, middle-class habits and preferences among the settlement's "low-browed" and "ill-favored" residents.[57] The settlement, whose residents represented more than twenty-one nationalities, mostly Italian and Portuguese, was integrated, but racial condescension was pervasive and white, middle-class habits were emphasized.[58] In keeping with contemporary reform priorities, when the settlement's young boys had finished practicing military drills and stamping leather, they received rousing instruction in "Scrubology" and "Soapology," coursework that echoed exactly General Booth's terminology.[59]

Also inspired by the Salvation Army, in 1899 the West Oakland Settlement began sponsoring a two-day-a-week salvage bureau. Not all volunteers were enthusiastic. Associating immorality and uncleanliness with used goods, they viewed the resale trade as antithetical to their goals of spiritual uplift and beautification. Proponents, however, thought that thrift stores would offer the poor a venue where they might develop the skills necessary to adequately negotiate the increasingly complex American marketplace. Buying was not just a necessity but an aptitude, one best honed in a setting that emulated the handsome, new department stores springing up in American cities. Thus, salvage bureau advocate Eva Carlin pointed out that "[e]very article of clothing" sold in the thrift store "is neatly wrapped up and tied, so that the transactions assume the dignity of store purchases."[60]

Occasionally, Progressive-Era reform groups organized "thrift clubs" designed to instruct immigrants on appropriate ways to extend their purchasing power through long-term investments and prioritized spending.[61] In many ways, thrift stores were the consumer's analog to thrift clubs. As shopping rapidly gained recreational value in the United States, it became, alongside an acceptably fashionable appearance, increasingly intrinsic to mainstream cultural participation. Protestant-led salvage stores extended the opportunity to refine that skill to the poor and foreign-born. The secondhand sales tied plans to reform residents by Americanizing them with a strategy to reform the secondhand trade by Christianizing it.

The New Philanthropic Capitalist

Rev. Helms followed a similar logic as the West Oakland Settlement volunteers when, in 1895, he became pastor of Morgan Methodist Chapel.[62] He and his wife changed the church's name to Morgan Memorial and extended to the community—populated largely by Italian, Hungarian, Czech, and Polish newcomers—childcare, direct almsgiving, and various Americanization programs, such as language training and fresh-air camps for children.[63] As part of these expansions, church members began collecting clothing for women and children in need. As both supply and demand grew, church leaders decided to charge a nominal fee for the goods. As money accumulated, the church hired unemployed women to repair and sometimes repurpose the cloth wares. Word spread, and donations swelled. In due course, Morgan Memorial distributed old food sacks among contributing housewives so that they could more conveniently set aside their unwanted articles for future donation. At first, bags were stamped with "The Morgan Memorial Cooperative Industries and Stores, Inc."; after 1902, they bore a more succinct branding: "The Goodwill Bag."[64]

In 1902, Helms officially launched Goodwill Industries, a secondhand goods program similar to the Salvation Army's. Goodwill Industries hired poor and often physically disabled people to assist with collecting cast-off goods, repairing viable items at large factories dubbed "cooperative industries," and selling those refurbished wares at secondhand retail stores. Materials beyond repair were sold to salvage yards.[65] In 1910, Rev. Helms established the first Goodwill organization outside of Boston, in Brooklyn, New York, not far from where the pushcarts of the Salvation Army salvage brigades first gathered urban discards. By the early 1920s, Goodwill had a fleet of trucks that amassed unwanted household goods and clothing from more than one hundred thousand homes. Within two decades, the modest Morgan Memorial Chapel had grown into a block-long complex, which included workers' living quarters and a six-story industrial plant.[66]

Those workers were key to Goodwill's public rhetoric. From early in Goodwill's operations, redemption through industry was a recurrent theme, one that reflected the authority of a new brand of "scientific" philanthropy—modern industrial-born charitable ideals that included a firm belief in hard work as the key to success and happiness. In actuality, many aspects of scientific philanthropy were mere reworkings of long-standing capitalist anxieties about the bulk of Americans' work habits, voiced in the United States since at least the time of Benjamin Franklin. The Protestant work ethic had never been an even or consistent aspect of American lives, and immigrants pushed back against the "scientific management" of regimented labor.[67] Goodwill publicists echoed a theme in American discourse from colonization forward. Work, the simple cure for the despair of poverty, served to discipline the masses: "Work is the great tonic. The man, broken and discouraged, who is put to mending chairs, repairs his own fortunes and hopes in the process. Each article repaired is made more valuable. To the garment, there is added the labor of the man or woman who works on it. So with people."[68]

Work provision was intrinsic to salvage stores from their start. In 1894, Rev. S. G. Smith of The People's Church in St. Paul, Minnesota, organized what was perhaps the first American thrift store, a small salvage bureau patterned after similar Salvation Army shops in London. In the 1890s, economic crises had sunk many people "in want, through no moral or intellectual defects." What they most needed was work, and "in the least conspicuous manner," according to Rev. Smith, who credited General Booth with the insight.[69] Other such programs sprang up across the country. Most were attached to settlement homes and churches, and at least loosely tied to the social gospel movement, which gave social welfare a Christian, often evangelical, purpose.[70]

Work's redemptive properties extended from the downtrodden laborers to the objects with which they toiled. Comparing the material hand-me-downs that were repurposed in Goodwill's factories with the people who processed them, Rev. Helms promoted his project with the slogan "Saving the Waste in Men and Things."[71] Goodwill advertised its work as restoring the unredeemed to usefulness, making out of the discards of a profligate society productive individuals and newly desirable commodities. Helms wrote, "The Goodwill Industries takes wasted things donated by the public and employs wasted men and women to bring both things and persons back to usefulness and well-being."[72] Using similar language, the U.S. Salvation Army commander at the turn of the century, Frederick Booth-Tucker, characterized the Salvation Army's industrial homes as places where "human wastage" was employed "in collecting, sorting, repairing and selling the material waste."[73]

By requiring labor in exchange for shelter—in effect vetting charitable recipients by testing their willingness to work—the Salvation Army and Goodwill Industries enacted emerging theories of philanthropic aid, which included replacing direct-giving charity with "scientific" or "systematic giving."[74] At the end of the nineteenth century, the percentage of those living beneath the poverty line grew precipitously, as did the roster of the super-rich. In the late 1870s, approximately one hundred individuals counted themselves millionaires; by 1916, that number had passed forty thousand. Some were millionaires many times over, such as Andrew Carnegie, who in 1901 sold Carnegie Steel Corporation interests to U.S. Steel for $447 million.[75] Since inflation rarely occurred during the period between the Civil War and the Great Depression, the actual gain in wealth for these individuals was significant.

The majority of the uber-wealthy gave away little during their lifetimes. A minority of the new upper class, however, recognized the nation's increasing wealth disparity as an incipient crisis and worried that the struggling masses would threaten the social order. The solution, as proposed by Frederick Gates, chief philanthropic advisor of John D. Rockefeller Sr., was scientific giving—large-scale, highly organized donations designed to better society at large.[76] Giving was "investing in," as Rockefeller put it, and the goal, Carnegie insisted, was to avoid wasting time, effort, and money on the "unreclaimably poor" and to concentrate, instead, on "stimulat[ing] the best and most aspiring of the poor."[77]

Rev. Helms read Carnegie's writings, and Helms's organizational tactics strongly reflected that influence. Goodwill Industries was so loath to compare its functions to old-fashioned, direct-giving charity that at its 1922 annual conference, the company adopted as its national motto, "Not Charity, But a Chance."[78] The motto appeared in nearly all company promotional materials,

FIGURE 1.2 Cover of *The Goodwill Magazine*, Milwaukee edition (vol. 1, no. 1, 1924).

such as the magazine shown in figure 1.2, which features Lady Liberty as Goodwill's benevolent, larger-than-life ambassador. Not coincidentally, by the 1920s, both the Salvation Army and Goodwill began to call their shops "thrift stores," eliminating references to either social aid or junk.[79]

Mass Production and Nostalgia

The reputations of pawnshops and junk dealerships presented obstacles for thrift-store organizers. Popular apprehensions about secondhand items clearly determined much about the groups' public relations strategies. They had help, however; at least one other sales format lent credence to thrift stores' claims of uplift and benevolence. In 1900, an author for one of New York's premier weekly journals, *The Outlook*, announced that the rummage sale was "sweeping over the United States like a cyclone, carrying all before [it]." A combination of an "Old Curiosity Shop" and "Rag Fair," it would soon outrank all other charity events, the writer predicted, and could benefit numerous causes, such as church, settlement home, community, and even political interests.[80] Selling donated and gleaned goods to the public became a popular tool among activists of all kinds, especially those with limited access to conventional political influence, such as women and African Americans.[81]

Rummage sales had their origins in charity fairs, which in the United States began around 1820. The events were irregularly held, often only annually. Originally organized around agricultural products or handmade items and comestibles, the largely female-run charity fairs did not feature secondhand goods until industrial production had become efficient and widespread. Once consumers could regularly and economically replace still-usable household and personal items with new goods, they began donating their used materials to charitable organizations, which then circulated them through established networks.[82] Engaging with a marginal trade that had been the assumed province of the foreign, the criminal, and the destitute, the largely middle-class and usually native-born women who ran rummage sales—frequently conducted in public, outdoor venues—brought respectability to resale and helped pave the way for thrift stores as well as flea markets, a central topic of the following chapter. Much like thrift stores, charity fairs were a way "for elites to co-opt the secondhand economy and establish order in place of the promiscuity that marked the secondhand trades in food, clothing, and household goods."[83] Thrift stores were even more thorough and successful in their efforts.

The popularity of rummage sales also indicated a growing interest in the collection of certain secondhand goods, ones that were more common and inexpensive than European antiques. Before the end of the nineteenth century, few people collected older objects crafted in the United States—the privileged elites who bought antiques focused on foreign-made items. But large-scale production and increased access to new goods spurred a heightened interest in some older objects handmade in the United States, fueled by nostalgia for an imagined "simpler" time in the face of rapid social change. A late-Victorian idealization of hearth and home, part of what historians have dubbed "the cult of domesticity," went hand in hand with a new admiration for colonial American household items.[84] Many old, soon-to-be-revered clocks, furniture pieces, and housewares made their commercial debuts as covetable articles at rummage sales. Such sales introduced the hobby of collecting to members of the middle class—an ill-defined social and fiscal category, members of which were eager to distinguish themselves from the working classes—and added a patriotic appeal to some pre-owned goods.[85]

Collectability would not be attributed to used clothing for decades, but the mass production of apparel did spur some interest in nostalgic dress styles, trends that forecast later recycling of discarded apparel. During the last quarter of the nineteenth century, the market for new ready-made wearables grew prodigiously. Before they were even available for women, ready-mades were standard for many men, who comprised most of the market during the middle of the nineteenth century (after the earliest recipients of crude ready-made clothes, African American slaves and sailors). This gendered order was in part a function of men's greater need for professional wear in addition to daily clothing and in part a function of what styles the technology could manage; men's comparatively loose, separately constructed garments were easier to size and mass-produce than the elaborate, tight-bodiced dresses favored by women. However, as the abilities of mechanized sewing improved, and particularly when separate skirts and shirtwaists became the rage in the 1890s, women joined in with seeming abandon, embracing a consumer ethic that promised relative freedom from the sewing machine and a new license to participate in a cultural form—shopping—which was increasingly recognized as feminine. From 1870 to 1900, capital investment in the United States' garment industry more than tripled, rising from $54 million to $169 million. The number of workers—nearly half of whom operated in New York state, and many of those in the city—almost doubled in total, with a much sharper spike in the percentage of female workers.[86]

Notably, at the same time that the employment, quantity, and value of clothing production in New York City rose, the number of garment factories themselves declined. According to the United States Census of Manufacture, the number of establishments counted went from 9,700 to 8,600, demonstrating an early trend toward concentration of production.[87] The growth of the ready-made industry and the simultaneous constriction of manufactories—a process that would accelerate throughout the twentieth century—affected both the supply of and demand for new and used clothing. Certainly, informal clothing sales like those of pushcart peddlers and at the Chatham Street market in New York City rose along with the quickening turnover of fashionable apparel. As newer styles became more quickly and consistently accessible for shoppers, the speed of clothing discard increased, too, rapidly swelling available stores of secondhand articles.

The end of the nineteenth century saw several reactionary dress movements, including rational dress, associated with the political ideals and suffrage advocacy of New Women. Rational dress styles allowed for more physical mobility and less attention to rapid shifts in fashion, imagining the wearer as a dynamic political subject. Another kind of dress reform impulse, however, the aesthetic or artistic dress movement, most directly reacted to changes in clothing manufacturing and had minimal political meaning for the women involved. Related to a broader artistic and decorative movement (also called the aesthetic movement), in the late 1870s and 1880s avant-garde women in the United States began to favor "artistic" dress, which included loose gowns composed of airy, light material with classical drape and little corseting.[88] The movement began when the social philosophies of John Ruskin and William Morris inspired London-based artists who called themselves Pre-Raphaelites. In attempts to reform contemporary visual art, the Pre-Raphaelites sought to undo what they saw as an academic preference for mannerism and classical poses, and looked to early Renaissance painters such as Botticelli and Donatello as more "natural" examples. In their view, adherence to natural colors and forms produced visual art with greater spiritual intensity.[89]

The aesthetic movement, like the Arts and Crafts movement (whose stylistic preferences helped spur the interest in collecting older American-made objects such as the clocks and furniture often sold in rummage sales), favored the homemade and one-of-a-kind over machine-made products.[90] Since the admired styles were far too antiquated for a literal adoption of the representative material, secondhand clothing did not play a physical role in the artistic dress movement. Proponents still relied on production methods—just more artisan ones than those of the new large-scale manufacturers. Also, artistic dressers reviled newly developed synthetic dyes, which were cheaper to produce and brighter in hues than the vegetable- or mineral-based dyes otherwise used. Florid shades resulted from the new synthetic processes—such as magenta, so-named for the particularly bloody Battle of Magenta, fought in 1859 as part of the Second Italian War of Independence. Clothiers specializing in artistic dress relied on a handful of fabric makers who preferred vegetable dyes, which lent fabric softer tones of unconventional colors, such as salmon, sage green, and amber-gold. Ideally, artistic dresses were intricately but delicately embroidered in Art Needlework style and had liberal smocking.[91] The final product was intended to be art. Aesthetic dress was not inexpensive.

Although Pre-Raphaelites relied on the production of new items for their oppositional style, the ideals reflected by artistic dress hinted at antiquated clothing's potential as social commentary. Fashion historians often refer to the artistic dress style as "a bohemian counter-fashion," a label some contemporaries adopted with pride.[92] In this instance, "bohemian" should not be read as synonymous with a reliance on secondhand materials, a practice that self-identified American bohemians cultivated beginning with post–World War I

Greenwich Village modernists. Late-1950s Greenwich Village Beats adopting early "hippie" flourishes through secondhand clothing called themselves "Beat Pre-Raphaelites," imagining an affinity with artistic dressers, one covetous of the literal materials of the original imitative movement.[93]

During the 1880s and 1890s, artistic dressers relied on high-priced, custom-made materials cut and patterned after pre-Raphaelite artists' depictions—or Oscar Wilde's well-publicized sartorial "dos and don'ts." In the turn-of-the century United States, it was not the well-off avant-garde who borrowed directly from the less fortunate to express class dissent; exception from the lower classes meant rejection of one mode of production for another more elite and costly one. Instead, we must return to the evangelistic Salvationists to find a better example of pre-WWI sartorial appropriation intended to showcase a rejection of status and utilizing old clothes. For a select group of "Hallelujah lassies," spiritual ambitions avowedly trumped societal ones and expressed themselves, once again, through unconventional secondhand dress.

Salvationists' Cross-Class Wardrobes

Members of the Salvation Army framed the desire for new, fashionable clothing as immodest and materialistic. As already mentioned, the uniform advertised the group's ostensible exception from worldly fashions, but Salvationists used other manners of dress to enact and advertise cross-class outreach.[94] Salvationists' adaptations of regulated dress allowed working-class Salvationists to dress "up" in order to consolidate members' status and legitimate public presence. At the same time, certain factions of Salvation Army soldiers dressed "down" in solidarity with the extremely poor, in order to "pass" as impoverished and to perform humility in a time of increasingly uneven wealth distribution. As Gilded Age excesses led economist Thorstein Veblen to coin the phrase "conspicuous consumption," Salvationists appropriated tenement garments to represent the group's nonmaterial ambitions.[95]

The Salvation Army's "slum sisters" lived among the very poor, offering practical aid and spiritual guidance. This lauded faction of soldiers abandoned their Salvationist uniform in favor of even meaner clothing, dramatizing a deliberate departure from their own class origins through the adoption of disheveled, outdated apparel. Blanche Cox, the English innovator of the slum sisters' prescribed apparel, often referred to as "Lower Still" dress, demanded that the slum sisters use insubstantial, torn, dirty, and relatively revealing dress in order to "put ourselves on a level with the people, entering into their sorrows and cares."[96] Ragwear, like the uniform, gave women from "decent" backgrounds entrée into places where most such women would never have ventured—while still relegating them to accepted feminine tasks of caretaking.[97] The Lower Still dress was a "total metaphor," worn with the intention of "passing" as a genuine subject of the realm, regardless of upbringing.[98] Even slum sisters who came from working-class backgrounds (as many did) were obscuring their origins by going "lower still" down the socio-sartorial ladder.

In London and New York City, these women were praised by press reports as much for their material abnegation as for the help they provided. Salvation Army Major Emma Bown, who headed up the Army's American slum work for many years, hailed from a middle-class background.[99] In 1889, a year and a half before Jacob Riis's *How the Other Half Lives* showed New York City slums in stark black and white photography, Major Bown ventured into those same quarters, and her Lower Still dress was central to media's notice. *Frank Leslie's Weekly* (1893) praised Bown's austerity, comparing her to a fourteenth-century "rapturous ascetic."[100] Other publications described her comportment as if it were that of a highly spiritualized fashion model. Bown was "tall, slender, and clad in a coarse brown gown, mended with patches. A big gingham apron, artistically rent in several places, is tied about her waist. She wears an old plaid woolen shawl and an ancient brown straw hat. Her dress indicates extreme poverty; her face denotes perfect peace."[101] The same clothing that on tenement residents would have indicated depravity and sorrow, apparently allowed the slum sisters' luminous piety to shine.

In their quotidian dress, slum sisters emulated Christ, "who, though he was rich, yet for our sakes became poor, that we, through his poverty, might become rich, and who has left us an example that we should follow in his steps."[102] Aside from the aim of sartorial alliance with the poor, the abandonment of the uniform signaled an added sacrifice—an extra step away from secular fashion in its expression of humility. The emphasis of Lower Still clothing was on modesty and servitude, as read in the plain calico print dresses and utilitarian aprons in figure 1.3, a publicity shot of Major Bown and a fellow slum sister caring for a tenement child, clutching the modest tools of their trade, a brush and broom. Cut-rate (presumably used, unless the organization disfigured new garments instead of relying on its stocks of secondhand items) calico and gingham dresses sought to redefine cheap as moral and idealistic instead of as promiscuous. Respectability was defined by willingness to work in aid of others, and this willingness was signaled by raiment appropriate to the adopted station. But like the uniform, ragwear also deviated from conventionally prescribed Protestant dress. John Wesley, who famously preached "Cleanliness is next to Godliness," wrote, "Whatever clothes

FIGURE 1.3 Major Emma Bown at left with unidentified tenement child and a fellow "slum sister," circa 1890. Courtesy of The Salvation Army National Archives.

you have, let them be whole; no rents, no tatters, no rags. These are a scandal to either man or woman; being another fruit of vile laziness. Mend your clothes, or I shall never expect you to mend your lives. Let none ever see a ragged Methodist."[103]

Useful parallels with the Salvation Army's ragwear may be found in turn-of-the-century masquerades or fancy-dress balls, which were very popular among the wealthy classes in Europe and the United States.[104] These lavish cultural events were opulent celebrations of prosperity, decadence, and an (often metaphorical) alliance with aristocratic ancestry. For example, the Vanderbilts' fancy-dress ball in 1883 was populated by specters of royalty, brutality, and fame, from Otho the Barbarian to Cardinal Richelieu and the Count of Monte Cristo. In addition to the requisite Marie Antoinettes, women favored symbolic representations, such as Light, Folly, Morning, Night, and Innocence.[105] While worlds away from the Vanderbilt mansions, the slum sisters also elicited romantic descriptions of their clothing as symbolic of vaunted characteristics.

Salvationists' ragwear may have inverted the robber barons' conspicuous spectacles, but they used sartorial display as much as did the elite community's fancy-dress ball gowns. Similarly to how a Marie Antoinette costume expressed unproven aristocratic affiliations, gingham and calico signified an unearned alliance with destitution. In this way, Lower Still dress represents some of the contradictions of self-conscious unfashionability, contradictions that would color secondhand styles throughout the twentieth century. The slum sisters chose selective representatives of this unidirectional sisterhood—after all, Salvationists had many emblematic outfits available in their coffers of used materials. Not all the impoverished dressed alike, and Salvationists did not emulate all "poor sisters." Despite the Army's focus on evangelizing to prostitutes, for example, slum sisters never tried to blend in with that subset of urbanites.[106]

In other instances, Salvationists even more directly dramatized a disaffection for individual wealth and fortune—and demonstrated the contradictions of their own brand of staged sartorial modesty. Evangeline Booth, the Salvation Army founders' seventh child who served as the commander of the U.S. Salvation Army from 1904 to 1934, before becoming the first female general of the entire organization, exemplified the organization's performative dress habits.[107] Christened Evelyne Cory Booth, and called Eva, Booth later changed her name to Evangeline under the advice of her friend Frances Willard, suffragist and temperance crusader. Eva Booth's personal dress performances describe the intersection of the Gilded Age Salvation Army's religious politics and a canny understanding of the importance of public appearances. From early in life, Evangeline Booth was theatrical, staging demonstrations that placed her at the center of crowds' attention. Her parents once feared she would leave the Army in favor of the stage, where her auburn hair, striking features, and bold demeanor might have been welcomed. Her role as commander of the United States Salvation Army, however, amply accommodated her desire for attention, power, and theatricality.[108]

Growing up in a privileged home, little Eva romanticized poverty even while sympathizing with its victims. Eva felt called at a very young age to work with the poor, which was, after all, the central mission of her father's organization. One laudatory biographer called her George Bernard Shaw's *Pygmalion* heroine in reverse. After devoting her life to the Army at fourteen, Eva, whom her father had already declared a born orator, turned to full-on masquerade to penetrate the London slums. She willingly donned rags and sold flowers in Piccadilly Circus, so the story goes, reportedly relishing her father's impressed dismay at the success of her disguise when she revealed herself. She took on another mythic role when she posed as a match seller, evoking the Hans Christian Andersen story of pathos and poverty. Her appreciation for the drama of poverty and the performance of dress often fused in displays of calculated Victorian sentimentalism.[109]

The adult Evangeline Booth continued to frankly view poverty as romantic, likening the Army's own struggle to that of noble indigence, proud though destitute: "This organization was born amid the roaring thunder of the darkest neighborhood of the great metropolis—London.... It was born in lodging houses, damp-polluted cellars, blind alleyways, fever-stricken courtyards, the deep recesses of the great bridge, where ragged forms staggered into darkness, and fair faces vanished for the last time."[110] For Evangeline Booth, echoing Lower Still dress imperatives, "ragged forms" became metaphors for virtuous struggle. She carried those notions and her predilection for theatrical rags across the Atlantic, where her father appointed her commander of the U.S. Salvation Army in 1904. Immediately after she assumed her position as commander, she began staging plays and dramatic readings for the public, including a musical titled "The Commander in Rags."[111] In a 1906 performance of the musical at Carnegie Hall, slum sisters clad in obligatory gingham formed the chorus to Booth's lead. Evangeline Booth regaled the gathered public with stories of her own slum work, glamorizing her organization's urban labor and sensationalizing the institutionalized dress. An article titled "Miss Booth's Slum Tales Thrill Crowd" described her clothing and demeanor much in the way a French paper might have lingered over details of an Irene Castle costume: a slim, little woman, Commander Booth wore "a tartan shawl, a tattered print skirt, and broken-heeled shoes laced with string."[112] By placing herself at the play's center, Evangeline Booth was able to showcase her leadership as well as her sympathy for the poor.

Evangeline Booth depicted respectful sympathy for the impoverished and relayed romantic tales of her own forays into its abyss. At the same time, she also cultivated a personal taste for fine things, such as high-end furniture and expensive musical instruments. At fifteen, she donned the Army uniform, poke bonnet and all, and continued to wear it during her American command—except when performing in rags. She did, however, hire a French seamstress to line all her uniforms with silk. Evangeline Booth lived among the rich, spending inherited wealth to outfit her two homes. She used this proximity to wealth in her position as Salvation Army commander; she was particularly gifted at recruiting moneyed patrons for the Army.[113] In contrast

FIGURE 1.4
Evangeline Booth posing in rags with a pedal harp, circa 1910. Courtesy of The Salvation Army National Archives.

to Booth's lavish personal expenditures, she often posed for public relations images clad in slum wear. At least thirty different photographs exist of the commander dressed in rags, sometimes in reenactment of her early subterfuge, gripping matches with expressions of patient wistfulness or forlornly offering flowers to her audience.[114] Figure 1.4 reflects maudlin Victorian sentiments, Gilded Age wealth, and Booth's romantic understanding of poverty. Evangeline Booth stands erect and posed, looking serenely away, seemingly occupied by otherworldly concerns. The pedal harp, an elaborate and expensive instrument, expressive of the grandeur of the Gilded Age but still emblematic of angelic piety, is juxtaposed with Booth's dramatically ragged clothing. Complex, concatenated modern identities drove Booth to supplement her institutional uniform, expressive of modesty and humility, with fine linings, and to masquerade on and off stage in ragged clothing.

The Conflicted Consumer

While all-out class masquerade was not the aim of the average consumer in the first decades of the century, those aims were anything but simplistic or well defined. By 1915, men and women—but particularly women—were greatly influenced by the formation of a spectacular, sensuous culture of consumption, a culture that "subverted, but never overturned, the older mentality of repression, practical utilitarianism, scarcity, and self-denial."[115] While seemingly pervasive in turn-of-the-century cities—which erupted with new and increasingly elaborate department store displays—firsthand shopping was hardly a universally approved activity. The buying public did remain ambivalent about the thrift-store system's use of discarded clothes and indigent labor to create alternatives to department stores, but also expressed uncertainty about the moral value of department stores.

In the early part of the twentieth century, consumers often linked personal restraint with principled propriety; proscriptive literature certainly advised frugality. Fiction authors, as well as secular and religious sermonizers, also portrayed the heightened recreational consumerism, boosted by an unevenly rising standard of living, as morally questionable. In Theodore Dreiser's *Sister Carrie* (1900), the enchantment, promise, and betrayal of department store wares ultimately proved ruinous for the covetous heroine.[116] But not much more than a decade after Dreiser's character willingly sank her reputation and any nonmaterialistic ambitions beneath a tempting tide of consumer enticement, a burgeoning medium expressed a very different view of the conflicts surrounding youthful material desire, feminine independence, and old-fashioned parsimony.

D. W. Griffith's short silent film *The New York Hat* (1912) cast consumerism, particularly "frivolous" dress, in a liberatory, modern part. The new consumer ethic included the promise of deliverance from familial patriarchy, a trope *The New York Hat* employs, with a young Mary Pickford as a rural heroine of consumer desire.[117] In this instance, Pickford's aged father, with his obsolete values of strict frugality—not much different from the father in *The Post* story about the disease-ridden blue silk dress—is a clear antihero. In the short film, a youthful minister, the obvious vehicle of moral instruction, carries out the mother's dying wish: to buy the daughter a few coveted objects with money painstakingly hidden from the patriarch's eagle eye. The minister's purchase of a lavish New York City hat spurs a town scandal as church biddies imagine an illicit link, but in the end, the girl and the minister are vindicated, while the community soundly reproves the curmudgeon father for his penny-pinching ways.

The ideal of thrift was certainly changing. Film, itself a new, urban recreational indulgence, joined eager advertisers in encouraging greater consumer abandon. But thrift was and is a stubborn standard. Thrift, which influential religious leaders had long stressed as a core Christian virtue—something that resonated with thrift-store entrepreneurs—was also a basic value of capitalism.[118] The seminal Scottish economist Adam Smith declared that "Parsimony, and not industry, is the immediate cause of the increase of capital."[119] As consuming ready-made goods became an essential activity of everyday life in the late nineteenth century, the concept of thrift was forced to more directly accommodate the impetus to buy. In 1920, Harvard economics professor T. N. Carver claimed, "[t]hrift does not consist in refusing to spend money or buy things." In fact, he contended, "the thriftiest people are the people with the highest standard of living."[120] It followed that the sort of educated consumer who understood the time-and-money-saving convenience of modern products promoted a brisker economic pace, spurred product innovation, and even encouraged the use of consumer credit. Rather than positing a necessary opposition between the goal of acquisition and the value of frugality, the growth of thrift stores coincided with a mass advertising appeal to fiscally sensible shopping in order to encourage consumer participation.

Still, American consumers continued to critique their own and others' materiality across categories of class and ethnicity, despite new and aggressive forms of advertising and marketing.[121] Thrift stores' reliance on goods donations accorded well with public sentiment about consumption. Even though more commercial items were available for sale and Americans' purchasing power was steadily increasing, consumers continued to associate profligacy with a weak moral character. Through thrift-store programs, people could abandon viable clothing and household materials, reassured that they were helping those with fewer means. In a business memoir reflecting on two and a half decades of success, Rev. Helms would include a special dedication to the thousands of "altruistic housewives" who aided in Goodwill Industry's success by supplying the raw materials for eventual sales.[122] In the first two decades of the twentieth century, thrift stores secured donations by recasting the abandonment of traditional domestic stewardship as charitable giving. Passing down her clothing a little sooner than she might have otherwise, the "altruistic housewife" exhibited a virtuous devotion to public thrift that also happily sanctioned her personal indulgence in new acquisitions. In this way, the practices of thrift stores served to increase buyers' participation in firsthand consumer capitalism. The "subverted, but never overturned" mentality of self-denial and parsimony worked well to secure thrift stores' supplies of consumer goods.[123]

The New York Hat hints at a changing societal position for that longtime vaunted virtue, thrift. It also suggests another problem for secondhand sale success—newly produced and aggressively promoted goods did rise in public esteem. By 1915, immigrants, the majority members of thrift stores' original target audience, were often surrounded by urban consumer opportunities, and like other buyers, they were conflicted by the myriad options—the practical, the glamorous, the frugal, the reliable, the fantastical. Upon arriving in the United States, the first imperative for many European, especially Jewish, immigrants was "to visit the stores and be dressed from head to foot in American clothing."[124] Basic English language skills were necessary for many jobs, but employment and social acceptance were more readily achieved when the applicant's clothing was neat, clean, and not markedly foreign. Thrift stores, which offered inexpensive American wares, would seem to have been ideally equipped to serve the needs of the ambitious immigrant. But historians like Peiss and Enstad—and novelists such as Dreiser—emphasize young aspiring women's ardor for department stores, well stocked with the ready-made options that enticed both native-born and immigrant wage earners.[125]

Passing preworn clothing through kinship networks was common to many newcomers' countries of origin, but the practice did not necessarily translate into buying strangers' discards, even though recent immigrants well understood the adaptive importance of clothing. Hand-me-down goods often have been presented as the stagnating, old-world way in a new economy of generational change and economic and social mobility by reflective historians, and by contemporary sociologists such as Mead. The fiction works and memoirs of the Poland-born Russian Jew Anzia Yezerskia sometimes agree with this narrative, but provide evidence of ambiguity from the perspective of the foreign-born consumer.

Yezierska's stories illustrate the centrality of clothing in early twentieth-century immigrants' lives. American-looking clothing was perhaps a greater priority for assimilatory Jews than for other immigrant groups because their traditional, Old World clothing set them apart at a glance as both un-American and non-Protestant. Despite the coercions of salvage stores, many immigrants avoided buying from secondhand venues, since adaptation to the New World included leaving behind situations in which they and their families were obliged to participate in "shadow" economies for survival. As emblematic of the cruelty experienced in harshly anti-Semitic countries, secondhand clothing was an unappealing option for Jewish immigrants hoping for greater opportunities in America.

In one of Yezierska's stories, a young Jewish immigrant, Shenah, illustrates this double-bind when she bemoans her orphaned plight. "Woe is me! No mother, no friend to help me lift myself out of my greenhorn rags," she complains.[126] Shenah's lament speaks to a 1913 Chicago study demonstrating that a newly arrived Jewish girl's stateside relatives considered themselves obliged to buy her American clothing "almost immediately."[127] Shenah, however, with no welcoming relations in the United States, lacks that advantage. To get the money she needs to buy a cheerful dress and hat decked with imitation cherries, Shenah pawns her "last memory from Russia," a featherbed her mother had made and bequeathed to her. The pawnshop Shenah patronizes is a clearly undesirable commercial zone. In one sentence, the space is described as "gloomy," its wares as "tawdry," and the proprietor's face as "grisly."[128] In Yezierska's stories, virtuous actors such as Shenah will reluctantly sell secondhand items to afford new ones, but they clearly balk at buying used goods.

Yet a converse enthusiasm for new, ready-made clothing was far from absolute. If Yezierska's entire body of both fictional and autobiographical work is taken into account, the author's awareness of the performative importance of clothing did not translate into simple ambitions of upward mobility or a clearly assimilatory appearance. Yezierska's—and many of her fictional character's—employment in the garment industry represented the vocation of many young Jewish women, more than any other group, followed by Italian immigrants such as the Navy Street dancer. These sweatshop experiences grounded a deeply complicated ambivalence toward new, ready-made apparel, one that competed with the vexed associations with second-hand clothes. Yezierska described secondhand stores as "banners of poverty" in fiction, but her fraught experiences as a clothing producer in sweatshop conditions tainted her enjoyment of new and glamorous clothes, leading her to record in a memoir, "If my hands are sick from waists, how could my head learn to put beauty into them?"[129] Autobiographically, she recalls her childhood shame of her greenhorn rags but acknowledges that even after her success as a writer allowed her access to assimilatory styles, "perversity made me cling to my pushcart clothes."[130]

Consumer motives for buying secondhand, as the Navy Street dancer's aims and Yezierska's ambivalence show, were not guided strictly by the suppliers' philanthropic and assimilating objectives. Thrift stores, which provided alternatives to department store couture, had various important advantages over other sorts of secondhand sales. As legislation increased restrictions on informal economic exchange, thrift stores' reliance on donations helped them capitalize on Americans' mounting habit of disposing viable goods. While rummage sales had narrow precedence over the venues, thrift stores' permanent locations and chain-store standardization gained them loyal consumers and consistent donors by the 1920s. In the years around World War I, Salvation Army and Goodwill thrift stores matched, or even outpaced, the growth of chain stores such as Woolworth's and A&P, stores whose success threatened the sanctity of other colloquial means of food distribution, such as public marketplaces (and partly enabled the rise of another form of secondhand sales new to the United States, the flea market).[131] By the eve of the Great Depression, thrift stores' broader acceptability as affordable stand-ins for expensive department stores relied on their ability to echo the variety and organization of mainstream stores. Given that John Wanamaker, "the greatest merchant in America," was a longtime friend and supporter of the Salvation Army, thrift stores' success as an alternative to department stores was not entirely surprising.

Over time, the Salvation Army and Goodwill Industries backgrounded their salvage efforts' work provision and promoted consumer appeal. In figure 1.5, a Salvation Army pamphlet from the late teens/early 1920s shows a few choice images of "What the camera finds in a Salvation Army Industrial Home and Store." A venerable-looking older man labors in the "clockmaker's corner," evoking preindustrial nostalgia, perhaps tapping into the popularity of the Arts and Crafts movement of the time. A mechanic has a position, and even "men who have no other trade can always sort and bale paper." But the exultant consumer is in the very center of the pamphlet, from where a young girl smiles at a newly prized possession held aloft with pride: "A modish little top-coat made from remnants of automobile upholstery."[132]

The consumer item itself is telling, relying as it does on the sort of repurposing that nineteenth-century women had commonly performed, delegated now to massive philanthropic organizations. In the age of industrial capitalism, the stewardship of material goods was adapted to new commercial realities, and thus recodified, at the same time that new populations—both employees and consumers—were drawn into the free market economy of the United States. The satisfied workers skirt the periphery; the happy buyer is central.

The success of thrift stores made savvy businessmen of old-fashioned almsgiving missionaries. By 1909, Industrial Homes, under which the salvage programs functioned, was providing the Salvation Army with nearly $2 million annually and comprised the bulk of its $1.5 million real estate portfolio.[133] The mounting importance of maintaining this source of income was reflected in shifting institutional priorities. In 1923, for example, a handbook

FIGURE 1.5 Promotional pamphlet, circa 1920. Courtesy of The Salvation Army National Archives.

for evaluating officers valued the "ability to secure business efficiency from men" over "spiritual results in dealing with men."[134] The semantic rebranding of "junk shops" as "thrift stores" signaled that Christian-based social reform groups had, in effect, sanitized secondhand goods, both morally and physically. Much-maligned pawnshops underwent a similar transformation in the mid-twentieth century, when semiphilanthropic associations began to compete with independent owners. The most successful of these "benevolent" pawnshops was the Provident Loan Society in New York City, founded in 1929 and bankrolled by business elites such as Cornelius Vanderbilt and J. Pierpont Morgan.[135] Wealthier consumers who donated their cast-offs were encouraged to think of themselves as virtuous helpmeets in the Progressive Era's reform agenda, while poor, "ethnic," or disabled individuals were transformed into an army of workers as well as a niche market to be tapped. A prime example of doing well while also doing good, the Salvation Army's and Goodwill Industries' salvaging operations changed America's charitable giving as well as its culture of consumption by creating for the very same artifact both producers and consumers.

However, it would be a mistake to think of thrift stores as just an assimilationist success story, or as an example of the power of marketing strategies. Historians have widely agreed that the engines of industrial capitalism and advertising strongly influenced the acquisitive decisions of firsthand consumers at the turn of the last century.[136] But secondhand commerce illustrates how marginal consumers, many of them immigrants, reciprocally shaped marketing and conformed reform projects to their own desires. New philanthropy targeted immigrants with a view toward maintaining clean, orderly, and fully "American" cities. Philanthropic capitalists adapted the tactics of mainstream marketing not only to "remake" waste products but to "remake" public perceptions of that waste as well. In the process, goods salvaging programs also claimed to "remake" the men and women associated with that waste. Teaching American style and habits was part of the Salvation Army's and Goodwill's Americanization and reform programs, which included resale retail as a natural extension of social welfare projects. At the same time, however, most thrift-store consumers were uncurtailed in their purchase choices—and the ways in which they used the secondhand materials, as the Navy Street dancer demonstrates in 1902.

Secondhand clothing outlets like salvage stores did not simply replicate the "progress in consumption" that aroused and fulfilled wealthier consumers' desires for choice.[137] With a rise in the consumer demand for variety came a narrowing in the range of production as well. As manufacturing and advertising interests consolidated, new goods outlets were arguably as restrained by the time lines of trends as places like thrift stores were by fluctuations in donation levels. Despite their myriad adaptations to primary commercial procedures, thrift stores ran counter to an important capitalist trend emergent at the century's start: obsolescence. While some stores exerted efforts to adapt old materials to current styles—like the automotive upholstery turned girl's coat—for the most part, secondhand venues had the dubious distinction of containing multiple generations of style, goods, and apparel. The variability of such stock was a total detriment only if the desire for new was simple and absolute among consumers. At the same time that American cities grew and diversified, the urge for and definition of novelty expanded. Eventually, what was old became new again.

CHAPTER TWO

Dressing Dada and the Rise of Flea Markets

The hour of the pawns has come.
—"Midnight in a Pawnshop," Guido Bruno (1920)

The people I know don't wear clothes—that is—not what you would call clothes. . . . They wear ideas.
—"Chains of Dew," Susan Glaspell (1920)

In 1937, the *Washington Post*'s society editor boasted the advent of an open-air sale sure to attract "proper city folk" as well as those from "the fashionable hunt country." The market's organizer, Bettina Belmont, was known for her "flair for infusing a familiar setup with foreign atmosphere."[1] Paris's famed Marché aux Puces, widely considered the inaugural modern flea market, inspired the event. The avid sportswoman's upscale version of a flea market offered both new and used objects, featuring boots and saddles, handwoven tweed-cushioned dog baskets, and fine linens and glassware. In the 1930s, Belmont was not alone among D.C.'s debutante set in her use of French inflections or secondhand business acumen. For example, the Washington Arts Club hosted an entirely secondhand fund-raising sale called "Foire aux Croutes" (or "Fair of the Crusts)" annually throughout the 1930s.[2]

At the same time that secondhand sales were attracting the money and attention of D.C.'s high society, New York City mayor Fiorello LaGuardia was working hard to squelch the presence of pushcart dealers whose routes had steadily shrunk throughout the century. In the run-up to New York's turn to host the World's Fair, LaGuardia saw the city's "modern" status as at odds with the street-based economies.[3] This was no sudden impulse; New York City officials began trying to immobilize the mostly immigrant vendors thronging thoroughfares late in the nineteenth century. By the 1930s, city legislation had mostly succeeded in concentrating once-peripatetic peddlers in either legally designated zones or de facto markets in areas with poor regulation and enforcement. And now, the latter pushcart markets were in the mayor's crosshairs.

Both Bettina Belmont's upper-crust hunting-gear soirees and lower Manhattan's persistent pushcart markets were American manifestations of European-born flea markets, a varied and messy category of informal economy. The first example reflected a privileged enthusiasm for distinctive consumer goods, an expansion of recreational collecting to include some everyday items, and the chicness of French styles and habits. The Belmont event indicated a reframing of the notion of "novelty" to include the not-new in a way connected to, on the one hand, nostalgic sentimentalism forged by conservative patriotism, and on the other, transnational art movements tinged with political radicalism. Across the economic spectrum from Belmont's elite soiree, Manhattan's pushcart markets showcased the adaptability of marginalized workers and the related tenacity of informal economies. Similar sites formed the basis for many American city flea markets, and rural regions had their counterpart derived from farmers markets. Immigrants, country farmers, and black Americans introduced (and helped maintain) the retail practices, habits of valuation, and often the physical goods themselves that enabled the growth of an elite interest in secondhand exchange. Whether that interest was more related to the anticommercial ideals espoused by surrealist founder André Breton or to the patriotic fervor of uber-wealthy collectors such as automobile mogul Henry Ford, laborers relegated to the sidelines of American society were vital to the process, as were burgeoning forms of recreation and mass media. During the interwar period, art, fashion, and theater helped secondhand materials slowly gain new, positive meanings, disseminated through cultural borrowings, reinterpretations, and light-hearted parodies.

As voluntary secondhand consumers came into public focus, flea markets flourished. Versions of open-air markets have existed as long as commerce has, but dismissing the twentieth-century versions featuring mostly secondhand goods as simply throwbacks to preindustrial commerce is myopic. A closer examination reveals the flea market's oppositional significance in an industrial capitalist economy based on fixed prices and mass-produced materials. Admittedly, quantifying, or even concisely classifying, "flea markets" is a Sisyphean task.[4] Historically, hardly any elements evenly applied to all the venues, and even fewer *only* applied to them. Flea markets had no formal chronicles of their declared purposes and no centralized standards before the 1990s.[5] Exactly when flea markets can be counted as part of U.S. commerce is debatable—perhaps in the unrecorded moment when pre-owned objects became a critical part of urban public and rural farmers markets, or perhaps in the also-elusive instant when the name was first applied. What is clear, however, is that the addition of secondhand goods sustained city-built public marketplaces as their original, food-sales purpose faded attendant to the rise in chain grocery stores during the interwar period.[6] Similarly, secondhand goods enlarged the services of rural farmers markets in the face of farming crises and diminishing returns on direct-consumer distribution.[7] In short, secondhand sales saved the American public marketplace.[8]

During the 1920s and 1930s, tony secondhand venues hosted by members of high society and ragtag commerce relegated to ethnic neighborhoods or country back roads both conformed to the strictures of modernity, around which ideals of fashionability, nonconformity, practicality, and consumer marketability swirled and shifted. Perhaps the most modern thing about flea markets in this period was their resistance to various practices intrinsic to modes of firsthand sales. Based on some markers, these anticonsumer consumer venues were roughly analogous to "antiart" art movements of the time such as Dada or surrealism—associates of which themselves were devotees of flea markets. The practice of haggling over cost (antithetical to fixed-price chain and department stores) and the disorienting array of objects available (as opposed to the highly organized aisles at Wanamaker's or Macy's) gave the flea market an edgy air, which sociologists have called "libidinous," making it a "ritual and ceremonial venue for the experience of disorder."[9] This "experience of disorder" earned avant-garde artists' appreciation for secondhand exchange generally and flea markets particularly. For French-born André Breton, who defined the precepts of surrealism in the 1920s and coached its followers for decades after, flea markets were delightfully rife with "chance encounters" that might inspire transcendent artistic vision.[10] Foreign-born affiliates of surrealism and Dada—André Breton, Marcel Duchamp, and Max Ernst, to highlight a few well-known artists who spent time in New York City—along with American-born Joseph Cornell, elevated physical items removed by disuse from their original purpose to new heights of creative potency. However, it was the less well-known German-born Dada exemplar Baroness Elsa von Freytag-Loringhoven who best demonstrated the intricate links between the modernist investment in fashion, performance art, and the avant-garde reappropriation of secondhand materials. Through writings, personal appearances, and visual art enabled by castoffs, modernists declared that used items had liberatory potential, from capitalist labor and consumption, sexist assumptions, and an aesthetic rooted in realism. Moreover, materials found among garbage, in junk stores, on the street, or amidst flea-market dreft held particular personal meaning for artists who themselves were exiled or displaced.

Breton emphasized the *désenchaînement* of flea-market objects, which "can be found nowhere else, outmoded, fragmented, useless, almost incomprehensible, perverse in short."[11] The English translation connotes disenchantment or disconnection. At the same time that this conception of flea markets proved aesthetically useful, it ignored, or at least underplayed, the specific "local, ethnic, and class-bound" meanings of such items (and places of commerce), as critic Susan Sontag later pointed out.[12] Many of the chief participants at flea markets were poor and provincial, relegated to marginal careers and dependent on society's discards for subsistence. What to one viewer seemed magically surreal and antibourgeoisie, to another participant was a component of personal habituation to misfortune or prejudice. An increasingly diversified demand for secondhand objects spurred the growth of mostly used economies such as flea markets; recycled pushcart shoes warmed immigrant toes, industrial detritus conveyed abstract modernist concepts, and decades-old Americana fueled a conservative nostalgia for preindustrial life.

Contrasting forces shaped and encouraged secondhand exchange after World War I. In general, the 1920s were a time of conflict and contradiction. Americans' moral ideals, cultural habits, economic desires, and political priorities were varied and at odds, as the nation split between movements to preserve the status quo and efforts to progress beyond the constraints of nineteenth-century social standards.[13] Americans aghast at youth culture, urban heterogeneity, and the decadent pastimes of relative affluence sought to maintain an imagined simplicity—a simplicity that sometimes included racial segregation, religious oppression, and ethnic intolerance. Some vied for a dark, romanticized notion of "traditionalism," the kind that made *Birth of a Nation*—the epic film portraying Ku Klux Klan members as righteous, masculine heroes—a commercial success in 1915.[14] World War I accelerated many of these tensions; just as the war slowed European immigration to eastern port cities, the need for industrial wartime labor stimulated the mass northward movement of 1.6 million southern blacks eager to escape Jim Crow.[15] Black political, intellectual, and cultural communities flourished as Ku Klux Klan membership spread out from the South to peak nationally in the mid-1920s. Urban night life, bawdy theatrical revues, and modern youth culture thrived in conjunction with the apparent constraints of Prohibition.

Reactionary repression and outward-looking progressivism sometimes worked in concert toward the same end. Flea markets took shape in response to both impulses. Supplies of secondhand items grew as modern efficiency and innovations in manufacturing, production, and advertising quickened the pace of consumption and disposal. Clothing was a greater part of this consumer growth than ever before. Demand for used goods grew in apparent proportion. The origins of those demands ran the gamut: the poverty of many new immigrants and other victims of the growing inequity of wealth;

a popular attraction to wares branded "exotic" and specifically, all things French; an avant-garde anticommercialism; and finally, a rising conservative nostalgia for the preindustrialized American past.

Mounting constrictions on street economies shaped the location and design of emerging flea markets, with the advent of the automobile age spurring tighter control over all types of city traffic. At the same time, practical local politics and economic rationale eventually guaranteed small-scale entrepreneurship, and especially secondhand sales, a continued role in urban commerce. More "efficient" food systems—such as the chain grocery stores belonging to The Great Atlantic and Pacific Tea Company, better known as the A&P—left huge public markets half-empty, and the same city officials who worked to eradicate peddling from the urban streets invited secondhand salespeople into the dying public marketplaces, for a fee. Agile secondhand economies slid into the modern age like able shape-shifters, sacrificing form, retaining content, and strengthening function.

The hiccupping economies of the early twentieth century both shaped and accommodated the modern consumer. After a two-year recession following World War I's end, the standard of living rose for many Americans but continued to decline for others, including the nearly one-quarter of the population in the agricultural sector. Expanding corporations produced an array of enticing consumer items—some, like refrigerators, washing machines, and waffle irons, seemed to validate family life and domesticity, while others, like radios, cosmetics, synthetic fabrics, and of course, automobiles, advertised the new importance of mass culture, individualism, and mobility. Soon, consumers' material desires extended beyond the average worker's means. Though production outpaced consumption by mid-decade, for a few years credit extension and installment buying sustained the impression of unequaled and undiminishing affluence in an atmosphere of recreational consumer abandonment that characterized the 1920s.[16]

Amidst all these changes, fashion, dress, and clothing continued to expand their meaning for American buyers, especially women. Clothing producers and merchants began to consolidate, organizing around key French designers and establishing more corporatized models of manufacturing, distribution, and marketing; what would later be called the "fashion industry" took nascent form. Popular styles changed drastically. The silhouette of women's dress morphed from the S-curve of the tightly corseted Victorians to simpler, looser lines practical for the fast-paced dance moves popular in the 1920s. Hemlines rose, and cleavage lost regard. An American version of the brassiere was patented in 1914 as a liberating, comfortable alternative to crushing corsets; nevertheless, in keeping with social contrasts of the time, tightly corseted bodices and sheltered calves also endured for many, especially older women. But for modern sartorialists, variety, movement, and individual expression replaced class signification and social propriety. In addition, widespread access to reproduced images transformed individual dress and habituated trend followers to a faster pace of change. As fashion historian Anne Hollander observes, "After the public eye had adjusted to camera vision, spontaneity became a new ideal for dress design."[17]

The war brought increased exposure to styles reflecting European glamor and sensuality. Respect for French design echoed throughout commercial productions, from department store windows to clothing to Broadway musicals to architecture. Historian Morris Dickstein notes this growing adulation, but also connects it to a complementary ardor for self-consciously American style, as exemplified by American songwriter Aaron Copland, whose studies in France in the 1920s sparked in him a desire to produce folk music that, while new in style, *felt* to its audience very familiar and somehow classically American.[18] Similarly, Broadway adopted a supposedly European emphasis on the sensual female form but soon changed the bodily ideal to emphasize Americanism, embodying racialized nativist and eugenicist rhetoric. The defining of an "American" style of beauty coincided with a theatrical merging with haute couture. The American showgirl became in part a fashion model, promoting shifts in design trends.

Styles of the 1920s had multiple influences. The roomier, shorter feminine dress popularized during this period copied French designs like those of Paul Poiret and Coco Chanel, but they also stemmed from practical wartime considerations for working women and grew from grassroots artistic and social movements in places such as the new bohemian enclave of Greenwich Village, a small area below 14th Street in lower Manhattan where secondhand clothing was an approved creative and practical resource.[19] The flappers of the 1920s—the brash, young females who shaped the first modern American youth culture—crafted their identities from commercial stereotypes and reproductions of such avant-garde fashions and lifestyles, stereotypes consolidated on the theater stage, and eventually, on the silver screen. In the early 1920s, for example, Ziegfeld Follies comedian Fanny Brice and her performance of "Second Hand Rose" tied a representation of Greenwich Village bohemian style to the association of secondhand exchange with Jewish immigrants, and by way of humor, packaged both for mainstream consumption.

The Avant-garde Use of Secondhand Objects

The theater did reflect a slow-growing popular acceptance of secondhand materials including clothing, but other visual artists increasingly dissatisfied with the limits of representative art more actively embraced the inspirational potential of used goods beginning in the teens. Dadaists and surrealists were among the first to recognize secondhand commerce, especially flea markets, as "a model for a kind of cultural refuse dump that dissolves the relationship between art, history, and junk."[20] André Breton, French founder of surrealism, extolled the virtues of secondhand objects for the crafting of surrealist vision.[21] In his 1928 autobiographical work *Nadja*, Breton describes the chance discovery of a flea-market object as an experience capable of "admitting me to an almost forbidden world of sudden parallels, petrifying coincidences, and reflexes particular to each individual, of harmonies struck as though on the piano, flashes of light that would make you see, really *see*."[22] Breton's explanation of secondhand objects as material epiphanies resonates with Dadaist Marcel Duchamp's definition of "readymades," a term he coined in 1915 for mass-produced objects recontextualized as art, and epitomized by his porcelain urinal exhibited as *Fountain* in 1917. According to Duchamp, a readymade existed not as a physical thing, but as a *rendez-vous*, a meeting place between subject and object, and observer and observed.[23] During the interwar period, artists enunciated the role of secondhand things as being capable of breaching boundaries between time, space, gender, race, and class. Awareness of this liminality, useful in its performativity and deviations from norms, would remain central to secondhand stylemaking for the rest of the twentieth century.

Both Duchamp and Breton spent time in New York City, sifting through flea markets, thrift stores, and junk shops, not primarily out of fiscal necessity but for creative stimulation. Marcel Duchamp first moved to New York City from Paris in 1915, where he started The American Society of Independent Artists. He displayed the original *Fountain* in the group's first exhibition in 1917. Breton came to the United States much later—*Nadja*'s lauded flea market was Paris's Marché aux Puces—when the Vichy government in France banned his work as "the very negation of the national revolution."[24] Breton sought refuge in New York City in the early 1940s. During his time there, he continued to praise the place of secondhand objects in surrealist thought. He famously collected an array of secondhand things, often from unfamiliar cultural contexts, and led American artists and writers around to junk shops and flea markets in Lower Manhattan, entreating them to identify and respond to surreal items.[25]

The German-born surrealist Max Ernst also incorporated flea-market objects into his work. Objects from the Paris flea market inspired Ernst and his lover Leonora Carrington during their 1930s stay in France; a broken hobbyhorse prompted Carrington to create her first major painting, *Self-Portrait: At the Inn of the Dawn Horse*. The Nazi-accommodating government judged the Jewish Ernst an "undesirable foreigner" in 1939, and he was briefly interned in Camp De Milles near Aix-en-Provence before escaping to New York City. There, he married American art collector and tastemaker Peggy Guggenheim and remained until 1953. Like Breton, he also took acolytes to Third Avenue junk shops and Manhattan flea markets. Many of the collages he made during this period incorporated Victorian magazine clippings and other "found" objects.[26]

Similarly, New York native Joseph Cornell frequented Manhattan's secondhand venues to find materials for the construction of his oneiric assemblages from the 1930s until his death in 1972. Cornell's shadow boxes compiled found objects and images that bridged temporal gaps, combining elements of the present with objects from the past in a coherent aesthetic vision. When pairing contemporary movie stars such as Hedy Lamarr and Greta Garbo with relics from the Renaissance and Victorian eras, Cornell emphasized the value of dreams and dreaming in his "constructivism."[27] Artists influenced by surrealism often cited the importance of a dream-like merging of unlikely subjects. For Breton, flea markets themselves were sites of dreams within the realm of the everyday, where one found "the objects that, between the lassitude of some and the desire of others, go off to dream at the antique fair."[28] All these artists were connoisseurs of detritus and devotees of flea markets.

For modernist writers, too, secondhand objects figured as other than inert things, as part of increased attention to the role of consumerism in American lives. In Guido Bruno's 1920 short story, "Midnight in a Pawn Shop," the briefly animated articles in the pawnbroker's safe become protagonists telling "interesting and pathetic stories." The jewels and trinkets give voice to their discontented masters—many of whom bemoan the ruin of postwar recession and express disenchantment with the goals of democracy.[29] Stories like these echo Dickens's and James's nineteenth-century suggestions, recounted in chapter 1, that physical objects are imprinted with previous owners' attributes, giving secondhand objects an eerie agency. At the same time, modernist writing reflected the growing social value of dress and fashion. In feminist playwright Susan Glaspell's 1920 play *Chains of Dew*, one character fumbles to describe to a midwesterner how cosmopolitan New Yorkers dress: "The people I know don't wear clothes—that is—not what you would call clothes." The listener assents, adding, "They wear ideas."[30]

While the above-mentioned artists' use of secondhand materials rarely extended directly to personal dress, surrealist and Dadaist work acknowledged and articulated the importance of fashion, dress, and the body.[31] Mannequins, the common mode of displaying clothing for sale, preoccupied the work of several major surrealists, including Salvador Dali, Josef Breitenbach, and Wols. Their models, like Glaspell's characters, wore "ideas, embodying and displaying Surrealist aesthetics and principles."[32] It was directly through fashion itself that surrealism gained currency among the consuming public. In 1920s Paris, artists experimented with fashion design, and soon surrealist images inspired well-known designers, especially Coco Chanel's rival, the prominent Italian designer Elsa Schiaparelli. In the late 1920s, Schiaparelli created sweaters with surrealist trompe d'œil designs and paired up with Jean Cocteau to create evening coats. Some of her most famous designs were the result of collaboration with Salvador Dali—also a purveyor of flea markets—including her shoe hat and skeleton dress, and in 1937, a white silk evening dress onto which Dali painted a large lobster.[33] Man Ray, the one American who was included in both Dada and surrealist movements in Europe, financed his art and life with a career in fashion photography, a career that married art and commerce in a way that his artistic affiliates often disdained. Later fashion photographer Richard Avedon (whose own work helped popularize images of bohemianism after World War II), however, credited Man Ray with "breaking the stranglehold of reality" on methods of depicting clothing.[34]

Unsurprisingly, then, life models were intrinsic to avant-garde artistry of the time. Dadaist baroness Elsa von Freytag-Loringhoven, one of Man Ray's favored photographic subjects for a time, posed semiprofessionally and considered modeling a central form of her own extensive artistic expression. The baroness's work as both an artist's model and a creative innovator (especially during her residency in Greenwich Village in the late teens) brought into focus the relationship between avant-garde art, fashion and dress, and gender and body, often through the use of secondhand materials. By then, the figure of the bohemian artist's model was already established in the United States, thanks to the oft-read translation of George de Maurier's 1894 novel *Trilby*, which was about a perfect-footed, free-living (but virtuous) artist's model, literally put on a pedestal for adoring male art students. The book served as a popular example of cross-class bohemia—an ideal that continued to influence postwar bohemians, as chapters 4 and 5 relate—and its popularity was such that many everyday consumables, from shoes, hats, ice cream, clothing, cigarettes, foot remedies, and even a tourist-drawing town in Florida, bore the name Trilby.[35]

The baroness, however, was a less demure model, far less likely to be taken under Svengali's sway and apparently much less marketable. Baroness Freytag-Loringhoven was born Else Plötz in 1874, in Pomerania, Germany. As a teen, she left an abusive father to pursue acting and modeling, immediately taking a job as a burlesque model in Berlin. While in Berlin, Elsa experimented sexually and sartorially. After her first encounter with gonorrhea at twenty years old, she retreated for a time to live with a maiden aunt, who sought to establish her niece in a "legitimate" career in the theater. Before finishing acting school, however, young Elsa argued with her aunt, proclaiming "hopeless spinsterdom" as being at the root of objections to her liberal sexual habits. Kicked to the curb, Elsa earned a place as a chorus girl in the Zentral Theater, hired more for her "straight figure and nimble legs" than her singing. The role of a chorus girl in Zentral Theater in Berlin in 1895 was as fabled as the Ziegfeld Girl would be in the next generation in New York City. Such young performers represented a type of New Woman—bold, independent, and fun, but still certainly upholding the subordinate position of women, offering a way to contain, sterilize, and commodify the "social transgressiveness" of the female body.[36] They occupied a position that elevated chorus girls to the role of "showgirls," a position that served as an imagined portal to fame and fortune (often through lucrative romantic connections) rather than merely a repetitive pair of legs framing the upstage stars. Elsa's experience as a showgirl and as an artist's model, together with her innovative Dada art, would coincide in a precociously modern career, one sparsely recompensed yet highly influential.

In Berlin, Munich, and Italy, Elsa modeled, acted, posed, wrote, and painted until 1910, when she followed her second husband, the writer Felix Paul Greve, then known as Frederick Philip Grove, to Pittsburgh, Pennsylvania. The first public notice of Elsa Greve in the United States announced her arrest for inappropriate appearances on Pittsburgh's Fifth Avenue, where she was taken into custody for cross-dressing. The 1910 *New York Times* headline gasped: "She Wore Men's Clothes."[37] Legal censure failed to check her sartorial habits. The androgynous exhibitionist would spend thirteen years astonishing residents of various American cities, mostly New York City, with her audacious public appearance. Abandoned by her second husband in Pittsburgh, she found her way to New York City in 1913. There she met and married the penniless baron Leo von Freytag-Loringhoven, who provided her with little else besides her regal tile. The baroness (this time left alone when her third husband returned to Germany during World War I and committed suicide) soon became a seminal part of the artist movement in Greenwich Village, where rent remained cheap amidst rising housing costs.[38] The turn-of-the-century industrial boom bypassed winding Greenwich Village streets in favor of New York City's more predictably gridded areas, leaving its quaint meanderings to impoverished modernists, who soon established the first American bohemian enclave.[39]

Though hailed by her contemporaries as the mother of Dada—the Swiss-born, antiwar, antibourgeois avant-garde artistic movement with links to cubism, surrealism, and futurism, but with an urge to disaffiliate with all—the baroness found fame elusive. Her often-ephemeral artistic practices, her precocious gender disruption, and her disregard for convention disqualified her from even marginal marketability. The baroness had great artistic breadth and produced in various media, creating some of the first "sound poetry" and forging striking assemblage sculptures and readymades. Recent scholars suggest that the baroness, who was close with Duchamp, may well have given him the famous *Fountain* urinal, and the original piece might better be understood as a collaboration.[40] While versed in various media, the baroness's dynamic, performative personal appearance, including elaborate contrivances of clothing, was arguably her biggest contribution to twentieth-century art. She began to repurpose or adapt used objects in the creation of wearable art during World War I, perhaps sooner. Far from being acknowledged as art, attention to daily habits of dress was more often vilified as culturally eroding. For example, male critics saw the rise in fashionable dress (and the supposedly attendant catering to frivolous femininity) as contributing to the demise of theater as high art.[41]

Like other artists of the interwar decades, the baroness gleaned and repurposed discarded objects, adapting secondhand materials for artistic purposes. But unlike her male counterparts, she often used them to array her body in dissident scripts. This "corporeal art" never edited sexual content and relied on a style of spontaneous, public performance that blurred lines between life and art to the point of indistinction.[42] Drawing from her experiences as a model and showgirl, the baroness transferred theatrical practices and tropes to the unprepared city streets. To compose the costumes that ranged from eccentric to arrestable, the baroness gleaned and stole materials, relying on the flotsam of city life. In its outrageous flamboyance, her public appearance presaged later crafters of "camp" performances, including 1960s underground film guru Jack Smith (and his notorious rival/admirer Andy Warhol), as discussed in chapter 6 of this book. For the baroness, tomato cans found in gutters served as bras, predating by more than twenty years Schiaparelli's lacy bra designed with black satin hands cupping the wearer's breasts. Celluloid curtain rings, liberated from department stores, clattered in place of bracelets, and bicycle taillights flashed as bustles. The baroness roamed the city wearing headdresses of birdcages, peach baskets, and wastepaper bins. Sometimes she wore postage stamps on her face as beauty marks or donned kitchen cutlery as accessories.[43] As seen in figure 2.1 (unfortunately, extant photographs are rarer than are dismayed descriptions) she posed in acrobat's outfits and aviation gear, visually commenting on the war and her personal desire for motion, comfort, and liberation. Such comportment was strikingly *en vogue* in the attire of showgirls in popular New York City revues, which highlighted "jaunty showgirl versions of the New Woman as aviator or acrobat."[44]

The baroness's personal image and artistic production (often simultaneous) exemplified many of modernism's collapsing boundaries. Her poverty compelled improvisation, but it was artistic preference that drew her to secondhand objects, making her participation in secondhand markets emblematic of both the cultural elitism associated with certain used objects and the role of secondhand economies as stopgaps in a time of increasingly unequal distribution of wealth. Strikingly, her performative dress blurred the line between artist and muse, between subject and object, and between audience and participant. Social realist painter George Biddle recounts his first encounter with the baroness as such:

> Having asked me, in her harsh, high-pitched German stridency, whether I required a model, I told her I should like to see her in the nude. With a royal gesture she swept apart the folds of a scarlet raincoat. She stood before me quite naked—or nearly so. Over the nipples of her breast were two tin tomato cans, fastened with a green string about her back. Between the tomato cans hung a very small bird-cage and within it a crestfallen canary. One arm was covered from wrist to shoulder with celluloid curtain rings, which later she admitted to have pilfered from a furniture display in Wanamaker's. She removed her hat, which had been tastefully but inconspicuously trimmed with gilded carrots, beets and other vegetables. Her hair was close cropped and dyed vermilion.[45]

As biographer Irene Gammel observes, the moment the baroness cast aside her raincoat, Biddle was confronted with the imperative to recognize his model as an artist. In its details, the visual commentary of her array was abrupt and highly modern. The worn objects themselves were comestibles

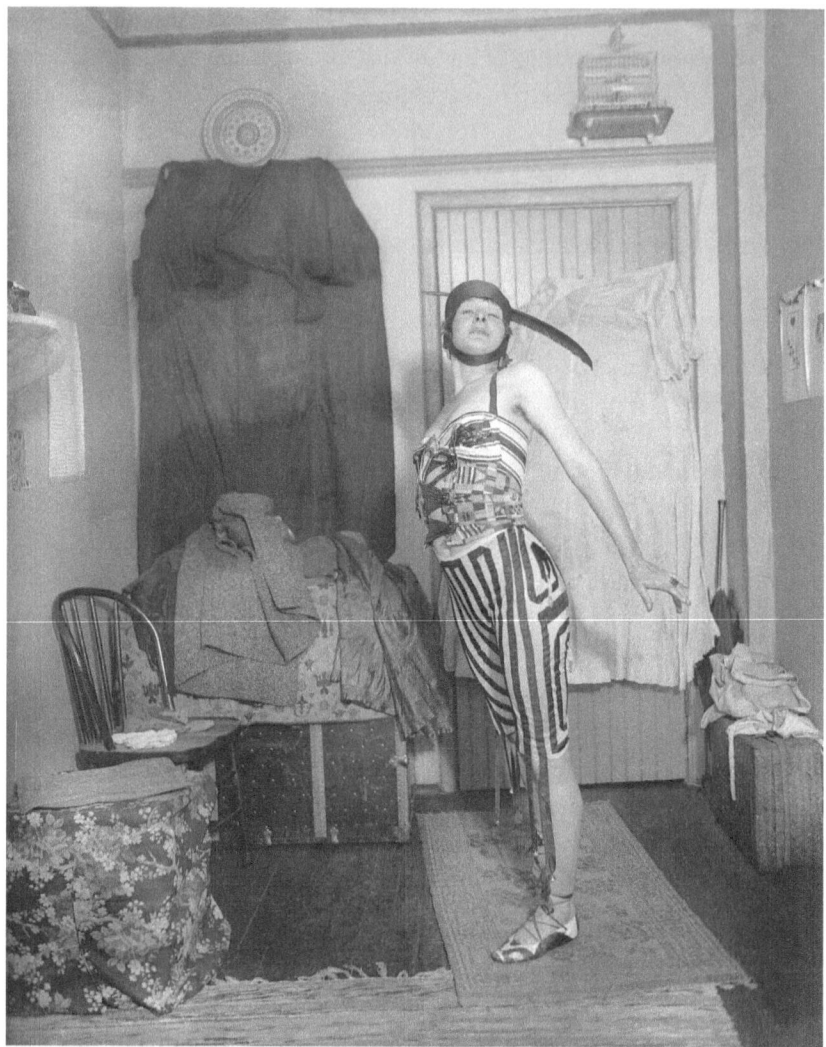

FIGURE 2.1 Baroness Elsa Von Freytag-Loringhoven working as a model, 1915. © Bettman/Corbis.

and industrial or household tools turned accouterments, noting the impermanence of consumer items or the absurdity of their relegation to particular uses.[46]

The baroness was rarely paid for her sartorial creations, though some of her readymades and assemblages did appear in exhibits, and a few publishers risked printing her poetry. Still, the incontrovertible physical figure of the baroness was acknowledged by many of her Village peers, if in ways that recognized its inevitable obscurity. "She is the future," Marcel Duchamp said admiringly and damningly of the artist around 1921, the year he and Man Ray made a film titled *Elsa, Baroness von Freytag-Loringhoven, Shaving Her Pubic Hair*.[47] Also in 1921, Man Ray wrote Tristan Tzara boasting of New York's claim to Dada. In his letter, Ray patched in a photo of the baroness's wirey, nude, shaven figure to form the "A" in *l'Amerique*, centralizing the role of her very body in American Dada.[48] The publisher Jane Heap faced rebuke for printing the baroness's colorful poetry, and debated recurring insistences that she drop the verse from the pages of *The Little Review*. In one refusal, Heap claimed that "The Baroness is the first American Dada" and is "the only one living anywhere who dresses dada, loves dada, lives dada."[49] In observing that the baroness "dresses dada," Heap validated clothing and personal appearance as a form of artistic expression. A kind of arms-length adulation of the eccentric German immigrant flowed from most members of "New York Dada," the group of American and European artists who, in the years after World War I, congregated in the uptown New York City salon of Walter and Louise Arensberg (but often lived in or around the more affordable Greenwich Village).[50]

Ultimately, the fact that the baroness was far more notorious than famous masked the breadth of her influence. The baroness's sartorial, sexual, and linguistic risk taking came at a price. Her *blitzkrieg* of radically sexualized art led to an erasure of the scope of her influence until the twenty-first century. Adding to the list of admiring luminaries, poet Ezra Pound composed "Canto 95" about the baroness's bold unmarketability, suggesting that dedication to an eccentric artistic vision cost her recognition: "the principle of non-acquiescence / laid a burden."[51] While she died in near-obscurity, art historians and feminist scholars have recently worked to restore to history her central role in the New York Dada scene.[52] I add that, in large part through her innovations in performance art, a genre unrecognized until well after her death, Baroness von Freytag-Loringhoven was a landmark figure in establishing secondhand apparel as a meaningful form of rebellion, of artistic commentary, and of gender disruption. Through deviant performances of gender and with her appropriation of quotidian objects for artistic symbols, the baroness regularly confronted American modernists with a rearrangement of feminine reality, sexual intensity, and consumer sensibilities, and few were prepared for her strategies and chosen media. However, through her fellow Dada and surrealist artists and by way of popular imitations, her effect on American culture is deceptively broad. Gammel notes, "Traces of the Baroness's élan are assimilated into the public media in much tamer form, while the wild Baroness herself was silenced and labeled insane."[53] Artists inspired by her brashness and experimentation, but able to temper the effect, succeeded. Representations of the baroness herself appeared in renowned paintings, drawings, and also writings of the time, indicating that the breadth of her usefulness as an artist's model extended beyond the visual. One of the baroness's closest friends, the novelist Djuna Barnes, used her as a model for a major character in her tour de force of modernism, *Nightwood* (1936).

Popular cultural representations offered sanitized versions of the baroness's bohemianism. Discussed at length later in the chapter, Broadway star Fanny Brice's hit songs, "Rose of Washington Square" and "Second Hand Rose," delivered a palatable rendition of the bohemian life of an artist's model *and* made comedic the previously reviled Jewishness of used-goods sales. While the baroness was unusual in the extent of her unconventional personal appearance, she lived in a time and place where women were testing the boundaries of acceptable self-presentation. In the years surrounding World War I, Greenwich Village women bobbed their hair, dispensed with restrictive undergarments, and favored exotic ethnic styles such as Russian peasant blouses, silk Chinese tunics, and Moroccan sandals. Others improvised their own attire, adapting existing styles and materials to suit their political, social, and artistic agendas. Although the baroness ventured to untenable extremes in her use of nudity and eccentric dress, in this milieu Dada adherents did recognize that clothing (and unclothing) had modern value. In 1915, for example, the Dada publication *Rogue* described graphic artist Clara Tice—who claimed she bobbed her hair before the credited trendsetter Irene Castle—as "an artist of undressing par excellence," demonstrating that feminine dress and bodily display were understood as artistic statements on occasion.[54]

In a pattern that would repeat midcentury, the first phase of shabby fashionability for the Greenwich Village was relatively short-lived, victim to its own panache. By 1920, rent around Washington Square had tripled, and the Village had become a tourist destination. However, the area retained its reputation as a haven for independent women, some of whom capitalized on the hipness associated with bohemian style and with the cachet of secondhand items. Single women ran teahouses, hat and batik shops, antique stores, and tour guide companies.[55] A 1919 faux tour guide by witty lyricist Robert Edwards poked fun at the increasing commercial dilettantism of both male and female Village residents—and incidentally revealed a market in secondhand goods by mocking the area's fashionable trade in used goods and clothing.[56]

The year after Brice's Victor Records recording of "Second Hand Rose" reached number three in national sales, poverty and alienation forced the baroness to abandon New York City for Paris, taking with her a deep bitterness toward her adopted country, the United States. By this time, stereotypes of Greenwich Village bohemia echoed in the details of her more commonly represented counterpart, the flapper. And by this time, secondhand sales in the United States included not just rummage sales, junk shops, and thrift stores, but a coalescing venue called the flea market.

The Magical Marché aux Puces

Of all the sites of secondhand exchange, flea markets especially attracted surrealists and Dadaists interested in breaking down existing artistic boundaries. The markets themselves were sites of blurred delineations, straddling public and private physical spaces, and selling both old and new goods. Many participants fluidly acted as both buyers and sellers within the same context. As time went on, vendors recognized the value of secondhand goods to both the wealthy and the poor, and catered to practical and creative buying motives. Half a century later, Susan Sontag would critique the surrealist assumption that the surreal—including gleaned secondhand objects—was something universal and psychological, something dredged from a shared primitive unconscious and brought to the surface by way of Breton's "sudden parallels." Actually, many of the objects and images they imagined transcending reality were the quite mundane products of unfamiliar-to-them ethnic, racial, and class backgrounds.[57] Accordingly, for some surrealist artists, the attraction to secondhand objects might be considered a sort of visual slumming.[58] Describing the growth of these markets grounds an examination of the erudite, avant-garde perceptions of used goods in the practical, dynamic economic purposes of secondhand exchange.

As Sontag wrote, "it was Breton and other Surrealists who invented the secondhand store as a temple of vanguard taste and upgraded visits to flea markets into a mode of aesthetic pilgrimage." Paris's Marché aux Puces, Breton's best beloved hunting ground and the premier so-named flea market served and still serves as the exemplar and prototype of the venue.[59] The origins of the market's name and situation are relevant to as well as prescient of U.S. flea markets' urban emergence. The genesis stories of the Marché aux Puces and its appellation are as numerous as its vendors quickly grew to be.[60] As is often the case with secondary economies, the development of this mode of used goods sales coincided with changes in firsthand economies, urban demographics, and social reformists' goals.[61] The Marché aux Puces emerged following an important phase in the systematization of primary consumerism—the advent of the department store and the institutionalization of fixed-price sales.[62] In 1867, a large new building was constructed for Paris's original *prix fixe* department store, Bon Marché. Considered by many to be the "first" department store in the world, Bon Marché changed the way French consumers shopped by codifying exchange interactions and introducing new elements of fantasy and recreation.[63] Previously, goods' prices were often negotiable and when listed were assumed to be more like guidelines than a done deal. Such mid-nineteenth-century *grand magasins* marked the waning of an important aspect of public sociability: the face-to-face interactions that accompanied haggling or price negotiation. Since the owners of such vast establishments relied on hosts of scarcely trained salespeople, fixed prices were considered a necessity to assure satisfactory profits and uniform customer service.

Before the late nineteenth century, Parisian peddlers both salvaged and hawked their wares in the street, as happened in many of the world's cities. An estimated thirty thousand Parisian *chiffonniers* (rag pickers), for instance, gleaned cloth scraps to sell to paper producers in the 1870s. Some, as in the United States, were part of the Jewish diaspora, scattered by anti-Semitic laws and violence, and often relegated to nonprofessional, menial labor. Parisian gleaning involved a good amount of repair and repurposing, some from very far down the scavengers' food chain: human hair fashioned into wigs, dead animals rendered into candles, and discarded bones turned into buttons.[64] As multiple *grand magasins* grew up along Paris's main boulevards, laws regarding street selling increased at the behest of department store owners and in response to increased traffic, a pattern that would repeat in the United States in succeeding decades.[65] In the last quarter of the century, new trash-related ordinances and vendor licensing measures impeded salvaging business within the Paris city limits. After international outbreaks of yellow fever inspired public panic, officials in France, as in the United States, began to systematize trash collection to prevent the spread of infectious diseases. An 1884 Paris ordinance requiring every building to include a standard, lidded garbage receptacle slowed street scavenging substantially; simultaneously instated ordinances limited the peripatetic sales of goods.[66] Around this time, *chiffonniers*, *biffins* (rag-and-bone men), and *les pêcheurs de lune* (literally translated as moon-fisherman) all began to sell at a large scrap-metal market in the Parisian suburb of Saint-Ouen. Increasingly undesired and legally restricted within Paris's city limits, dozens, then hundreds, of secondhand peddlers soon found the cooperative model to be effective. By 1885, enough secondhand merchants sold in Saint-Ouen for a newspaper to dub the congregation *marché aux puces*, or "market with fleas"—referencing the often-valid assumption that the secondhand cloth goods came with parasites. The French flea market grew rapidly after the turn of the century, becoming renowned as a carnivalesque shopping experience and prestigious destination for American and European travelers by World War I.[67]

While flea markets emerged partly in reaction against the institutionalization of retail practices through the development of department stores, participants were enabled by the same factors supporting the large stores' success, such as greater quantities of cheaper ready-made goods and advances in transportation. As more Parisians could afford new items, still viable objects were more quickly abandoned than before, increasing the pool of secondhand consumer goods. And in 1908, a completed metro line connecting Paris north to south secured Parisians' easy access to these flea market items. As the Marché aux Puces expanded, the market's managers organized and structured the rows of goods, at least loosely categorizing the types of items to facilitate shopping—following the marketing schematics of department stores.[68] In its combination of mainstream and alternative consumer attributes, the Marché aux Puces represents how the adaptability of informal economies helped determine the flea market's format in the modern economic context. Also, as the Marché aux Puces grew more attractive to consumers internationally, its success indicated and stimulated the popularity of collectibles and antiques, a transnational trend that extended beyond avant-garde artistry and would support American secondhand commerce as well.

Immobilizing American Peddlers

The formation of what would become flea markets in eastern U.S. cities was, as in the case of Marché aux Puces, a response to local politics and regulations, many of which relied on xenophobic and racist rationales.[69] At the end of the nineteenth century, peripatetic pushcart peddlers presented new problems for growing East Coast cities. In the late nineteenth century, from New Orleans to Philadelphia, officials sought to manage street sales by building a central public market aimed to stabilize and standardize the distribution of goods, especially food. As populations grew and as trucks replaced farmers' wagons for transportation, those public markets became more congested and bewildering to shoppers. Individual peddlers selling an array of foods and other wares acted as conduits from the central markets, distributing goods into neighborhoods and enclaves. Peddlers multiplied along with immigrants, and lawmakers rapidly responded with high licensing fees and regulations limiting their domain.[70] As early as 1894, newspapers periodically reported the imminent demise of pushcart peddlers, as retail merchants and lawmakers sought to staunch their rapid growth in what were dubbed "pushcart wars."[71] New York, Chicago, Washington, D.C., New Orleans, Omaha, and Milwaukee all took steps to reduce or eliminate pushcart peddling, with varying results.

A large influx of immigrants, especially eastern European Jews, shaped the particularities of all types of informal trade at the turn of the century. Jews in the United States also were often barred from professional vocations and forced into low-status jobs at the margins of the economy. While no one group ever entirely dominated informal city commerce, Jews were especially instrumental in establishing systems of secondhand exchange in numerous U.S. cities, where they adapted old-world survival tactics. For example, Chatham Street in New York City nearly replicated East London's Jewish-run old clothes trade by World War II.[72]

After their great migration out of the South began during World War I, African American peddlers joined or replaced Jewish salespeople—some of whose financial circumstances improved by the 1920s. Black Americans, much like Jewish immigrants, were often barred from professional employment, and so were similarly relegated to informal economies for subsistence. African Americans first became active in secondhand industries in the nineteenth century, many opening their own storefronts, others working as street vendors. Like eastern European Jews, black southerners also brought with them the knowledge of informal trade; as historian Alison Isenberg argues, African American antique dealers were central to the creation of a trade in Americana as early as the 1890s.[73]

Although no single model can accurately represent all such sales venues, the evolution of flea markets on the Lower East Side of Manhattan and Maxwell Street Market in Chicago illustrate the various motives and shifting participants vital to establishing designated city areas as sites of largely informal sales. Before it was mostly moved and partially dismantled in 1994, Maxwell Street Market was one of a handful of American flea markets that claimed the title of the country's "first" flea market.[74] At the time of Chicago's great fire in 1871, eastern European immigrants were already creating Jewish enclaves in multiple parts of the city and practicing the sorts of informal trade familiar overseas, including the collection and sale of used goods. The fire consumed residences and businesses in and around the Loop. Another conflagration in 1874 ravaged the Near South Side where many poor eastern European immigrants lived. Burned-out businesses relocated to Jefferson Street near Maxwell Street, just outside the fires' paths, as did the displaced Chicagoans themselves.[75] The number of peddlers grew, spilling over onto Maxwell Street. By 1893, pushcart peddling had become enough of a spectacle to warrant a special mention in the World's Fair guidebook as one of the city's most interesting sights.[76]

While the 1893 World's Fair guidebook boasted of the unique display Maxwell Street provided, not all contemporary commentaries were quite so positive. According to one reporter in 1896, Maxwell Street festered with the raucous commerce: "oratory, profanity, gesticulation, and fisticuffs are so often connected with the sharp bargainings of the street that the Maxwell Street Police Station exerts a not inconsiderable influence upon the trade of that whole section."[77] The same journalist also reported that despite the abject poverty of this area, there were no pawnshops. Why not? "Everything is too hopelessly second-hand. There's never anything new in the neighborhood except babies."[78] At times, critics assigned early makeshift flea markets a status even lower than much-maligned pawnshops. Racial references riddled the author's detailing of the unembarrassed haggling intrinsic to exchanges. The buyer must be unsentimental as "he seeks to buy for the least money which his small Shylock will accept."[79]

As part of wide-ranging municipal efforts to limit pushcarts, dealers had to pay a yearly license tax higher than storefront merchants—fifty dollars in 1896.[80] Despite these hardships, activity swelled in Chicago's increasingly Jewish Near West Side (by 1910, 90 percent of the area's residents were Jewish). Complaints also mounted—from buyers about bad products or dishonest exchanges, from dealers about municipal favoritism, and from store owners about unfair competition. In 1912, the city formally certified Maxwell Street as an open-air market—a step intended, hypothetically, to increase oversight of the goings-on there.[81] Scarce relevant legislation favored the street merchants, however. As the baroness's arrest for cross-dressing in Pittsburgh in 1910 demonstrated, city officials wished to maintain control over both individual and collective urban appearances. That control extended to the sights and sounds of pushcart peddling. City thoroughfares were contested zones and would become more so as automobile traffic increased. In the first decade of the century, a series of Chicago-wide antinoise laws curtailed the "crying of goods" that Near West Side peddlers deemed vital to their livelihood. The Nineteenth Ward alderman argued that the restrictions were weakly disguised discrimination against immigrant and working-class street vendors. The sellers rebelled, continuing to cry their goods, despite sporadic arrests and futile court disputes resulting in the Supreme Court upholding the statute. On 26 July 1911, peddler strikes and protests culminated

FIGURE 2.2 Merchants and shoppers along Maxwell Street, Chicago, 1917, featuring a sign advertising secondhand clothing. Photograph by the *Chicago Daily News*. Courtesy of the Chicago History Museum.

in "a day of rioting and wild disorder such has not been seen in Chicago since the garment workers' strike."[82]

Multiple arrests and exorbitant fines dampened the rebellion for a while, and the designation of Maxwell Street as a formal market area (see figure 2.2) helped to contain noisy peddlers who persisted in violating the ordinance. Still, peddlers insisted they had a right to use the streets as they saw fit. Finally, in 1913, the peddlers won a partial victory: the passing of a new ordinance allowing "the crying of wares by peddlers between 11 a.m. and 6 p.m."[83] The new resolution did not end public legal disputes over market authority and the terms of commerce. Immediately after the market's formal designation, decades-long outrage erupted over the Maxwell Street Market master's unfair fee system. The conflict included recurrent fistfights and public law suits.[84]

FIGURE 2.3 Daddy Stovepipe on Maxwell Street, Chicago, November 1959. Photograph by Clarence W. Hines. Courtesy of the Chicago History Museum.

In many eastern cities, efforts to control the informal sales escalated in the 1920s, as automobiles became more common and as the addition of blacks fleeing the oppression of the Jim Crow South—and their presence selling on public avenues—amplified white northerners' prejudices against streetsellers. Despite resistance, secondhand commerce persisted, even increasing as a percentage of total informal sales. By the 1930s, many of the Jewish families that had populated Maxwell Street dispersed to other neighborhoods. African Americans who moved North in the Great Migration of the 1920s became the new majority participants at Maxwell Street Market.[85] By this time, secondhand goods were crowding out comestibles as chain grocery stores cornered the market on food distribution. Cultural forms migrated alongside the wares and trade knowledge of southern blacks, and Maxwell Street soon became a renowned center of jazz and blues performance. Itinerant blues and minstrel musician Daddy Stovepipe began playing at Maxwell Street at the height of the Great Migration in the 1920s, after almost two decades of performing in southern minstrel acts. Stovepipe continued to perform on Maxwell Street into his nineties, even after several recording deals.[86] As figure 2.3 attests, secondhand material such as Daddy Stovepipe's trademark nineteenth-century hat made up a large proportion of Maxwell St. trade.

Similar patterns—of peddling growth followed by restrictions and regulations, and of African Americans joining Jews and other poor workers—repeated in other cities, though the scale of Maxwell Street's commerce was unusual. In 1904, Manhattan's Commissioner of Street Cleaning assigned five city blocks to the city's 5,000 licensed vendors in the hopes of isolating the "nuisance." Some clearly thought the peddlers ought to be grateful, opining that "[b]y making himself a public nuisance the Manhattan push-cart peddler now gets from the city, absolutely free of charge, one of the finest market stands in the world."[87] Many peddlers protested the arrangement, however, preferring to remain peripatetic. Banding together, these working-class entrepreneurs fought against rising reformist notions of progress, modernity, and order. In 1906, the East Side Push Cart Peddlers' Association wrote New York City mayor McClellan, demanding to retain their "little privileges in order to make a living for ourselves and our families," or else they would march to City Hall and "show to this metropolis how its poor are treated."[88] Nostalgia, as part of an idealized vision of urban spaces, sometimes influenced defenses of roaming pushcarts. Journalists portrayed recommendations for designated pushcart market space alternatively as a win for the poor immigrant workers and as a sad victory for "utility over the picturesque." According to one author, "the series of markets for the use of small dealers" would rob "drab, somber tenement streets" of a rare source of vibrancy and attractiveness.[89]

As the number of peddlers continued to grow, the mayor's new Pushcart Commission recommended a fresh tactic, the opposite of bounded markets for the peddlers. The commission could "see no reason why the City of New York should go into the business of providing shop space for dealers in any class of supplies, at a large annual loss, nor why taxpayers should be called upon to bear such a burden." Instead, the commission proposed a diffusion of pushcarts by limiting the number of peddlers allowed per block. Again, massive protest meetings and the threat of boycotts on the part of the United Citizens Peddlers' Association helped guarantee that the commission's suggested regulations were never pursued by the city.[90] Instead of formal actions, selective prosecution and harassment of peddlers continued, which effectively concentrated pushcart activity, as officials in some areas were more tolerant than those in others. The Lower East Side—again, an area with a high concentration of Jewish immigrant residents—was a popular trading spot by 1912, as the debate over what to do about "the pushcart evil" continued in New York City.[91]

Sometimes, Jewish organizations led calls to reform pushcart licensing, recognizing that dishonest or noisy peddlers increased public animosity toward the Jewish population and also hoping to fight against extortionist politicians. The frequent solution was to erect or occupy existing permanent structures designed to contain and centralize the peddlers and to remove licensing from subjective control. Advocates argued that honest peddlers and the consuming public would benefit from such arrangements. Some peddlers agreed, at least in part. In New York City, thousands of peddlers organized the Push-Cart Peddler's Trust to protest existing licensing restrictions and to propose that permanent sites be built instead.[92] As in Chicago, permanent market zones, when established, did not solve Manhattan merchants' problems. In 1922, Lower East Side peddlers mobilized to fight weekly fees for market stands, alleging extortion and corruption among the politicians and market owners and generally echoing the complaints of Maxwell Street vendors.[93] In many cities, middle-class reformers continued to complain that peddlers swindled unsuspecting housewives, compromised sanitation and traffic safety, made disruptive noises, conducted illegal exchanges, and contributed to a system of bribes stemming from uneven regulation of licensing laws. Undoubtedly, some peddlers skirted regulations and made bad deals, but frequently, this was attributed to their ethnic or national origins. Anti-Semitic language colored pushcart critiques, and Chicagoan council members even considered restricting licenses to native-born peddlers. Storefront merchants and disgruntled consumers described peddlers as "parasites."[94]

Yet when peddlers were successfully banned, there were also city shoppers who bemoaned the loss of the competitive advantages, picturesque atmospheres, and proximal conveniences. Even store-bound merchants sometimes found peddlers' presence economically beneficial. In 1925, over one hundred retailers and landlords in Brooklyn sought an order to *compel* pushcart vendors to sell in front of their shops. The businesses across the street, where merchants were permitted to park, were doing much better as the result of a general stimulation of trade.[95] Mediating between extreme views, temperate reformers admitted that the pushcarts were not an inherent nuisance and could even save consumers time and expense, but they also begged that the carts no longer be allowed "to obstruct the streets and impede traffic, to scatter disease-breeding refuse, and to produce congestions that are dangerous in time of fire."[96] The growing popularity of the automobile in the 1920s boosted complaints as the battle for the public thoroughfares cast the cart peddlers in the role of "traditional"—or outmoded, depending on perspective.

The success of chain grocery stores proved decisive in solidifying the role of secondhand sales in cities and describing the shape and location of flea markets. In 1915, the Great Atlantic and Pacific Tea Company, or A&P, became the largest retailer in the United States, starting what many consider to be its first chain store (a tally that does not consider Salvation Army and Goodwill thrift stores). Subsequently, the public marketplaces built to accommodate food vendors increasingly suffered for lack of stall renters, as profits diminished for food dealers *not* part of the chain grocery business. As a result, vendors of other goods, including secondhand items, were more likely to be welcomed into established city marketplaces.[97]

Hoss Mondays and the Rise of Collectibles

The relationship between nineteenth-century modes of food distribution and the early twentieth-century development of flea markets was not consigned to cities. Many rural flea markets evolved from agricultural trade fairs and farmers markets. As they did in urban public markets, secondhand goods sustained farmers markets during decades of decline, until the local foods movement in the late twentieth century would bring about a resurgence in their popularity.[98] Farmers markets, like open-air markets generally, have a long and varied history. The direct sale of produce and homemade comestibles to consumers often combined with other community efforts. In the nineteenth century, particularly in southern states where year-round outdoor sales were a possibility, rural produce sellers coordinated their transactions with county court days. For example, first Monday Trade Days in Canton, Texas—another self-proclaimed "first" U.S. flea market—began as a trading market for produce and livestock decades before the term flea market was applied.

In the 1850s, the circuit judge came to Canton, the Van Zandt county seat, to hold court and conduct legal business the first Monday of every month, a practice common in rural areas at this time, particularly in the American South. These "Court Days" became the day to trade livestock, and sell and buy produce and other goods in the town square—and perhaps stop to watch a murder trial or hanging.[99] First Mondays seemed to some designed to guarantee fine attendance, since Van Zandt County had a long-standing reputation for notorious criminals. In one oft-recounted tale, a group of outlaws lured James Hogg, the first native Texas governor, over county lines and shot him in the back (he recovered and went on to bear four children, one of whom, the auspiciously named Ima Hogg, would become quite the connoisseur of secondhand goods at the vanguard of elite American collecting in the 1920s).[100]

By 1930, Canton's trade days attracted sojourners from surrounding states, often looking to swap or buy mules, horses, hunting dogs, and wagons. Secondhand farm implements, household goods, and clothing were added to the mix as the market covered more and more of the square. Known to many by then as "hoss Mondays," the event attracted big enough crowds to provide buyers for almost anything. Swaps were often sweetened (and tight wallets loosened) with locally made corn whiskey or home brew. While women were newly permitted to attend, their presence was still dissuaded, and the trade days maintained a rough and ready reputation. One story from the 1930s illustrated just how much was considered fair game for swapping. A Texas oil worker recalled that two mule-traders drove into town with their families—the "women were slatternly, and the kids were as wild as coyotes"—and left having traded out their companions, children and all.[101] One slightly different version had the couples legally married; accordingly, they went to the District Clerk to try for a validated swap.[102]

In other county seats in the South, flea markets emerged from similar circumstances. In Maysville, Kentucky, and Emporia, Virginia, Court Days—and de facto market days—fell on Wednesdays and grew into flea markets. The Monday Market in Webster, Florida, also began as a farmer's market but soon included secondhand goods. In 1937, a group of central Florida farmers dissatisfied with their distribution options formed a co-op. Scraping together their own assets and materials (including cypress harvested from nearby swamps), they built a market in the center of Webster from which to auction their produce.[103] Since a local blue law prohibited the sale of any goods on Sundays, market day was Monday.[104] The market adapted to changes in local farming trends, with merchants replacing the vegetable auction with a cattle auction when changing weather patterns compromised produce production. Empty stalls soon housed secondhand clothing and goods, which were sold directly instead of auctioned. By midcentury, Monday was devoted to Webster's flea market—featuring used goods—and Tuesday was reserved for a cattle auction.[105]

The seeming popularity of secondhand goods in rural locales, like the rise of city flea markets, owed to multiple factors. Necessity played a role as farmers faced increasing economic hardship; both buying and selling used items served as money-saving strategies. The types of goods offered at rural flea markets nationwide expanded beyond immediately useful farming equipment as the interested clientele grew. The rise of motoring as a wealthy consumer pastime coincided with a rise in travel and vacations, correlative to increased incomes (for many not in agricultural careers) and automobile ownership.

Some motorists sought to acquire items in a newly popular category of collectibles, Americana. At the beginning of the century, an "aesthetic revolution" in antiques changed the nature of collecting. Some older goods were newly valued for their utility as well as a fashionably handmade look, and after World War I, patriotic nostalgia heavily determined the types of favored items and the meaning of collecting.[106] The rough definition of "antiques" expanded to include more recently made but still secondhand items, as well as more quotidian objects. Around the same time that the Salvation Army and Goodwill started calling the "junk shop" a thrift store, the "curio shop" or "Old Curiosity Shop" became an antique store.[107] A spate of museum exhibits displaying American decorative arts, beginning with the Metropolitan Museum's 1909 Hudson-Fulton Celebration and culminating in the establishment of the Metropolitan's acclaimed American Wing in 1924, verified the artistic merit of these goods.[108]

While the inclusion of more accessible, American-made items extended the hobby of collecting to those of somewhat more modest means, the uberwealthy maintained their primary cultural position in establishing and defining the popularity of such goods. Prominent citizens and avid collectors such as automotive millionaire Henry Ford led the shift in taste by advocating a move away from European antiques and toward rustic, American-made collectibles. "Colonial corners," or whole rooms decked out in antiquated U.S. goods, underscored the popularity of this fad among the well heeled. The powerful elites who supported this surge in preserving American heritage applied a material vision of history emphasizing a nationalistic celebration. Henry Ford—whose oft-quoted 1921 retort, "History is bunk," is usually taken out of context—iconized and romanticized the American past as a collective and democratic experience that ought to be physically preserved as a means of visual instruction. His disparaging remarks about history, he later clarified, applied mostly to written history, not the material representation of it.[109] A description of Henry Ford's chief aims in opening the Ford Museum and Greenfield Village in Dearborn, Indiana, in 1929, defined the ostensibly antielitist intentions of many new collectors. Rather than focusing on "association pieces"—items connected to notable persons—Greenfield Village aimed to preserve human achievements through "the acquisition of the things that portray the doings of the mass of men as they went about their daily routine of working and living."[110] Greenfield Village tried to recreate Early American life, with samples of many of the material objects required in the daily lives of an imagined—and idealized—preindustrial village, including accurate eating and cooking utensils, farm implements, and personal apparel. Tellingly, the inspiration for this revision of the purpose of heritage was modernity itself. As Ford said, "Improvements have been coming so quickly that the past is being lost to the rising generation, and it can be preserved only by putting it in a form where it may be seen and felt. That is the reason behind this collection."[111] Ford's seeming ambivalence about changes in the United States is well noted. Almost in the same breath, Ford could boast of prime responsibility for the creation of modern American life and disavow its moral value. Similarly, this "man of contrast" who invested in the preservation of the past sometimes dismissed history as pointless to a generation that ought to "live in the present" and only care about *making* history, not remembering it.[112] Such inconsistencies framed the purpose of American heritage preservation and by extension, the role of secondhand markets for the middle-class masses.

In response to an expanding demand for more everyday collectibles, early twentieth-century dealers swept the countryside for attractive Americana at the same time that small-scale farmers' agricultural fortunes were declining.[113] Small-time dealers or "pickers," as they were known in the trade, roamed the countryside searching for saleable objects. Because of their door-to-door methods, such bottom-rung traders were also called "knockers" or "rappers."[114] Pickers initially relied on the naiveté of country farmers—as well as their increasing poverty—but rural homeowners soon became aware of the monetary value of their attic wares. As early as 1910, knowledgeable antique dealers suggested that even in the countryside "people who have antiques to sell nowadays have a pretty clear idea of their value."[115]

While New England held the distinction of the first developed antique market in the United States, southern regions also had their own systems of Americana exchange before the twentieth century. Former slaves were intrinsic to establishing trade routes; black southerners recognized and emphasized the value of certain older goods as early as the 1890s.[116] By the 1920s, Americana collectibles were popular nationwide. Museums in the Midwest and West cultivated their own Americana displays, indicating the extension of those goods' popularity and knowledge of their value.[117] Collectors lived throughout the country as well. Ima Hogg, the daughter of the Texas governor shot in Canton, Texas, was vital to the national collecting scene of the 1920s and lived in relative proximity to the famous First Mondays.[118] Hogg joined Henry du Pont and Henry Ford in bidding wars at important New York auctions of the era, but she also cultivated relationships with more than twenty dealers, who canvassed smaller venues throughout the country and were personally acquainted with her tastes, as was common practice for a growing class of very wealthy collectors.[119]

Mid-range dealers who owned their own stores began to buy from pickers, expanding modest secondhand businesses into antique markets, increasing their profits along with their knowledge of valued goods. Some mixed less expensive everyday items and mid-range collectibles with high-end antiques, tempting the more modestly financed patrons who fantasized about the expensive pieces with items in their price range.[120] These developments in the collectibles game coincided with the rise in the inclusion of secondhand items in rural farmers markets as well as urban public markets.

Popular media demonstrated the allure of collecting and the multiplication of objects deemed collectible. For example, Mabel Urner Harper's syndicated newspaper column, "The Married Life of Helen and Warren," traced the rising interest in pre-owned objects for those who had a cultivated interest in collecting but lacked Henry Ford's expansive resources. "Helen and Warren" began in 1915 and ran for thirty years, regaling a broad reading audience with the adventures of an antique-collecting couple. Helen's collecting specialties were cross-stitch and needlepoint work, underscoring the shift in interests in high-end items to everyday memorabilia. Helen and Warren were somewhat omnivorous in their tastes, however, and the articles showcased the author's knowledge about collectibles ranging from valuable furnishings to obscure knick-knacks. For city residents, automobiles facilitated travel outside urban areas in pursuit of valued secondhand items. The urban elite viewed motoring vacations to the country as healthful excursions.[121] Fictionalized New Yorkers Helen and Warren were no exception; in 1916, an "Auto Tour" led them to a farmhouse stay, where they coveted prime Americana.[122] Several times in the 1920s, a "Sunday Motor Trip" resulted in the purchase of some choice object, such as an old table with a "real pie-crust edge."[123] They haggled over such objects with shrewd farm owners, showing the widening knowledge of collectibles' worth.

The 1930s ushered in a period of economic distress for many Americans—for farmers, this was nothing new. By the time the stock market crashed late in 1929, the U.S farm sector had been in crisis for almost a decade. High agricultural product prices in the early 1900s were followed by an expansion of demand during World War I, marking a brief sort of golden age for farmers. However, after Europe began producing again in the early 1920s, competitive prices, increased importation, and decreased exportation seriously compromised the saliency of many small farms.[124] Then, the Great Depression stalled the expansion of most business sectors (including thrift stores), while things continued to worsen for small-scale agriculturalists. In the 1930s, more Americans hung onto their viable goods as fear and destitution prevented new purchases, curtailing many forms of secondhand sales. On the other hand, the acquisition of collectibles or antiques among the upper-middle and upper classes actually grew in popularity. In fact, in the wake of the stock market crash, many were attracted to forms of investment that might survive financial market collapses. The belief that well-chosen objects responsibly maintained would only increase in value gained traction throughout the first decades of the century.[125] Coupled with nostalgia for premodern goods, the wisdom of investing in tangibles increased the appeal of farming families' outdated furnishings.

During the lean 1930s, Mabel Urner Harper's stories of collecting junkets took readers overseas as well as to the countryside, vicariously entertaining those for whom international travel was but a fantasy and instructing those for whom it was possible. The heightened esteem of collectibles and nearly universal concern with affordability encouraged interest in European flea markets. Various international flea markets joined Marché aux Puces as hyped tourist destinations, about which "Helen and Warren" educated their readers. The markets' appeal to travelers during the Great Depression included flea markets' cost-cutting value as well as their festive airs. A 1931 *Chicago Daily Tribune* article recommended that "every right minded American in Rome" visit the "rag market" in the campo dei Fiori, for the atmosphere as well as for the deals.[126] Harper's column emphasized the importance of a bargain at such markets. At a market in Milan, Helen mused over potential purchases, assessing objects for appropriate traveling size and weight and "good value—that almost an obsession."[127] In the 1930s, a myriad of shops responded to this trend by renaming themselves flea markets, from the Maxwell Street Market in Chicago to Hollywood's "new and swanky interior decorator's shop on Sunset which advertises itself as specializing in 'glass bathrooms and lovers' boudoirs.'"[128] Throughout this growing appeal of secondhand objects and the rise of flea markets, old clothes retained many of their stigmas and for the most part remained relegated to the Maxwell and Chatham streets of flea market sales. The meaning of dress and the role of fashion in American lives, however, drastically changed, setting the stage for a soon-to-be increasing popularity of secondhand styles.

Fashion, Broadway, and Secondhand Roses

The quickening pace and heightened commercialism of modern life inspired changes in the popular perception of secondhand commerce, changes rooted in a preindustrialist nostalgia aptly defined by Henry Ford as well as anticommercial avant-gardism. Of course, Dada and surrealist art was not the average cultural fare of American consumers, and while Ford may have strived to democratize collectibles, his vision only obliquely extended to clothing, and only in a limited preservationist mode. Fashion's link to a rising ardor for used materials remained obscure, as artists such as the baroness failed to gain public approval. Despite a slowly growing fad for some secondhand sales and products, no large-scale fashion trends requiring visibly outdated or secondhand materials emerged before World War II, unless you count a minor smattering of Greenwich Village bohemian embellishments. In mainstream fashion, stylistic appropriation was key to the interwar fame of French designers such as Paul Poiret, whose sartorial Orientalism altered the world of haute couture in Europe and in the United States, but such design adoptions relied on new, expensive fabrics, much as had the artistic dress movement of the 1870s and 1880s.[129]

The spontaneous, adventurous fashion model cast in theatrical performances and in movies, however, did crack the door to the voluntary consumption of secondhand clothes, offering a few examples of quite nearly acceptable secondhand dress. In general, the importance of fashion to the urban theater grew in the first decades of the century, especially in New York City, where clothes-making and stage performance both flourished. Whether on Broadway or through exposure to more Burlesque varieties, young women began to view the formal stage as a source of information for personal appearances.[130] Early in the century, actresses' endorsements of clothing served to convince female consumers, perhaps especially older ones, of the advantages of manufactured dress items—as opposed to handmade or tailored. By the time World War I ended, ready-made clothes were the norm and the theater attendee assiduously scrutinized stars' clothing for hints on how she might improve her own sartorial panache and for information regarding upcoming designers. Interest in fashion mounted among a cross-section of working and leisured youth, subsets judged to be both impressionistic and demanding. Critics—male critics—complained that the increasingly female audience decentered the proper theatrical focus on content and made the stage all about clothes.[131] Although the theater's relationship to fashion was mostly in support of new gowns and up-to-date designers, Broadway performances in the teens and twenties also offered a liberal dose of the exotic and experimental.

A fascination with and increased access to exotic materials and designs influenced not only the Paris runway (and bohemian enclaves such as Greenwich Village) but also Broadway's stages. Theatrical mimicry of foreign or marginal appearances and styles ranged from performances in blackface to subtler, sartorial imitations of Japanese geishas, Egyptian princesses, and

Turkish harem girls. Such "national or cultural drag," far from indicating cultural inclusivity, enunciated the "American" whiteness of showgirls while capitalizing on the appeal of the exotic. These performances preserved established gender and racial hierarchies at a moment in which the dominant citizenry felt threatened by female autonomy and "nonwhite" immigration.[132] As xenophobic sentiments rose in the United States, the female performers promoted by slick Broadway producer Florenz Ziegfeld exemplified a shift from the glamorous, sexually suggestive European performer to the ultimate Ziegfeld type: the tall, thin, Anglo-Saxon "Glorified American Girl." Ziegfeld's Follies Girls reigned on Broadway from 1907 to 1931 and served in a similar cultural role as had Berlin's Zentral Theater girls (like young Elsa before she was the baroness). Packaged as ideally American, the Ziegfeld Girl with her distinctive Ziegfeld walk, pale-skinned, Anglo-Saxon good looks, wearing carefully curated materials and accessories, "worked as a powerful icon of race, sexuality, class, and consumerist desires."[133]

Although many Broadway spectacles began incorporating fashion display into their billings by 1910, Ziegfeld productions were especially adept at presenting what were essentially haute-couture fashion shows as plays in his renowned revues. Such genre-blending was an indication of the Follies' avant-gardism. In one distinctive Follies affect illustrating the intimate relationship between female forms and consumerism, costumes transformed showgirls into commodities such as lingerie, lace, or gems. The models/showgirls became living advertisements, posing as the highlighted objects through the medium of dress. In the 1919 *Frolics*, for example, women appeared as precious gems in the number titled "Beautiful Jewels."[134] Such displays of sexualized allegories of consumer desire were very much akin to the baroness's habit of transforming everyday objects, often detritus, into elements of dress, changing her own body into an abstraction or parody of consumable life. The taillight bustle converted the baroness into a form of transportation, and the postage-stamp beauty marks made her mail-able. These two examples not only denoted the modernist preoccupation of mobility in the age of the automobile but bore curious similarity to the "City Girls" who appeared in the *Passing Show of 1916*, a production by another set of famed producers, the Shubert brothers. Whether the baroness gleaned ideas from Broadway shows or whether she and Broadway costume designers were both inspired by the modern context, the similarities are striking.

The Shuberts were Ziegfeld's competitors, Broadway entrepreneurs who owed their sudden success to a determined corporatization of theatrical programming. From the beginning of the century, the brothers aggressively courted advertising and collaborated with a host of factory owners, venture capitalists, clothing companies, and fashion designers on theatrical tours.[135] *The Passing Show of 1916* offered advertisers the opportunity to "name" a showgirl who would represent the location of the business's home office. The costumes used illustrate how thoroughly "the Shuberts cemented their relationships with advertisers through the literal commodification of female performers."[136] The costume designer Homer Conant instructed the use of actual car parts in the making of "Detroit Girl," for example, including a bodice contrived of skidding chains, a skirt trimmed with a "Detroit Cadillac 8" tire, and most teasingly, a car door and handle in the middle of the performer's body—costume details reminiscent of the baroness's bicycle taillight bustle. Conant's "commodity costumes" also included "Postage Stamp Girls" around the same time the baroness took to using stamps as beauty marks.[137]

Whether the Detroit girl's costume used excavated car parts or factory-fresh components, formal theatrical performers had a well-cultivated relationship with secondhand materials in the first decades of the twentieth century. At the same time that Broadway embraced its role as fashion informant, many of its players still relied heavily on secondhand materials for both stage design and costuming—habits persisting from the days when dim, non-electric lighting meant corners could be cut and audiences kept, well, in the dark. Even after lighting improved, modestly funded theaters kept using secondhand materials to increase the variety of options while minimizing cost.[138] In the first decades of the century, a new imperative arose that the biggest stars appear always in fashionable dress, especially as their reproduced images became commodities. In addition, by World War I, realism in costuming for narrative plays required Broadway performers to don high-quality wardrobes if befitting the part. While this may have required financing the latest designers, conversely, Salvation Army Commander Evangeline Booth was perfectly in line with (even precocious of) theatrical form when she appeared onstage at Carnegie Hall in credible rags in 1906. Appearances in *either* down-at-the-heels or flush-to-the-gills roles might persuade actors—who, until they reached star status, often had to buy their own wardrobes—to shop secondhand.

Performers wishing to go beyond chorus-girl status but without much fashion knowledge or monetary means might resort to secondhand styles for networking and social appearances. Fanny Brice, famed Ziegfeld Girl and performer of the 1922 hit recording of "Second Hand Rose," did just that. The third child of parents of Hungarian-Jewish descent, Fania Borach was born in New York City in 1891. Growing up on Second Avenue and then Henry St., in the heart of the predominately Jewish Lower East Side, Brice had little opportunity to learn much about shopping. Even though her first job was, like many of the era's fair-featured, light-skinned girls, in a department store, she handed over her paycheck intact to her mother. A talented singer and born ham, Borach embraced the idea of performing during adolescence. She dropped out of school in 1908 to work in a burlesque revue and was soon headlining for the Ziegfeld Follies—around the time she adopted the "whiter" surname "Brice." According to her own account, when she landed a choice position with the Ziegfeld Follies in 1910, she only had enough money to "nose out a secondhand shop where the maids of fashionable ladies disposed of their mistresses' wardrobes."[139] Like the *Washington Post*'s 1884 cautionary tale about being "outed" as a secondhand shopper recounted in chapter 1 of this book, Brice recalled her embarrassment when her elaborately garish—and thus identifiably ethnic—secondhand outfit choice appalled her patron at a fine dinner. According to Brice, in reaction, Florenz Ziegfeld gave her $200 and the instructive tastefulness of his paramour Lillian Lorraine to update her style to be appropriately white and middle class.[140]

Brice did assimilate, but she also maintained her Jewish identity, and even capitalized on it. Overall, Fanny Brice's fame as a Ziegfeld Girl, along with the national popularity of "Second Hand Rose," written as a Follies performance, was atypical. Her success with "ethnic" numbers and a rare comic gift set her apart from the regal, Anglo-Saxon appearances of the by-then standardized Ziegfeld beauty. She headlined in the fast-paced, raucous numbers that punctuated the longer parades, where "living curtains" of lithe female bodies filled the stage with drawn-out sensuous performances. Fanny Brice's somewhat off-brand, comedic style demonstrated the migrating role of Jewish women in culture and society. The popularity of her hit song "Second Hand Rose" likewise indicated (or precipitated) a shift in the perception of used clothing. Brice first introduced the character of a Greenwich Village bohemian artist's model in "Rose of Washington Square" as part of the 1919 *Ziegfeld Midnight Frolics* featuring "Beautiful Jewels." She offered a sort of prequel, "Second Hand Rose," in the *Ziegfeld Follies of 1921*. The next year, she recorded "Second Hand Rose" for Victor Records, where it landed at third on the sales charts. By then, Ziegfeld had a well-publicized reputation for having, as he himself put it, "invented the showgirl." By the 1920s, the premier Broadway showgirl image was that of a desirable, ultimately American, fashion model.

While Brice did perform in roles that served as "contrast"—like those of charmingly awkward Vaudeville cowboy Will Rogers—to the bevies of elaborately dressed beauties, she was also not *not* a Ziegfeld Girl, despite how historians and filmmakers have emphasized her skinny, gawky legs and

"Jewish-looking," prominent nose. Glamorous publicity shots show a lean, long, fair-skinned body very much on display, quite the type of fashion model-cum-showgirl Ziegfeld claimed he culled and perfected from the ranks of "All-American" beauties. Brice, in turn, assimilated to the accepted white, middle-class styles of Broadway fashionability, not only changing her name from the recognizably Jewish Borach to the perky Brice—by no means the only instance of name-changing among Ziegfeld Girls—but even conforming her physical features by having her nose operated on by "an expert in recontouring." Her nose, she jested characteristically, was the only part of her that persisted in growing, and in 1923, she had it pared down from "prominent" to "merely decorative."[141] Despite conforming to expected aesthetic standards, though, Brice maintained and even leveraged her affiliation with Jewish life in New York City by comically identifying with varying aspects of Jewish stereotypes. Unlike Ziegfeld's early model for showgirl sexuality, the Polish-born Anna Held (along with numerous other Follies stars), Brice did not deny her Jewishness, but used it for comically self-deprecating effect. Such identity-based humor catered to the increasingly successful second-generation Jewish American audience. But the success of Brice as well as other Jewish showgirls exemplified not so much the rupture of categorization in understandings of racial beauty as the continuous permeability of race and the constant effort required to define "whiteness" in a decade rife with anti-Semitism, racism, and xenophobia, even as the children of some immigrants gained measurably in status.

Ziegfeld *himself* echoed the language of nativists and eugenicists of the 1920s, whose white supremacist rhetoric and accompanying pseudoscientificism was approved by widespread anxiety over the influx of "new immigrants"—those from southern and eastern Europe rather than England and northern Europe. In countless beauty advice and expert columns, Ziegfeld simultaneously emphasized the democracy of "American beauty" (the showgirls came from all the regions and classes of the country) and touted the superiority of English and Irish (white, Christian, northern European) heritage. Nativists relied on a loosely binary categorization, where northern European whites were alone in one tier, and Mediterraneans, Jews, Asians, and African Americans crowded the lower tier. The second category was hierarchical, however, and Jews, as visually white and often eagerly assimilative, came closest to "passing," which accounts in part for their presence in Ziegfeld's cadre of "Glorified American Girls."[142] Underscoring Brice's appeal as a confounding racial device was the fact that Ziegfeld first cast her as a "coon singer," which required high yellow or café-au-lait blackface—a role frequently assigned to Jewish performers.[143] Later, Brice's somewhat conditional Jewishness set her up for the portrayal of a female type in the process of becoming conditionally accepted as American. And through her performance of Rose, a secondhand-reliant bohemian, she also parodied the use of a category of consumerism in the process of becoming conditionally accepted as American.

The hit status of "Second Hand Rose" gestured toward an increasing romanticization of the Jewish ghetto by second-generation Jewish Americans, one that was apparent in varying ways in the work of many Jewish writers, including Anzia Yezierska's stories, but also Greenwich Village resident Michael Gold's *Jews without Money* (1930) and Henry Roth's *Call It Sleep* (1934).[144] Again, Yezierska's abashed admission of her own gravitation toward pushcart wares long after their cheapness was no longer the chief draw has complicated indications—rejection of the inequity of American capital, acknowledgment of an ethnic heritage, and nostalgic reminiscence, all of which encouraged a voluntary consumption of possibly secondhand items.

Rose's debut song, "Rose of Washington Square," came to epitomize the unconventional life of Greenwich Village bohemians for generations of Americans, and periodically reappeared throughout the twentieth century, along with filmic retellings of Brice's own life, her several interesting marriages, and connections to known criminals.[145] The songwriters supposedly based their character on an artist's model living in the Bronx, but moved their Jewish muse to Greenwich Village, figuring the more widely recognized bohemian enclave a fitting setting. In the song, Rose appears as a Judaized version of Baroness von Freytag-Loringhoven (who herself, like many of her modernist compatriots, unfortunately evinced occasional anti-Semitic sentiments). Rose was the "queen of the models" in the Bronx who wandered "down to Washington Square / and Bohemian Honky Tonks." There, her "Roman nose" pleased her "artistic" Beaux who wore "secondhand clothes, / and nice long hair."[146] Together with "Second Hand Rose," the song connected bohemian Greenwich Village—of which Washington Square was then considered part—to the surrounding area's predominantly Jewish trade in secondhand clothing. Indeed, the links between Village artists, secondhand materials, ethnic boundaries, and "Second Hand Rose" abound. For example, art historian Bradley Bailey suggests that Marcel Duchamp modeled his female alter ego Rrose Sélavy after Brice's Rose. According to Bailey, Duchamp habitually adopted various personas, and Rrose grew from an aspiration to cross both religious and sex boundaries. Initially, the Catholic artist sought to adopt a Jewish name but opted instead for crossing gender boundaries— though Rose was a common name for Jewish American women, including

FIGURE 2.4 Man Ray, "Marcel Duchamp as Rrose Sélavy." © Man Ray Trust/Artists Rights Society (ARS), NY/ADAGP, Paris 2016.

Brice's mother. Like Rose of Washington Square, who boasts in a very baroness-like way, "I'm terrible good as a model/the artists are stuck on my charms,"[147] Duchamp's Rrose was an artist's model. The lyrics of "Rose of Washington Square" go on to detail Rose's influence as a muse, inspiring the likes of Rube Goldberg—the cartoonist creator of impractical machines with whom Duchamp found some affinity. In the song, Goldberg (also distinctly Jewish by name) admires her figure, but dresses her in a veil, perhaps alluding to an other-than Anglo-Saxon profile. The baroness, too, was often admired for her lithe and muscular form, but critiqued for her hard and masculine face; Fanny Brice's figure conformed to Ziegfeld Girl standards, but her facial features deviated from the outlined formula for "pretty girls." Rrose Sélavy emerged, in name and in a posed Man Ray photo of Duchamp in drag (see figure 2.4) in 1921, well into the baroness's association with Duchamp, amidst many popular reiterations of "Rose of Washington Square" and the same year "Second Hand Rose" debuted on stage. If Duchamp saw something appealing and imitation-worthy in Ziegfeld's Rose, it is also likely that Duchamp recognized in her his good friend, the artist's muse and secondhand aficionada Baroness Elsa von Freytag-Loringhoven, with whom both R(r)oses have so much in common.

Performed in 1921, "Second Hand Rose" furnished Rose with a backstory. In this song, the pouty protagonist good-naturedly bemoans her fate as the daughter of a used-goods dealer: "Father has a business, strictly second hand. / Ev'rything from toothpicks, to a baby grand. / Stuff in our apartment, comes from Father's store, / Even things I'm wearing, someone wore before. / It's no wonder that I feel abused. / I never have a thing that ain't been used."[148] Everything in Rose's life is secondhand—including her "man," who has been married before. Everyone knows she's "Second Hand Rose," from Second Avenue. Like the "Roman" nose, Rose's secondhand status elides ghetto Jewishness and fashionable bohemianism. Second Avenue—where Brice's mother, also Rose, and father, first set up their household—was in a respectable section of the Lower East Side that became a hub of Jewish culture in the early 1900s. For Vaudeville listeners who might not pick up on these "subtleties," Brice's comically Jewish accent and liberal peppering of Yiddish surely clued them in.

In the song, Second Hand Rose is an imposter. Beneath the comedy, if there is a moral to the song, it is not far afield from the 1884 *Saturday Evening Post* story recounted in chapter 1, or from Brice's real-life dinner tale. Like the *Post's* comely protagonist, Rose uses secondhand materials to cut a fine figure and to emulate higher class, with her pre-owned pearls, grand piano, and fur coat (Duchamp, in his poses as Rrose, crosses gender boundaries with the aid of similar accessories). Rose "strolls"—an action implying not just movement but proud display, a flaneur-like promenade—through the posh lobby of the Ritz-Carlton, seemingly well-enough appareled not to be displaced, until a girl there outs her attempts at class-passing by loudly recognizing the coat as her own cast-off.[149] The humor of the song relies on the listeners' recognition of types: certainly of the "ghetto Jewess," but also of the secondhand consumer as a status imposter, but it does so in a lighthearted, approachable way, creating a character who is sympathetic and recognizable to upwardly mobile Jewish audience members. As the decade went on, representations of class imposters grew less and less condemning, until in the 1927 silver screen hit *It*, the class-climbing Clara Bow could be a plucky heroine. Playing a clothes clerk, Bow's character repurposes accessories and refashions her cheap wardrobe, improvising an edgy flapper look for a cross-class performance also to be enacted at the Ritz, still the stand-in for the authentic upper class. By then, such subterfuge was cute and gutsy—and moreover, it absolutely succeeded. Bow got her (very wealthy) man.

Second Hand in Demand

Improvisational wardrobes took on a much less flippant tone in the 1930s, as did fashion or dress generally. As the Great Depression deepened, the average expenditures on clothing plummeted alongside national employment. Financial panics, production stoppages, and rapidly spreading unemployment disrupted many economic trends. For numerous industries producing new goods, production outpaced demand years before the stock market's crash further undermined consumer confidence, causing rapid declines in sales, and spurring corporate slowdowns. The problems for secondhand commerce were converse—demand increased while supplies diminished. As unemployment rose to peak at more than 25 percent by 1933, more Americans viewed used goods and clothing as necessary resources.

Thrift-store interests scrambled to keep profits stable. In 1934, when President Franklin D. Roosevelt announced his request to the Boy Scouts to collect used clothing and household materials to give free to the nation's needy, the Salvation Army helped with these efforts for more than altruistic reasons. So few items were coming their way through the usual routes (and those that did were in such bad condition) that it had become a challenge to provide clothing even for the men working in the salvage centers. The Salvation Army helped gather goods for the government partly to keep damaged items their workers might repair or repurpose into something fit for use or sale by the organization.[150] By then, Goodwill Industries' mostly employed physically or mentally disabled workers as its lower-level employees. President Roosevelt's New Deal labeled this group "unemployable" and advocated for the growth of "sheltered workshops" such as Goodwill so that such potential workers would not compete on the open market with able-bodied men. Amidst continuing national unemployment and economic disarray, Congress passed the Fair Labor Standards Act of 1938. Much of the legislation was ostensibly intended to protect workers rights and urge more equitable distribution of available work. For example, it mandated a raise in the minimum wage for certain employees, limited the weekly number of hours an individual employee could work, and outlawed child labor, wherein a child was defined as anyone under the age of sixteen.[151]

Goodwill Industries benefitted from the terms specified in section 14(c) of the Act, which permitted employers to apply for a special wage certificate granting the right to hire people with disabilities at a subminimum rate. During the Great Depression, Goodwill often overhired, underestimating the dearth of donations, and were unable to provide much income to its workers—at times even just "paying" employees in vouchers for store goods.[152] However, in the 1950s, when secondhand donations surged as hordes of Americans rushed to update material belongings with which they had been required to "make do" and demand kept pace as well, Goodwill Industries did not significantly readjust their wage scale for the disabled as corporate profits grew, nor have they as of this writing.

Secondhand commerce's limited supplies continued amidst the government-ordered rationing of World War II. Secondhand markets, as ever, adapted. "Junk men" still turned a tidy profit collecting scraps for industry and paper for the war effort.[153] Wood pulp and rag recycling for the production of paper helped sustain independent gleaners as well as Goodwill and the Salvation Army through the 1930s and into the 1940s.[154] After the Allies won the war, clothing demand continued to outstrip supply while factories were being reconverted to peacetime production, and because liberation efforts absorbed the bulk of donations. For example, instead of Goodwill seeing an immediate spike in donations as soon as citizens were able to purchase new clothing, the United National Clothing Collection's drive to send American discards to newly liberated Europe preempted expected donations, as Americans continued the habit of war-related civic efforts by emptying their closets in anticipation of new garments. Still, some secondhand vendors profited from liberation efforts. In the informal economies of secondhand, the price of used goods rose with demand. Old-clothiers hiked prices fourfold in the "frowsy streets" of the Bowery, sales zones inevitably compared to Paris's flea market.[155] And at the war's end, the Bowery's estimated $3,000,000-a-year business earned the bulk of its profit from the Procurement Division of the Treasury Department. According to the *New York Times*, in May 1945, the Army was the Bowery's old clothes wholesale merchants' biggest buyer, with twelve and a half million pounds of clothes on order, all headed for liberated areas, reportedly ahead of the United Nations Relief and Rehabilitation Administration.[156]

Between 1897, when the Salvation Army started its first U.S. salvaging business, and 1945, when the Army bought over six thousand tons of discarded clothing from a coordinated group of street merchants, formal and informal streams of secondhand sales firmly imbedded themselves in American economic life. Still, in many ways, clothing was the last frontier for those who did not need to rely on cheaper, pre-owned goods, the last major material realm of secondhand goods to be upgraded to antique or collectible. At the end of the war, the cultural value of pre-owned clothing remained abstracted and sparsely recognized. Avant-garde artists, a few popular performers, and historical reenactors in Henry Ford's employ notwithstanding, it would take over a decade more of economic and social changes among the bulk of Americans to arrive at any widespread revaluing of certain used clothing. Before that happened, the expanding numbers of middle-class Americans would introduce their own colloquial mode of secondhand sales, one arguably even more popular and widely accepted than thrift stores and flea markets—garage sales.

CHAPTER THREE

Garage Sales and Suburban Subversiveness

Maybe the garage sale is a metaphor for the mind.
—Performance artist Martha Rosler, 1973

In August 1972, *Life* magazine listed the items going for cheap at a garage sale, a phenomenon that over the past decade and a half had "mushroomed throughout the nation's suburbs."[1] Piles of old toys, chipped plates, a faded rug, pillows, aquariums, and an antiquated popcorn popper all heaped onto a manicured lawn would once have announced "that the junkman was on his way," but by the early 1970s, they were par for the Saturday morning course. According to *Life*, the happy Eriksons family hosting their featured garage sale (see figure 3.1) netted a neat $442 from eager buyers who "blitzed" their home, clearing out nearly every one of the 1,500 offered items and leaving them with "a fistful of dollars—and room to start again."[2] Twenty years before, as masses of Americans migrated from cities to suburbs in World War II's wake, garage sales had no part in the consumer experience. Neither did regional shopping centers or Tupperware home parties. By the end of the 1960s, all of these were integral to middle-class suburban lives.

Garage sales were the premier postwar used-goods market innovation. Burgeoning suburbs fertilized the idea and a new secondhand economy was born, as were thrift stores and flea markets, of necessity and pleasure, to provide recreation and profit, and to fill civic and political gaps. Even more clearly than earlier secondhand exchange innovations, garage sales signified changes in the relationships between individual consumers, material goods, and the act of shopping. In the Cold War United States, amidst the raging ideological war between capitalism and communism, the process of honing a personal identity increasingly revolved around consumer choices. Garage sales well represented the conflicts and alliances between domesticity and consumption; separate sets of expectations for men and women conflicted with and eventually adapted to the imperative for Keynesian-style economic growth, which required as many earning and buying citizens as possible.

Influential individuals from early in the century, such as Evangeline Booth, André Breton, and Fanny Brice, helped set the stage for voluntary secondhand consumption. Popular imagination—and some historical discourse—assigns postwar Beats and hippies principal roles in articulating oppositional meanings

FIGURE 3.1 The Ericksons' garage sale. *Life* magazine, 18 August 1972.

of used clothing specifically. Straight-laced, Valium-laden suburbs are not usually canvassed for evidence of consumer rebellion, but these television-buying, commuting postwar adults not only supplied much of the physical material exchanged on secondhand markets for decades to come but also helped forge a lasting nexus between secondhand objects and creative individual identities among the middle class, whose ranks rapidly swelled.

Garage sales first popped up in the mid-1950s, amid the rampant building of single-family homes in the undeveloped regions beyond cities—and around the time economist John Kenneth Galbraith penned *The Affluent Society*, marking a shift in some economists' attention from problems of poverty to the worries of wealth.[3] Also called carport sales, yard sales, moving sales, lawn sales, attic sales, cellar sales, or bargain sales, the events were informal, irregularly held and privately hosted, usually in or around a single-family residence.[4] Women structured the shape, content, format, and growth of garage sales. A 1971 devotee quipped that there were only "two kinds of women in the world"—"those who go to garage sales and those who *give* them."[5] Actually, as the number of garage sales rose seemingly in proportion to unemployment and inflation, many suburban women in the 1960s, and certainly in the 1970s, both bought and sold in a kind of lateral recycling that underscored still-broadening definitions of novelty.

From the 1950s inception of the sales, hostesses sold mostly used household goods and clothing, sometimes supplemented with handcrafted items and comestibles. The vibe was social: browsing, bargaining, and gossiping were intrinsic to the practice. The sales reacted to both the isolation of new extraurban neighborhoods and the emphasis on close-knit interactions within those communities. The practice adapted community fund-raisers such as church rummage sales to an at-home format suited to the milieu and reflective of popular "home sales" tactics pioneered in the early 1950s by the Tupperware and Avon companies. Suburban garage sales provided a way for home-bound housewives to earn income, participate in politics, and build community networks despite, and often in accordance with, the spatial circumscriptions of suburban communities and postwar gender expectations.

As mass production again expanded at the end of World War II, advertisers more ardently than ever billed shopping as recreational. Garage sales signified an increasing preoccupation with material possessions, since they served to, as *Life* put it, make "room to start again." But these rogue economies only partly obeyed postwar economic directives. They reached outside the spatial limits of new, corporatized commercial zones such as regional malls. They charted aesthetic territory counter to the historical assumption of economic envy and consumer escalation—or, "keeping up with the Joneses."[6] Anthropologists have qualified garage sales as "suburban subversiveness" in part because of their open rebellion against mainstream commerce and marketing pressures to have the latest and newest.[7] Furthermore, the intimacy of garage sales countered the continuing depersonalization of firsthand exchange systems—trends that began with fixed prices in those mid-nineteenth-century Parisian stores such as Bon Marché ending what Friedrich Engels called the practice of *Schacher*, or haggling, trends that expanded with the postwar multiplication of shopping centers.[8] Haggling also persisted in street sales and at flea markets, and to a lesser degree, through fund-raising fairs and rummage sales.

The clearest innovation of the garage sale was location, which transformed peripheral, semiprivate areas (garages, porches, lawns) of single-family homes into quasi-public arenas of consumer exchange. As fund-raisers with various personal and communal aims, garage sales mapped localized changes in community engagement, political activity, and charitable aid. In this era of mounting civic participation, a greater percentage of Americans than ever before or since were joining churches, clubs, and formal organizations. The 1950s and 1960s growth in civic associations is largely attributable to suburban women. Since those same hyper-joiners were more likely to have a larger number of young children than previous generations, and, at least until 1970, many of them were unlikely to have reliable access to an automobile during the workweek, incorporating activities centered on the revered domestic realm made practical as well as ideological sense. And, like hostess or home parties devoted to the sale of Tupperware or Avon products, garage sales conformed to cultural assumptions of women's roles as mothers and wives, while offering opportunities for remunerated work. Despite the *Father Knows Best* image of postwar families with working dads and stay-at-home moms, by 1960 as many of 30 percent of mothers did some sort of formal paid work to supplement the household coffers.[9] That number disregards the contributions of informal economies; garage sales supplied housewives with a small occasional income without appearing to question the masculine position of breadwinner.

Certainly, garage sales were considered by many participants simply to be fun. The recreational pastime of collecting antiques and other older goods grew in popularity among suburbanites, and gleaners happily added garage sales to the list of likely sales sites. In popular media and through advertising, antiquing junkets were presented as suitable activities for happy couples, and counted as many men as women among its enthusiasts. Though women were the chief movers in the garage sale world, men, too, encouraged the venues' success through their own leisure-time interests. Secondhand goods provided the raw material for many home-centered hobbies, such as do-it-yourself home building and repair, which postwar men pursued with new zeal—possibly as a counter to the rote intangibilities of middle-management labor, one of the largest-growing sectors of employment. At least indirectly, suburban men also supported the phenomenon of garage sales.

Historians have barely glanced at garage sales, despite their significant monetary function and iconic cultural role in suburban life. According to the few estimates given in the 1980s, after what seemed like a peak in popularity (or at least popular attention) in the 1970s, more than ten million garage sales were held every year, and more than a billion dollars changed hands. This is no insignificant economy. Anthropologists and other social scientists have addressed these sales, agreeing on their social and recreational importance.[10] However astute, such research treats only recent examples. To understand the embedded cultural meaning of secondhand economies, we need to see the context of their emergence. In the decades after World War II, garage sales' growth resembled the evolution of thrift stores and flea markets in many ways—particularly in their consistency with the pattern of new secondhand venues emerging in boom times and during times of population rearrangement—but garage sales also offer us new insight into suburban consumers. Garage sales were keen representations of suburban postwar Americans' altered relationships to material goods, gender roles, home, labor, and community in ways that sometimes disrupt the still-common narrative of suburban conformity.

Cars and the Suburban Home

The name "garage sale" indicates the centrality of location to the mode of exchange. Integral garages, or at least carports, were first consistently included in home building during the 1950s.[11] As more Americans spent more time in motor vehicles to get to work in cities remote to new homes, cars took on greater personal importance, becoming viewed as identity markers for owners, a development stimulated by and responded to with design variations and feature options.[12] Gone were the days of Henry Ford's democratically practical black Model Ts; car buyers in the 1950s embraced General Motors' guru Alfred P. Sloan's more expansive and individualized marketing ideology.[13] Cars linked the deepening meanings of consumerism and the increasing physical gap between many Americans' places of work and living spaces. Vehicle storage became a home building priority, and many architectural designs accommodated cars with the addition of a specially designated liminal space, the garage.

Automobile ownership was part of what made it possible for more and more families to move away from crowded cities, where housing had been a problem for decades but where most employment remained. After the war, the automotive industry worked overtime to meet the backlogged needs of eager consumers whose acquisitiveness had been waylaid first by economic crises and then by rubber rationing, an industrial preoccupation with military supplies, and governmental inducements to consumer saving. When American industries reconverted to peacetime businesses, large-scale producers capitalized on the widespread interest in new cars.[14] By the mid-1950s, four out of five American families owned automobiles, and about the same percentage of newly built homes included garages or carports.[15]

The government contributed to efforts of suburbanization partly through federally funding the building of highways connecting suburbs with cities. As the Cold War between the United States and Russia escalated after the Soviet Union developed their own atomic bomb in 1949, and after a proxy war between capitalism and communism erupted in Korea, arguments for "defense through decentralization" supported government subsidies. When President Dwight D. Eisenhower signed the 1956 National Interstate and Defense Highways Act into law, he cited the need for convenient evacuation routes away from target atomic blast areas as one justification for the funding.[16]

The backlog of demand for home construction was even greater than that for cars. Similar "defense through decentralization" rationale supported aggressive government financing for homebuyers looking to move to the peripheries of cities. Thanks to cars and highways, many city employees could choose to move to these more spacious residences, and thanks to yet more federal subsidies and new liberal home loan policies, unattached, single-family homes were within financial reach of more Americans than ever before. The establishment of the Home Owners Loan Corporation (HOLC) in 1933 made obtaining lifetime mortgages easier and lowered the risk of foreclosure. Along with the efforts of the Federal Housing Administration (FHA) to improve mortgage plans and the passage of the Servicemen's Readjustment Act of 1944 (or GI Bill), these federal changes made home ownership an option for many working-class citizens, as well as their wealthier peers.[17] While these practices somewhat leveled the playing field across economic classes, the same cannot be said for race. Appallingly, the HOLC's and FHA's rating systems, which undervalued older, racially nonhomogeneous, or densely populated neighborhoods, erected obstacles to the movement of African Americans and other minorities from the city to the suburb, creating de facto racial segregation in many areas and limiting possibilities for minorities' financial and physical mobility. The resonating effects of such structural racism continue to compound inequality in the United States to this day.[18]

Despite the limited opportunities for some groups of Americans, at least 83 percent of the population growth in the United States during the 1950s was in the suburbs.[19] By 1955, the phenomenon was marked enough for panelists at the Boston Conference on Distribution to characterize suburbanization as "without question the greatest and most rapid shift in the pattern of living in history."[20] This mass migration inevitably affected commerce, including secondhand exchange. As opposed to central factors in thrift-store success earlier in the century, the fact that suburban transplants had *more* rather than *less* room shaped the format of garage sales. Turn-of-the-century cities' populations included record numbers of immigrants and rural migrants, and many residents lived in very close quarters. To accommodate ready-made, convenient, and increasingly affordable consumer goods, urbanites had to discard existing older items, as storage was not an option for most. A continual supply of unwanted but still salvageable goods helped the Salvation Army and Goodwill Industries establish national chains of thrift stores.

Lack of space was not an immediate problem in the postwar suburban context. For most new homeowners in the late 1940s and 1950s, their residences had more space than their former city dwellings—though often still not as much as they would have liked. Suburbanites also had a much greater variety of newly manufactured household goods from which to choose than their prewar counterparts, and oftentimes, an increased disposable income with which to buy. The marketing imperatives to buy a greater variety of goods, more often, ratcheted up the inducements to acquire. Even when cash flow was insufficient, there were remedies; the immediate postwar years brought rapidly increasing access to and use of consumer credit lines.[21] Consumer spending increased 60 percent from 1945 to 1960, concentrated in the domestic arena; spending on household goods, from appliances to televisions to furniture, increased by 240 percent.[22] So even though suburban families did have some space in which to store unused or outdated items, before long these spaces, too, were overstuffed. To compensate for what quickly became seen as inadequate space in the average suburban home (and to accommodate trends in do-it-yourself crafts, as discussed later in the chapter), *Popular Mechanics* advertised in 1952 a "new trend" in garage design that included added space with various cabinets that might serve as storage or as a workshop.[23] By the mid-1950s, when hostesses began advertising garage sales in newspapers, new goods were edging out older items, which filled garages or attics. The space available made it possible for a single family to acquire and retain enough unwanted items for a stand-alone sale—though garage sales did sometimes involve multiple families, whole neighborhoods, or members of civic organizations, increasing their value as community-building ventures, as examined below.

Why not just give these things away or throw them out? William H. Whyte, one of the most outspoken critics of postwar American life during the time, declared in a 1956 *Fortune* magazine article titled "Budgetism: Opiate of the Middle Class" that as "a normal part of life, thrift now is un-American."[24] Whyte's assessment, which assumed that rising credit debt and diminished savings signaled a forfeiture of responsible personal control over finances, failed to consider practices such as garage sales and the overall rise in secondhand consumerism as at least mitigating factors. Granted, as rebellions against rising commerce, garage sales compromised, serving as they did to assuage

FIGURE 3.2 Powers of persuasion: poster art from World War II. "Use It Up—Wear It Out—Make It Do!" 1941–45. Courtesy of the National Archives and Records Administration.

sellers' apprehensions over increasing their firsthand spending and to make room, as the 1972 *Life* magazine article noted, "to start again."[25]

Still, rather than simply tossing excess goods out, housewives flung open garage doors and invited neighbors in to rifle through their discarded belongings, usually for a modest profit. After the war's end, thrift as a value did not wholly disappear with the diminishment of its immediate necessity. Frugality espoused by older generations or learned during the Great Depression was elevated to the level of patriotism during World War II. Wartime propaganda "enlisted" housewives into war efforts as "militant consumers" whose "budget is their battle plan."[26] The U.S. government formally urged American consumers entering the second decade of a worldwide depression to continue to "make do" (see figure 3.2). Such insistent, long-standing messages of community aid and good stewardship were not gleefully abandoned but rather tailored to postwar affluence.

Also, simply giving away large quantities of old belongings was not actually so easy following the end of the war. Neighborhoods were assembled rapidly, and other community infrastructure, including shopping facilities, lagged behind home building for some years. In cities, families could conveniently donate old goods to Goodwill or the Salvation Army, but such thrift stores did not immediately appear in suburbs, nor did convenient pick-up routes extend to the freshly minted communities. Chain salvage stores worked to catch up—Goodwill Industries tripled their number of stores in the 1950s.[27] But the lag time between a critical mass of stockpiled unwanted goods and the spread of Goodwill Industries, Salvation Army, and other thrift stores to the suburbs likely encouraged the emergence of garage sales as an alternative secondhand exchange system, one fittingly centered on the increasingly important family home.

At least one more aspect of suburban houses themselves stimulated participation in secondhand shopping. While the popular models of new housing, such as prefabricated ranch homes, were made affordable by government subsidies, full employment, and higher salaries, suburban houses by no means pleased all buyers. In the 1940s, the cost of building rose (in part because construction labor cost rose in accordance with demand). Mass-produced homogenization of styles and sacrifice of space were ways builders maintained quality while keeping cost down. Critiques of the homogeneity of postwar suburbia echoed in stories, articles, poems, and songs of the time, such as Malvina Reynolds's 1962 song "Little Boxes and Other Handmade Songs": "Little boxes on the hillside / Little boxes made of ticky tacky / Little boxes on the hillside / Little boxes all the same."[28] Although millions of buyers accepted the trade-off of residential distinction for ownership and comfort, their acquiescence does not imply wholesale acceptance of uniform domestic style. Many homeowners were disappointed at the size of the house they could afford as well as the repetitions in design and floor plan.[29] Clearly, suburbanites resisted implications that their lives replicated their neighbors and hesitated (if only momentarily) to purchase cookie-cutter homes.

As much as critics such as William Whyte painted suburbanites as eager conformists, many of them expressed a desire to distinguish their domestic personalities—even if, in capitulation to the epoch, this was often done by way of purchase choices and through material display. Historian Lizabeth Cohen asserts that suburbanites used consumerism "to express their individuality as much as their conformity in the homes they created."[30] While the popular *negative* perception of postwar suburban homes was that which John Keats expressed in *The Crack in the Picture Window* (1956) as places "inhabited by people whose age, income, number of children, problems, habits, conversations, dress, and perhaps even blood-type are precisely like yours," Cohen emphasizes that the cross-class inclusivity of suburban growth meant that many new residents carried with them the habits and proclivities of second-generation Americans.[31] Because of the relative diversity of income and ethnic backgrounds—though *not* race—some suburbanites carried with them habits regarding home repair, the maintenance of handed-down family objects, and receptiveness to secondhand acquisitions.[32] And increasingly, for already established middle-class, Anglo-Saxon families, quirky items from garage sales or church rummage sales might serve as markers of credibly unusual taste, aesthetic acumen, and prized individuality.

Allying Work and Shopping in the Suburbs

Undoubtedly, the 1940s and 1950s were acquisitive years for many Americans. As they had at the turn of the century and during the 1920s, patterns of shopping and goods disposal changed after World War II's end. Many of the same American consumers who had faced wartime rationing and scarcity on the heels of a worldwide depression were eager to replace those items with which they had long made do. A wide array of tempting new products emerged from reconverted factories, and full national employment assured a strong cohort of shoppers. Urging along this capacity to buy, promoters of many consumer goods followed the lead of the automobile and fashion industries by making planned obsolescence part of their marketing schemes.[33] Nervous producers theorized that one way to prevent the consumer fatigue that preceded the market failure of the 1930s was to require incessant consumer updates and frequent replacements. Thanks also to the maintenance of a wartime economy through the building of what Eisenhower dubbed the "military-industrial complex," the postwar boom time was in fact extended beyond a predictable span. Employment stayed high, so production spiked while costs decreased, allowing consumers to keep pace with industrial output. As the 1955 *Economic Report of the President* noted, "perhaps at no time in the past has the desire for material improvement played so large a role in the economy as it does today."[34]

Initially, there were some practical impediments to trading in war bonds for a new washing machine and a Dacron sports suit. For pioneer postwar suburbanites, firsthand commercial outlets, as well as salvage businesses such as Goodwill, were not always conveniently available. Until the mid-1950s, suburban shopping options were limited. Although many new residents had expansive consuming needs and increased incomes, few early developers of suburban communities took the more quotidian consumer demands under immediate consideration.[35] Shoppers sometimes had to drive miles to get to the nearest "market town" or return to the city to make family purchases. Most primary earners (usually men) still worked in the city all day, and the suburbs often bound the daily activities of housewives since the family car ferried the husband to his job. Even when a vehicle was available, urban commercial districts were not designed to accommodate automobile-dependent shoppers and therefore provided inadequate parking.[36]

The types of primary businesses established for suburban consumers were not just extensions of existing commercial models but rather innovations that accommodated the new economic standards and demographic situation of the United States. At the end of World War II, only a few hundred regional shopping centers—the original malls—existed in the United States. Before long, businesses fought to tap into the enormous, growing consumer demand in the suburbs, and a large, multibusiness outlet was the adopted model. In the mid-1950s, shopping centers began peppering the landscape. Frequently, these complexes were situated to serve several prefabricated communities at once to maximize profit. Thus, driving was usually still required, except in suburbs closest to metropolitan areas, which might have access via bus systems (along routes that were often manipulated to exclude poor minorities whose business was not considered ideal to center developers).[37] By 1958, developers had erected 2,900 centers nationwide; by 1963, 7,100; and by the end of the 1970s, more than 22,000 regional shopping centers provided for outlying communities. Many of these centers had from fifty to more than one hundred stores, included chain and department stores, and sought to provide comprehensive consumer services.[38]

While a number of shopping centers did emulate urban downtowns in providing community services beyond the sale of goods, they ultimately represented a continuation of the commercial shift from public to privatized (and isolated) shopping. Although city department stores have been described as one step in this direction, even major ones continued to tie commercial activities to the immediate community, through health fairs, planning boards, charities, and events such as Macy's Thanksgiving Day Parade. Also, urban department stores were flanked by bars, hotels, post offices, and courthouses, and looked out on pedestrian sidewalks and busy streets. Some larger postwar shopping center plans did include community activity centers and childcare provision catering to the consumer needs and recreational desires of housewives, the malls' largest audience, but soon it was clear that malls' services failed to extend much beyond commercial transactions.[39]

City planner Ann Satterthwaite points out that "sociability became a casualty" of mainstream commerce by the late 1950s partly because shopping center developers did not build for a single or even for existing neighborhoods.[40] Chain stores needed large selling areas to efficiently use their mass merchandising methods, and large-scale development was further encouraged by the hefty acreage needed for ample parking spaces. Fueled by federal tax policies encouraging commercial real estate development in greenfield locations, builders paved remote cornfields in anticipation of subdivision expansion. Soon, suburbs were following the shopping centers. These proactive practices hobbled organic community integration and increased privatization.[41]

Changes in consumer markets came under scrutiny. Economists, philosophers, and other social scientists paid mounting attention to the subjects of consumer satisfaction and corporate interests in the 1950s. While classical Keynesian interpretations of market growth emphasized the importance of consumer demand (supported by government funding), others accused corporate capitalism of leading or creating those demands. One of the most controversial chapters of Galbraith's 1958 edition of the best-selling *The Affluent Society* forwarded the idea of consumer sovereignty as a myth, noting the overwhelming power of advertising and marketing in formulating buyer preferences.[42] Along with William Whyte's best-selling *Organization Man*, published in 1956, Galbraith disseminated critiques of conformity and mass culture to the general public, whose eager response to the studies at least implied agreement.[43] Eight years later, Herbert Marcuse would even more forcefully insist that "advanced industrial society" relied on a system of creating false needs that entrapped consumers in unceasing cycles of production and consumption, dulled their ability to rebel and innovate, and ultimately, created a "one-dimensional man." His dystopian vision of a world comprised of William Whyte's people-pleasing organization men incapable of opposition and innovation even eliminated the possibility for a Marxian revolutionary proletariat.[44]

The idea of the commercial creation of needs as paramount to postwar lives has become the standard narrative. Accordingly, there even evolved consumer outlets for anticommercial desires, which in effect, dampened the force of potential social and political action. To an extent, secondhand commerce was an imperfect rebellion against the commercial cooptation of anticapitalism. Indisputably, consumption increased enormously in the 1950s and 1960s. Material possessions became, for many, a key avenue of personal expression. Including secondhand commerce in this equation does not counter observations about the middle-class's preoccupation with material acquisition, but it does help explain the subsequent consumer backlash of the 1960s and 1970s, which may not have been as sudden and generational as it seemed. Shopping centers failed to combine community and commercial life. Consumers did not abandon the outlets en masse as a spontaneous or organized response, but they did diversify, dispersing their buying power to various places as a response to corporate constraints. Corporations sometimes adapted to consumer preferences and created alternative shopping modes and products. For example, Tupperware, Inc., was an unsuccessful endeavor until Brownie Wise came up with the home-based party plan system in the 1950s.

Even scholars who describe mass culture, including shopping, as a site of both oppression and dissent as is now de rigueur in many academic circles, usually still ignore the creation of alternative, dismissed as marginal, modes of commerce.[45] Secondhand exchange demonstrates that consumer capitulation to advertising for new goods was at no point wholesale. Non-new content aside, the garage sale's format itself was rebellious. Rather than further impersonalizing the experience of buying as did shopping centers, garage sales (like Tupperware parties) upped the intimacy of sales transactions by inviting consumers into the home, or at least a semiprivate extension of it. Moreover, garage sales welcomed critical examination of the personal, sometimes sentimental items of near-strangers, a fact that disrupts the characterization of postwar families as domestically insular. A love of bargains or a fashionable ardor for collecting were obvious motivators for shoppers, but one avid 1967 garage sale goer, who averaged ten sales per week in the peak months of April and May, insisted she was not alone in adding human curiosity to her reasons for this hobby. She insisted the offered items revealed intimate details about their owners' lives, at least when browsing was coupled with the ability to analyze material goods. "With hair dye and face lifting, you can't always tell a woman's age. But a pretty good indication of how long she's been married comes from her furniture. Is it fumed oak or limed oak? Either one gives her away."[46]

Buyers who opted for secondhand choices were at least marginally maverick consumers, whether they willfully ignored commands to abandon budgeting or to have the latest model and style, or whether their incomes forbade conformity to primary market dictates. Garage sales' sellers, too, operated as at least lightly rogue capitalists, pursuing profit outside established and taxed corridors. While those studying garage sales later in the century downplay the importance of income to garage sale hostesses, an early 1970s study revealed that earned income was a significant factor. By this time, periodic economic recessions probably heightened the association of garage sales with financial gain, but pressure to maintain increasing standards of living dated back to the 1950s and 1960s, when rising numbers of housewives worked outside the home at least part time.[47] Despite the impression of unlimited affluence, postwar economic growth was fitful and unpredictable, marred by intermittent recessions that brought forth the still-looming specter of the Great Depression.

Immediately after World War II, many working women—about two million of the six million employed in wartime—surrendered their paychecks, often in favor of marriage and children. The marriage age decreased and the birth rate rose. Women were discouraged from seeking work outside the home. Although twice as many wartime working women chose to or felt compelled to continue working as did not, television shows and commercials, magazines, and self-help books emphasized in countless ways that "[w]omen have many careers but only one vocation—motherhood."[48] However, the mounting belief in Keynesian economic growth as the cure for not only domestic economic toils but as proof of capitalism's supremacy over communism convinced economists that the United States needed more earners as well as more spenders. In 1958, the National Manpower Council argued that women workers were necessary additions to workplaces. By 1960, the number of wives working outside the home exceeded 30 percent, although about 80 percent of women's jobs were "pink-collar" ones—that is, they fell into categories of employment stereotyped as female, which included clerks in retail outlets and other consumer-related functions. Women's roles in professional careers did not grow nearly as rapidly. The rise in the service sector accounted for much of the increase in women's work. Throughout the 1950s, the increase in nonurban, regional shopping centers mirrored the increase in working wives and mothers. In 1957, a Stanford Business School professor assured managers of chain store branches that most suburban stores have access to "a large number of housewives and nonemployed women who have been willing to work." These arrangements furthered business's interests; by employing many part-time workers, store managers avoided doling out full-time benefits and could more easily impede union growth.[49] Often part-time or without benefits, and usually with little opportunity for advancement, pink-collar jobs emphasized the perennial idea that female employment produced only supplemental incomes—pin money.[50]

Polls taken of those employed wives showed that about half worked "to buy something"—a much smaller proportion worked for a sense of accomplishment.[51] The desire for material acquisitions extended to less conventional types of employment as well. This echoed in the personal stories of Tupperware saleswomen and distributors throughout the 1950s, 1960s, and 1970s. Midwestern housewife, Lavon Weber, ventured into the field in the 1950s because she coveted a blonde coffee table, and an extra like that "was not on the list."[52] To earn the money herself, either in an area where other pink-collar jobs were scarce or in a way that did not go against ideals of domesticity, Weber and thousands of other women became Tupperware party hostesses. These home parties, or "hostess parties," appeared as newly discovered, quaint yet modern, social yet productive, housewife activities. Even husbands reluctant to have working wives often acceded to such a feminine and convivial event as a Tupperware party. Home parties were a solution to the tension between the societal ideal of women focusing their attentions on the home and the increasing consumer imperatives. Some women, like Brownie Wise herself, head of the Tupperware sales division and mastermind of the "party plan" marketing system (and the first woman to appear on the cover of *Business Week* magazine, in 1954), were divorced and lacked the skills or opportunity for lucrative income elsewhere. A rising number of these women—again, like Brownie Wise—had the added responsibilities of single parenthood.[53]

Tupperware, Inc., struggled with low profits and poor distribution until Brownie Wise established the party plan system in the early 1950s. Companies such as Tupperware, Avon, and Stanley Home Products saw suburbia as the ideal scouting place for both party hostesses and product consumers. Wise described the suburb as "a picnic ground for direct selling," citing the "increase in household expenditure, women doing their own housework, and child-centered consumption" as prime reasons for success.[54] In addition to in-home gatherings, Tupperware hostesses were encouraged to seek out community events in the society pages, with the recommendation of combining a Tupperware party with "a bake sale, a white elephant sale, a rummage sale, or bazaar."[55] Three of these events featured used goods exchange and usually supported community groups, such as churches, sororities, or charities. Tupperware may well have paved a smoother path for garage sales, but secondhand fund-raisers first cleared the heavy brambles.

Ever the critic, Whyte cited commercial "parties" as an example of coffee-klatching conformity and "lowest denominator-seeking" among suburban housewives. Whyte and other detractors considered such "neighborism" to be disingenuous and intellectually homogenizing.[56] But at-home money-making schemes were not just opportunities for dulling neighborhood gossip. They were examples of conciliatory resistance to gendered family arrangements, in which the financially responsible husband drove to work in the morning and the domestically inclined wife tended home and children. Integrating work with the duties of caring for home and family, which overcame material obstacles such as child care, circumvented concerns about feminine breadwinning. The responsibilities of such tasks allowed women to lay partial claim to the family car—or to argue for and afford the addition of a new one.[57]

Like home parties, socializing and profit were both motives for hosting garage sales. In a 1970s survey of residents in the suburbs of DeKalb, Illinois, most hostesses, some of whom had been conducting sales semiregularly since the early 1960s, did not work outside the home. Several reported feeling "guilty about not being able to make a cash contribution to the family income."[58] Garage sales' profit-making potential was signaled in more formal ways, too. By the late 1960s, local legislation in many parts of the country regulating frequency, size, and taxation of the events indicated that the sales had become an effectual enough means of income to attract official attention—possibly through complaints by more formalized competing businesses, such as established and taxed secondhand stores and antiques shops. As had previously happened with rummage sales, pushcart peddling, and flea markets, zoning requirements and limits on garage sales' recurrence were established in many areas by 1970. However, municipal attempts to limit the number of garage sales or require permits were frequently disregarded and difficult to enforce.[59]

At the same time that garage sales inverted trends of depersonalized commerce, they also conformed to patterns of increasing privatization of commercial outlets and assumptions about shopping as women's province. Large shopping centers were privately owned and had stricter limitations, even in the outdoor portions, on public discourse and activity than downtown shopping areas in cities. Owners catered to women, targeting them as their primary shopping demographic—even, patronizingly, increasing the size of parking spaces to accommodate "female drivers."[60] Home parties, as female-run and held in private homes, even more starkly represented the trend toward privatized and feminized sales. Through garage sales, secondhand commerce kept pace, combining and reforming aspects of postwar consumerism to suit the needs and limitations of suburban housewives—needs that were not only monetary but also social, communal, and political. While the regional shopping centers relied on depersonalization and corporatization of their facilities for rapid expansion, garage sales, featuring personal interactions, haggling, bartering, socializing, and grassroots politicking, inverted the trend toward mass customer service. Similarly, garage sales negotiated societal scripts that limited the labor opportunities for women after the end of World War II, offering monetary opportunities within domestic spheres and further blurring the line between private and public.

Civic Involvement

As anthropologists Gretchen M. Herrmann and Ruth H. Landman point out about garage sales later in the century, such ventures were not only—or maybe even primarily—for personal profit.[61] Affiliated charity work, political fund-raising, neighborly socializing, and other civic pursuits compounded the sales' community importance. Even when motivated by personal profit, some hostesses saw the events as mutually advantageous forms of philanthropy. Respondents to one survey suggested that needy recipients would feel better having paid a small price rather than having accepted a handout. And for some, by the early 1970s, suspicion of the institutions controlling charity made garage sales' more direct interactions with needy community members preferable to the increasingly bureaucratic workings of the Salvation Army or Goodwill.[62] By at least partially relocating community sites of secondhand exchange from public spaces to nearer the private realm of home, the act of divesting unwanted goods was transformed into a directly personal affair, as opposed to an anonymous donation. The satisfaction of monetary gain and the more individualized mode of home sales made garage sales an attractive alternative to thrift store donation, and one that could still be imagined as charitable.

Contemporaries studying 1960s suburbs called them "hotbeds of participation" and labeled community members "hyperactive joiners."[63] Much of this increase in civic activity is attributed to housewives; women organized charity clubs, political organizations, Neighborhood Watch Groups, and Parent Teachers Associations, to name only a few types of groups whose membership skyrocketed in the decade and a half after the end of World War II. In addition, churches and synagogues expanded community functions, creating youth programs, recreational outlets, and social events. Church membership rose from 64.5 million in 1940 to 114.5 million in 1960.[64] By the mid-1950s, community involvement was widely recognized as an important facet of ideal suburban life. And like their close relatives, rummage sales and church bazaars, garage sales combined commercial exchange with civic involvement, this time in convenient proximity to the family home.[65]

As was the case with shopping, limited mobility circumscribed housewives' community activities, spurring innovation and encouraging neighborhood-centered interactions. Ford Motors recognized the restraints of a single-car household in the suburbs and began marketing a second car as a means of increased civic and social involvement for housewives. One television ad from 1956 shows a pretty young mother accepting a social invitation over the telephone. After hanging up, she tells viewers that before her husband bought a second car, she could not have accepted the summons. "I was practically a prisoner in my home," she pouted. "I couldn't get out to see my friends, couldn't take part in PTA activities—well, I couldn't even shop when I wanted to!"[66]

These three activities—shopping, socializing, and participating in community events—were the bread and butter of daily life in the suburbs, and not coincidentally, the three defining purposes of garage sales. Proximity to the home was important because despite Ford's bid in these early ads, many Americans managed their super-participatory lifestyles without an additional vehicle. In 1969, the majority of households still had only one car. Getting a second car came to be considered a necessity rather than a luxury sometime in the 1970s and 1980s, after garage sales were established localized venues.[67]

In fact, contrary to Ford's advertising claims, scholars posit a correlation between automobile dependency and *decreasing* community involvement in the last decades of the twentieth century. Kenneth T. Jackson has argued that a "major casualty of America's drive-in culture is the weakened 'sense of community.'"[68] However, *limited* access to automobiles possibly contributed to increased community involvement, partly because more planning and firmer commitment was necessary. For example, carpooling created mutual dependence, making it more difficult for an individual to skip an event once obligated. In the age of carpools and pick-ups, accomplices had to make more of an effort to bow out than when traveling solo.

Centering civic involvement on the home encouraged participation for broader political reasons as well. As historian Elaine Tyler May argues, the anti-Communist Cold War policy of "containment" was reflected domestically in the retreat of the family unit to their own private spaces, a retreat that represented an urge for both physical and ideological security.[69] Home and family-centered activities meshed with the generalized paranoia that led many McCarthy-era Americans to erect at least a guise of conformity to middle-class heterosexual values. With governmental crackdowns not only on aberrant political behavior—such as socialist or communist inclinations—but also on "deviant" sexual orientations, societal pressure to join in on the family-friendly festivities of marriage and child-rearing were at an all-time high in the 1950s.[70] Uncertain of whether they met the shifting criteria for

Americanism, some chose the appearance of conventionality that life within single-family homes provided.

For Kenneth Jackson, the retreat to the home replaced a nebulously defined "sense of community." "The real shift," he argues, "is the way in which our lives are now centered inside the house, rather than on the neighborhood or the community. With increased use of automobiles, the life of the sidewalk and the front yard has largely disappeared, and the social intercourse that used to be the main characteristic of urban life has vanished.... There are few places as desolate and lonely as a suburban street on a hot afternoon."[71] Maybe, but on Saturday mornings during prime garage sale season, suburban sidewalks, or at least driveways, were often crowded and convivial. Garage sales straddled public and private space, and extended from inside the home to out in the street and community—literally spilling the personal contents of private life outside and inviting inhabitants of the public sphere quite nearly inside the domestic sanctuary. The retreat, though marked, was never absolute, as garage sales' popularity illustrates.

In fact, garage sales helped reanimate stagnant elements of prewar civic life. Like most forms of consumer-based economic exchange, twentieth-century community fund-raising suffered in the lean economic times before 1945. During both the Great Depression and World War II, church bazaars and rummage sales declined in number and popularity.[72] Problems acquiring secondhand clothes and other goods for resale persisted after the United States joined the war effort in 1942. Rationing, along with government-sponsored war propaganda, urged personal conservation. Donations continued to be paltry. A similar pattern emerged with church bazaars, club rummage sales, and other civic fund-raisers. During World War II, ladies societies and church groups rerouted fund-raising energies to help provide for soldiers or citizens of war-torn countries. War relief shops substituted for fund-raising fairs across the country, featuring gently used and handmade items. Sometimes, multiple groups joined forces to compile enough items to sell.[73]

Almost as soon as the war ended, community fund-raising fairs returned with a renewed vigor, as did thrift store growth. After the war's end, the Salvation Army and Goodwill grew bigger and stronger than ever before. Goodwill's earned income, in real dollars, increased by a full 580 percent between 1948 and 1966.[74] Donations skyrocketed, as consumers rushed to update wardrobes and furnish their new homes in relevant styles—notably, purchasers for the discarded goods were also in no short supply. At the same time, the frequency and size of bazaars—one name for fund-raisers featuring used goods—and rummage sales rose at the same time that membership to community clubs and churches did likewise. In 1955, the preface to *McCall's* full-length guide to bazaars insisted that there "has *never* been a money-making method so ideally suited" to all organizations as the bazaar.[75] Groups that had previously hosted bazaars returned to the practice with new zeal and an increased bounty in theme ideas, food, and homemade and recycled goods. Other groups held fund-raisers for the first time, including churches, synagogues, and homemaker's clubs.[76]

Considering the popularity of rummage sales and bazaars, garage sales may seem redundant or selfishly motivated, but garage sales shared their civic role with bazaars and rummage sales in the postwar era without diminishing the importance of any of them. Over time, each specialized. After garage sales invaded suburbia, handmade items, family activities, and comestibles increasingly replaced used goods in other public fund-raisers. The form of these fund-raisers remained consistent, while the content shifted.[77] By the early 1960s, the types of goods sold often determined nomenclature. The appellation "garage sale" indicated sales of mostly used goods, even when the event was held at a public venue or organized by a community group. In 1958, for example, the Lyre of Alpha Chi Omega announced the results of a rummage sale. Just five years later, the same publication reported a successful "Garage Sale," which was held at the same location and offered similar sorts of donated used items as the 1958 sale. Other events that continued to call themselves rummage sales or bazaars increasingly featured handmade items such as macramé pieces, placemats and pot holders, Christmas ornaments, and sentimental cross-stitchings.[78] The categories continued to be fungible, but garage sales claimed a large portion of the suburban territory of community secondhand exchange by the late 1960s.

As civic involvement increased throughout the 1950s and 1960s, newspaper society pages reported garage sales whose profits supported clubs, societies, and churches, most of which were female-dominated. Garage sales also served as political fund-raisers and in doing so, intervened in male-dominated territory. Garage sales in Los Angeles suburbs raised funds for both the Democratic and Republican parties in the 1960s and early 1970s, with Republican women's clubs more frequently represented. As historians Lisa McGirr and Matthew Lassiter argue, housewives' coffee klatches in this era provided a popular setting for the suburban grassroots politicking that spawned new conservatism—garage sales also seemed to contribute.[79] Sponsors organized at individual homes but often represented groups—such as the Brentwood Republican Women's Club Federated, whose 1970 "GOP Garage Sale" took place in the home of "Mrs. Charles George."[80] Similarly, the 24 August 1967

"Datebook" section of the *L.A. Times* reported a "pool, lawn, and garage sale" held by the Palisades Republican Women's Club Federated, hosted in the private home of a club member.[81]

Garage sale fund-raisers supporting Democratic candidates often involved younger participants. Although contemporary studies and anecdotes reported limited garage sale activity among youth before the mid-1970s, electoral fund-raisers seem to have been an exception.[82] In 1968, a garage sale was one fund-raising option, alongside bake sales, house cleaning, and soda bottle collecting, organized and run by high school and college students. The proceeds of all these endeavors went toward the Democratic presidential nomination of Senator Eugene McCarthy.[83] Sometimes the liberal candidate supported by the fund-raising was notably young, too. In Montana, a garage sale helped fund Dorothy Bradley's successful bid for state representative. Described as "an attractive 23-year-old ecological activist and Phi Beta Kappa graduate in archeology," Bradley was the only woman elected to the Montana House of Representatives in 1970. Her platform, environmentalism, dovetailed with her fund-raising tactic; Democratic women in her district helped her coordinate a huge garage sale, touted as a means of reuse and environmental stewardship as well as financial support.[84] By 1970, the year in which the first Earth Day was held, secondhand commerce was affiliated with the goals of the environmental movement, a correlation further explored in chapter 5. Garage sales were posited as ecologically responsible consumerism, a type of communal recycling.

Garage sales connected grassroots efforts to strengthen neighbors' economic standing, promote civic organizations, and build political networks. They did not represent a full retreat to the home or a forfeiture of former systems of community support, such as church rummage sales or bazaars. Rather, when part of formal organizations such as women's clubs and churches, garage sales expanded the role of the home in community action. Decades-old practices of donating unwanted goods to charities and participation in various secondhand fund-raisers acclimated women (and some men) to the idea of moral and civic good associated with passing along gently used goods. Garage sales helped diversify community fund-raisers.

Collecting and Do-It-Yourself

While garage sales became the common name for sales of mostly secondhand goods, bazaars and rummage sales in the 1960s and after increasingly reflected the growing Arts and Crafts movement, a fad similar to that of the

Progressive Era, when amateur artisanship and home crafting were also valued and the products deemed saleable—many times through female-run charitable bazaars.[85] In both periods, the popularity of handmade goods coincided with nostalgia for a bygone era and emphasized anticommercialism. Since secondhand materials were often useful in popular do-it-yourself projects, garage sales provided raw materials for a variety of popular postwar hobbies that involved hands-on building. So far, it may seem that women were solely responsible for the existence of garage sales. While it is true that most direct participants were female, suburban men's interests also fueled the sales' growth. Of course, even when women served as the primary buyers for the home, they did not consume everything they bought.[86] Secondhand materials were no exception. Men as well as children and other family members benefitted from the purchase of pre-owned household goods, and from any profit attained from the sale of the same. But garage sales also provided a specialized resource connected to a rise in hobby pursuits, including collecting and antiquing, which rose in popularity as a recreation and attracted male adherents. Men used the secondhand materials found at garage sales in do-it-yourself home handcrafts and building.[87]

Suburban men's reasons for home construction were various—frugality, recreation, and an eagerness to "achieve something different." A survey quoted in a 1955 *Better Homes and Gardens* issue showed that 63 percent of homebuyers did some of their own construction and 23 percent did all of it.[88] The magazine's content reflected this shift in homeowner's attention; the number of articles on building, renovating, and home furbishing increased alongside the magazine's growth in overall size—but the space devoted to gardening remained the same. In fact, beginning in 1945, the size of the words "and Gardens" on the cover appeared in shrinking type. Simply put, the editors got better advertising support for items relating to the burgeoning DIY movement than for gardening. Accordingly, the magazine also redoubled its efforts to attract men as well as women—though it had sought a coed audience since its seminal 1922 issue.[89]

The popularity of collecting as a hobby had been slowly gaining popularity throughout the century but spiked in postwar years. After World War II, more Americans could afford the leisure and expense antiquing and collecting entailed. Like consumption in general, collecting democratized, and collectibles expanded to include more common manufactured items and not just high-end antiques. The extension of hobbyist collecting to other than the uber-wealthy began with the popularity of everyday Americana earlier in the century, but reached a quirkier array of goods in the 1950s and 1960s. Postwar museums such as the Strong Museum in Rochester, New York, and the Lightner Museum in St. Augustine, Florida, celebrated everyday items like toys and shaving mugs, elevating them to new cultural heights.[90] Like with the museum collections mentioned in chapter 2, which began to include nineteenth-century Americana, museum decisions validated the arrival of certain used goods to an elevated status and increased value.

An emphasis on design in new manufactured goods encouraged and reflected the same consumer interest in distinction that spurred antique collecting. Historian Thomas Hine dubbed the 1960s "the Populuxe era," and pointed out that the design of common objects, "from salt shaker to house," included elements of fantasy and personalization. Populuxe, a contraction of "popular" and "deluxe," suggests the process of democratizing luxury.[91] Coupled with the perception of shopping in general as recreational, consumers' awareness of the aesthetic details of everyday objects and the value of material distinction meant that buying secondhand could signal personal creativity rather than material need. Therefore, even those without the means to frequent expensive auctions could pursue inexpensive collecting or distinctive decorating through secondhand venues like garage sales.

The significance of secondhand shopping as recreational is apparent in media sources of the 1960s. Auctions were portrayed as respectable and amusing outings for both men and women—often, as something a couple could enjoy together as part of a personally fulfilling relationship. One Du Pont ad from 1965 featured in *Better Homes and Gardens* addressed men, telling them, "Enjoy a day rambling through the country together, like you've promised yourself for so long. Your wife has a baby-sitter. And you have the time—thanks to Du Pont LUCITE House Paint."[92] The ad illustrates several relevant recreational trends, as well as important expectations of masculinity in the domestic sphere. First of all, Du Pont addresses the man of the house, assuming that it is his weekend task to paint the house, reflecting the rise of do-it-yourself home building and maintenance. In addition, the postwar era emphasized familial closeness; camaraderie, a good sex life, and shared interests became important aspects of a successful marriage and a secure home life.[93] The couple's outing includes not only an auction but an antique car show, illustrating the prevalent interest in material objects of previous generations as well as the romanticization of automobiles.[94]

Aesthetically, decorating with choice collectibles pointed to a desire for personalized style in an era dogged by assumptions of conformity. The nonmonetary worth of secondhand items increased when they became meaningful representatives of creativity—a shortcut, one that required varying degrees of knowledge and expense, to showing individual style. Critics of suburbia argued that aggressive corporate tactics and the increased number of "necessities" in the American middle-class culture of mass consumption led to the homogenization of suburban life. At the same time, though, suburban residents pursued hobbies and recreations that belied this supposed disintegration of stylistic variety. Personalizing the décor in a new home through older or handmade items showed individual taste, as well as some specialized knowledge of material styles other than newly manufactured, easily accessible products.[95] As new goods became more affordable for more Americans, shoppers perceived a scarcity in original or distinct items, including those available in secondhand venues. Following a classic supply and demand model, such scarce commodities were valued at a higher rate.

A 1957 short story in *Ladies' Home Journal* shows the value placed on nonnew household goods. A young couple wanted their personal possessions to be expressive and distinctive. In "The Chippendale Chest," a woman not long married voices a strong desire to replace their bland furnishings with "beautiful, priceless, *authentic* antiques." The current tables, chairs, and sideboards were "*awful*" because "they don't *mean* anything."[96] The story's two protagonists struggled with finances, yet they managed to scrape up enough, together, to place a winning bid on a small, highly desired Chippendale chest and individualize their new suburban home with an object that was not manufactured in a newly reconverted factory but reflected a belief in their own specialness—through the acquisition of a distinct material object. Such stories reflect not only the deepening significance of possessions but the variety of meaning attributed to them. The dewy-cheeked wife uses the word "authentic" in opposition to the meaningless of newer (phony) items. This near-personification of inanimate objects illustrates the extent to which postwar Americans identified with their possessions, and the ways in which buying choices reflected anxieties over personal status in the wake of rising median wealth in America. The popularity of antique and secondhand objects at the same time as the rise in market segmentation and aggressive admen at least partially contradicted confident assertions that consumer sovereignty was wholly illusory. Although the Chippendale couple stayed mostly on script by using material objects to express something about their personalities, they ad-libbed a bit. After all, McCann Erickson—or other major advertising corporations of the time—could not count as clients many auctioneers and certainly no garage-sale hostesses.

Consumers also expressed a disdain for new, mass-manufactured goods through building, repairing, or modifying home furnishings, and adding decorative accents. Horace Coon, who wrote about postwar hobbies at the time, cited the monotony of contemporary work as motivation for the do-it-yourself trend. Hobbies in general provided an "escape" from the stultifying repetition of the middle management labor that accounted for more and more American jobs; crafters especially, according to Coon, rebelled against hegemonic industrialism.[97] As paid work became more and more abstracted from physical final products, DIY tasks provided an antidote to or at least compensation for alienated labor by making goods production a healthful hobby rather than a livelihood.

After World War II, patterns of leisure changed dramatically. Initially, in the late 1940s, Americans satisfied their pent-up longings for entertainment by viewing motion pictures and attending sports events. As the number of births rose, however, the nature of leisure choices changed, and Americans opted for "private leisure" rather than "public leisure"—toys, radios, television, and home building and crafting equipment all counted as expenditures in this area.[98] Hosting garage sales only partly complied with this trend (staying true to their characteristic hybridity) since they counted both as work and recreation, and both as private and public. Purveyors of secondhand goods were often participating in or enhancing some form of postwar leisure activity, such as hunting for collectibles or purchasing raw materials for at-home projects. Historically, both men and women collected—at times, more men than women. The do-it-yourself trend was decisively associated with men. The DIY craze, which included household repair work, furniture-building, kits, and many other handicrafts, was depicted as a return to traditional values, that is, to a deeply rooted American spirit of independence and ingenuity, but that perception owed much to false nostalgia. Before the Great Depression, it was uncommon for middle-class men to take such an interest in the state of their dwellings. Nineteenth-century couples were far more likely to hire experts for even the simplest fix or improvement.[99] Our Du Pont-buying, auction-going husband would most likely have hired a professional painter to do the job in the 1890s.

In speaking of the craze of home repair and workshop craftsmanship in 1952, *Business Week Magazine* called the era the "age of do-it-yourself."[100] Soon, only reading and watching television were more popular as forms of recreation among married men.[101] While sometimes portrayed as things an entire family could do together, DIY tasks tended to be male-dominated activities, involving dad and perhaps a trusted son or two. During the 1950s, the maintenance of paternal authority within the domestic realm became an issue of concern among influential writers and media producers. Philip Wylie's

Generation of Vipers got the ball rolling early, in 1942, by notoriously vilifying mothers, and pronouncing that excessive female influence prevented boys from becoming properly masculine men. Alongside critiques of domineering mothers were denouncements of absent fathers, whose lack of influence supposedly left suburban sons susceptible to vices and unapproved ideologies, including communism, homosexuality, or simply juvenile delinquency. These anxieties resonated not only in the abundant self-help literature of the 1950s and 1960s but in fiction and hit films like *Rebel without a Cause* (1955).[102] Wylie called fathers "mice"; in October 1954, *Parents Magazine* titled one article with the directive, "Fathers Shouldn't Try to Be Mothers."[103] One way dads could better prepare their sons for a manly life was by reaffirming their control over parts of the "feminized" home. DIY building, often in the garage or other peripheral home spaces, was a popular route to guarding against excessive feminine influence. The pages of *Popular Mechanic* magazine were littered with father/son projects intended to educate, masculinize, and influence young men through crafts and hands-on building. The projects ranged from the simple—like those of the father who finds secondhand furniture to strip and refinish with his son—to the complex and costly, such as the 1956 feature, "Father and Son Build a Sports Car."[104] Hot rods were extremely popular father-son projects for many years."[105]

Many such projects were conducted in the garage. Since the interstitial structures often included more room than required to house the family car or was not at all used for that purpose, garages were adapted for multiple uses. They were the wild card of home spaces; their use was a matter of negotiation between residents. Men tinkered in garage workshops, teenage boys (and a few girls) began garage bands, and housewives held garage sales. The sacred sphere of Dad's tools was featured in popular sitcoms of the time, such as episode 37 of *Leave It to Beaver* (1958), in which Beaver runs away after being reprimanded for allowing his friend to play with his father's tools, resulting in a hole in the wall of—where else?—the garage.[106]

By the mid-1960s, *Better Homes and Gardens* regularly ran project suggestions—usually addressing men and sometimes their sons—ordaining specific uses for extra garage space, like "a Playful Playroom," "a very Serviceable Sewing Room," or the rather ambiguously designated "Good Times Room."[107] Many of these projects entailed repurposing existing materials, including the "under $100" projects annually highlighted in 1960s' issues of *Better Homes and Gardens*. One suggestion from 1965 suggests the reader "[l]iberate a piece of junk and turn it into a jewel of an end table! This not-quite antique spool chest (a youngster of only 50 years) started life in a dress factory and almost ended as kindling."[108] While the cost of the goods used could be low if salvaged, in many ways do-it-yourselfers practiced a form of elitist simplicity—the flip side of Populuxe's democratic luxury. Trendy craftsmanship often required expensive tools and took the luxury of time to produce relatively simple objects. At the same time, the value-added of the craftwork involved in refurbishing made the purchase of a discarded item expressive of the ability to pursue a leisure activity rather than an admission of fiscal weakness.

Scholars have succeeded in breaking down many myths and exaggerations about conformity and homogeneity in the burgeoning suburbs of postwar America.[109] However, the assumption of at least one major allying factor persists: consumption. In her book on Tupperware, Alison Clarke sells her own topic short when she claims about suburban shoppers, "Old world values and diverse social backgrounds might divide them in the realm of production, but through consumption they were redefined as a culturally bound, aspiring middle-class group."[110] Yet families' conversions from urban, ethnic, and working class to suburban, Americanized, and middle class did not follow set paths. Hand-me-down furnishings and home building were part of the transition for many, and these tasks carried specialized resources and skills into established suburban lives.[111] Garage sales enabled, exhibited, and expanded these diverse consumer attributes.

The links between primary and secondary consumerism abound. Oftentimes, scholars portray formal, firsthand economies as monolithic, crowding out more informal means of trade and imagining secondhand exchange as relegated to historical irrelevance by the march of capitalist commerce. But the relationship is much more layered, and informal economies have always been much more adaptable and obdurate than such assumptions allow. When historian Beverly Gordon describes what she sees as the decline of fund-raising fairs after World War II, she declares the community aspect sacrificed to the altar of mass commerce. As an example, she points to bazaar organizers resorting to shopping malls for their events, taking their outdated affairs "to the people." As a result, the groups responsible were hobbled in what items they could offer, limited to handwork and simple baked goods so as to not compete with mall retailers. To Gordon, in such gatherings, "the community is reduced to something fleeting and illusory: it is a community of consumers."[112] By looking more closely at garage sales, however, it becomes clear that community, recreation, and socialization survived as part of goods redistribution. Like much of white America, secondhand sales adapted to the suburbs.

The Garage Sale in the 1970s

The postwar years of idealized togetherness and relative political unanimity did not last. The late 1960s saw the breakdown of what historians dubbed "the liberal consensus." During the 1960s, an already faltering belief in the reliability of government and liberal politics died, as did thousands of unwilling American soldiers in Vietnam, and, in a string of high-profile assassinations, revolutionary leaders, including Malcolm X, President John F. Kennedy, Martin Luther King Jr., and Senator Robert Kennedy. Moreover, by the early 1970s, faith in endless economic growth (of the kind that John Maynard Keynes in 1930 had promised would provide "[e]conomic possibilities for our grandchildren" by *solving* the economic problem one hundred years hence) seemed misplaced to the many struggling to find work.[113] Garage sales persisted amidst these changes. By the 1970s, depending on your viewpoint, garage sales were considered a mounting nuisance, a practical stopgap, or a reliable recreation. They became symbols of American life, passing into the realm of artistic and social commentary. In 1973, writer Ken Kesey published *Ken Kesey's Garage Sale*, in which he offered a patchwork of materials—letters, plays, photographs, interviews—that bridge the space between the Beat writers' 1960s psychedelic drug culture and the economic crises of the early 1970s.[114] These secondhand offerings required some consumer labor in the form of sifting and contextualizing, roughly analogous to the efforts made in analyzing what fumed oak versus limed oak revealed about the seller's age.

Also in 1973, feminist performance artist Martha Rosler staged her first *Monumental Garage Sale*, an event advertised as an actual garage sale as well as an artistic installation at the University of California in San Diego. In a 2012 interview about her upcoming solo exhibition at New York City's Museum of Modern Art, *Meta-Monumental Garage Sale*—where again, everything was available to browse and buy—Rosler encapsulated the key enduring, suburb-born elements of garage sales: "It's a form of community ritual behavior, but it's also an unwitting portrait of yourself—and an effort to make money so that you can continue to consume."[115] Rosler ran audio clarifying the exhibit's purpose of highlighting the contradictory meanings of the garage sale, framed in part by a quote from Karl Marx: "A commodity appears, at first sight, a very trivial thing, and easily understood. Its analysis shows that it is, in reality, a very queer thing. . . . in it the social character of a person's labor."[116] Garage sales embody the collective imaginative effort involved in turning an object into a commodity, in ascribing material things with value. Producer, distributor, and consumer have sometimes-disparate and ever-fluid perceptions of material worth in all exchange, an economic variability especially highlighted in the world of secondhand commerce. The settled-upon appraisal of goods is a matter of intense and ongoing negotiation.[117]

Clearly, by 1973, garage sales were established as useful and meaningful to American social and cultural life. For dispassionate observers, the piles of flotsam hocked on suburban lawns might have underscored the accelerated consumerism of the postwar years and the dangers of Keynesian beliefs in the economic salubriousness of unchecked spending. But a more determined gaze might also uncover the basic materials for an alternative economic form whose social meanings opposed decrease in face-to-face consumerism, countered imperatives for commodity obsolescence, and dovetailed with nascent environmentalism. Garage sales entailed a displacement of goods from their domestic context, an uprooting of material meanings—André Breton must have approved, and Joseph Cornell certainly did participate. Garage sales are disjunction events and often performed as rites of transition, hosted after spring cleaning, when a child moves away to college, or when a couple divorces.

Writer Raymond Carver explores the latter context in his famous short story written in the mid- to late 1970s, "Why Don't You Dance?"[118] The story begins with a garage sale host sipping whiskey and observing his bedroom, displaced onto the front lawn. The lamps, the record player, and the television are all plugged in via extension cords, in a vision of a private life disrupted, hiccupped out of its usual position of domestic containment. The intimacy of the garage sale host's disemboweled house briefly reanimated on his lawn captures the queerness of the venue, and the blushing revelations such sales may portray. A young couple ventures onto the scene, and the disjunction intensifies as the three characters (boyfriend, girlfriend, and an uncoupling suburbanite) drink whiskey in the morning and dance to records on the lawn, flouting neighborly rites of discretion. The couple goes home with many of the items splayed on the lawn (for a nominal cost; profit appears to be inconsequential to the tale). The story ends with the girlfriend's obsession with the transaction and its meaning. Her uneasiness with the new acquisitions implies a lingering assumption that secondhand objects retain traces of previous owners' discontent—a theme portrayed in fiction for over a century at least and recounted in this book already by way of Charles Dickens, Henry James, and others. The girlfriend struggles to describe the exchange to guests in their home, which is now tricked out with the accessories of the whiskey-drinking yard-sale man's defunct marriage. She eventually gives up trying to convey the weirdness of the experience. The story ends with her frustrated last line, "There was more to it."

Despite—and soon enhanced by—continuing apprehensions about secondhand materials, garage sales, along with other community fund-raisers, helped integrate secondhand economies into the American middle class. Practical in the wake of mass consumption, yet malleable to individual purpose, garage sales, perhaps more than any other single form of secondhand commerce, expanded the social role of used goods in the United States. Over the course of the 1950s and 1960s, used goods became a tool of personal taste and collective rebellion. And for the first time, secondhand clothing would take center stage, as growing numbers of Americans expressed their discontent with presumably middle-class conformity through the adoption of various modes of secondhand style.

CHAPTER FOUR

The Invention of Vintage Clothing

Coast to coast ads offering ancient raccoons for college wear boasted...
a "snobby seediness."
—*Life* magazine, 9 September 1957

You had to be monumentally narcissistic and have time on your hands,
and just about enough money to do it.
—Designer/antique dealer Christopher Gibbs, on mid-1960s London
vintage dress

In August 1957, the *New Yorker* ran a short, chatty article about three Greenwich Village residents who found themselves at the center of the latest college fad—wearing raccoon coats from the 1920s.[1] The "rousing, cheerful tale of a freakish business success" marked the well-advertised arrival of "vintage clothing" to the American marketplace, an arrival that connected hip Village parties, fashion magazines, high-end department stores, and trendy collegians with vastly more disposable income than those of generations past. The craze for "true raccoons" gleaned from thrift stores and boys' clothing warehouses, peddled by no less accepted sources than Lord & Taylor and Macy's, brought the growing popularity of secondhand objects into the realm of popular fashion.[2] No notions of anticonsumerist rebellion, vocalized ideologies of breaking down capitalist fashion hegemonies, fighting for feminist agendas, or allying with the poverty-stricken accompanied the furry fad. Rather, an imagined affinity with past affluence, elegance, and class privilege described the induction of clothing into the category of vintage.

Many postwar Americans eagerly consolidated the nation's global role as prime exemplar of capitalist consumerism, and the recirculation of quality used materials in every venue of secondhand commerce grew apace with firsthand buying. As fashion interests consolidated internationally, planned obsolescence became the industry norm, and advertisers honed their audience-targeting skills in the postwar years. Reacting against a perceived democratization of fashion, "vintage clothing" became a sort of brand, one that distinguished its elite wearer from the presumably conformist middle class. An overall decrease in the cost of firsthand clothing, an increase in the average number of articles of clothing Americans and Europeans owned, and the rise of a distinctive rock-star image all helped make eclectic, recognizably secondhand styles fashionable. The process of branding vintage clothing was transnational. Reacting to the popularity of the working-class Mod styles, young members of the English nobility embraced a dandified, antiquated image that recalled times when their status was unquestioned, and when the very eras—Victorian, Edwardian—were named for powerful royalty and boasted alternate titles such as "the Age of Opulence."[3] Secondhand dressers in the United States also reacted against the prevalence of British Mod style by adopting Victorian accents. But in what might be deemed a show of antiestablishment patriotism, San Francisco secondhand styles added Old West and Native American flourishes to their elaborately performative secondhand outfits.

Over the course of the 1950s, and especially the 1960s, used clothing commerce and styles became markers of social defiance, emblems of generational discord, and tools in political protest. The next two chapters will look at two distinct but intersecting paths by which old apparel became accepted, celebrated, and coveted in the decades following World War II. At the same time that secondhand wardrobe accents emerged as a transnational means of elite distinction, a dramatized appearance of what I call elective poverty served to signify social and political dissent.[4] Both styles renounced membership in the presumably conformist and growing middle class.

First I examine the invention of "vintage clothes," which effectively upgraded certain older apparel by acknowledging the time, effort, and money it required to be a notable bohemian dandy. Vintage, a word originally associated with wine and extended to valuable automobiles and furniture in the late 1920s, described sartorial performances that were ostentatious, expressive of erudite knowledge and means, and often openly narcissistic and exclusive. Although the appellation appeared only briefly in the late 1950s, the sentiment persisted and expanded—and the term "vintage" reemerged in the late 1970s, seemingly for good. Premier postwar vintage style was the realm of Ivy League collegians, wealthy and titled English socialites, and rock stars. Mostly, the market in vintage clothing avoided overtly political implications, while nevertheless delighting in rankling established proprieties. An exultation of wealth, individuality, and fame surrounded this vein of secondhand popularization.

Chapter 5 examines the often-politicized practices of what I call elective poverty, the voluntary denunciation of visible middle- or upper-class status. In the postwar years, privileged white youth frequently adopted cultural forms—including fashion—originating from the working class and racial minorities in order to distance themselves from their inherited class positions.[5]

On the face of it, the styles associated with elective poverty were minimalist, communicative of nonmaterialistic priorities, and usually expressive of a cross-class or cross-racial affiliation. However, to retain a dissident or ironic conveyance, something usually remained in the context of the "poor dress" that communicated the voluntariness of the attire. Ultimately, the success of elective poverty relied on material hints that the performance was not one of total necessity but born of awareness and defiance—higher status traces such as expensive jewelry or quality shoes; a fine car or nice furniture; even a certain haircut or expert makeup. Elective poverty changed markedly over the course of the 1950s and 1960s, emerging as part of noncomformist—but often apolitical—Beat style, taking on definitive political valences amidst a national antipoverty movement, and blossoming into full-scale theatrics in reaction against late-sixties "hip capitalism."

The image-oriented, mass culture–catering roots of vintage dress were not wholly disparate from the social and political protests of cross-class identification. Chronologically coincidental, key figures in establishing secondhand styles migrated from one category to the other, or claimed elements of each. Still, chapters 4 and 5 separate their developments to avoid conflating different objectives. As part of distinguishing between vintage exhibitionism and elective poverty, I eschew the too broadly applied term "counterculture" coined by scholar Theodore Roszak in 1968 to apply to mostly white youth living self-consciously against middle-class values. In doing so, I hope to avoid automatic associations of rebellious attitudes with New Left political engagement, acknowledge the occasional radicality of mass culture, and accept the limits of the overtly revolutionary. As Alice Echols suggests, for example, "the hippie subculture mirrored the values of the dominant culture, especially in regard to women and gays."[6] If "counterculture" can apply to any group selectively countering mainstream ideals, the list is too long to be useful in historical discourse. There was no single, unifying rationale for the political, aesthetic, social, or economic use of used commercial goods, just as there really was no such thing as *the* movement in the late 1960s.

Many secondhand dressers avowed happily apolitical priorities. And those using secondhand commerce to express anticapitalism ultimately relied on the same political economy being critiqued, thus compromising their protest. Neither of these facts eliminates the possibility that secondhand clothing exchange and display were part of meaningful or effective protest. As Thomas Frank rightly insists in his persistent thesis on the "conquest of cool," profit motive did not eliminate the potential for nonconformist innovations and youth culture appeal. The reverse is also true: playful, creative expressiveness did not automatically discount politically radical, anticapitalist intentions.[7] On the one hand, jet-setting British nobility helped inspire international rock-star styles reliant on carefully culled "vintage" items that signified originality and privilege, and influenced Americans' style from Haight-Ashbury to the Lower East Side. Often, such carefully crafted personas stemmed from and appealed to those who could afford to stand out, to not conform to common standards of appearance; such dress exemplified a modern-day version of Veblenian conspicuous consumption and leisure. On the other hand, a coinciding interest in visibly secondhand dress evolved based on outspoken political grounds. Activists donned obviously old clothes and advocated for secondhand commercial practices to protest and counter a number of societal ills, many of which were seen as results of corporate capitalism, including war, poverty, sexism, and environmental degradation.

Dissimilar groups with varying aims relied on and fundamentally altered the same marginal economies of styles. Sartorial claims of both class erasure and class distinction based on secondhand materials shared at least one common denominator, marking almost all types of voluntary uses of secondhand clothing in the postwar years. Secondhand styles nearly always signaled disaffiliation from the middle class, with its connotations of conformity, plasticity, and consumer democracy—whether the resultant style included the "beat" jeans and Goodwill T-shirts of Japhy Ryder, Kerouac's proto-environmentalist star of *Dharma Bums*; or the bricolage effect of resurrected designer clothes from the 1920s, Moroccan sandals, and Victorian lace on titled London youth.

The Short-Lived Raccoon Coat Craze

While some older cars, furniture, and other objects gained added worth throughout the first half of the twentieth century, the new valuation of used goods was slow to extend to clothing. As Goodwill's Rev. Helm observed early in the century, "We have been taught to look askance on discarded clothing."[8] That doesn't mean that there were no innovations in the use and meaning of secondhand clothing before World War II: Evangeline Booth and the Salvation Army slum sisters dramatized their work's moral worth with ragged clothes; Baroness von Freytag-Loringhoven's corporeal art disrupted boundaries of gender and performance; and Jewish comic singer Fanny Brice lampooned the image of a secondhand dresser for a popular audience, reframing the disrepute of secondhand commerce as at least harmlessly humorous, and presenting the curated use of secondhand objects as shorthand for bohemian identity.

But before World War II, the United States lacked any firm example of clothing fads that relied entirely on obviously secondhand materials. Some historians suggest that zoot suits, the radical outfits worn by black and Hispanic youth before and during the war, derived in part from secondhand materials. The voluminous zoot suit, emblematic of ethnic exception from mainstream comportment, was controversial during the United States' involvement in World War II in part because it demanded more material than deemed patriotic; ration order L-85, issued in 1943, limited the civilian purchase of certain fabrics used to make uniforms and other war paraphernalia. Men's suits were restructured during this time for a trimmer, slimmer cut sometimes called the "Uncle Sam suit." Conversely, zoot suits formed their striking silhouette with outsized jacket shoulders, long tails, and exaggeratedly baggy pant legs dramatically pegged at the ankle. One story of the zoot suit's start proposes that impoverished people and ill-paid workers began the fad by simply wearing old clothes. Since secondhand materials were in high demand during the Depression and amidst wartime rationing, such shoppers could not be picky about fit. With adept sewing skills, a too-big pant could be faddishly pegged at the ankles and taken in at the waist to produce the outrageous-to-some zoot suit style.[9] If the zoot suit genesis is accurately associated with pre-owned materials, then the fad may count as the first hugely contentious and (maybe) consciously political style that began with secondhand goods.[10] But sailors on leave clashed with ununiformed zoot suiters partly because of the assumption (not always correct) that the fabric was new and breached the limits of government rations. Certainly, many such suits were advertised and sold as new products, before and during the war—but often using fabric not on the rations list. While secondhand materials may have enabled the growth of the fad, they were not intrinsic to its public meaning.

The first definitively secondhand clothing trend of any proportion did not emerge from marginalized communities, led by black and Latino youth either making do or making a political point. It started at the Greenwich Village apartment of a hip and prosperous couple, the Salzmans. In 1957, the Village's second bohemian era—this one marked by the residency of artists and writers associated with the Beats, discussed in greater detail in the next chapter—was just about played out. The year 1957 was when Beat writer Joyce Johnson declared that wealth had officially changed the Village, along with the cost of rent. Area bohemians began to drift to the more affordable Lower East Side, leaving the Village to those who could pay the increase—like the Salzmans. That August, young, "good-looking" architect Stanley Salzman offered the *New Yorker* an account of his wife's sudden success selling raccoon coats. For the interview, Stanley Salzman wore a "fashionably ancient T shirt and duck pants," an outfit that might have fit in with the casual milieu of the still-Beat Village but that also hinted at the Ivy League habit of dressing down, a practice by members of a class so confidently established as upper that displaying well-worn or working-class items broadcast a privileged disregard for middle-class propriety.[11] The "duck pants" may have referred to durable hunting pants, the sort popularly featured in the product catalogues of L.L. Bean, Inc., a company that catered to an upper-class clientele—or it may have suggested working-class material designed to last under the duress of manual labor.[12] Certainly, Salzman's background suggests elite societal membership. The ambitious thirty-three-year-old Harvard alum helped launch one architectural firm at a mere twenty-three years of age, and, two years before the interview, opened his own firm, all in addition to his duties as a professor at the prestigious Pratt Institute in Brooklyn.[13] Whether his outfit's style inspiration was Village Beat, Cambridge couture, or both, the overall impression Salzman gave was one of class confidence and cultural cachet.

According to the dapper Stanley Salzman, he and his wife Sue threw a small party in December 1956. To the gathered company, Sue reminisced about a gorgeous raccoon coat she spotted at a Salvation Army. After hesitation, she lost the coat to a more decisive customer. Several party attendees agreed that a "true raccoon" from the fad's roaring twenties heyday would have been a sartorial boon.[14] As it happened, a party attendee, one of Stanley Salzman's former architecture students, volunteered a potential source for not just one but a small pile of the old coats, left over from when the original collegiate trend of the late 1920s abruptly ended alongside national confidence in stock-market stability. A relative of his, the owner of a boys' clothing store, had bales of the things stored away for decades, unsure of how to unload the once-expensive material.

The original fad for raccoon coats nodded to the raucous affluence of the 1920s at a time when the number of collegians rose alongside average incomes. The coats were particularly associated with Ivy League college men—though some spunky girls also sported the heavy and unwieldy furs, as did members of the black middle class, whose ranks were also growing. Fur in general in the 1920s was very popular, but many kinds remained out of reach for most Americans even at the height of that decade's wealth. Raccoon furs—as the cheapest and most plentiful animal skins—on the other hand, were lush representatives of a new democratic ideal of consumer luxury. "Democratic" though they may have been, comparatively, the coats were still undeniable emblems of wealth, often retailing at between $350 and $500—about $5,000 at today's value. Still, around the same time that collegians were gulping goldfish, full-length coonskin automobile coats were the "it" accessory for cruising around a cold New England college town in a Model T—and certainly the most appropriate gear for attending the wildly popular college football games.[15] Football star Red Grange and silent movie heartthrob Rudolph Valentino helped launch the fad, and it spread quickly, peaking in popularity between 1927 and 1929. In 1928, George Olsen and His Music recorded "Doin' the Raccoon," featuring the lyrics "College men, knowledge men / Do a dance called raccoon / It's the craze, nowadays, / And it will get you soon. / Buy a coat and try it, / I'll bet you'll be a riot, / It's a wow, learn to do it right now."[16]

The coats were such icons of male collegiate life that the cover of the 16 November 1929 issue of *Saturday Evening Post* featured an Alan Foster illustration of a chorus of five dapper college men clad in the flamboyant outer wear. But as fashion historian Deirdre Clemente notes, the look was not universally perceived as a wholesome part of college life but sometimes associated with drunken revelry, "a false standard of affluence," deplorable male vanity, and sloppy, sophomoric comportment. Critics found fault in the garment both for its emblematic extravagance and as an example of the younger generation's increasingly slovenly dress.[17] Though primarily associated with white, male youth, the coat also had cross-cultural significance. James Van Der Zee's 1932 photograph *Couple in Raccoon Coats*, an enduring image of the Harlem Renaissance's "New Negroes," features the lush raccoon covering. Although by then the fad had mostly ended, for Van Der Zee, the fur-shrouded black couple posing in front of a Cadillac symbolized the attainment of prosperity for some urban blacks.

Such symbols of wealth, recreation, and youthful frivolity quickly became indefensible in the fiscally lean 1930s, and clothing outlets were left holding the bag. For more than twenty years, thousands—by one estimate, as many as two million—of those coats moldered in storehouses.[18] Then along came the 1955 Walt Disney hit film *Davy Crockett: King of the Wild Frontier*, a popular celebration of American individualism in the wake of widespread recognition that this was the "American Century."[19] In it, the hero, played by Fess Parker, donned the trademark raccoon fur hat—and suddenly, every little boy wanted one. Stanley Salzman's former architecture student knew about his relative's supply of raccoon coats because he had been offered a summer job chopping them up to make hats. Happily for the Salzmans, some intact coats remained after the coon hat fad played out. Not only did Sue get her coveted fashion statement, but they also passed one along to each of the dozen guests from the party. Initially, Stanley Salzman insisted, there was no profit motive;

RACCOON TYCOON Sue Salzman sits in her apartment surrounded by old coats. A '20s fan, she wears floppy cloche and dangling beads typical of the era.

FIGURE 4.1 Sue Salzman posing for "Raccoon Swoon," *Life* magazine, 9 September 1957.

Sue was just "on a real twenties kick." But in her blue-black lipstick, floppy cloche hat, and dangling beads (see figure 4.1, from a story in *Life* magazine), "she was a walking ad." Friends of the fur-clad partygoers and strangers on the street alike queried the lot about their coats. Before long, Sue Salzman and a lawyer friend named Benjy Bejan—also goofy for his warehouse-musty coat—decided to go into business.[20]

The coat commerce was an immediate success. By canvassing thrift shops and clothing warehouses, Salzman and Bejan managed to turn a profit on about four hundred of the coats by late in the spring of 1957, at the brisk pace of about forty a week. They suited whole Broadway shows and sold one to actor Farley Granger, a favored lead of Alfred Hitchcock. Then, in June 1957, *Glamour* magazine published a photo of one of the coats, naming the Salzmans as suppliers. Phone calls and letters poured in, including an astonishing request from Lord & Taylor, the department store be-all and end-all for college fashions. After securing the Salzman's biggest order yet, Lord & Taylor advertised "vintage raccoon coats" in a promised "state of magnificent disrepair."[21] College students embraced the idea en masse. Following Lord & Taylor's trusted lead on the college demographic, other department stores, including Macy's, Peck's in Kansas City, and I. Magnin in San Francisco, quickly exhausted their own supplies and begged the Salzmans to help them keep up.[22] Advertisements (see figure 4.2) promised looks that were

FIGURE 4.2 Reprints of various vintage raccoon coat ads, *Life* magazine, 9 September 1957.

"down-at-the-heel," "shabbily genteel," full of "lovely holes," and achieved a "snobby seediness."[23]

Soon though, the moment was over, and not because of the short attention span of young consumers. Thanks to "[t]hat Crockett!" they ran out of coats. Stanley Salzman guessed in 1957 they could have sold fifty thousand coats if they had them, but call after call to clothing retailers brought the same answer—most of them had been cut up during the Davy Crockett boom, recycled to make boys' novelty hats.[24] The waning of "authentic" product led to a quick burst in new raccoon accessories, but the attempt at reproduction never fully caught on with consumers.

The coonskin coat trend of 1956–57 traveled both inside and outside of major fashion corridors. From a hip Village flat to those "in the know" to a major fashion magazine to an influential department store to college dorms, the furry fad gained momentum. The Salzmans were not selling out. They were simply selling. As for the buyers—well, the nostalgia for the excess of the 1920s on the part of young, affluent college students full of a sense of their own possibilities was more narcissistic than rebellious. For the really with it, the only "true raccoons" were the 1920s models; the old coats were part of a popular fascination with the era and appealed to "lovers of the Lost Generation, sports car enthusiasts, lady fashion magazine editors and high fashion models." They fit a gangster's idea of luxury. The Salzmans fueled the furs' romantic image by reporting that "in one coat, they found a revolver and a mask; in another, a list of speakeasies."[25] This secondhand trend referenced opulence instead of poverty, and excess over thrift. The Great Gatsby–themed fraternity soirees are easy to picture.

The Postwar Fashion Industry

By advertising the furs as "vintage raccoon coats," Lord & Taylor established the practice of upselling used clothing by foregoing words such as "old" or "used." Although "vintage clothing" is usually a label attributed to the late 1970s or early 1980s when it reemerged and stuck, the 1950s raccoon coat fad helped brand a newly valued category of old clothes that was widely unacknowledged in the United States before that decade. Among other indications, an aesthetic interest in older clothes showed a grassroots movement on the part of young women determined to mix into their wardrobes a flair of casual androgyny—one as of yet unsanctioned by mainstream department stores. The original raccoon coats were boys' and men's outerwear, but 1957 advertisements show them on perky young women, posing in the classic juniors section, legs-akimbo style. And years before the Salzmans' coup, young female collegians, their numbers rising, were already keen on older styles, if not the actual antiquated materials. As early as 1949, *Life* reported on fall back-to-college trends favoring past fashions—all very different from the nipped-waisted, Christian Dior New Look most prominently touted and popularly remembered. Instead, some college girls opted for flapper-style shingle haircuts, turn-of-the-century pocket watches, whipcord pants, and "frank copies of the 1920s' slickers, raccoon coats, and short evening dresses."[26] Many of these looks had defiantly masculine elements, but until the Salzmans and their business partner cashed in on the interest, the touted products were all still reproductions, newly made versions of the old items. That 1949 article emphasized "strange sources" of retrospective styles, but those sources were boys' clothing stores and the rare, high-end designers working to reproduce past styles in new clothing—for a hefty price.

The Salzmans' coats were not expensive. Unlike in their first iteration, the Salzmans' recycled outerwear were special not because of an exorbitant price tag—$22.09 at Macy's—but because their scarcity demonstrated the wearers' obscure fashionability and up-to-the-minuteness. Most important, perhaps, was their "authenticity"; like the coveted Chippendale chest from the 1957 *Ladies' Home Journal* story, the coats demonstrated consumer discrimination and originality. Historian Grace Elizabeth Hale argues that middle-class white Americans in the postwar decades changed the meaning of authenticity to signify a discerning, rebellious outsider status, and included artifacts, music, clothing, and attitudes usually associated with nonwhites, the poor, the foreign-born—essentially anyone clearly on society's margins.[27] The proudly wealthy and elite also employed a refashioned definition of "authenticity" to include scarce or exotic items, which were also from "outside" the contemporary times and middle-class sensibilities. The reams of posh, new items affordable to an increasing proportion of the masses did not seem scarce to many postwar consumers. Since elite buyers sought distinction in their purchases, relics of the past held fresh aesthetic and social appeal. Advertisers urged consumers to identify with their purchases and feel as though their choices in cars, clothes, food, and home goods reflected the deepest, sincerest parts of their identities. For some with generous financial means, new items were too easy to come by, too common and homogenous—exactly what William Whyte accused suburbanites of being. New was no longer novel.

Social critics were pulling back the curtains of the advertising world and revealing its wizards, heightening readers' sensitivities to their consumer choices. In 1957—the same year Jack Kerouac's *On the Road* was published and the vintage 'coonskin coat trend peaked—Vance Packard's *The Hidden Persuaders* warned Americans that business advertisers were manipulating Americans into the "kind of catatonic dough that will buy, give or vote at their command."[28] For those attentive to such critiques but still determined to participate in the celebratory mass embrace of postwar recreational buying, secondhand materials offered an appealing alternative, a way to express exception from the easily duped masses and removal (in both directions) from the apparently repressed middle class aching to buy anything marketers offered, even if the product would be obsolete in a season.

The appeal of vintage clothing dovetailed with the fashion industry's intensification of planned obsolescence, a concept first honed by Alfred P. Sloan in the 1920s as the automotive industry reached saturation. During the 1940s and 1950s, magazine editors, fashion designers and other intermediaries, and major distribution chains agreed on rapidly changing seasonal lines, and contrived to help make last year's fashions passé to modish crowds. In 1950, the chairman of Allied Stores Corporation, one of the largest American department store chains, instructed more than four hundred fashion world leaders, "We must accelerate obsolescence." By the end of that decade, the garment industry served as a model of planned obsolescence for other industries seeking to increase product turnover and profits.[29] True, variety in what was fashionable did increase within a given year as items' shelf lives diminished. However, the clipped-pace consensus among industry leaders on momentarily suitable cuts, colors, and fabrics also established greater uniformity across income groups in the types of clothing worn—tending toward a specialization by activity and more informality in general.[30] The number of articles of clothes many Americans expected to own increased along with the multiplication of types of leisure activities: specific outfits were sold for tennis or golf, for college functions, for cocktail hour, for business meetings, for casual luncheons, for fund-raising events. Yet within each of those multiplying categories, variations diminished as fewer accessible designers worked outside the "system" or deviated from the agreed-upon seasonal styles and color palates.

The United States emerged from World War II with a remade fashion system: who, what, and how clothing was made changed forever over the course of the war. For decades, the United States, specifically New York City, had competed with France and Great Britain for the distinction of the largest manufacturer of clothing—the United States especially cornered the market in mid-priced ready-made women's apparel. However, most of the clothing

Americans made was based on de rigueur Parisian designs. From early in the century, American designers, usually working for a big label and without individual recognition, annually traveled to Paris fashion shows to bring back ideas to mimic. Most American designers produced cheaper versions of French styles in relatively large runs. A handful of U.S. designers vied to create a recognizably American style during the 1920s and 1930s, but with limited success until World War II. In 1940, Nazi occupation of France halted the annual travel to Paris fashion shows. With French products inaccessible and patriotism on the rise, New York City became the new fashion center for Americans, with local designers creating practical, wearable, and affordable choices. The war changed not only who made fashion but also how they made it.[31] Rations on materials used in wartime manufacturing, particularly leather and wool, posed challenges for manufacturers during the war; hemlines shrunk and fabric-heavy design details such as pleats diminished. A simplified wardrobe emerged, a trend encouraged by the demands of a growing, affluent college demographic.[32]

After the war ended, a whole new array of materials became available, materials that changed the look of clothing much as synthetic dyes had done the century before. Synthetic-blend fabrics developed from wartime technologies transformed the production and cost of clothing, and influenced styles, cuts, and colors. Although the chemical company DuPont first touted Nylon as the solution to dependence on Japanese silk panty hose in 1938, the War Production Board took over all nylon yarns for military purposes on 11 February 1942, halting the public availability of nylon panty hose.[33] After the war, when reconverting factories for civilian production, DuPont not only resumed production of legwear but also began to incorporate synthetics into other articles of clothing. Other companies followed suit. Polyesters, nylons, acetates, and acrylics abounded in the 1950s, parading under numerous brand names that read like the cast of a science fiction novel: Dacron, Terylene, Trelenka, Orlon, Crimplene.[34] These wool and cotton substitutes made dresses, shirts, blouses, and suits that could be tossed in the washer and then quickly dried, requiring little ironing or extra maintenance. The new fabrics suited the sportswear styles representative of the recently emerged U.S. designers and marketed as the "American Look," a casual style antithetical to the posh runway qualities affiliated with French fashions.[35] While the end of the war did bring a resurgence in American adulation of Paris designers, American sportswear persisted as a strong influence, even in stateside interpretations of Dior's "New Look."

The visual distance between pre- and postwar clothing designs—and between new and most secondhand items—was suddenly vast. The new fabrics took dyes differently, accepting and retaining more vibrant shades than did natural materials. An emphasis on comfort, affordability, and ease of maintenance characterized American postwar clothing, cutting across classes.[36] In 1954, the French-born American historian Jacques Barzun remarked on the differences in sartorial class-enunciation between France and the United States. In France, haute couture was available to the few, the wealthy, the visibly privileged. In the United States, Barzun said, "you will hardly see any difference between farm girls and the tidy numbers swinging their hips on Fifth Avenue."[37] At the same time that homogeneity in dress rose, the mass relocation of families from cities to suburbs brought alternatives to firsthand retail out from attics. Trunks and crates of clothing and household items carefully saved and maintained during leaner times found their way into secondhand outlets. A fast-mounting repository of antiquated fashions, already noticeable for their public renunciation of postwar styles and synthetic fabrics designed for domestic ease and democratic affordability, emerged.

The new identifiability of secondhand clothes, combined with consumer desire for variability and distinction from middle-class tastes, helped brand vintage clothing as fashionable and elite. For many, the cheap, new fabrics and rapidly rotating styles flooding the postwar clothing market visually defined the middle class. Among the New York high society set Tom Wolfe derides in *Radical Chic* (1970), the "need" to have a weekend place away from the city was proxy for the need to separate oneself from the "fat mommies with white belled pants stretching over their lower bellies and crinkling up in the crotch like some kind of Dacron-polyester labia."[38] In some circles, among elite consumers, certain high-quality secondhand clothing became the antithesis of mass-produced, egalitarian wardrobing, flagging the supposedly discerning and separating them from the masses, not unlike a house in the Hamptons.

Secondhand Venues

Meanwhile, secondhand exchange venues multiplied. Throughout the twentieth century, the shapes and formats of secondhand exchange accommodated demand and responded to shifts in firsthand retail models. For the most part, secondhand venues were morphable designs rooted in foregoing models of used goods trade but adapted to contemporary sales innovations, changes in population demographics, and new technologies. Turn-of-the-century cities spawned international chains of thrift stores as an urban response to increased manufacturing, sanitation crises, wealth disparity, and xenophobia. Thrift-store organizers transformed established patterns of junk collecting and street peddling to more closely correspond to the tastes of white, middle-class America; they codified, sanitized, and Christianized an increasingly profitable subeconomy. Thrift shops flourished in the 1920s, with Junior Leagues and the women's auxiliaries of hospitals giving Goodwill and Salvation Army some competition.[39] During the Great Depression and World War II, thrift-store donations declined and sales suffered, but major salvage programs continued to profit as tax statuses changed and the Fair Labor Act of 1938 established subminimum wages for disabled employees, especially advantaging Goodwill Industries.

After World War II ended, the Salvation Army and Goodwill Industries multiplied their products, storefronts, and revenues. With a sudden spike in supply as many Americans shed hoarded goods to make room for new purchases, other religious groups started or expanded lucrative thrift businesses, including the Catholic-run St. Vincent de Paul and the Mormon-operated Deseret Industries.[40] Secular charities began using newly established not-for-profit tax statuses to do the same. For example, the Military Order of the Purple Heart Service Foundation started a salvage business to support veterans and military families, but smaller organizations like these struggled to stay in business. By the 1960s, most solvent thrift stores relied on the receipt of large quantities of donations, multitiered managerial organization, and multiple locations to turn a substantial profit. Smaller thrift stores could not compete with the mammoth chains, either for bulk of product or efficient resale. In 1969, William Ellison, the son of a Salvation Army thrift store manager, offered the struggling Purple Heart Foundation thrift-store businesses a compromised solution: he would buy, in bulk, the goods donated to Purple Heart and sell them to the public, absorbing the costs (and most of the enormous profits) involved in marketing and distributing the goods. With the agreement, Ellison, a former Purple Heart Thrift Store manager himself, started Savers, Inc., the United States' first for-profit thrift store. Ellison soon signed up other charities as "collection agents only" and paid them a nominal per pound rate for donations. Savers (also known as Value Village) became a competitive international salvage chain whose for-profit, noncharity status was not transparently advertised.[41] By the late 1960s, whether philanthropic or not, many successful thrift stores followed a corporate model.

Early in the century, U.S. city flea markets reacted to many of the same developments as did thrift stores, but automotive use, transnational precedence, and independent entrepreneurialism also determined location, layout, and content of the sales. In rural regions, flea markets—often addendums to farmers markets—leveraged a growing popularity for everyday collectibles to supplement decreasing incomes for direct-to-consumer foods. Whether city or country, interwar flea markets reacted in part to the success of chain grocery stores, which hobbled foregoing systems of food distribution. Flea markets maintained the open-air market format established primarily to sell food, but venders adjusted content according to demand. After the end of World War II, flea markets, like other secondhand venues, prospered. Beginning in the 1950s, creative entrepreneurs eyeing the popularity of antiques started flea markets from scratch—such as Russell Carrell, generously (and inaccurately) dubbed the "granddaddy of U.S. flea markets." Carrell held his first "one-day rural flea market" in Salisbury, Connecticut, in 1958. Carrell called the event "antiques in a cow pasture," and swore that when he began, some who paid the fifty-cent admission fee expected to see a literal flea circus.[42] By the 1970s, such events were common.

Not all outdoor recreations similarly flourished. That same decade, drive-in movie theaters plummeted in popularity as in-home television broadcasting poached suburban clientele. The coinciding switch to daylight savings time in many states contributed to drive-ins' decline by decreasing the hours when the sky was dark enough for the screen to be seen and effectively eliminating a daily showing for part of the year.[43] So for some landowners looking to use the large, open lots (without the expense of converting them into shopping malls, another lucrative option), flea markets were convenient ways to offset declining drive-in profits. Some drive-in owners entirely abandoned their theaters, simply shifting to flea-market management. Other flea markets served as models of improvisational integrated economies, in which space is used for one business to defray the costs accrued by another. At a time when drive-in theaters had begun quickly closing across the country, this incorporation of daytime flea markets allowed some theaters to continue running—and many still exist as hybrids today.[44] Amidst a changing economy, flea markets begun as financial stopgaps soon proved rewarding undertakings.

To many postwar observers, flea markets popped up out of nowhere. As California "swap meets"—the West Coast synonym for flea markets—attracted young suburban expats selling and buying used and handmade goods, news reports called the events "a phenomenon of the 60s." Soon, the markets were loosely associated with the drug culture and patchwork fashions of hippie youth. By the 1960s, many flea markets or swap meets had uniform markers: large, outdoor settings with anywhere between twenty to one thousand different vendors, mostly selling used and handmade goods. California rapidly became the nation's "swap meet" headquarters, followed by Texas and Florida—states where longer warm seasons sustained outdoor ventures. The rise in California markets especially correlated with the decline in drive-in theaters, which had once enjoyed more success in that state than in any other.[45] The *New York Times* estimated in 1965 that in Southern California there were at least twenty weekly swap meets, events "which embrace ingredients of an oriental bazaar and the Paris Flea Market."[46] In this era, increased immigration from Pacific Rim countries accounted for much of the "exotic" market content, which began to include inexpensive newly manufactured import goods. Conservative nostalgia for prewar goods, the avant-garde appeal of quirky, out-of-date items, and financial need all continued to support flea-market success. Owner profits and large-scale organization increased at flea markets, but the individual stall renters who comprised the bulk of dealers remained mostly autonomous in their choices of what and how to sell to an omnivorously consuming public.

The concurrent growth of garage sales reinforced the popularity of flea markets in part by acclimating younger generations to practices of secondhand exchange within suburbia. In fact, more than one 1970s observer mistakenly identified flea markets as expansions of garage sales.[47] Although flea markets well predated garage sales, they both responded to the influx of new consumer items in the 1950s and 1960s. Individuals and families—especially those in the new suburbs—used stand-alone garage sales to periodically clear room for new items, recoup stagnant value in unused merchandise, participate in community building, and socialize. By and large, secondhand commerce continued to reflect and often support the expansion of firsthand commerce.

The recirculation of used goods was not restricted to thrift stores, flea markets, and garage sales. In addition to pawnshops and junk stores, longstanding systems of casual bartering and familial gifting continued; for the many Americans still outside the new affluence, secondhand exchange served practical purposes. But secondhand goods, including clothing, also appeared in postwar community events, introducing the civically minded, well-to-do consumer to alternative views of secondhand clothing. Secondhand clothing exchange extended beyond charity rummage sales. Postwar journalists detailed benefit sales, impromptu flea markets, and fashion shows featuring older gowns and other elegant, prewar wearables proudly out of tune with the dressing down of America. The end of the war brought a quick escalation in the number of all sorts of charitable community events, as mentioned in chapter three. As early as 1947, hostesses—such sponsors were overwhelmingly female—applied the word "vintage" to older clothing as a way of upgrading items from "used" to something with more panache, and more economic value. An association of secondhand goods with France, and the recognition of Paris as the site of the famed Marché aux Puces, aided in both the popularity of secondhand sales and the branding of vintage clothing as something special and desirable, indicative of the consumer's fine taste and worldly perception. In the aftermath of Allied victory, America renewed its romance with France, a nation greatly hobbled by the war. Various clubs across the country, mostly women's groups, staged "Parisian" markets sometimes supplemented by fashion shows to raise money to rebuild France in the wake of German occupation.[48] In society-page accounts, clothing descriptions increasingly approximated the production date or "vintage" of fine gowns and other clothing, showing the hostesses' specialized knowledge and elevating rummage sale goods to a higher status.

The word vintage came from wine making. Originally, a "vintage wine" denoted one whose grapes were all from a single specified year; vintage also indicated the highest quality and best year for certain grapes and/or vineyards. Commonly, vintage became understood (incorrectly) to indicate particularly old or excellent wine for all varietals.[49] It was not until the late 1920s that "vintage" was applied outside of enology. Collectors or dealers of older automobiles and then furnishings applied vintage in conjunction with a specific year or sometimes by itself, relying on the wine-born connotation of quality and age.[50] The designation worked its way slowly into association with clothing in the 1940s and 1950s, first by specifying year: "smart ensembles of 1895 vintage" or "a slinky satin and beaded evening dress of 1926 vintage."[51] Over the course of a few years of dutiful coverage of postwar benefit events, the word migrated to the adjectival form when precise clothing genealogy was unknown or when referring to an aggregate wardrobe. For example, at a 1954 Town and Country suburban fashion show, the Batavia Woman's club members modeled "[v]intage gowns."[52] Mid-1950s' reporters often put the adjective in quotations—"ten 'vintage' gowns"—suggesting novel usage.[53] The more frequent application of vintage to modify descriptions of clothing indicated that those materials were becoming objects worthy of collecting, like Model Ts and colonial grandfather clocks. Once Lord & Taylor advertised their coveted vintage raccoon coats, there were no more quotations. Fashionable secondhand clothing had arrived in the United States—and its meaning was far less a marker of rebellion than a show of nostalgia for elitism, and a disdain for the common availability of new, simpler clothing styles.

The vintage label did not persist immediately, fading out of usage by 1960 until its reemergence in the late 1970s. However, secondhand outlets of various sorts aimed at wealthier clientele began to appear regularly in the 1950s. Such outlets often took the form of consignment shops, such as Henri, a chic Washington, D.C., consignment shop that, according to a 1958 *New York Times* article, bore "as much resemblance to an ordinary second-hand store as a Wedgewood cup does to a beer bottle." The stock at Henri included designer evening gowns and mink coats—some of which were too new to be vintage, but too fine to go to Goodwill. Clientele included "not only the upper echelon of capital society, but also white collar girls, busy housewives and other thrifty soul [sic] who want a bargain."[54] The consignment model, whereby someone might consign their lightly worn items to the store proprietor in return for a cut of the profit, helped women with demanding wardrobe needs but without a commensurate budget; the article mentions wives of diplomats and congressmen, who were required to attend multiple parties a week and hesitated to duplicate gowns. The popularity of consignment boutiques would rise in the coming decades, after the 1960s split wide open the door to voluntary secondhand dress.

London's Bohemian Aristocracy

Arguably, posh postwar fashion benefits and Lord & Taylor's validation of a flash-in-the-pan Ivy League fad had restricted cultural resonance. While these U.S. fads did indicate a growing predilection for used clothing among the elite, they flew under the radar compared to the internationally renowned secondhand styles that emerged in the 1960s. In England and the United States, secondhand materials had a heavy hand in establishing the "hippie" aesthetic—brightly flowered fabrics, velvet and lace accents, and a layered eclecticism that blended genres and eras, particularly Victorian and Art Nouveau. In London, a microeconomy of secondhand traders, aspiring designers, and antique dealers flourished alongside those responsible for the internationally recognized Mod movement. Retailers of Mod clothing—initially based on futuristic, streamlined designs—gradually included more and more retrospective elements to their newly made goods. Key to this melding of old and new was a tribe of wealthy, young nobles, titled and well-traveled, who helped establish Victorian-inflected looks *and* stocked the rarified boutiques that sold them. The hybridizing Mod fashion house Biba was chief among the era's firsthand retailers to incorporate nostalgic "retro" details into newly made, even futuristic, clothing, but wealthy globetrotters introduced many of the physical fabrics of past eras. This period hailed a distinction between vintage clothing, reliant on the actual old materials, and "retro" styles, newly made clothing reproducing or incorporating elements of older fashions. Like vintage, the term retro would not gain consistent currency until the late 1970s, but by the mid-1960s, in England and the United States, the sartorial fascination with the imagery of the future made room for the past. As historian of London fashion Alistair O'Neill claimed about clothing, "It is generally agreed that around 1965, as with other areas of pop culture, the demand for ever-evolving newness forced a distraction from innovation and invention toward a plundering and interpretation of historical styles."[55] Once again, new was no longer novel. Clothing was not the only commodity that turned to Victoriana for aesthetic inspiration—Dodo Designs Ltd, founded in 1966, sold an array of "revivalist kitsch" objects, from nineteenth-century insurance company enamels to Victorian fob-watches, and "yesterday's advertisements" stormed the poster art industry.[56] Films, furniture designs, and advertising all began to plumb the archives of the past in the late 1960s.

Starting as early as the late 1950s, members of London's "pop aristocracy" gave highly stylized public faces to the Victorian romance and Edwardian exoticism associated with hippie clothes. This tight-knit group of rebellious young noblemen and women helped jump-start the "peacock revolution"—the media-given name for the late-1960s revival of dandyism in men's fashion—and helped synthesize the sartorial irony of some secondhand couture into a lasting component of rock 'n' roll style.[57] Using new and used goods gathered in India, Africa, and the middle East, and gleaned from European and American secondhand shops and flea markets, rich dandies curated cohesively colorful, eclectic wardrobes. By culling the undesirable dreft from the secondhand stalls on Portobello Road and area "charity shops"—the more common name for thrift stores in England—finding or commissioning experimental designers and traveling widely, these Londoners elevated buying to an art.

Beginning with Granny Takes a Trip, which opened in February 1966 on King's Road, a series of boutiques blended new and old materials and styles. In addition to becoming premier shopping destinations, King's Road shops became the center of an upper-class and celebrity scene, one that included not only princes and titled nobility, but the new nobility of rock 'n' roll, such as members of the Rolling Stones. Sheila Cohen, one of the masterminds of Granny Takes a Trip, collected Victorian clothes, especially army coats, ostrich-plumed hats, pony-skin shirts, and velvet jackets, for years before opening the shop. Soon, other similar boutiques opened: I Was Lord Kitchener's Valet (IWLKV), Cobwebs, Antiquarius, and Past Caring. Colonial relics, including brightly colored Victorian military apparel, were especially popular—and inspired the brightly-colored military tunics featured on the cover of the Beatles' 1967 album, *Sgt Peppers's Lonely Hearts' Club Band*. The stores sold a blend of new and old, and deviated from the thrift-store model in curation, cost, and cachet.[58]

For about a decade before the mid-1960s, the flea-market stalls on Portobello Road had seen a brisk trade in Victoriana, including clothing and especially military accouterments. IWLKV began in 1964 as a stall on Portobello Road specializing in Victorian military uniforms—and newly made replicas of the same—alongside other Victorian accessories. Proprietors John Paul and Robert Orbach helped define the 1960s rock-star image. Shop manager Robert Orbach recalls the turning point in the popularity of their stand-alone Portobello Road store one morning in the spring of 1966, shortly after it opened. John Lennon, Mick Jagger, and Cynthia Lennon walked in to browse. Jagger left with a red Grenadier guardsman drummer's jacket—probably gleaned from the British Army Surplus. Jagger wore the red tunic on the popular British rock/pop television show *Ready! Steady! Go!* According to Orbach, the store opened to a line of one hundred people wanting similar styles, and the shop sold out by lunchtime. Other rockers embraced the Victorian military style, including Eric Clapton, Jimi Hendrix, and all the Beatles, whose *Sgt Peppers's Lonely Hearts Club Band* cover costumes were inspired by an I Was Lord Kitchener's Valet window display. London boutiques such as IWLKV and Granny Takes a Trip supplied wealthy bohemians with Victorian undergarments, 1920s flapper dresses, military uniforms, 1930s Chicago gangster suits, and exotic accents like Arab headdresses. IWLKV's owners collected some such wares from British Army Surplus stores or Moss Bros, a still-extant men's fine apparel company; the 1960s fad for dressing with Victorian military accents relied on sources similar to those of the raccoon-coat craze—but vastly more plentiful. The prices soared beyond those of the Salvation Army.[59]

The popularity of Victorian apparel was partly a reaction against the nearly ubiquitous Mod style, but keen Mod retailers soon incorporated the trend. Mod was shorthand for modernists, initially used to describe jazz musicians and enthusiasts, but it extended to dress and style in the 1950s. Rock critic and sociomusicologist Simon Frith calls Mods the "clothes-conscious children of Jewish rag trade families" who met up with semi-beatniks in London's Soho coffeeshops—which sounds quite like the "Second Hand Rose" of

1920s Broadway.⁶⁰ Major Mod London fashion designs appealed to many, but especially caste-resisting, working-class postwar youth, who were self-sufficient and sartorially experimental—and ideally, physically diminutive. The Polish-born owner of the popular London boutique Biba, Barbara Hulanicki, described her customers as "postwar babies who had been deprived of nourishing protein in childhood and grew up to be beautiful skinny people: a designer's dream."⁶¹ The aptly named model Twiggy represented this generation of underfed sartorial experimentalists.

Biba, which opened in 1964, was only one of a rash of hip, new-clothes boutiques that opened alongside Granny Takes a Trip and its ilk. Mod designs often relied on wartime innovations, plastic and synthetic blends that achieved experimental silhouettes. They were priced to sell. While edgier and less casual, Mod styles shared vital characteristics with American trends of the time, including affordable and washable designs. Mod, however, soon mixed in older styles and fabrics, too—Biba frequently featured velvet Victorian-style articles—reflecting the growing attraction to old, or at least old-looking, things. The venue itself acknowledged the growing vintage trend. In the original Abington Road Biba, the dresses were new but displayed on antique coat racks next to a nineteenth-century mahogany vanity table spread with jewelry.⁶²

Even when Mod clothing mimicked older patterns, it was not secondhand. In fact, in both London and the United States, the Mod emphasis on futuristic materials encouraged detractors to veer away from postwar fabrics and patterns and embrace pre-Raphaelite ornamentation. Yet many observers use Biba to symbolize the shift from futuristic to nostalgic.⁶³ Astute music writer Simon Reynolds finds it paradoxical to contrast the *Chicago Times* 1968 comment that "the whole Biba scene makes you feel like you're in tomorrow" with *The Face*'s recollection of Biba in 1983 as "the first fashion house to define the present as a modern-baroque restatement of the past. . . . As a trading company, Biba spanned the years 1964 to 1975. As a design factory it began around 1890 and ran a clear line through most of the Twentieth Century." Though only extant for eleven years, Biba's success stemmed from its versatility and adaptability, from Hulanicki's skills not only as a tastemaker but as a trend-spotter. Later, Hulanicki recalled seeing Jane Ormsby-Gore, the scioness of a long-standing Celtic dynasty, enter her store wearing an eclectic mélange of used and new, remade and layered clothing, and was both inspired and fascinated by the elements. In 1966, Ormsby-Gore, one of the vintage-loving London aristocrats and a "prime mover to the revolt of the British upper-class during the '60s," married Michael Rainey, the proprietor of another

King's Road boutique, Hung on You, further demonstrating the intimate links between London retailers and young aristocrats. For the event, she wore an antique lace chemise.[64]

Not unlike the Harvard Americans draped in decades-old raccoon fur, many of the secondhand London entrepreneurs and fashionistas honed their sense of style at elite schools such as Eton, an expensive boys' boarding school in Berkshire England. Christopher Gibbs, credited as "the most avant-garde dresser" England ever boasted, attended the Sorbonne in Paris after getting kicked out of Eton, where he'd already earned a reputation as a dandy dresser.[65] A young Gibbs opened an antique shop in the late 1950s in Chelsea, where he displayed an ever-growing collection of antiques and garments, much of which was collected in his travels abroad, especially in North Africa.[66] While he did sell some of his curios—mostly to his fellow bohemian aristocrats—he saved the most elaborate outfits for himself. Gibbs admitted that to dress like him and his group of flaneurs, "You had to be monumentally narcissistic and have time on your hands, and just about enough money to do it."[67] Among his other sartorial firsts, Gibbs is popularly credited as "the first man in England to wear flared trousers, back in 1961."[68] Gibbs is sometimes assigned a central role in the peacock movement, which by the mid-1960s was strongly associated with London's young Carnaby Street designers and their extravagant boutique items, including early bell-bottoms and tight flowered shirts with widening lapels.[69] Gibbs, as a wealthy antique dealer-cum-style icon, solidified his sartorial reputation in 1965 when he became an editor of shopping guides in *Men in Vogue*.

The male edition of *Vogue* magazine lasted from 1965 to 1970, coinciding with the peacock revolution. Though variously defined, the peacock revolution described the styles associated with mid-1960s "Swinging London," especially the newly made flamboyant menswear garnering international attention. In Europe and to a lesser extent the United States, men's flared trousers, fitted, wide-lapeled shirts, flowered patterns, and velvet fabrics had an industry-wide moment in about 1968, coinciding with the inclusion of unisex departments in mainstream stores.[70] A rush of colorful, detailed men's clothing emerged from and coincided with the ardor with which London embraced Victorian and Edwardian styles and older actual materials—though it was also associated with designers from other parts of Europe and the United States, such as French Pierre Cardin, Austrian-born Rudi Gernreich, and American Bill Blass. Intended as a challenge to the (again middle-class) drabness and homogeneity of midcentury men's clothes—especially the iconized gray flannel suit—softer fabrics, elaborate design details, and an expanded color palette defined the movement, participants of which boasted that the change was permanent. In reality, tight velvet britches and Edwardian collars did not kill the gray flannel suit, which reemerged as the recommended business dress by 1975. Even in its heyday, the peacock revolution was much more limited than popular imagination and news reports suggested; swift backlash arose in response to the fashion's association with effeminacy and homosexuality.[71] Short-lived though the movement was, secondhand outlets such as the Portobello flea market definitely influenced the florid accents of the peacock revolution.

Gibbs was not the only high-born, vintage-wearing member of London society to be drafted into service by *Vogue*. In 1966, *Vogue* also asked Jane Ormsby-Gore, daughter of the titled British ambassador to the United States during John F. Kennedy's presidency—and, as Mick Jagger's one-time girlfriend, the reputed inspiration for the Rolling Stones song "Lady Jane"—to join their British staff. As socialites of a new order, the handsome, fashionable (and sometimes troubled and drug-addicted) Ormsby-Gore siblings sought to do away with the arduous formalities of the old nobility; they were youthful, eccentrically dressed, world-traveled partiers. Jane Ormsby-Gore publicized a style that mixed high fashion with rare secondhand pieces such as embroidered Russian boots, feathers, and other fantastic items, many that she embellished or combined herself, to gypsy-like effect.[72]

For much of the late 1960s, Ormsby-Gore haunted high-end fashion shows in layered adaptations of reigning styles, peppered with whatever ethnic or antiquated details took her traveling fancy. In retrospect, Ormsby-Gore would attribute her intermixing of styles to a desire to break down class boundaries. "I always longed not to be contained within my class," she claimed decades later. And on its face, the outrageous style of the bohemian aristocracy represented by Gibbs and Ormsby-Gore did signal a departure from the structure and formalities of English life among the established upper class.[73] Yet, when examined, the very particular old clothes required signaled privilege and opportunity, as Gibbs admitted—and perhaps a desire to distinguish oneself from affordable, working-class styles. According to *Vogue*'s 1966 article on Ormsby-Gore, "Jane Ormsby-Gore: Fashion Original," her wardrobe reflected nothing more than a "detestation of all things commonplace."[74] On the one hand, some of her clothing hailed from the open-air stalls of Portobello Road (which *Life* called that same year, "no fashion center but a flea market of some twenty years standing"), but on the other hand, "a lot of her clothes are made by dressmakers," which was not a penny-pinching prospect.[75]

FIGURE 4.3 "Jane Ormsby-Gore: Fashion Original," *Vogue* (U.K.), January 1966.

Vogue ended the article by describing Ormsby-Gore as "a medieval monarch surrounded by her courtiers," hardly the image of a classless revolutionary identifying with the peasantry.[76]

An examination of one of Ormsby-Gore's featured outfits in the *Vogue* article (see figure 4.3) reveals the role an elite knowledge of modern fashion history, personal wealth, and ample leisure played in creating Lady Jane's brand of creative eclecticism. The striped, Portobello-Road coat is by Paul Poiret, the early twentieth-century fashion innovator. Renowned before World War I as a premier French designer, Poiret died in 1944, poor and forgotten; in 1966, interest in his designs was only recently revived, along with those of his designer friend, the Italian surrealist Elsa Schiaparelli.[77] Ormsby-Gore's choice showed esoteric knowledge in very recent fashion trends (and her own influence on them) through the specific revivalist choice of then-obscure avant-garde fashion elements. The Edwardian motoring hat belonged to her great-grandmother. A rare piece from the advent of automobile transport, it bespoke of a familial lineage that participated in new technology at its outset. Ormsby-Gore found the handmade cream silk shirt at a trip to Paris's Marché aux Puces—a regular shopping sojourn the possibility of which, once again, indicated wealth and leisure. A military belt from the late eighteenth century finishes the outfit, the sort of touch that would become invested with strong parodic protest by American Vietnam War protesters—but not before rock stars Eric Clapton, John Lennon, Mick Jagger, and Jimi Hendrix all performed and posed in military jackets, many reportedly purchased at I Was Lord Kitchener's Valet.[78]

By the late 1960s, King's Road and Carnaby Street teemed with similar eclectic looks. Not everybody approved of military uniforms paraded as street fashion, which served to boost the look's reputation among the young and rebellious. IWLKV flourished in part because of high-profile antiestablishment stunts, like the time Lord Chamberlain admonished the owners for selling five-shilling replicas of the Royal Coat of Arms, all left over from the 1952 coronation celebrations. The thousands of souvenirs on hand sold out before any action could be taken.[79] By 1967, Londoners were desperate to uncover forgotten caches of old clothes everywhere. Large department stores threw huge divestment auctions that were elaborations on the Lord & Taylor raccoon coat coup, digging into stores of unsold stock from bygone eras. Heirs brought heavy trunks out of cold storage, revealing dead marchionesses gowns and musty-feathered hats. Amateur playhouses marketed hoards of century-old clothing. Sotheby's auctioned a rediscovered stockpile of ballet costumes from the founder of the Ballets Russes in the first decade of the century—the details of which had, incidentally, strongly influenced Paul Poiret's own designs, which in the celebration of the wealthy rebels of the 1920s, became covetable again in the 1960s.[80]

Postwar London's focus on secondhand style at least rivaled that found anywhere in the United States, and emerged from a similar class dichotomy. British cultural theorist Angela McRobbie examines this context in one of the few existing scholarly considerations of secondhand fashion.[81] "Second-Hand Dresses and the Ragmarket" focuses on the "existence of an entrepreneurial infrastructure" within subcultures, one that gave working-class young people after World War II opportunities to be fashionable during times of recession. McRobbie emphasizes the roles of young students and self-conscious bohemians in establishing the fashionability of secondhand clothing. Many of these actors had "cultural capital" without significant financial means.[82] For the most part, McRobbie examines elective poverty—"stylized images of poverty"—as central to postwar secondhand venue participants, all the while underscoring the "thinly-veiled cultural elitism" required to pull off the precise look, an observation that applies to many of the subjects of the following chapter.[83]

McRobbie only briefly acknowledges the costlier, higher-profile London boutiques. I argue that the most successful and influential entrepreneurs of secondhand style in postwar London were not young fashion school dropouts, but world-traveling nobles jockeying for international attention by earning recognition for their erudite tastes. In addition, while postwar recession in England may have accounted for eager participation among the less well-off, the twentieth-century United States charts interest in secondhand styles that rose alongside affluence, attendant to firsthand supply. Insightful as it is, McRobbie's analysis lacks an explanation for the wealthy exhibitionists who helped make Jimi Hendrix's purple military tunic an iconic garment of the time. However, viewed alongside a consideration of upper-class London's posh dabblings in secondhand apparel, the working-class ragmarket scene demonstrates how multifaceted and reactive the development of secondhand economies and styles were.

The wide-spanning styles of "Swinging London" (fashions that both relied on and invited retro indulgences, such as the turn-of-the-twenty-first-century *Austin Powers* movie franchise) saw a decade-long merging of modern and retrospective dressing. Early 1960s Mod designs, wildly popular, distinctive, and forward-looking as they were, quickly became devalued in part due to their easy availability and democratic appeal. But even as romantic figurings of bygone eras emerged, sartorial representations of what was to come remained. The past was integrated into perceptions and idealizations of the future, a melding that framed and sustained the coming postmodern aesthetic—an aesthetic that continued to travel along the parallel tracks of fashion and music.[84]

Dressing America's Edwardian Hippie

In both fashion and music, the "British invasion" of the 1960s influenced American culture substantially, but secondhand dressers stateside also innovated.[85] San Francisco was the premier American site of psychedelic styles, and as such, influenced Europe in return. Competition and interchange between London, New York, and San Francisco especially fine-tuned the "bright plumage" that was associated with hippies and utilized secondhand materials. While clothing boutiques stockpiled elaborate colonialist military uniforms and Portobello Road's antique stalls helped the bohemian aristocracy add Victorian accents to their posh family homes, San Francisco secondhand style began to emphasize "the lore of the frontier West and the American Indian" along with the requisite velvet and brocade.[86]

Many credit Haight-Ashbury in San Francisco, the center of a quickly flourishing antiestablishment culture celebrating liberal sexual attitudes, drug use, and rebellious personal appearances, with the honing of a specific aesthetic associated with the psychedelic drug LSD. However, some claim that the psychedelic San Francisco scene of the late 1960s actually began three hours away in the renovated ghost town of Virginia City, Nevada. About a hundred years before, Virginia City was the center of the Comstock Lode silver rush and a hub of Wild West prospecting. In 1965, Virginia City was the hailed headquarters of the new Wild West. A couple of hip entrepreneurs moved in and restored a large Victorian house, complete with bat-wing doors and a shaded wooden sidewalk. They named it the Red Dog Saloon, a common name for saloons in the 1860s. The last element for this outlaw-themed psychedelic bar was a new band, the Charlatans, organized and designed by George Hunter, a student at San Francisco State.[87]

Like many future Haight-Ashbury residents, Hunter originally moved to San Francisco hoping "to be part of the Beat Generation," only to find the scene strung-out and abandoned.[88] Hunter soon moved to the Haight, where he spent hours perusing the many area thrift stores to fine-tune his and his bandmates' "look."[89] Openly more style than substance, the Charlatans had reportedly never played until their audition at The Red Dog Saloon, but their cracked cowboy boots, wasp-waisted coats, and straw boaters or cowboy hats were a perfect match for the Red Dog Saloon's velvet curtains, crystal chandeliers, and antique bar.[90] Their image was that they were all image.

The Charlatans are often credited with pioneering acid rock, incorporating light shows, and creating the first psychedelic art poster. Along with Ken Kesey and his Merry Pranksters, The Charlatans' performances in Virginia City, Nevada, galvanized the hippie community in the summer of 1965.[91] Hunter infused both hippie fashion and publicity graphics with a Victorian flair—the latter especially owing to his admiration for artist Maxfield Parrish.[92] Generally, the swirls and dips of Art Nouveau designs swarmed San Francisco in the mid-1960s, inspiring museum exhibitions, revivalist household objects, and mass-produced wallpaper. The ardor was such that in 1967, *Time* magazine proposed renaming the city "Nouveau Frisco."[93]

Hunter relied on thrift-store finds to distinguish the Charlatans' look from British hipness, especially Mod. The bolo ties, handlebar mustaches, belt buckles, and accompanying swagger referenced solidly and singularly American myths and history.[94] The choice of Old West fashion in 1960s California was good publicity. Reared on the fantasies of the Hollywood Western film, those coming of age in the 1960s were expert readers of the symbolisms of the

FIGURE 4.4 The Charlatans, 1964. Photograph by Robert H. Ballard, from Mike Wilhelm Collection.

style. In figure 4.4, a publicity photo from 1964 (before the band had ever played in public), the Charlatans' pose communicates individualism. None of the members touch each other. For everyone but Mike Wilhelm, in the center, posture and hand placement suggests self-protectiveness. Wilhelm's hands dangle at his side, but with his level stare and slightly curved fingers, he looks ready to draw a six-shooter from his holster. The picture is an old-fashioned showdown, referential and coolly patriotic.

The Charlatans may have been the first to set the tone for image-conscious psychedelic bands, but countless other individuals contributed. Through her close affiliation with singer Janis Joplin's meteoric rise, fashion designer Linda Gravenites, the adopted daughter of wealthy Los Angeles Republicans, further refined the psychedelic dress styles of hip San Franciscans in the mid- to late 1960s. Gravenites rigged up bell-bottoms from old slacks or skirts, embroidered on everything, and repurposed Victorian lace and velvet—all mixed with new synthetics. From no working-class background herself, Gravenites moved to North Beach in 1959 after getting kicked out of Whittier College, but quickly saw the Beat movement lose its literary and artistic focus and decline, according to her, into "a subculture revolving around speed." In a few years, she followed other disappointed would-be beatniks to the Haight-Ashbury neighborhood—where she met Janis Joplin, for whom she designed stage costumes, including Joplin's much-touted Woodstock outfit: lace slacks and a tunic cannibalized from a secondhand tablecloth.[95]

Gravenites's aesthetic arose as a part of her disenchantment with the beatnik ideal, which she dismissed as "a rejection of all worldly values—including beauty." According to her, "North Beach was a study in black and white; the Haight-Ashbury is a crazy quilt of living color."[96] Gravenites sold some of her creations at local boutiques, but mostly she created outfits on order, catering to individual whims. Los Angeles competed with San Francisco for West Coast style innovation, but Gravenites dismissed her home city's boutique clothing scene by saying "Los Angeles was where you went to shop at stores that *sold clothes*," whereas in San Francisco, "you went to the Goodwill, or made it yourself or had a friend who did."[97]

On 16 October 1965, members of the nascent hippie community strutted and preened in front of each other at a dance held by the Family Dog commune at Longshoremen's Hall in San Francisco. The display of sartorial rebellion was resplendent and various, from Allen Ginsberg, quietly clad in the white hospital orderly outfit he had affected since his return from India, to the younger bohemians, "in Mod clothes, Victorian suits, and granny gowns, Old West outfits, pirate costumes, free-form costumes."[98] Like Ormsby-Gore's more outlandish gear, the impracticality of these costumes confounded the association of secondhand with either elective poverty or spiritual simplicity. The outfits signified a firm removal from mainstream society—rejecting pursuit of a "straight" nine-to-five job—and a complete commitment to antiestablishment lifestyles. In their extremity of deviance, such antiestablishment garb echoes aspects of economist Thorstein Veblen's 1899 discourse on "conspicuous consumption." Veblen called "elegant clothing" an "insignia of leisure," demonstrative of "the wearer's abstinence from productive employment." In most of 1960s America, the daily donning of a pirate outfit hobbled someone in search of mainstream employment much as a polished French heel negated the likelihood of manual labor seventy years prior.[99]

In 1968, Gravenites joined many in leaving Haight-Ashbury to the throngs of newcomers, and attributed the decline of the hippie haven to hip capitalism, saying, "off-the-peg looks were antithetical to the iconoclasm of the original community." A battle began between long-term residents' style and "store-bought hip that didn't come from the soul"—a battle led by some of the most vocal (and visible) proponents of elective poverty.[100] Late 1960s San Francisco, like Portobello Road in London, certainly saw the intersection of vintage exhibitionism and elective poverty. Secondhand goods acquired special status in the postwar years. A group of young, wealthy elites eager to distinguish themselves both from other classes and from other generations embraced the idea of "vintage clothing." And in a process not precisely oppositional to the vintage movement, but still distinct in its social and political aims, members of the same proximate generation used secondhand clothes to suggest downward affiliation. Exhibitionist vintage-clothing dress and politically engaged performances of elective poverty shared trademark images and popular icons, such as Beat writer Jack Kerouac and television-courting activist Abbie Hoffman; both individuals are central to the following chapter.

The Salzmans, Lady Jane Ormsby-Gore, and the Charlatans are only some of the major representatives of a hip, wealthy genre of stylization, one that romanticized the past not as more responsible and conservative, but as more fun and experimental, as unabashedly classist, as elegant, as wild and unrestrained. Yet politically motivated elective poverty and vintage displays did often mingle—especially in recollection. Years after the sixties ended, Jane Ormsby-Gore claimed her motivation for eclecticism was natural at a time when "everything was being broken down," especially "social strata."[101] However, her class status, abundance of leisure time, and family fortune is exactly what allowed her to curate the image of supposed class indifference. Descriptions of the raucous youth cultures of the 1960s often succumb to the temptation to ascribe all with political intent.

The transnational, backward-glancing trends emerging between about 1957 and 1966 were not guided by a consolidating fashion industry, but neither were they a rebellion from below, a grassroots story of unexpected success. "Ragamuffin chic"—a fashion term reminiscent of the "shabbily genteel" advertising peg for those raccoon coats in 1957—relied heavily on the influences of elite individuals, such as London socialite Jane Ormsby-Gore, nobleman retailer and dandy Christopher Gibbs, and the Whittier College dropout who designed Janis Joplin's wardrobes, Linda Gravenites. Mainstream magazines and highly visible popular rock stars helped to distribute the styles to an eager mass audience. New-clothes retailers such as Biba embraced the trend and encouraged the new production of old-fashioned clothing. Around the same time, similar patterns of apparent appropriation in San Francisco would excite the political ire of activists angry at what they saw as commercial interference in hippie lifestyles. The distinction between politically motivated secondhand dress and elitist vintage exhibitionism blurred and melded by the 1970s, making retrospective disaggregation of the sixties' secondhand trends increasingly difficult.

CHAPTER FIVE

Elective Poverty and Postwar Politics

Everything belongs to me because I am poor.
—Jack Kerouac, 1951–52

Clothes make the poor invisible too: America has the best-dressed poverty the world has ever known.
—Michael Harrington, 1962

A utopia would rise out of the garbage.
—Abbie Hoffman, 1968

In 1962, political theorist Michael Harrington published a popular book countering the era's confidence in widespread abundance and unending economic growth. In *The Other America*, Harrington extended Kenneth Galbraith's concerns about social apathy among the well-off, who were increasingly shielded from the effects of poverty. Poverty, Harrington argued, had not disappeared but had grown less and less visible. The ghettoization of inner cities, the rise of a geographically separate white, middle-class suburbia, and the appearance of "urban renewal"—cosmetic efforts in cities which often alienated the very poor even more—made it possible for the bulk of the population to never physically be confronted with the continuing effects of poverty in America.[1]

Along with residential segregation, an apparent democratization of clothing masked the true appearance of poverty: "There are tens of thousands of Americans in the big cities who are wearing shoes, perhaps even a stylishly cut suit or dress, and yet are hungry." The democratization of American couture that Jacques Barzun observed in 1954, according to Harrington's concerns, fueled rather than stemmed social inequity by masking the poor. Not only was new clothing made more affordable through the application of wartime technology and materials, but, Harrington implied, charitable habits of donating used goods and providing affordable, presentable apparel for the poor helped produce a deceitful uniform. Even if not formally calculated, "it almost seems as if the affluent society had given out costumes to the poor so that they would not offend the rest of society with the sight of rags."[2] Donating lightly worn clothing to philanthropic charities like Goodwill and the Salvation Army treated societal wounds with cloth Band-Aids.

By convincingly arguing that up to 25 percent of Americans lived in poverty, *The Other America* ushered in an era of attention to the poor in America. President John F. Kennedy read the book after a *New Yorker* review brought it to his notice, and two years later, President Lyndon Johnson declared "War on Poverty" in his state of the union address. Historians often attribute the expansion of Social Security benefits and the establishment of Medicare, Medicaid, and food stamps to Harrington's ideas.[3] The New Left, organized and articulated largely by college students in the early 1960s, took ending poverty as their central cause before the Vietnam War demanded a reorganization of priorities. But with that ironic twist to which fashion seemed increasingly drawn after World War II, at the same time in which "[e]ven people with terribly depressed income [could] look prosperous," people with the benefit of comparative fiscal security began to emulate poor dress, sometimes out of political intent, other times out of a vague sense that an "authentic" way of living was more accessible to those living on the margins. Like rock 'n' roll's appropriation of black musical styles, the adoption of visibly secondhand clothing, as well as Native American and Old West costumes, relied on the white, middle-class conviction that sincerity, depth, passion, creativity, and even social equality were more accessible from the margins of society—past and present.[4] As public appearances and personal identities became central to the social and political conflicts of the era, a dramatized appearance of elective poverty—often by way of secondhand consumption—joined other visible means of middle-class, usually white, social rebellion.

Nostalgie de la Boue

Tom Wolfe coined the term "radical chic" to describe the late 1960s practice of New York liberal intellectuals adopting a radical cause associated with oppressed minority groups, such as Cesar Chavez's grape workers, the Young Lords, or the Black Panthers. According to his satirical essay in *New York* magazine (1970), radical chic included throwing benefit parties and inviting outré radical figures to plumb the wallets of high-society members, who received in turn the thrill of "elegant slumming."[5] Though run through with Wolfe's own personal efforts of status rejection, the essay incisively dissects the "delicious status contradictions and incongruities" of the "cause parties" the liberal elite threw in late-1960s New York City. By way of an imagined Black Panther fund-raiser party hosted by composer Leonard Bernstein, Wolfe focuses on the overcompensating insecurities of the nouveau riche, particularly the formerly ostracized—here, wealthy, Jewish New York intellectuals.

He describes two ways, often used in tandem, newcomers to high society had of "certifying their superiority over the hated 'middle class' ": they might take the high road and mimic aristocracy with lofty architecture, numerous servants, and extreme formality—or, "they can indulge in the gauche thrill of taking on certain styles of the lower orders."[6] The French long ago dubbed the latter impulse *nostalgie de la boue*, literally translated as nostalgia for the mud. During the postwar years, this impulse to emulate the less well-off or those of lower status or with diminished freedom was a recognizable way for many groups and individuals to disdain middle-class politics and aesthetics. However, this supposedly imitative dress, as Wolfe points out, failed to actually resemble the poor or marginalized. After all, as Harrington points out, the truly poor often did not look it. I argue that the wardrobing was not always a failure of imitation, as Wolfe would have it, but instead more broadly symbolic of dissidence; middle-class whites dressing below their station defied social order in a way parallel to dandy-dressing radical blacks abandoning the vaunted civil rights "politics of respectability."

The term *nostalgie de la boue* has roots in early- to mid-nineteenth-century France, in the wake of the rising bourgeoisie there—significantly, around the same time the first so-designated "bohemians" emerged. Henri Murger sketched the archetypal 1840s bohemian artist in his autobiographical *Scènes de la vie de Bohème* (published in 1851), through which creativity gained a romanticized affiliation with cultivated poverty.[7] Mid-nineteenth-century Parisians' particular brand of ostensible destitution did not include principles of steady, mindful thrift; rather than being the result of misfortune, bohemian poverty was born of wild flings of profligacy, followed on their heels by humbled circumstances.[8] The bourgeoisie trappings of thrift and security were posed as antithetical to artistic endeavors.

Obvious visual distinctions were needed to materialize bourgeoisie status rejection in part because "bohemian" and "bourgeois" were vague, indefinable, and overlapping concepts. Much of bohemian life in Paris was thus marked by "the appropriation of marginal lifestyles by young and not so young bourgeois, for the dramatization of ambivalence toward their own social identities and destinies."[9] Similarly, many of those adopting secondhand styles in the 1950s and 1960s were not forging a simple counterimage to the postwar bourgeoisie. Rather than being an immediate and wholesale rejection of all that was firsthand or familiar, secondhand styles forged an admixture of old and new, masculine and feminine, expensive and cheap, exotic and ordinary, utopic and pragmatic, high-end and street-born, and past and future—as we saw in late sixties London as well. The sartorial bricolage "dramatized ambivalence" toward their social status more often than it represented a total rejection.

Appearances in this earlier bohemian era divided into two performative categories not unlike the postwar secondhand styles laid out in this and the previous chapter. On the one hand, nineteenth-century Parisian bohemians were often flamboyant, colorful, and excessive, sporting wardrobes set off by romantic medieval touches. Theatricality, fueled by the popularity of costume balls and historical dress references, influenced daily wear for self-proclaimed outsiders—a presentation that implied the luxury of at least time and often money, and that certainly signified outré employment. But in a converse yet equally performative style, humble dress also reigned among some factions: Champfleury commented in 1855, "Today poverty forms the basis of the painters' costume ... only ancient hats, jackets and trousers stained with oil, and shoes whose owners tremble at the least sign of rain."[10] Like the postwar Beats and hippies in the United States, many Parisian bohemians hailed from an at-least bourgeoisie background. Some sought refuge from middle-class ennui in florid displays of privilege, while others sought the virtuous comfort of *nostalgie de la boue*. According to Balzac, the "Bousingots" of the Restoration period, middle-class malcontents, sported filthy fingernails, long beards, crooked cravats, and greasy coats.[11]

Wolfe cites another foregoing example of *nostalgie de la boue*. Concurrent with the rise of the French middle class, Regency-era London socialites borrowed the habiliments, hairstyles, dancing fads, and wild driving habits of tavern girls, prize fighters, and coach drivers. These early nineteenth-century affectations, however, did not primarily express affiliation or sympathy for the working-class plight, but gave an aristocratic middle finger to middle-class niceties in the wake of the temporary upset of the status afforded by noble title.[12] A sense on the part of the privileged that the poor and labor-bound had some mystical strain of authenticity unavailable to them—some core way of living that was more viscerally expressive than those inured to comfort—linked into a desire to shock and defy. From at least the nineteenth century onward, the romanticization of the marginalized often coincided with fads emulating casual and seemingly unrestrained styles of dress alongside the rejection of less visible class markers. In 1968, cultural theorist Stuart Hall identified the American "hippy" moment as reliant on performative poor dress—and a dismissal of formal education as classist brainwashing. While it fits that a widening middle class and increasingly disaffected generation of young people (with the numbers to support the impression of collectivity) encouraged an existing tradition of poverty mimicry, evidence of class rejection well predates hippies in the United States as well as in Europe. In addition to France transmitting its image of the bohemian to Americans via authors such as Henri Murger and George du Maurier, the United States had its own versions of and motivations for the middle-class imitation of poverty.

During the Great Depression, a full quarter of the working population was unemployed, bread lines lengthened, and suicide abounded. Class guilt played a role in a subsequent romanticization of poverty, evident in the documentary tradition of the 1930s. Coffee table tomes like *You Have Seen Their Faces* featuring the heroically styled photography of Margaret Bourke-White and the plainspoken text of Erskine Caldwell, captured images of rural poor in a humanizing, even glorifying, light. A cheap copy of the book paid homage to the poor in nearly every "progressive" household in Depression-era America. Bourke-White, whose bold photos speckled the book, loved to frame shots from below, staging monumental postures for her subjects.[13] This tradition of documenting poverty with a romantic lens went hand in hand with a sentimentalizing of the poorest region of the country, the rural South. James Agee and Walker Evans famously chronicled southern Depression-era poverty in *Let Us Now Praise Famous Men*.[14] Evans's photographic style set the book's tone as more candid and evidentiary than did Bourke-White's, emphasizing inhabited spaces and clothing as well as less dramatized, head-on portraits of members of three tenant farming families. In *Let Us Now Praise Famous Men*, though, Agee's text feels more central than Caldwell's, forming the bulk of the book, while the pictures at the start make a sort of visual preface. Often maudlin, the narrative pleads with the viewer to identify and sympathize with the oppressed cast—without actually letting them speak for themselves for fear that rural dialects would perpetuate stereotypes of ignorant vulgarity.[15] In the text, even while acknowledging their distress, Agee also imbued the sufferers with special wisdom and virtue, viewing them as purified by their struggles. In his painstakingly detailed, thirty-page description of the tenant families' clothing, he aligns their bedraggled sartorial state with the heroic efforts, dignity, and strength of character defining the laboring women who strive to keep their prodigious families clothed. Very often, he is extravagantly generous with the beauty he ascribes their simple, cheap articles. Scarcity, he seems to argue, makes the objects more beautifully worn.

Agee, biographers agree, suffered momentous guilt over his own inherited privilege while documenting his rural Alabaman subjects. Agee wore clothing that was "deliberately cheap" because he believed high quality clothing would be read as a claim of social superiority. According to Walker Evans, however, Agee's frank, personal enjoyment of class rejection interfered with any professed altruism. According to Evans, Agee's determined dressing down resulted in a "knowingly comical inverted dandyism. He got more delight out of factory-second sneakers and a sleazy cap than a straight dandy does from waxed calf Peal shoes and a brushed Lock & Co. bowler."[16] Like 1960s hippies also would, Agee, out of admiration and respect for his tenant-farming subjects, disdained the advantages of an upper-class education. The paltry years of study afforded his subjects in Alabama, he claims, did not negate individual growth. He turns the discourse to a bitter reflection on his own breadth of instruction: "I could not wish of any one of them that they should have had the 'advantages' I have had: a Harvard education is by no means an unqualified advantage."[17] In such ways, Agee falls just short of describing poverty as a stroke of luck, as a special sort of destiny—and Ivy League opportunities as contemptible.

Many secondhand dressers in the postwar decades echoed Agee's self-deprecating sentiments about formal education alongside his habits of wearing "deliberately cheap" clothing. Electively poor appearance marked the countenance of Beat writers, antiwar activists, feminists, and early environmentalists, among others. More specifically than just dressing on the cheap, the marked innovation of the time was the widespread use of secondhand clothing markets in order to express stylized admiration for the poor and oppressed—even as the poor were increasingly difficult to identify based on dress.

From the Margins to the Middle Class

In the decades after World War II's end, white, middle-class youth bought, sold, stole, traded, borrowed, gleaned, decorated with, and wore secondhand items with increasing frequency and visibility. Pre-owned goods made manifest postwar insecurities over the cultural position of the middle class amid anxieties of possible nuclear war, increasing class conflict, the black rights struggle, anti–Vietnam War protests, and second-wave feminism. Although the radicalism of the 1960s owes an enormous amount, politically and aesthetically, to African Americans fighting for a parity of rights, black activists themselves did not consistently adopt used dress for overtly political purposes. When black activists did dress down instead of up, the aim was to visibly ally middle-class, non-southern activists with the working-class communities they supported or helped organize.

Not unlike Salvation Army "slum sisters" adopting ragged calico earlier in the century to work and proselytize in tenements, black and white members of the Student Non-Violent Coordinating Committee (SNCC) began, in the early 1960s, wearing a "uniform" of denim pants or bib overalls. Black SNCC women stopped chemically processing their hair and "went natural" not only as a visual expression of African heritage, but in solidarity with poorer southern black women.[18] Aside from this instance, most black activists in the 1950s and 1960s followed the "politics of respectability." Civil rights leaders directed activists to dress "modestly, neatly . . . as if you were going to church," dictating a middle-class comportment.[19] When black activists disregarded injunctions to dress respectably, radical dress tended toward the ethnically inflected or paramilitary—like the black-clad, mutton-chopped, gun-toting Black Panthers that so appealed to Wolfe's critiqued New York elites.

A long history of involuntary poverty that necessitated secondhand acquisition caused many blacks to associate used clothing with the limits of structural racism. Actor and playwright Ossie Davis, for example, underscores this association when writing in 1965 about the obstacles facing black playwrights—specifically, he is remembering Lorraine Hansberry, the playwright best know for *A Raisin in the Sun*—when white audiences refuse to recognize poetic or political expressions outside of their specific expectations of the black arts movement. "Our limits," Davis writes, "are handed down to us, like second-hand clothes, from the white man. But what else is there with which to clothe our nakedness?"[20] For recipients of insufficient and patronizing philanthropy, there was little point in adopting clearly secondhand styles as markers of defiance. Similarly, in describing the limited opportunities that attracted southern blacks during the Great Migration, Amiri Baraka calls their neighborhoods, houses, schools, and jobs, all "secondhand." For striving blacks, hand-me-downs were emblems of oppression, not wedges into freedom from a stultified middle class.[21]

Despite rarely using poor clothing to dramatize their demands, marginalized groups played a vital role in establishing voluntary secondhand styles of dress for white, middle-class youth. For one thing, those for whom the rapidly multiplying opportunities for upward mobility were not available remained disproportionately represented among urban secondhand sellers as well as goods recipients; as mentioned in chapter 2, African Americans replaced Jews as the predominant dealers in street markets such as Maxwell Street in Chicago. But of course, many of the young people who would come to embrace an elective poverty in the 1950s and 1960s grew up in the suburbs. Beat writers, certainly, mostly hailed from middle-class backgrounds, as did many antiwar, antipoverty, and environmental activists. Second-wave feminism, criticized for its racialized and classist exclusivity, similarly counted white, suburban baby boomers central to their ranks. In suburbs, cross-class and cross-race interactions frequently revolved around participation in secondhand exchange—thanks to the popularity of benefits and community fund-raisers. In fact, the radicality of middle-class secondhand dress stemmed partly from a visual reversal of charitable roles; those taught to donate lightly worn apparel became the purveyors of those same sources.

Radical feminist Alix Kates Shulman grew up in midwestern suburbia. Shulman first gained widespread attention as the author of the controversial 1969 article "A Marriage Agreement," which detailed methods for dividing child care and housework equally between men and women. Shulman went on to become one of the most well-known feminist authors of her time. Her best-selling debut novel, *Memoirs of an Ex-Prom Queen* (1972), examines the contradictory expectations of privileged young women before the 1960s. Her second autobiographical novel, *Burning Questions* (1978), contextualizes the rise of the women's liberation movement—and in doing so, consistently highlights the importance of secondhand objects and elective poverty in materializing radical identities in the 1950s and 1960s. The book begins with a suburban rummage sale, described as formative in the life of her protagonist, Zane. A child of postwar suburbia, Zane aspires from preadolescence to have the "life of a rebel," a quest that carries her from a midwestern suburb to 1950s Greenwich Village, and from a beatnik bohemian youth through a marriage of compromise, to her eventual arrival as a key actor in second-wave feminism.[22] Zane's participation in her junior high rummage sale honed her nascent yearnings for rebellion—for distinction from middle-class rules and conformity.

Sponsors of such sales saw the events as a way to raise school funds and as a means of "character building" for the young suburbanites. As mentioned in chapter 3, such public fund-raisers demonstrated a postwar suburban commitment to civic responsibility—and relied on the frequent amassing and discarding of still-usable goods. In showing white, privileged kids how "the other half lived," such charitable work also introduced young suburbanites to perceptions, habits, and styles that went against suburban strictures. At the rummage sale, Zane encounters nonwhite, nonsuburban, nonaffluent people. The first aspect of difference she remarks on is not that of skin tone or mannerism but of fashion. The rummage sale patrons dressed in color combinations that "were forbidden" in her suburban hometown of Babylon.[23] "Such combinations as green with blue, orange with red (or red with pink or pink with orange), brown with black, or purple with anything were considered quite untenable. Such breaches of taste variously called loud, gauche, stupid, Italian,

Jew, were simply prohibited without anyone's ever questioning why. And now gradually the room was filling up with people who so consistently violated these simple, basic rules that one could only conclude they were unaware of it."[24]

That evening, Zane lays out her cherry-red sweater and pink pleated skirt, vowing to her picture of a shorn-headed Joan of Arc that she will "wear the forbidden combination to school."[25] Her first deliberate act of cultural rebellion is sartorial, inspired by the rummage sale's racial, class, and cultural heterogeneity, and exposure to style choices undictated by familiar propriety. Assumed by some to be limiting, the hodgepodge array available at secondhand venues, coupled with more lenient dress practices, invited imaginative costuming. Through decades of personal striving for an activist life, Zane relies on secondhand commerce to define her own image as one anchored by defiance and originality—and as pointedly un-middle class.

After high school, Zane soon left her suburb for New York City, joining throngs of white middle-class youth in a reversal of recent migration patterns.[26] Nationwide, "white flight" from urban centers like New York City drained cities of economic resources and increased ethnic and racial heterogeneity in the postwar years.[27] Young refugees from the isolation of the suburbs and the influences of homogenous mass culture filled some of that abandoned space.[28] For a second time, a postwar industrial boom bypassed Greenwich Village, leaving affordable urban housing. New manufacturers looked outside of cities, and especially to the Sunbelt states. Even before the term "Beat" was brought to a broad audience in John Clellon Holmes's 1952 article "This Is the Beat Generation," a collection of college dropouts and urbanizing thrill-seekers recognized that while New York City (and specifically the Village) was declining economically and politically, its cultural influence was expanding.[29]

Burning Questions portrays the importance of neighborhood and housing to the self-consciously bohemian identities of some new urbanites. In considering whether to move into her first Village "quasi-legal, cold-water flat," Zane is swayed by the place's bohemian past. The history is more than architectural—though the tin ceilings and gingerbread moldings have their own special éclat. Evidence of hip revolving-door tenancies is scattered throughout the rent-controlled walk-up: sculptures strewn about from three occupants ago, a glass bookcase with "the complete works of every writer who's ever lived here," and most appealing, a general sense of intentional unkemptness. "It's shabby disrepair had its own value: to free you of responsibility."[30] Barely a decade after widespread housing shortages, which peaked in the early days of the wartime baby boom, the practical, tidy, and affordable tract houses were anathema to a growing number of youth renouncing their middle-class backgrounds.

The Beat Generation

In the late 1940s and 1950s, the Village's "shabby disrepair" once again, as it had in the years surrounding World War I, drew those looking to be freed of certain expectations—of religion, family, class, or gender. Among those migrants were the poets and artists whom magazines would soon stereotype and homogenize as black-wearing, cigarette-smoking "beatniks" for a disapproving and fascinated public.[31] White men like Jack Kerouac, Allen Ginsberg, Neal Cassady, and William S. Burroughs were quickly recognized as central figures of the "Beat Generation," while white women such as Joyce Johnson and Diane Di Prima, though important to the emerging literary (and sartorial) aesthetic, struggled to attain the intellectual acknowledgment of the androcentric group and its followers. Innovative black writers like LeRoi Jones (later Amiri Baraka) and Ted Joans were cast as peripheral members and had political voices that rang beyond the bounds of most Beat reflection. As East Coast Beats gathered in the downwardly mobile Village, the North Beach of San Francisco and Venice, California, attracted similar crowds. Some individuals criss-crossed the coasts in a continental ping-pong game of Beat socialization like that depicted in some of Kerouac's novels.[32]

Allen Ginsberg asserted that "the essence of the phrase 'beat generation' can be found in one of Jack Kerouac's most celebrated axioms, 'Everything belongs to me because I am poor.'"[33] This fundamental maxim was part of the spontaneous prose added to the original manuscript of *On the Road*, which became part of *Visions of Cody*, Kerouac's experimental novel, written in 1951–52 (published in 1972). In *Visions of Cody*, the phrase appears consolatory at first, evoked in the wake of yearning for a beautiful, unattainable girl outside of St. Patrick's Cathedral. Kerouac's mission to "sanctify the world" from profane visions places the book's narrator at the cathedral, remarking wistfully on his own holy poverty, that is, his lacking of both material possessions and sexual accomplishments.[34]

"Everything belongs to me because I am poor" was a renunciation of worldly pleasures, but particularly of both material and familial middle-class trappings. The idea that creative abandon required a life of spontaneity, necessarily untrammeled by possessions (as well as most interpersonal commitments) ran throughout Beat literature and poetry. While in practice, Beat simplicity sometimes involved theft and wasteful living, many Beats at least periodically embraced the material minimalism of Ralph Waldo Emerson, Henry David Thoreau, and Zen Buddhist philosophies. As Beat poet Lew Welch wrote in the 1950s, "Going to Mexico by motorcycle would be the coolest, but / Thoreau warns against any undertaking that requires new clothes."[35]

Admiration of poverty dovetailed with the Beats' renowned fascination with African Americans. Kerouac recycled "Everything belongs to me because I am poor" in 1959 for a short piece sold to a cheap girlie magazine, *Escapade*.[36] "The Beginning of Bop" cast key architects of bop—Dizzy Gillespie, Charlie Parker, and Thelonious Monk—as "12th Century monks high in winter belfries of the Gothic Organ." They waited "like witchdoctors," "miserable cold and broke," saying "Everything belongs to me because I am poor."[37] Poverty was a way of spiritual, intellectual, and aesthetic transcendence; elective poverty was a way of expressing solidarity across the social boundaries of race, class, and mystical beliefs.

The Beat preoccupation with jazz performers and black hipsters articulated the romance of racial outsiderness to mainstream America. An appearance of elective poverty had at least implicit links to black hipness as well. In his 1957 essay "The White Negro," Norman Mailer described how white "hipsters" grafted expressions of black experiences onto the suffering of white outsiders. Or, as Werner Sollors put it, "for the sake of convenience, the Bohemian might call 'Negro' everything he thought white America unjustly repressed."[38] Certain, not necessarily poor-looking, aspects of fashion popularly recognized as Beat, and then beatnik by the late 1950s, relied directly on African American influences—sometimes by way of Paris bohemians, as Paris had long been a sanctuary for black performers. Fashion historian Linda Welters attributes at least three elements of beatnik appearance—beret, eyewear, and goatee—to Dizzy Gillespie specifically. Though Gillespie did not use heroin like many jazz musicians of the time, he had sensitive eyes due to repeated infections and wore dark glasses on stage against the glare of stage lights, preferring horn-rimmed glasses—like those favored by Allen Ginsberg—for their durability. The goatee reportedly cushioned his trumpet's mouthpiece and prevented skin irritation. The beret Gillespie picked up from his French travels, adopting the style in 1937, sometimes using the soft hat as a back-up trumpet mute. In adopting black musicians' affectations, middle-class white Americans were following sartorial standards set in bohemian Paris and filtered through an American jazz sensibility—especially that of bebop, whose rhythms permeated Beat writing.[39]

Although supposed patterns of Beat style emerged over time, neither male nor female Beats displayed the level of black-clad uniformity portrayed by the popular press (and adopted by young followers who, in turn, would rebel against that image by becoming colorfully clad "hippies").[40] Before popular magazines such as *Life*, *Look*, and *Time* forwarded a persona of dark, minimalist disrepair in 1956 and 1957, Beat costumes were not easily defined, aside from a general preference for casual clothing such as chinos, jeans, sweatshirts, T-shirts, and flannel. Even that tendency, as evidenced by William S. Burroughs's habitual suit, tie, and hat, was by no means standard. Perhaps as the Beat born closest to genuine upper-class status, Burroughs felt less determined to disavow standards associated with middle-class propriety by dressing down.[41]

The attire worn to Allen Ginsberg's famed reading of "Howl" in October 1955 at Six Gallery in San Francisco illustrated the variety in Beat garb and underscored the prevalence of a secondhand aesthetic at this, the Beat movement's cohering event. In Michael McClure's account of the gathering, master of ceremonies Kenneth Rexroth presided "elegant in a handsome thriftshop suit," a 1920s-ish, pin-striped one specially purchased at Goodwill for the occasion.[42] Ginsberg wore a conservative charcoal gray suit, white shirt, and tie, though Kerouac describes him in a fictionalized account of the reading as one of several "hornrimmed intellectual hepcats with wild black hair," and McClure as a "delicate pale handsome poet . . . (in a suit)."[43] Gary Snyder provided the most variety in Kerouac's fictionalized account. Among poets in "various costumes, worn-at-the-sleeves corduroy jackets, scuffly shoes," Snyder's character didn't *look* like a poet, in "rough workingman's clothes he'd bought secondhand in Goodwill stores."[44]

In addition to the thorough mix of clothing styles at Six Gallery, used goods of other sorts were well represented at the reading, which featured artist Fred Martin's found objects.[45] Secondhand goods had powerful currency among Beats on both coasts as delegates of delinquency from middle-class environs. They also served as inspirational tokens, in ways akin to—and referencing—surrealist interpretations. Whether, as with Snyder, the used clothes emphasized rough experiences camping and working as a logger (rather than his formal Reeds education), or, like Rexroth, thrift shopping produced a parody of an authoritative style of "gangster" rebellion, used goods expressed nonconformity and a belief in reinvention.[46]

Scholars have described the middle-class backgrounds of Beats as formative to their literary and personal styles, often as the things against which they reacted.[47] Almost uniformly, they sought stimulation outside the cultures of their upbringing.[48] Since for many, familiar society was an affluent, consumer-oriented, middle-class one, elective poverty (and secondhand commerce) offered imagined entrée into beathood. Tellingly, Beats from genuinely downtrodden pasts, like Neal Cassady, Kerouac's original Beat icon, had more conflicted ideas about secondhand clothing. Cassady, born into down-and-out circumstances, did not share other (more affluently raised) Beats' associations of secondhand or "beat" clothing with freedom. After his mother died when he was ten, Cassady grew up with an alcoholic father, dividing his adolescence between skid row and reform school. In his autobiographical novel, *The First Third*, Cassady's protagonist wakes next to his father's "drink-swollen face" early in the morning and dons "hated remnants of brother Jimmy's clothes; too-short shoes and knickers which crept above my knees." He walks past "musty-smelling secondhand stores."[49] Though reluctant to rise economically by ordinary "respectable" paths, Cassady resisted a classic romanticization of poverty, instead glorifying fast cars and complicated amorous entanglements.

Jack Kerouac's own relationship with a secondhand aesthetic was ambivalent, as were most of his ideals and desires. Generally, he vacillated between a conventional urge to "live, work, and raise a family" and a periodic craving to divest himself of those goals and indulge in the madness of his friends.[50] Yet sometimes Kerouac's romanticization of poverty was a defense of what was to him tradition rather than a deviance from social norms. Kerouac's parents were of working-class backgrounds, and his father moved his young family from Canada to Lowell, Massachusetts—where Jack and his sibling grew up—to take a job running a small newspaper, elevating the clan to only marginally middle-class status.[51] The family's tenuous status suffered more after Kerouac's father began to gamble. Young Jack sought to rescue the family with a football scholarship to Columbia but dropped out as his father succumbed to alcoholism; Jack then took to hanging out with Ginsberg, Burroughs, and Cassady in New York. After his father died, Kerouac and his mother were periodically poor. In *Desolation Angels* (written in the late 1950s), Kerouac describes the "junks of life" he and his mother pack in preparation for a move from Florida to California. In regarding their piles of "essentials," he evokes the deprivation of the Depression with a childish nostalgia for days when "old men with burlap bags at night fished thru garbage cans."[52] But in "1957 prosperous America," people laughed at their junk much as they laughed as Kerouac's own unfashionable love of his mother and the peace he derived from her passé domestic skills. Kerouac's tender description of "memere" mending his raucously rended clothing, and his admiration of her adeptness of reuse, signals his belief in material and spiritual redemption and in his mother's ability to attain it for him: "A minor cigarette hole in old jeans is suddenly patched with pieces of 1940 jean."[53] Here, old things, secondhand patches, are icons of nostalgia and simplicity, emblematic of home, security, and maternal love.

Kerouac often depicted a struggle between desiring, on the one hand, the stability of his mother's care or his own "traditional" family, or both, the discipline of hard work, and the guilt and comfort of his native Catholicism; and on the other hand, the stimulation of wild, drunken, craven ramblings like those in the autobiographical *On the Road*, which details Kerouac's and Cassady's travels through the United States and Mexico. In the work that would make him famous, Kerouac's fictional stand-in follows the impetuous Dean Moriarty (modeled on Neal Cassady), the patron saint of irresponsibility and emblem of the freeing potential of destitution.[54] Antimaterialism is an uneven refrain in *On the Road*. Without altogether foregoing material delights, the hero Moriarty conspicuously eschews earnestly acquired ownership, preferring illegitimacy and theft.

In *On the Road*, clothes are approvingly tattered, old, washed-out, cracked, frayed, ragged, baggy, greasy, bug-smeared, torn, belly-hanging, and yes, beat, but their manner of acquisition or secondhand status goes unmentioned.[55] It is not until *Dharma Bums*, Kerouac's 1958 follow-up to *On the Road*, that Kerouac assigns secondhand acquisition a philosophical meaning, one that reflected his (and other Beats') exploration of Eastern mysticism, which for a time funneled Kerouac's attraction to Catholicism into an updated spiritual pursuit. In *Dharma Bums*, Kerouac's fictional foster self pursues a role model quite unlike Cassady, one who represents transcendent asceticism and a usually more restrained and studious version of freedom than that of Cassady. The new role model, Japhy Ryder, fashioned after poet Gary Snyder, is a college-educated "Northwest boy" whose "real" education derived from deep in the woods of eastern Oregon.[56] Not only did Ryder's style signal blue collar, but his clothes, which served him on his mountain hikes, campfires, and hitchhiking, were recycled from the cast-offs of men who actually made livings from logging and construction. In a positive twist on how previous generations feared the physical contagions clinging to pre-owned clothes, voluntary secondhand patrons sometimes imagined a mystical transference of the donors' supposed aptitudes.

Ryder (Snyder) derived much of his inspiration from Eastern philosophies, especially Buddhism, at a time when interest in Buddhism in the United States was just starting to rise. A minimalist "Zen Lunacy" inspires

Ryder's prophecy of "a great rucksack revolution," including masses of wandering youth, praying in mountains and refusing to work for the "privilege of consuming."[57] Ryder needs just a rucksack, food, and a good pair of shoes. Recalling that elective poverty often depended on some clue that the apparent destitution was voluntary the details of that footwear are important: "mountain-climbing boots, expensive ones, his pride and joy, Italian made."[58] Schulman outlines a similar signifier in *The Burning Question*. On the cusp of her first affair with a woman, a consummation of her feminism and recurrent defiance of middle-class life, Zane pauses to assess the setting, finding her soon-to-be lover's home décor consistent with that of "the sordid romances" of her beatnik youth: "Lumpy mattress on the floor beside a whitewashed brick wall in the upper reaches of a heatless walkup. Posters on the wall in place of prints, cheap California wine, marijuana, stacks of precious books, and even an expensive hi-fi (the one invariable luxury marking the poverty as partly voluntary, decade after decade)."[59]

Consistent with elective poverty's imperative to signal the owner's voluntariness, Ryder does not represent a wholesale rejection of consumption but a selective adjustment. Where and how he consumes is as important as how much. Despite his near-phobic avoidance of other retail sites, Ryder scours thrift-shop aisles for old hand-me-downs with a "bemused and happy expression," proving he can derive joy from shopping.[60] For Ryder, thrift stores are approved ways to consume, and in his abandonment there he echoes the inverted dandyism of James Agee's delight in factory seconds—and ignores the corporatized structure of many postwar thrift stores and their role in encouraging an accelerated pace of consumerism. Once again, the perceived *désenchaînement*—to echo Breton—of secondhand commerce validates a limited arena of shopping for anticapitalist artists. This key term Breton used, *désenchaînement*, can be roughly translated as "disconnected," but also as "disenchantment"—redolent of a comedown or degradation—and well suits elective poverty.

For poet Gary Snyder himself, secondhand commerce merged a political concern for the destruction of natural environments and a spiritual interest in self-denial. Snyder studied Zen Buddhism in Japan, and in an article encouraging the combining of two disparate traditions, "Buddhist Anarchism," he advocated for, among other things, the adoption of "voluntary poverty."[61] Snyder's choice of natural settings for his poems, and his advocacy for the preservation and enjoyment of wilderness earned him the label "poet Laureate of deep ecology."[62] Snyder's environmental focus foreshadowed widespread concern over natural ecosystems even before Rachel Carson documented the detrimental effects of pesticides in *Silent Spring* (1962), inspiring public protest of chemical company practices and jump-starting the modern environmental movement.[63] Snyder vocally opposed an economy based on a throwaway culture, and relatedly lauded the moral superiority of secondhand goods, prefiguring the environmentalist slogan "Reduce, Reuse, Recycle."

In "Bubbs Creek Haircut," mostly penned in 1960, Snyder portrayed secondhand sales venues as not only positive consumer spaces but as pathways on a journey to understanding wilderness, both inside oneself and in the natural environment.[64] Before beginning his trek, the narrator gets a haircut and goes to Goodwill to look for a sweater, where he imaginatively animates the "unfixed junk" and demonstrates empathy for the abandoned goods—in a way that is reminiscent of Guido Bruno's 1920 modernist tale, "Midnight in a Pawn Shop."[65] As he begins a long trek through the Sierras, Goodwill reappears in reminiscences as part of a spiritualized triumvirate of thrift stores alongside St. Vincent de Paul and the Salvation Army: "A.G. [Allen Ginsberg] and me got winter clothes for nothing," a statement arguably ignoring or undervaluing the poorly recompensed labor of Goodwill workers.[66] A ways up the trail, boulders transform into the "sag-asst" chairs of Goodwill, and the question arises of whether the proprietor is "King of Hell" or leader of a paradise of sorts, ruling over objects "freed" of their originally imposed purposes. Throughout the narrator's journey, Goodwill especially signifies, with the commercial space standing in for the attribute. In the course of an eco-spiritual journey, thrift stores became sacred spaces. After ecstatic meditation, the objects in the Goodwill basement become the wild nature: "a room of empty sun or peaks and ridges / beautiful spirits, / rocking lotus throne: / a universe of junk, all left alone."[67] Garbage becomes something beautiful in its unviability, or its potential as something unplanned in the original production, a sentiment that is Dada-esque in its reflection, if not its poetic format.

The New Left and the Rise of the Hippies

Throughout the 1960s, secondhand advocates attributed anticommercial, political meaning to an appearance of elective poverty, to secondhand shopping itself, and even to (a curated category of) "garbage." Along the way, the look of elective poverty changed. By 1960, when Snyder published "Bubbs Creek Haircut," it seemed to many aspiring Beats that their image had been commodified and sullied by an eager press. Once again, rent in Greenwich Village grew costlier as the image of the Beat generation "sold books, sold black turtleneck sweaters and bongos, berets and dark glasses, sold a way of life that seemed like dangerous fun—thus to be either condemned or imitated. Suburban couples could have beatnik parties on Saturday nights and drink too much and fondle each other's wives," according to Beat writer Joyce Johnson.[68] The fall of 1957, Johnson observed, marked the moment when Village painters began to make money and "turn up self-consciously in stiff new brown corduroy suits." That same fall, the Village-housed, upwardly mobile Salzmans scrambled to fill their raccoon coat orders for Ivy League collegians. By 1960, Greenwich Village had emerged from another fashionably downtrodden postwar moment. As rent increased, a new wave of bohemian youth drifted to the East Village side of New York City, just as North Beach in California gave way to Haight-Ashbury as the hip, affordable Bay Area destination. Secondhand persisted as a symbol of bohemian lifestyle, but it adopted new aesthetics. According to Johnson, some of the "old ladies" in the area retaliated to both media stereotypes and new-money styles "by picking up the wilder stuff in thrift shops—Spanish combs and beaded dresses from the twenties that ripped under the arms if danced in too energetically. They draped themselves in embroidered piano shawls, put on purple mesh stockings, and called themselves Beat Pre-Raphaelites."[69] In other words, Beats began to look like hippies, a term used but not widespread until 1967, when applied by Herb Caen, the same San Francisco journalist credited with coining the term "beatnik" shortly after the launch of the Russian satellite Sputnik in 1958.

The sixties—a term intending to convey the activities of an era, not strictly the decade—were full of contrasts and contradictions, yet readily reduced to iconic images. Not unlike in the twenties, the same epoch that saw a rise in radical leftist politics saw the flourishing of encroaching conservatism. The same group of youngsters critiqued for their apolitical self-centeredness and carefree licentiousness counted members who fought for the equal rights of minorities and women, and against an increasingly unpopular war. Fashion of the decade met with similar divergences and intersections, even when limited to voluntary secondhand styles. The uses of secondhand clothing well illustrated the shifting range of sartorial motives in the sixties. From antiestablishment Beats to politically engaged members of the New Left, to radical anticapitalists such as the San Francisco Diggers, secondhand clothing was integral to the disjunctive journey of sixties society.

The same year Harrington's *The Other America* took the country by storm, the Students for Democratic Society (SDS) produced the manifesto of "the New Left," expressing disenchantment with the United States' postwar capitalist agenda and linking the material goods consumption valued by older generations to problems as diverse as domestic poverty, racial inequality, and war—that list would continue to expand, including gender inequity and environmental destruction before the end of the decade.[70] The first paragraph of the original 1962 draft of the Port Huron Statement ended with a list of "problems so serious as to actually threaten civilization," the last of which was that "we treat newness with a normalcy that suggests a deliberate flight from reality." In echoes of the words of social scientists such as Vance Packard, the statement describes the oppressive nature of American consumerism, with business practices of planned obsolescence, "commodity glut," and the psychological creation of "pseudo-needs" forcing the isolated individual into work undertaken solely to satisfy material desires.[71] Among other recommendations, New Left students advocated for a government "program against poverty."[72] Indeed, President Johnson's administration would soon move in that direction, only to be derailed by the economic, political, and social costs of an unwinnable war in Vietnam.

One oft-repeated narrative about the (mostly white and middle-class) New Left youth is that their enthusiasm waned as the decade went on, as the civil rights movement spawned such divergent reactions as the black power movement and Nixon's "southern strategy," and as movement cohesiveness proved illusory. Love-ins, drugs, sex, and rock and roll, in this simplified story, replaced sit-ins, protests, and organized political efforts. This version elides disparate actors and ignores complicated overlaps, but an apolitical subset of bohemians did coalesce in certain regions, eventually attracting thousands of experimental young people to places like San Francisco and New York City. On 5 September 1965, journalist Michael Fallon wrote about the Blue Unicorn coffeehouse in Haight-Ashbury, referring to it as a "new haven" for a fresh generation of beatniks drifting into the area from North Beach: hippies (who, incidentally, could browse the free secondhand clothing boxes there, taking what they needed).[73] Older Beats observing the styles on the East Side in New York City also adopted "hippie" as a term of derision, employing the diminutive to suggest hipsters who did not quite get it.[74] Even earlier, the word purportedly referred to white emulation of blacks, echoing the impressions of hipsters charted in Mailer's "White Negro." For example, in his 1964 memoir about 1940s Harlem, Malcolm X recalls "hippy" as a word African Americans used to describe white men who "acted more Negro than Negroes."[75]

In the early 1960s, North Beach beatnik life lured the young and rebellious to the proximity of Haight-Ashbury, where cheap bedraggled Victorian houses both enabled a new bohemian enclave and helped describe an emerging aesthetic. Media descriptions of free love, drugs, and a communal repudiation of productive society soon made Haight-Ashbury a key destination for dropouts and runaways, and the center of a hippie life pursuant of exception from everything middle class, including politics. An imagined idyll of free love and nonmonetary interactions soon gave way to a harsher reality that included heavy drug use—notably heroin—which diminished community resources and decreased personal safely (spurring many instances of rape and violence).[76] For many of its older habitués, Haight-Ashbury was well downhill by 1967, when the "summer of love" brought approximately one hundred thousand (mostly young) people to the neighborhood.[77] New, firsthand businesses mass-marketing hippie styles greeted the influx of aimless dropouts and runaways—some who came with financial support, and many who were deliberately profligate with what little they had, in true, well-charted bohemian form. By the time of the Monterey Pop Festival, a three-day concert held in Monterey, California, in June 1967, famously featuring secondhand-dressing rock star Janis Joplin, "hip capitalists" were elbowing original designers and makeshift co-ops for storefront space along Haight-Ashbury.

Chapter 4 of this book details the transcontinental evolution of a Victorian-inspired 1960s hippie aesthetic—a style more properly the realm of vintage exhibitionism than elective poverty, though claiming elements of each. But at the same time that a florid and showy hippie aesthetic blossomed at the Golden Gate Park and young acid heads were dropping out, student activists at San Francisco State were staging historic antiwar and antipoverty protests. In *Mau-Mauing the Flak Catchers*, his companion piece to *Radical Chic*, Tom Wolfe lampoons the elective poverty styles of these white, middle-class San Francisco students, who wore clothing that was "righteous and 'with the people.'" Wolfe's point is that they missed the sartorial mark, that the students' "real *funky* jeans, and woolly green socks, the kind you get at the Army surplus at two pair for twenty-nine cents" were a far cry from "authentic" ghetto style, where James-Brown dressers donned ruffled white shirts and slick new accessories.[78] True, the Panthers, with their tight leather, visible weapons, and Afros, looked very different from a midwestern suburban-bred young women wearing secondhand Levis and "lumpy lumberjack shirts," but the styles were parallel expressions of radical defiance. Wolfe assumes styles of direct emulation, but in reality, student protesters and Black Panthers were each thumbing their noses at middle-class authority in ways distinctly suited to their disparate backgrounds.

Free Stores and Utopian Garbage

Whether newly purchased or cobbled together and homemade, whether plain and ugly, or elaborate and flashy, the eclectic, dissident styles of late-1960s youth underscored the tumultuousness of a time marked by growing social, political, and economic instability. By 1968, media coverage of student protests, open drug use and displays of sexuality, draft dodging, political assassinations, and dissatisfaction over the Vietnam quagmire portrayed a country in turmoil. The styles attendant to what appeared to be generational discord—but were actually the early battles in a decades-long culture war that criss-crossed age brackets—evolved throughout the sixties. Mainstream commercial interests attuned to what *Vogue* editor Diana Vreeland dubbed a "Youthquake" marketed newly produced clothing and other goods reflecting the latest rebellious aesthetic.[79] In the mid-to late-1960s, advocacy of secondhand commerce and styles grew alongside protests of just such market targeting, as well as protests of war, poverty, and sexism.

Angry responses to hip capitalism produced an increasingly politicized advocacy for elective poverty, combining New Left politics, radical theatricality, and reactionary hippie fashions, especially in places with growing hippie populations such as Haight-Ashbury in San Francisco; East Side, New York City; and Little Five Points, Atlanta. Underground newspapers and community organizations expressed the terms of discontentment with hip capitalism. In San Francisco, activists and improvisational actors (mostly from the guerilla theater group the San Francisco Mime Troupe) formed The Diggers in 1966 in part to combat store-bought hip. The group, which took their name from Protestant agrarian radicals in mid-seventeenth-century England, called themselves "community anarchists." They vied against the general apoliticism of the Haight-Ashbury crowd and criticized groups profiting from "helping" the young pilgrims who rapidly discovered that the Haight's resources were not infinite—groups that, for example, paid newcomers very little to make hippie handcrafts in turn sold to other Haight-Ashbury sojourners.[80]

The Diggers—of whom Emmett Grogan and Peter Coyote were perhaps the most well-known, though the group's philosophy advocated anonymity and professed equality among members—distributed protest pamphlets, gave goods and clothing away at free stores, served free meals at the Golden Gate Park, and staged theatrical protests such as the October 1967 "Death of the Hippie March," a faux funeral protesting the commercialization of hippie aesthetics.[81] As one of the most "recognizable symbols of hippie politics," the Diggers fought against a pattern of mounting political disengagement among their peers.[82] "Free stores" featuring secondhand items were part of the Diggers' proposed solution to social problems—the cultivation of a society not dependent on monetary exchange. According to Digger Peter Coyote, "The Diggers understood that *style* was infinitely co-optable. What could not be co-opted was doing things for free, without money."[83] Similarly, many politically inspired secondhand dressers argued that while styles based on secondhand materials could be co-opted, the actual use of recirculated, reused, and repurposed goods was much more difficult to commandeer—a claim that, while not entirely inaccurate, again dismisses the corporatized systems of much secondhand distribution.

For the Diggers, though, secondhand status of items was not the primary emphasis—free was. However the goods were acquired and whatever their previous statuses, the important part was free redistribution. In Diggers' broadsides and pamphlets proposing antimonetary systems, they provoked "hip capitalists" and tried to politicize hip consumers. In a pamphlet titled *The Trip without a Ticket*—also the name of the free store—the Diggers allied monetary commerce with war, oppression, self-loathing, insanity, and interpersonal estrangement.[84] In addition, the original free store name, "The Trip without a Ticket," perhaps references one of London's premier clothing boutiques offering vintage selections, "Granny Takes a Trip." Approving commentators referred to the store as a "hip Salvation Army"—even though according to Emmett Grogan only a "fraction of the goods used and accepted were secondhand and they were made available and displayed to affect a Salvation-Goodwill-salvage cover to conceal the fact that the rest of the stuff was new and fresh and had been stolen."[85] The Diggers' radical aims and their open willingness to steal firsthand consumer items obscured their endorsements of the principled *re*-use of commercial goods.

The Diggers clearest success was in establishing attention-getting theatrics and humor as part of hippie politics. Influenced in part by Diggers members, Abbie Hoffman and Jerry Rubin, along with Anita Hoffman, Nancy Kurshan, and Paul Krassner, founded an absurdist political party intending to link cultural separatists and political protesters. Members of the Yippies or Youth International Party (so named late in 1967, well into their nationally noticed antics) loosely choreographed massive protest events, using underground media networks to galvanize previously apolitical hippies. Hoffman especially saw in secondhand commerce common ground between aesthetic and political rebellions—between the New Left ideals and the hippie image— and he and Rubin were the chief forces behind Yippie renown, as well as its rapid decline. Older and more educated than most of the summer-of-love dropouts, Hoffman's civil rights actions in the 1950s while earning his master's degree in psychology at the University of California, Berkeley, and his participation in SNCC's Freedom Summers in Mississippi in 1964 and 1965, well primed him for activist leadership.[86]

In 1966, Hoffman moved from California to a New York City East Village tenement, recommitting himself to activism (after a divorce) by opening Liberty House—a cooperative store selling homemade goods produced by the Poor People's Cooperative in Mississippi to raise funds for the civil rights movement—and regularly contributing to underground papers, such as the *Village Voice* and *Liberation*.[87] At first, the apolitical attitudes of the East Village hippies disturbed Hoffman, but their creative appearances attracted him. Much like the Beats from North Beach transformed into the Haight-Ashbury hippies, would-be Greenwich Village bohemians moved into the East Village, and in greater numbers than either the 1910s Greenwich Village modernists or the postwar Beats. Secondhand clothes fueled theatrical parades at St. Mark's Place, and the most devoted actors increased the outrageousness of their appearance in resistance to the fashion industry's imitation of secondhand styles—much as older female Beats had begun to do a few years before in Greenwich Village. By 1967, New York City bohemians had moved backward from a 1920s flapper dress fad (after mainstream department stores mass-produced new versions), introducing more whimsical elements of Victorian and Edwardian style, reminiscent of and influenced by San Francisco and London styles.[88]

Hoffman and Rubin sought to ally cultural and political radicals by including psychedelic public displays of style, music, and rebellion in practices of the antiwar coalition.[89] Secondhand goods played a direct role in many Vietnam War protests. For example, when planning for the absurdist exorcism of the Pentagon on 21 October 1967 to protest U.S. involvement in Vietnam, Hoffman relied on the creative community to costume participants. The two van loads of materials came mostly from secondhand stores, rummage sales, and the Diggers-style Free Store in New York City. The collectively costumed attempt to levitate the government building has been called an example of Dadaist art, "one of the significant collective aesthetic antiwar protests of the period."[90] Once again, secondhand goods and surrealism joined forces as twelve hundred people dressed as priests, witches, rabbis, gurus, sorcerers, and so forth, invoked deities, and chanted (mostly "Out Demons Out") in the parking lot of the home of the U.S. Department of Defense. The spectacle generated massive attention to the antiwar cause, and included the participation of diverse luminaries, from Dr. Benjamin Spock to Norman Mailer, who recounts the event in his dual historical text/novel *Armies of the Night: History as a Novel, the Novel as History*.[91]

Abbie Hoffman also used a Diggers-style Free Store to generate media attention and publicity for poverty aid and antiwar activism in the Lower East Side. At the store's opening, he invited neighborhood kids to congregate and play dress-up. Hoffman's successful publicity for the store attracted the growing class of professional used clothing dealers, who took advantage of the free stock.[92] While the store did succeed in getting Hoffman and related issues even more recognition, it was a practical failure. Responsibility for the store's management passed haphazardly to whomever was available, from hippies to bikers to transients, and for a while the store became the focus of cross-class, interracial tensions in the area, resulting in destruction, violence, and rape on the premises.[93] Mostly undeterred, Hoffman clung to the idea of a free store as capable of creating self-sufficient community; he claimed that free networks of all kinds—free housing, free medicine, free clothing, and free food—could be sponsored by the excess of mainstream consumer society. "A utopia would rise out of the garbage," Hoffman later declared about the concept of free goods in his theatrical autobiography *Soon to Be a Major Motion Picture*.[94]

By the late 1960s, garbage was on many American minds. Just months before the first Earth Day in 1970—where the establishment of the slogan "Reduce, Reuse, Recycle" again expanded the political resonance of secondhand exchange—President Nixon's State of the Union highlighted the national importance of the growing environmental movement, asserting that "wealth and happiness" were not synonymous. *Time* agreed, warning the populace that "[t]he U.S. environment is seriously threatened by the prodigal garbage of the world's richest economy."[95] For environmentalists, reuse also became an ecological imperative, one that could be linked to cultural creativity and used to solve the problem of suburban isolation and artistic stagnation. From the beginning of the popular call-to-arms over environmental distress in the United States, conversations centered on the harm of affluence—and its relation to effluence. In rhetoric such as Hoffman's and the Diggers', "garbage" became useful. In "Garbage or Nothing," the Diggers called trash "a medium." "Let's use it to act out our fantasies, use it for unimaginable gratifications." In rebelling against the perceived fastidiousness of older generations, whose experience with the necessity of reuse bred contempt for the practice, "garbage" became a resource. "Diggers assume free stores to liberate human nature," they proposed, quoting Gary Snyder's proto-environmental claim that "Distrust of wildness in oneself literally means distrust of Wilderness."[96] By quoting poets such as Gary Snyder, the Diggers and Hoffman bridged a gap between the

Beat movement and the emerging environmentalist movement in part by advocating for the use of secondhand materials.

Hip Capitalism and the Underground Press

The Yippies most renowned event took place in Chicago during the 1968 Democratic National Convention, when they staged a "Festival of Life" to counter what many believed was a mockery of liberal politics. The Yippies sought a media blitz, and police teargassing the unpermitted revelers in Lincoln Park was nearly as widely broadcast as the proceedings inside the convention center. Hoffman, Rubin, and six other radicals were charged with conspiracy to incite a riot. The "Chicago Seven" stood trial (Black Panther Bobby Seale's trial was conducted separately) after Nixon took office in 1969, signaling the temporary defeat of the Democratic Party in national politics.

As indicated by their name's implied disregard for Old Left politics, New Left activists had scarcely more faith in the existing liberal politicians than in conservative ones. Harsh critique plagued status quo politics in general following the breakdown of the liberal consensus. By the mid-1960s, the mainstream media, increasingly concentrated in fewer and fewer hands, had joined the ranks of the untrustable old guard. Underground newspapers sprouted up in American cities as part of a widespread youth movement's suspicion of "establishment media." Independently published newspapers, many originating from college campuses, sought to break the perceived press monopoly. In May 1964, the *Los Angeles Free Press* became the first underground paper to publish regularly. Within four years, the *Free Press* boasted a circulation of one hundred thousand and a $2 million budget.[97] For the most part, underground papers focused on issues relevant to self-identified antiestablishment youth, and most reporters participated in the protests, concerts, love-ins, and demonstrations about which they wrote—both approvingly and critically.[98]

Underground newspapers from Berkeley's *Barb* to Atlanta's *The Great Speckled Bird* took ending domestic poverty and opposing the Vietnam War as central to their papers' mission, and regularly excoriated capitalism as complicit in both problems. Early in 1969, a *Speckled Bird* journalist looked around at the commercialization of Atlanta's Little Five Points, an area comparable in its postwar bohemian transformation to Haight-Ashbury and New York City's East Village. As the Diggers saw in Haight-Ashbury and Hoffman saw in the East Village, the radicality of Five Points had been diluted by a new, hip version of that anathema, the middle class: "Bread and chicks and the all-American middle-class scene all over again, only this time with bell bottoms and long hair."⁹⁹ Hippie enclaves simultaneously overrun by slumming middle-class youth and new hip capitalists highlighted the paradoxes of the success of dissident styles. In another *Speckled Bird* article, chiefly about the musical extravaganza Woodstock, a reporter roasted those buying brand names in imitation of the genuinely poor. Referring to the mostly white, relatively privileged festival attendees as well as hip Five Points residents, the author negatively compared a cheapened, newly produced style of elective poverty to cross-cultural musical appropriations. The "revolutionary energy of rock and of the movement is a response to oppression—it grew out of the blues, out of the poor white country music, out of the emancipated poverty of the street people and their drug scene."¹⁰⁰ A related "emancipated poverty" also encouraged newly produced versions of liberated styles "cut from finer cloth—bell bottoms, groovy vests, mucho hair, svelte girls in granny glasses. On the poor side, it's hip . . . on the rich side, it's a schuck, it's an Imitation of Hip. It's fancy boutique clothes cut to look like old surplus clothes which the street people once wore out of poverty, thereby creating a style."¹⁰¹

The article identifies cross-class appropriation of fashions as more problematic than white appropriation of black musical styles and also assumes that the roots of secondhand styles were solely found among the genuinely poor and oppressed. Often, *The Bird* touted secondhand consumerism as a solution to the rising new goods market for culturally rebellious styles, frankly advocating for a boycott of new goods, executed by a reliance on thrift stores—highlighted as useful receptacles of the "middle class's garbage."¹⁰² Those readers embarrassed to shop at such places, many of which were situated in parts of town associated with "the poor" and "winos," were "being *had* by the same wonderful folks who brought you the Cambodian invasion—and poverty in the first place."¹⁰³ Such entreats to shop at the Salvation Army neglected discussion of the conservative, corporate models to which chain thrift stores adhered, but expanded the cultural value of secondhand commerce, all the while highlighting emergent problems with its subsequent popularity.

Commerce and Community in *Rags*

By 1970, voluntary secondhand dress could be an elitist aesthetic, a political stance, a casual choice, or a composite. In the first year of the new decade, *Rolling Stone* rock photographer Baron Wolman started an underground fashion magazine, *Rags*. The self-consciously un-slick, rag-paper publication ran for just one year, piggybacking on the success of underground newspapers. The twelve issues Wolman produced consolidated many of the conflicts over used clothing and hip capitalism. Overwhelmingly, secondhand consumerism was presumed to be culturally and politically superior to newly made apparel, in part because of the artistic attention required to cultivate a secondhand wardrobe. In *Rags*' opening mission statement, Wolman called fashion a "safety valve," "a bit of joy" in a time of serious social problems. He invited the reader to admit to the ego boost of dressing up (and suggests the Salvation Army as an inexpensive, legitimate source of good "threads").[104] He also insisted *Rags* was not frivolous. The magazine's writers often remarked in various ways, "Clothes are politics."[105] Discussions of poverty and gender inequality were central to many of the issues.

The by-then-popular feminist assertion that the "personal is political" echoed in such claims. *Rags* magazine, as did underground papers nationwide in 1970, addressed the women's liberation movement as well as the rising gay liberation movement, in this case through the valence of clothing. For example, an article called "What Gay Women Wear," quoted Susan Walsh proudly claiming that "getting all dyked up" meant shiny boots and "Salvation Army–tailored, snazzy, comfortable clothes." Walsh wore hand-me-downs, bought from thrift stores, or occasionally stole from a chain store. Walsh's ideological preference for secondhand clothing followed from the "women's liberation analysis that consumerism oppresses women."[106] Again, such analyses dismissed the conclusion that shopping at secondhand stores was, in fact, still shopping, and that many thrift stores were also chains. *Rags* exhibited a rising emphasis on the personal in politics and on the trope of individually liberatory shopping, more than a structural intervention against inequalities between men and women—or among women.

A standard recognizable "feminist dress" never emerged, partly because the goals and ambitions among feminists varied so widely, exemplifying, for one thing, the obvious diversity among women.[107] Generally, the overwhelmingly white and middle-class complexion of second-wave feminist leadership erected obstacles to cross-class and cross-racial solidarity. By the 1980s, feminist critics questioned the effects of gestures of capitalist dissidence—such as secondhand dressing. Reflecting on white feminists' efforts to reach out across class and race boundaries in the mid-1980s, feminist critic bell hooks insisted that "Wearing second-hand clothing and living in low-cost housing in a poor neighborhood while buying stock is not a gesture of solidarity with those who are deprived or under-privileged."[108] However, feminist theorist Kaja Silverman, also writing in the mid-1980s, defends the feminist use of secondhand goods and supports the transcription of women's liberation analysis onto secondhand *dressing* (if not shopping): "By recontextualizing objects from earlier periods within the frame of the present, retro is able to 'reread' them in ways that maximize their radical and transformative potential."[109] The debate here is over the comparable importance of structural inequality and individual expression, between buying and wearing, and between economics and culture.

Using consumption, no matter how "alternative," to protest the societal harms of capitalism, was clearly a compromised tactic. *Rags* paid unusual attention to modes of acquisition, focusing on the ways hip dress could be attained as much or more than the looks themselves at times. For example, *Rags* advocated for "communal closets," flea markets, and clothing co-ops, and featured independent designers and street fashion. Unavoidably, though, the magazine remained a business reliant—as were most magazines—on advertisements. Wolman funded the paper's production in part with advertisements for hip companies pandering to anyone looking to conform to an aesthetic alternative, such as Truth and Soul Fashion, whose ads, as seen in figure 5.1, announced sentiments such as, "To hell with cookie pattern clothes," and "Most Americans wouldn't be caught dead in our clothes. We wouldn't be caught dead in theirs."[110]

In the seventies, secondhand venues further expanded their consumer audience. Financial crises, marked variety in clothing styles, and a greater acceptance of used apparel than ever before all helped thrift stores, flea markets, and garage sales thrive. In 1971, Abbie Hoffman started a publishing company of his own after more than thirty publishers rejected the book that would become an icon of subversion and a bestseller, *Steal This Book*.[111] Parodying the faddish how-to and self-help genres of the time, *Steal This Book* included advice on how to fight against corporations and the government. The book's advice blurs the line between violently criminal and merely subversive, including sections on how to make bombs and on organizing food cooperatives. The chapter "Free Clothing & Furniture" instructs the reader in the best ways to shoplift new clothing from department stores, but also includes advice on how to get secondhand clothing. By 1971, the number of free stores had diminished, but Hoffman included other ways to get discarded clothing: impersonate churches, ask people in the process of moving for clothes they intend to leave, fabricate a food and clothing drive for victims of a natural disaster, scour the lost and found at bus stations. Although Hoffman mostly advocates not spending money, he also mentions the cheap prices at the Salvation Army.[112] By the end of 1971, Hoffman had sold more than a quarter of a million copies of *Steal This Book*.[113] The level of acceptance of secondhand shopping as a means of recreation and acquisition had never been higher. And, as the protest movements of the late-1960s gave way to

FIGURE 5.1 Advertisement for Truth and Soul Fashion. *Rags*, February 1971.

disillusionment, secondhand dress retained some of its markers of dissidence, even as participants recognized the potential contradictions of anticapitalist consumerism and dress. As *New Yorker* fashion editor Kennedy Fraser remarked in 1975, flea-market fashions took on an "ironic stance."

Some studies cast thrift-store style as a clear representation of the antiestablishment sentiments associated with the late 1960s, as a youth culture backlash to mass-produced clothing and to a consumeristic society.[114] These generalized stories of defiance invest unexamined faith in the power of individual "rebellion" and take at face value personal accounts (often retrospective) of the political meaning of style. On the other hand, recent scholars have reacted to similar claims of resistance by denouncing the radical potential of many cultural forms, especially describing economic resistance as short-lived and trivial.[115] According to this narrative, savvy and creative postwar admen co-opted cool and hijacked hip, bringing recalcitrant baby boomers into the industrial capitalist fold by offering mass-produced tie-dyed, ethnic-inflected, and unisex styles.[116] Both of these accounts simplify the intentions of style, overlook the historical underpinnings of fashion trends, and ignore the implications of how and where objects are acquired.

Elective participants in secondhand commerce often critiqued the consumer-based culture without fully abdicating their preordained roles as consumers. For these patrons, consumer dissidence consisted of what, where, and how much to acquire, but not usually whether to engage in acquisition at all. Many sought to articulate the complex associations and sentiments surrounding used goods in the decades after the end of World War II; perhaps as many or more simply incorporated secondhand objects into their consumer identity with little more than a vague perception of their meaningfulness. Secondhand goods were part of the substantial detritus of consumer society, and the cultivation of dissident styles consisted of actions (buying, stealing, finding, or making) still reliant on the system in question. Partly for this reason, the fashion and clothing industries against which those styles inveighed were easily able to mass-produce new approximations of secondhand trends. Even so, the political implications of secondhand consumerism and the use of actual secondhand materials persisted and increased throughout the 1970s and beyond.[117] While not without contradictions, secondhand style provided a lasting legacy in its model of partially subversive consumerism and enhanced the role of dress in visible activism and protest.

For children raised in America's new postwar suburbs, the modes of acquisition—scavenging Vaudeville trunks' contents, rummaging through flea-market wares, or exploring aged relatives' attics—were as important to opposition as were the materials attained. Buying from places like thrift stores defied the middle-class standards of earlier generations still able to recall the material deprivations of the Great Depression and World War II, for whom a place like a Salvation Army store was "a terrifying reminder of the stigma of poverty, the shame of ill-fitting clothing, and the fear of disease through infestation."[118] Moreover, through the act of purchasing secondhand items, middle-class "rebels" upended the accepted order of class charity, wherein they offered donations and members of poorer classes accepted them. Elective poverty became integrated into the growing panoply of national fashion options, all the while retaining the requirement of something indicating voluntary poor dress. A 1975 guidebook to dressing titled *Cheap Chic* reported the necessity of a "touch" of richer apparel to do secondhand style well: "If you look closely at a woman with a strong individual style, you will discover there is almost always something in her outfit that costs a lot."[119] Alongside Army-Navy Surplus finds and thrift-store scores, the authors advise, budget for an expensive pair of boots or a high-quality leather belt.

In the first issue of *Rags*, a brief blurb about an artist called "Charlie Nothing" underlined the paradoxes of elective poverty as means of antipoverty protest. Nothing described his elaborate, handmade "suit of rags," designed for an art opening: "There are many colors in the rags, mostly faded. The rags are a ceremonial outfit which symbolically depicts the opposite of itself. For example, putting on clothes symbolizing poverty, and yet practically containing a great deal of work, implies poverty purchased at a price."[120] Charlie Nothing's statement summed up the philosophical paradox inherent in Jane Ormsby-Gore's claims of class deviance and in the elaborateness of hippie dress in general.[121] By the 1970s, the conflation of elective poverty styles and exhibitionist vintage was well established, and many questioned the political value of secondhand dress.

Secondhand styles may have taken on a more markedly ironic stance by 1975, as Kennedy Fraser opined. Still, her claim that voluntary secondhand styles tended to say "something quite intense but only in a footnote" underestimated the persistent radical potential of secondhand dress.[122] In the 1970s, some secondhand dressers did not quote in footnotes but spoke louder and more declaratively than ever—but the conversation changed. Secondhand clothing's use as a political tool in protest of wars and economic inequality did not end with the 1960s, but as other social issues rose, particularly those of gender and sexuality, secondhand dress diversified. The "ironic distance" Fraser dismisses proved an effective tool for revealing the arbitrariness of dress standards—and an effective tool for the disruption of accepted standards of sexuality and gendered appearances.

CHAPTER SIX

Genderfuck and the Boyfriend Look

Every revolution begins with a change of clothes.
—French fashion critic René Bizet (1913)

In a 1964 episode of the caveman cartoon *The Flintstones*, Fred Flintstone desperately wants to go to a baseball game. Barney has only one ticket, but as it is ladies' day at the ballpark, he can bring a female guest for free. Inspired by a box of his wife Wilma's unwanted clothes intended for a rummage sale, Fred decides to try to "pass" as Barney's date. That plain box filled with "old clothes" opens the door to gender masquerade of the vaudevillian order—and of course, light-hearted confusion based on mistaken identities and the comic value of a caveman dressed in pink frills and a hat fit for British royalty.[1]

In general, the humor of *The Flintstones* hinges on juxtaposition. Set in the Stone Age, *The Flintstones* features gender tropes and household objects more or less contemporary to the airing of the show, reinterpreted through a rough idea of Stone Age "technology" (dinosaurs and small animals stand in for most household objects, from a triceratops juicer to porcupine sewing needles). Wilma and Betty even dress in modish minis—jaggedly unhemmed for a prehistoric touch. In the above-mentioned episode, gender assumptions are layered on top of the show's theme of blending modernity with antiquity—fittingly, through the use of discarded clothing. Those discarded clothes, in a liminal state of belonging—neither Wilma's anymore nor yet anyone else's—presented the possibility for gender transgression in a way that would not have been so readily suggested were the dresses still lined up beside Wilma's Sunday best in her cave closet.

Four years later, at a 1968 press event held in a New York City Montgomery Ward, acclaimed American fashion designer Rudi Gernreich scorned the popularity of used clothes—"costumes from a vaudeville trunk, or great-great-grandmother's wedding dress, or flea market finds, or the rags off the backs of hippies."[2] Gernreich, considered one of the most important American antiestablishment designers (and famous enough to have graced the cover of the 1 December 1967 issue of *Time*), simultaneously recognized and dismissed secondhand fashion's claims to political engagement.[3] Romantic, historically evocative outfits, according to him, only protested the world's ills by "evading the issue or pretending. They're not true, by being someone else, somewhere else."[4] Gernreich, himself a gay rights advocate, argued that the new unisex clothing designs—like his own—had much more currency than secondhand items as "a way of breaking down conventional attitudes of sexual behavior."[5]

This chapter argues that contrary to Gernreich's possibly self-interested assessment of used goods, secondhand clothing was uniquely equipped, both as a commodity and as a vehicle of social expression, to go beyond normative boundaries of gender and sexuality identification. While breaching the sex-segregation of apparel, Gernreich's unisex line of clothing created yet another category, whereas secondhand outlets invited consumer disregard of classifications. Structurally, new clothing outlets imposed more stylistic boundaries than did more informal outlets, by organizing clothes by brand, cost, size, gender, and even age. The comparatively open organization of most recirculated clothing displays invited consumers to play fast and loose with many sartorial signifiers and to consider a broader arena of fashionable play and discourse, one more open to experimentation; in fact, in a large secondhand retail setting, imagination is required to cultivate preferences. In addition, and in some cases, more importantly, secondhand venues had few sales clerks working to steer shoppers toward items deemed appropriate for their class, race, generation, and—one of the most arbitrary yet uncompromising clothing classifications—gender.

During the 1960s and 1970s, gender-neutral dress, secondhand commerce, and a national focus on gay rights all grew in popularity.[6] Much emerging gender-neutral dress, like Gernreich's unisex lines, went hand-in-hand with the increasingly visible politics of gender and sexuality equality—for those able to afford the designer duds. Compared to these brand-new styles, secondhand clothing provided a wider range of affordable items and invited gender-disruptive interpretations, like Fred Flintstone's. Like Fred, new owners of old garments often reimagined their acquisitions' originally intended purposes. This chapter examines the role of used goods in the development of gay rights advocacy and queer identities, in part through images of glam rock, punk, underground art and film, and performance art. From female impersonator José Sarria to Bowery-browsing punk fashion icon Patti Smith, thrift-store wares, flea-markets finds, junkyard discards, and street jetsam were central to the art, politics, and performances of many gender-transgressive figures of the 1960s and 1970s. Some secondhand enthusiasts, such as Sarria, used secondhand exchange to explicitly question homophobic public perceptions and to support gay rights. Others who came after Sarria, such as underground filmmaker Jack Smith and Hibiscus, founder of the psychedelic drag troupe the Cockettes, presented a more ambivalent relationship to gay rights, citing anarchic, antimonetary motivations for avoiding firsthand consumption and for presenting a queer appearance. So while members of the early homophilic movement appropriated philanthropic capitalism for specialized political means, anticapitalist ideals, rather than notions of sexual equality, undergirded subsequent artistic expressions, leading to recognizably queer appearances through the use of a trash aesthetic. These later gender nonconformists often combined the vintage-associated practices of dressing "up" with the dressing "down" suggested by the visibly torn and worn apparel favored by elective poverty.

An anticommercial aesthetic popular among the postwar avant-gardists improved the cachet of used materials and defined the look and the content of underground theater, much of which looked back on the era of Florenz Ziegfeld's reign for aesthetic inspiration. As founder of the Theater of the Ridiculous Charles Ludlam remarked about the reuse habits of queer theatrics, "To have a new idea is as gauche as being seen in a new suit."[7] Or, as Jack Smith simply said, "Art is one big thrift shop."[8] As part of experimental "Off-Off-Broadway" theater, Ludlam, Smith, John Vaccaro, and Ronald Tavel were among those who used, sometimes exclusively, secondhand materials. In the process, these performers defined a persistent aesthetic component of queer display—and of sartorial "camp"—for following generations, including for members of the San Francisco-based psychedelic drag troupe, the Cockettes.

The original Cockettes—who performed mostly in San Francisco from 1970 to 1972—included gay, straight, and bisexual men, women, and even babies. In a 1974 article in the magazine *Gay Sunshine*, the author applied the term "genderfuck" to the troupe, ostensibly to account for a broad array of styles that indicated non-normative sexualities.[9] While the term *genderfuck* had long been included in gay vernacular, it emerged in more mainstream sources toward the end of the Cockettes' performance reign. Sociologist Laud Humphreys's 1972 book *Out of the Closets: Sociology of Homosexual Liberation* refers to "gender fuck" as "a form of extended guerilla theater"—not unlike the Diggers and the Yippies.[10] In explaining glam rock style, the August 1972 issue of *Rolling Stone* called the term "gender-fuck" a more vulgar reference to the "new 'macho' transvestism," a kind of satirical female impersonation.

Almost always, commentators applied the term to gender-bending men in dresses with hairy chests, glitter in their full beards, and long hair—men exemplified by the outrageous founder of the Cockettes, Hibiscus. The glitter-boy style of glam rock emerged from this flamboyant look, as several Cockettes members went on to work as stylists and designers, and for some time, relied on repurposed secondhand materials to infuse an already appropriative rock-star style with extra gender ambiguity.

Glam's flip side, its dirtier, do-it-yourself correlate, punk, also has firm roots in a secondhand aesthetic; "punk" and "hippie" are the two style categories most readily linked to secondhand.[11] The erotically charged development of Patti Smith's iconic fashion underscored consistency in the use of secondhand items in androgynous dress for both sexes. However, the public reception of cross-gendered dress suggested that men in women's clothes were more deviant, socially threatening, and politically radical than the converse. Descriptions of women in men's clothes as sporting "the boyfriend look" in the 1970s downplayed but did not erase possible feminist interpretations of cross-gendered dress.[12]

San Francisco and The Black Cat Café

Before Charles Ludlam's Theater of the Ridiculous and Jack Smith's *Flaming Creatures* in 1960s New York City, before the Cockettes' parodic camp, and before punk, there was the grande dame of the Black Cat Café, José Sarria, aka Carmen, and later, Grand Empress of the Imperial Court. The Black Cat was already a favorite stomping ground for Beats (part of Jack Kerouac's *On the Road* was set in a fictional version of the bar) by the time Sarria began his performances in the mid-1950s; figure 6.1 shows him performing circa 1963, near the end of the Black Cat's operations. In the years following World War II's end, amid the "Lavender Scare" of the McCarthy Era, Sarria's politically charged, satirical renditions of *Carmen* and *Turandot* helped make the Black Cat one of San Francisco's gay-friendliest spaces, prompting Allen Ginsberg to call it "the greatest gay bar in America."[13]

Beginning in 1948, the bar's owner, Sol Stoumen (a heterosexual man), fought against harassment from the San Francisco police department and the Alcohol Beverage Control (ABC) Commission over the Black Cat's increasingly homosexual clientele. In 1951, Stoumen took the state to court over his suspended liquor license. In *Stoumen v. Reilly* (37 Cal.2d 713), the California Supreme Court ruled, "[i]n order to establish 'good cause' for suspension of plaintiff's license, something more must be shown than that many of his patrons were homosexuals and that they used his restaurant and bar as a meeting place."[14] The case, which restored the Black Cat's liquor license, was one of the earliest cases upholding the rights of gay people. The court qualified its opinion, however, by stating that ABC might still close gay bars with "proof of the commission of illegal or immoral acts on the premises," a caveat that

FIGURE 6.1 José Sarria performing at the Black Cat, circa 1963. Courtesy of the San Francisco GLBT Historical Society.

might be interpreted to include any same-sex contact, such as dancing.[15] Sarria, one of the Black Cat's premier performers, personally fought to keep the bar open until Stoumen permanently lost his liquor license on Halloween 1963.

Sarria's story is often repeated by scholars as an example of pre-Stonewall gay rights activism and political transvestism.[16] At a time when homosexuals were deemed potentially treasonous security risks by the government and the American Psychiatric Association labeled homosexuality a mental illness, Sarria was unapologetically "out," both socially and politically.[17] In the midst of years when San Francisco law, like the law in many U.S. cities, forbade the wearing of attire produced for the opposite sex, Sarria persisted in his chosen career as a female impersonator, a title in which he took professional pride. For Sarria, drag performance was a second career threatened by laws concerning gender and sexuality; after being arrested and convicted on "morals charges," he was forced to give up hopes of being a certified teacher, toward which he had been studying.[18]

Sarria abhorred the double lives he saw many homosexuals living. His performance at the Black Cat became a political platform. In between songs, he preached "Gay is Good." He ended each show with a rousing parody of "God Save the [Nelly] Queen," encouraging the crowd to join in, "to get them realizing that ... we could change the laws if we weren't always hiding." His advocacy culminated in a bid for Board of Supervisors a decade and a half in advance of Harvey Milk.[19] In 1961, Sarria became the first openly gay man to run for public office in the United States. He conducted his campaign partly in drag, in his by-then renowned shows.[20] By then, Sarria's wardrobe of gowns, heels, and hats was prodigious, but his penchant for dresses and women's shoes began long before, at the home of his Columbian-born single mother, a domestic servant who had only occasional care of her son. Both his mother and his aunt indulged Sarria's boyhood delight in dressing up in gowns and heels, playing a duchess, and acting out narratives of royal balls.[21] José's first drag costumes were secondhand clothes he scavenged from the closets of female relatives. His evolution into full drag also relied on hand-me-downs. In early performances, Sarria tinkered with women's slacks and makeup, but wore loafers until a female patron gifted him the pointed, high-heeled Capezios from her feet, a footwear style he favored ever after.[22]

As Sarria transformed himself into Carmen, diva of the Black Cat, and later, the Empress of the Imperial Court System, he relied in part on the city's many thrift stores and flea markets. At least by 1960, Sarria was buying women's clothing from the Salvation Army, Goodwill Industries, and the Purple Heart Thrift Store. Later handwritten accounts also reflected a budget for—and an income from—flea market sales.[23] Sarria supplemented both his wardrobe and his personal income through the exchange of secondhand clothing. The task of constructing Carmen and his other personas would have been more difficult without inexpensive, used clothes and the relative permissiveness of secondhand commerce venues.[24]

The legal dangers of purchasing women's clothing firsthand compounded the difficulty of affording a double wardrobe—male dress for everyday public life and female dress for his career and enjoyment. As secretary of the first gay civil rights organization he helped start in 1961, the League for Civil Education (LCE), Sarria reported the dangers of mainstream shopping for those venturing outside of gender normative dress: "Macy's still continues to be a source of revenue for attorneys defending silly queens who insist on going there to shop at the T room."[25] As long as wearing the clothing of the opposite sex was illegal, shopping for clothes (as well as dates) in a department store meant risking not only reputation but arrest.

While not very popular or effective, the LCE set the stage for two more gay organizations Sarria helped start, the San Francisco Tavern Guild (1962–95) and the Society for Individual Rights (SIR) (1964–76). The Tavern Guild was the first gay business association in the United States, established by gay bar owners and liquor wholesalers in reaction to police harassment that closed several bars.²⁶ The Tavern Guild, while successful in many endeavors, could not prevent the final closing of the Black Cat in 1963. His work place shuttered, Sarria joined forces with other activists to form SIR, which became the largest grassroots homophile group of the era. SIR modeled new trends in gay activism by demanding fair legal treatment while openly and noisily protesting police oppression. The group became a model for similar organizations in major U.S. cities.²⁷ In 1965, Sarria rounded out his record of community building by establishing the Imperial Court System, of which he crowned himself Empress. The group created a gay social network and provided a platform for public expression by and for homosexuals—especially the "nellies" Sarria so supported—often using drag events to fundraise for gay charitable causes.²⁸

These homophile organizations all participated in secondhand commerce for various, sometimes contradictory, purposes, including raising funds for gay rights advocacy, providing "straight" clothing for those seeking employment, and distributing elaborate gowns in preparation for the annual Hallowe'en Ball—the one day of the year drag was not an arrestable offense. In the mid-1960s, SIR's monthly newsletter, *Vector*, printed warring views of appropriate dress for gays seeking public acceptance, and proposed similarly divergent uses of secondhand items. These discussions of clothes trace a transition from assimilatory homophilic rhetoric to the blossoming of a broader queer community. As radical as Sarria's own life and dress was, he occasionally acquiesced to mainstream expectations, such as during his 1961 bid for office. While he informally campaigned as Carmen during his act at the Black Cat, Sarria reportedly purchased his first men's suit for more formal civic presentations.²⁹ Sarria took his run seriously and extended his platform beyond issues of homosexual rights. The suit he posed in for the photo in figure 6.2 indicated a partial adaptation to straight constituents' expectations. Sarria frequently maintained that not all of the six thousand votes he received were from gay voters.³⁰

The *Vector* published assimilatory rhetoric during the publication's early years, in accordance with the mission statements of some early homophile affiliates, such as the Community Services Committee of SIR, sponsors of the very first gay community center in the United States.³¹ In 1965, an article outlined the Community Services Committee's chief aims, among which was to gain rights for homosexuals by "teaching the Heterosexual that he is not so different."³² To do this, a spokesperson advised that "the Homosexual" show a normative face by preventing the "the spread of the conception of the stereotype homosexual racing about in semi-transvestic garb."³³ The same issue of *Vector* in which this plea appeared also requested the donation of

FIGURE 6.2 José Sarria dressed "straight" on a promotional flyer when running for city and county supervisor, 7 November 1961. Courtesy of the San Francisco GLBT Historical Society.

used clothing in good condition for people coming to the committee for employment referrals. The garb requested was very "straight"—suits, ties, white shirts, versions of the conservative, gender-conventional dress male picketers outside the Civil Service Commission were careful to don when protesting the ban on the federal employment of gays that same year.[34]

In an issue of *Vector* just one year later, however, SIR's co-op and thrift store, the SIRporium (by 1966, one of three primary sources of income for the group), boasted of a wide array of "Hallowe'en gowns" for their annual drag ball.[35] Although Halloween was indeed the one night when drag was legal, police officers often waited outside the ball venue, ready to catch gown-clad men after midnight, in a modern-day, cross-dressing Cinderella plight. At that year's ball, Sarria helped circumvent the law against cross-dressing, which included the phrase "intent to deceive," by handing out tags in the shape of black cats for male ball-goers to display visibly on their dresses. The tag read, "I am a boy."[36] The Tavern Guild, which sponsored the ball, also frequently raised funds with the sale of secondhand goods destined for cross-gendered wear. Between 20 March and 9 April of 1967, the Tavern Guild held an auction series consisting of eight fund-raising auctions, featuring performances from San Francisco's most "outstanding stage performers," as well as the sale of "the clothes off their backs." The profits went to the creation of a Gay Community Fund.[37] In even earlier examples, in August 1964, the premier homophile organization the Mattachine Society, which presented a publicly assimilatory front, reported three different fund-raising auctions for the group, auctions held at gay bars known for cross-dressing. Reportedly, auction attendees could look forward to seeing drag ball gowns modeled and "resold at bargain rates."[38]

In the mid-1960s, inside and outside of gay communities, changes in attitudes about gender-nonconformist dress emerged and spread, and this transition period could account for some of the contradictory ideas about dress expressed in *Vector*.[39] By 1967, *Vector* journalists openly acknowledged the influence of hippie dress on public perceptions of gay dress. The author of "Drag—Is It Drab, Despicable, Divine?" argued against conforming to ideals of "social acceptability" in clothing. The "'drag dress' problem" extended to all men and women, the author wrote, because choices of style should not determine public assumptions of wearers' sexual identification. In this respect, the author argued, hippies "show maturity and logic in dispensing with this inhibiting social claptrap."[40] This sentiment suggests the emergence of a queer aesthetic not directly connected to a specific sexual orientation.

A few years later and just a few blocks away from the site of the Black Cat, a group emerged whose secondhand style epitomized this "maturity and logic": the Cockettes. Despite their proximity, key members of the Cockettes were completely unaware of the existence of Sarria or his organizations. This disconnect between neighboring queer communities reveals the disparate intentions and affinities of nearly interlocking movements. The differences between the Cockettes and Sarria showcase the broad range and meaning of styles and politics that were considered part of "cross-dressing," as well as the equally various motivations for participation in secondhand clothing exchange. Though the Cockettes' psychedelic performances are often referred to as gay liberation theater, most members described their lineage as more related to hippies than "the old generation" cross-dressers—not all members were gay, or even male. Two of the original Cockettes, Rumi Missabu and Fayette Hauser, made it through the twentieth century without ever hearing of Sarria or his political agenda, testifying to their own disinterest in direct gay liberation politics or San Francisco's homophile history. To Fayette, "Cross-dressers were another old generation . . . these fat men who'd put on old ball gowns and bad wigs."[41] Sarria *was* the establishment, part of the old economy of style and sexuality.

Sarria was not an anticapitalist. However, many of the influential gender-transgressive secondhand aficionados of the 1960s and 1970s premised their performative appearances on anticommercial ideals—not unlike those of the

San Francisco Diggers—including members of the "queer theater" emerging at that time, shaping underground cinema, performance art, and eventually, popular musical styles and even mainstream fashion. For centuries, movements of social and sexual liberation had been associated with campaigns of radical anticapitalism. The original, English Diggers took part in the civic unrest of the mid-1600s to advocate for community building that emphasized expression of free love and a rejection of wealth and consumption. In San Francisco, the political performers who named themselves after the English Diggers considered liberation from money and the making of a "free" society as the rationale behind ideals of sexual freedom; in fact, the theatrical troupe began in 1967 and only pronounced sexual liberation as part of their mission following the summer of love, seeing the trend as a path to spread anticapitalist ideology.[42] When sexuality, whether clearly "straight" or not, was presented as not procreational but for personal expression, it often acted as a critique of capitalism.[43]

Jack Smith and New York City Avant-Garde Theater

The Diggers themselves do not account for the aesthetic and political differences between José Sarria and the Cockettes. Across the continent from the Black Cat Café, in New York City, the theater of the Ridiculous emerged in the mid-sixties as "a definable sensibility in American theatre" associated with the playwrights Kenneth Bernard, Charles Ludlam, and Ronald Tavel, and director John Vaccaro, who started the Play-House of the Ridiculous in 1965. The genre of Ridiculous Theatre was a highly self-conscious style that broke with dominant trends of naturalistic acting and realistic settings. It tended toward "camp, kitsch, transvestism, the grotesque, flamboyant visuals, and literary dandyism."[44] Ridiculous often relied on parodies of icons and artifacts of the American entertainment past—old movies, popular songs, advertisements, and television. Just as important, it cultivated a trash aesthetic dependent on the use of secondhand materials for costumes and sets.

While these directors were vital to disseminating Ridiculous theater, Jack Smith, actor, artist, photographer, and underground filmmaker, is the acknowledged "father of the style."[45] Film and theater critic (and son of playwright Bertoldt Brecht) Stefan Brecht quoted Ludlam as admitting, "Jack is the daddy of us all."[46] Vaccaro cited Smith as "[p]robably the biggest influence" on his life and "*the* pure artist of our day."[47] From Andy Warhol to "pope of trash" John Waters to David Lynch, experimental filmmakers credited Smith's influence. Art photographer Cindy Sherman and performance artist Lorrie Anderson acknowledged his work, as did musicians Lou Reed and David Byrne, to name just a few of his admirers. Richard Foreman, acknowledged pioneer of avant-garde theater, went so far as to say that Smith was "the hidden source of practically anything that's of any interest in the so-called experimental American theater today."[48] Not unlike the baroness Elsa von Freytag-Loringhoven in the 1920s, Smith was imitated without acknowledgment or monetary compensation—though the latter was never Smith's direct goal, as he adhered to the belief that artistic creation should be severed from commercial activity. And Smith never abandoned anticommercialism to establish the popularity of a trash aesthetic. Rather, other ambitious artists who admired Smith's work used his visibly secondhand aesthetic to create widely admired art not intended to take a stance against affluence or a capitalist system.

Smith's work created and typified the Ridiculous sensibility, and it did so with a near-obsessive reliance on secondhand materials. Jack Smith embraced a trash aesthetic in his work from the start of his career, which began with photography shortly after he moved to New York City in 1953. There, he furnished his apartment from discards found on the street. He continued to layer his abode, a loft that would become the site of plays and movies, with fabrics and objects meticulously arranged.[49] As Brecht described it, the feet-deep layers of refuse, including a junk-filled old toilet, feathers, netting, bottles, metal, and plastic, were all defined by the "disruption of function," and presented "a sensitively restrained encroachment on a chance disorder."[50] There, Smith would construct, conduct, and perform in long, time-bending shows, displays that both included and disregarded its audience with sets that privileged elaborate arrangements of discarded materials. He himself appeared dressed in outfits "fresh from the thrift shop."[51]

Much of Jack Smith's work relied for its compelling effects on his elaborate use of junk as representative of desire—personal, collective, and abstract. Smith's creations were slipstream bricolage, flitting through categories of time, subject, and even medium. His style culminated in a form of expression later labeled "expanded cinema." Through his multidisciplinary art (prose, film, photography, performance), he "collapsed the distinction between the development of an event and its performance." His use of time was an aspect that Warhol, who referred to Smith as the only man he would ever copy, especially admired.[52] Smith's use of objects "out of time" was intrinsic to his temporal experimentations, aiding in disorienting the observer with disjunctive settings. Brecht emphasized the specific metaphorical importance of Smith's cluttered settings: "the bottles, containers, old Xmas trees, signs, broken toys, baby carriages that compound his stage setting . . . have all been carefully arranged and this has taken a long time because many minute rearrangements were needed."⁵³ As a result, "The heap glitters melodiously. It is clearly exotic, a landscape of desire."⁵⁴ Smith used abandoned materials to represent the potential beauty in people, ideals, and aesthetics considered "low" by middle-class consumers. Smith's aesthetic universe illustrated Abbie Hoffman's claim that "utopia would rise out of garbage," paired with a surrealist detachment of objects from their commercial intentions.⁵⁵

A touching quality of naiveté and hopefulness resides in his work, masked by seemingly disjunctive accessories and settings. Gender disruption underscores the subject matter in such a way that makes for striking images and reinterpretive content, as in figure 6.3, a photographic staging of Eve in the garden, eating the forbidden fruit. The serpent as a peahen and a gender-ambiguous Eve (and perhaps the slightly outré choice of pomegranate as the fruit) remove the iconic scene from its common context while providing commentary on gender presentation. The inelegant peahen acts to remind viewers that the preening sex in many species is not, in fact, female. Additionally, this early photograph (c. 1958–62) reveals Smith's sartorial philosophy. Instead of a mere fig leaf, Eve is entirely swathed in reams of wrinkled, blue, uncut fabric. Smith mocks a central purpose of clothing, modesty, by completely covering Eve's body. At the same time, by creating a sexually ambiguous Eve in conjunction with the drab peahen, he parodies the role of dress as a mode of gender identification—dress as extended to include makeup and jewelry.

Though his photographs might be his most highly regarded artistic works, Smith is best known for his sexually graphic film *Flaming Creatures*, which contains many of the distinguishing elements of Ridiculous theatrics. Smith claimed he intended the film to be a comedy "set in a haunted music studio."⁵⁶ A satire of Hollywood B movies, *Flaming Creatures* featured Smith's obsession with Dominican Republic–born actress Maria Montez, star of Technicolor costume adventure films of the 1940s, such as *Arabian Nights* (1942) and *Ali Baba and the Forty Thieves* (1944). *Flaming Creatures*' central character, Mario Montez, paid tribute to the "Queen of Technicolor."⁵⁷ However, many did not see the eerily colored panoply of sexual gyrations as the humorous homage Smith considered it. *Flaming Creatures* became the center of anti-porn controversy for a time, shocking censors with close-ups of flaccid penises and jiggling breasts, and surrealist displays of odd sexual interactions between men, women, transvestites, and a hermaphrodite, culminating in an apparently drug-fueled orgy. Police promptly seized the film at its premier on 29 April 1963, at the Bleeker Street Cinema in New York. As one film critic supposed, *Flaming Creatures* was "probably the only American avant-garde movie ever described in the *Congressional Record*."⁵⁸

FIGURE 6.3 Jack Smith, *Untitled*, circa 1958–62. © Jack Smith Archive. Courtesy of the Gladstone Gallery and the Jack Smith Archive.

According to Smith, though, *Flaming Creatures* shocked not because of its depictions of sex acts between same, mixed, and ambiguous genders, but because of its aesthetic of imperfection, including the use of old clothes. His critics were, he said, "[s]hocked by the seaminess of images of sexpartners not attired in brand new garments moments fresh from the dry cleaners."[59] At least to Smith, the choice of torn and obviously outdated clothing was a greater form of subversion than the absence of clothing. The old fears about used clothing as vectors of disease—moral as well as physical—endured. The desire for clothing to project an orderly external appearance was part of the aftermath of original sin, as implied by figure 6.3 Critics of the film assumed that bedraggled appearances signaled depravity. To Smith, both disarray and nudity signaled removal from the corruption of commercialism and, thus, innocence. His antipathy for commercialism translated to a respect for sexual expression in the abstract. Defining the exact nature of sexuality was distracting to artistic and sensual merit—as was the masking slickness of newly produced and neatly composed clothing.

Critics struggled to categorize the eroticism of Jack Smith's work and "queer theater" in general. Brecht tried repeatedly to articulate the meaning and effects of queer theater, a more encompassing genre than that of Ridiculous, to which Smith's work, once again, was central at the time. However, Brecht's assertion that "the queerness of queerness is that it is asexual" was facile in its dismissal of any eroticism not easily cast as homosexual or heterosexual.[60] Smith and his actors modeled sexualities not intended to be productive, not strictly homosexual, but certainly not asexual. Susan Sontag, in defending *Flaming Creatures*, agreed that it was a shame to miss the film's value by labeling it homosexual. She attempts to categories the desirous expressions of the film by claiming, "[t]he truth is that *Flaming Creatures* is more about intersexuality than about homosexuality."[61]

Smith often argued that his own sexual orientation—whatever that may have been—was not responsible for the qualities found in his art.[62] Smith pronounced himself queer but was frequently obsessed with women and railed against "garden-variety homosexuals."[63] His casual disdain for the mainstream gay community was reciprocated. When *Flaming Creatures* was confiscated and censored, gay rights organizations did not exactly rally around: the director of the Homosexual League of New York admitted he found *Flaming Creatures* "long, disturbing and psychologically unpleasant.... Why don't the filmmakers produce an authentic film about a love affair or something between two boys which takes place in the contemporary homosexual setting?"[64] Smith's artistic mission, however, was to strip artistic representations of capitalist influence, not to normalize supposedly deviant but clearly demarcated sexualities.

Smith was more comfortable with public revilement than with success, especially financial success. Filmmaker and writer Jonas Mekas built much of his career on top of his arrest and notoriety for persisting in showing *Flaming Creatures* as well as Jean Genet's banned film *Un Chant d'Amour* (1950). For the rest of his life, Smith castigated Mekas (or, as he called him, Uncle Fishhook) for profiting from others' art.[65] Smith's art was against "the conspiracy," as he considered it, that enforced conformity through artists' reliance on a capitalist system, which included promoters and advertisers. Smith "intended nothing less than the socialization of the function of art," and was dedicated to composing new art "from the trash heap of what he considered a bankrupt and puritanical culture." His views on the necessity for communal nonconformity made him dependent on others for collaborations, but his inflexible demands and eccentricities made him a difficult work associate.[66]

From railing against the "landlordism" that required he pay rent to a rigorous no-budget approach to his art, Jack Smith's political views and aesthetic passions were of a piece. The use of secondhand materials in the film was absolute, form and function. Smith recorded *Flaming Creatures* on outdated color-reversal film stock of "dubious provenance," which gave the black and white images "the flickering ethereality of a world half consumed in the heat of its desire."[67] His devotion to discarded objects was intrinsic to his message of a free-form, anticapitalistic artistic priority, one reflective of his urban surroundings. Because the materials used were methodically stripped of any foregoing usefulness—"in demonic purity junk"—they isolated and amplified an ambiguous, humorously serious sentiment that, to him and other avant-gardists, described New York City's particular urban decay. Smith worked and lived with the trash generated by "the big city's desires."[68]

New York City vied with Old Hollywood for Smith's aesthetic affections, however. Smith's obsession with the sets and décor of 1930s and 1940s Hollywood B movies focused especially on any productions starring Maria Montez, who, according to Smith, was never properly hailed for her talents. "To admit of Maria Montez validities," Smith wrote, "would be to turn on to moldiness, glamourous rapture, schizophrenic delight, hopeless naivete, and flittering Technicolor trash!"[69] Smith's fixation on Montez underlined the trash aesthetic extension of reuse from the physical incorporation of discarded goods to the resurrection of cast-off themes and characters from art and film, a habit of queer theater that became rather reductively known as "camp." As Susan Sontag points out in her assessment of camp, it is not merely a light, mocking sensibility but an expression of a denied critique of accepted ideals.[70] Smith's work critiqued reflexive habits of newness and novelty in art—habits that would be simultaneously mocked and codified by one of Smith's most famous admirers, Andy Warhol—advocating instead for renovation and resurrection.

And Smith *did* turn people on to "flittering Technicolor trash," through his own art and by his participation in theatrical productions. Smith's many jobs included costume design for John Vaccaro's Play-House of the Ridiculous in the mid-1960s. When Ludlam left the Play-House in 1968 and started the Ridiculous Theatrical Company, Smith followed him, helping to define and popularize camp performances. Sontag includes as one of her "[r]andom examples of items which are the canon of camp," 1920s women's clothing—feather boas, and beaded and fringed dresses.[71] Smith loved boas and beads, as well as glitter, and he was expert at creating desired effects out of lesser materials.

Ludlam attributed his theater's trash aesthetic almost entirely to Jack Smith, who was "a genius at doing things for no money. Jack Smith could take people and objects that everyone else considered worthless and transform them into the most exotic creation."[72] Following Smith's lead, the Ridiculous Theatrical Company immediately "threw out the idea of professionalism and cultivated something much more extreme than amateurism. Actors were chosen for their personalities, almost like 'found objects.'"[73] Ridiculous theater ideals echoed those of Goodwill Industries' founder Rev. Helms decades ago, when Helms claimed, "[t]he Goodwill Industries takes wasted things donated by the public and employs wasted men and women to bring both things and persons back to usefulness and well-being."[74] The camp critique of novelty wound up sustaining embattled early-twentieth-century ideals of stewardship and reuse, ideals previously promoted by politically conservative, Christian-affiliated interests.

The Ridiculous Theatrical Company presented lavish, relatively unrehearsed productions for three years, all without any funding, only with volunteers and donated materials. The sets and costumes grew more "environmental," taking over the stage, depicting an entirely different, abstracted world, much as Smith strove to do with his loft—his stage and home. The stage became not just a setting for a play, but installation art in its own right. At the same time, the content became more experimental and surreal. Ludlam was accused of—or credited with, depending on the viewpoint—removing plot from drama.[75] Ludlam fully embraced the use of secondhand goods for a time, even working at a secondhand store to make ends meet—and to get first dibs on donations. He was a vocal advocate of cultural and material reuse in theater, referring to his company's productions as "ecological theater." After Smith quit—never one to hold a position dependent on others for long—the theater continued to employ the trash aesthetic, partly with the help of Smith's ingénue, Mario Montez. Montez applied techniques learned from Smith to Ludlam's plays. The Ridiculous Theater's extravagant costumes emphasized the application of often-scavenged sequins, baubles, glitter, bangles, and beads. Volunteers crafted lavish looks out of used clothing and found materials.[76]

Ludlam admired Smith's adept use of discards, but his own use of pre-owned theatrical props and costumes was based on necessity rather than a holistic principle of anticommercialism. Ludlam's and his associates' poverty was *not* elective; however, to some critics, lack of funds was "one of the company's greatest assets." When the production of *Eunuchs of the Forbidden City* scored a $10,000 grant from the National Endowment for the Arts, supplemented by a more modest amount from the New York State Council on the Arts, their "look of tacky opulence" was comprised. According to at least one reviewer, "Money is endangering the Ridiculous Theatrical Company."[77] What criticisms of Ludlam's new sets and costumes implicitly recognized was the centrality of the process of acquisition to the final effects of the trash aesthetic. Where the materials for Ridiculous performances came from defined and inspired its content, for clothing and sets every bit as much as for the old B movies or classical theatrical characters referenced in scripts. Jack Smith often said that the costume *was* the character. The actor only brings it to life.[78] Ludlam recalled a beautiful gown found at a thrift store by actor Everett Quinton, who bought it especially for Ludlam. That gown, which Ludlam compared to a Charles James—an American designer most renowned in the immediate post–World War II years for his highly structured, lavish ball gowns—inspired the creation of the play *Galas*, based on the life of Maria Callas.[79] The costume became the character became the performance.

The pre–World War II avant-garde artists who appear in chapter 2 of this book, and whose work inspired many avant-garde artists of the 1960s, agreed that the acquisition of materials was part of art—not just part of the artistic process, but of the art itself. When Breton wrote in 1928 about stumbling across a copy of Rimbaud's *Oeuvres Complétes*, "lost in a tiny, wretched bin of rags, yellowed nineteenth-century photographs, worthless books and iron spoons," he specified that the surrealist spark of a thing depended on the circumstance of its discovery.[80] Eliminating the setting of acquisition compromised inspiration. The easy purchase of mass-produced glitter and glamorous costuming for the Ridiculous Theater effectively denounced the troupe's trash aesthetic premise.

Gleaning was intrinsic to the aesthetic on which Ridiculous was based. Irving Rosenthal, San Franciscan native, one-time editor of *Chicago Review*, sometimes beatnik, and close friend of Smith's (he even acted in *Flaming Creatures*), described the widespread cohesion of anticommercialism in postwar New York City. According to Rosenthal, in the late 1950s, avant-garde performers and artists defined themselves against what they were not or did not need: Hollywood, the mass media, academic poets, and money. "We were really poor and it was alright to be poor. It was our aesthetic to use whatever was at hand. Everybody went out 'junking.'"[81] With Rosenthal's support and participation, that ideal blossomed on the West Coast around the same time "hip consumerism" invaded Haight-Ashbury's hippie community along with thousands of hippie migrants. In 1967, Rosenthal left New York for his hometown San Francisco, taking with him his anticapitalist politics, his trash aesthetic, an eighteen-year-old named George Harris Jr., and a whole room's worth of theatrical "drag": feather boas, petticoats, gowns, hats, and more. Most of these fabulous articles were by-products of Jack Smith's own perpetual gleaning. Rosenthal stored them under lock and key in a room of the commune he immediately formed along with members of the now-disbanded Diggers.[82]

"Complete Sexual Anarchy"

Once established in San Francisco, young Harris renamed himself Hibiscus, grew out his hair and beard, pierced his nose and wore skirts "culled from garbage bags, remainder bins, thrift shops and leftover piles."[83] He lived with Rosenthal at the commune, and on New Year's Eve 1969, Hibiscus and a group of self-proclaimed "anarchists" wheedled the drag room key from its keeper—Rosenthal was out of town. Arrayed in their elaborate secondhand plunder, ten men, three women, and a baby ushered in the new decade on the stage of the Palace Theater in North Beach, California, cancan-dancing to the Rolling Stones. The reception was enthusiastic, and launched the newly christened Cockettes on a year and a half of cult fame.[84]

The Cockettes' debut performance was poetically timed, closing out a decade that, despite its initial conservatism, would be defined by war protests, sexual revolution, and a visual aesthetic inspired by psychedelic drug use, and ushering in an era shaped by economic crisis, glam rock and disco, and gay liberation. George Lipsitz summarized John Street's analysis of the 1970s' supplanting of the previous decade as "[S]equins for beads, decadence for politics and open plagiarism for originality."[85] The Cockettes did not choose—one era did not oust the other: they pasted sequins onto their beads, and their decadence was often at least perceived as political, and by way of plagiarism—of musical numbers and of antiquated styles—they were wildly original. Their fantastical clothing and improvisational theater captured the cusp, exemplifying emerging ambiguities in sexuality, gender, and artistic performance, without displacing the psychedelicism of the 1960s.

Central to nearly every contemporary description of the troupe's outrageous style was their patched-together thrift-store look.[86] An eclectic mélange of found materials shaped their style, and borrowed cultural references and parodies comprised the content of their shows. Clothes were central to the identities of the performers, who often dressed (and undressed) in life as on stage. Members of the troupe, the original cast of which appears in figure 6.4, stole, bartered, bought, borrowed, and wheedled their way into the chaotic costumes. They combined glamour and the gutter, the East and the West,

FIGURE 6.4 The Cockettes, circa 1970. Courtesy of the San Francisco GLBT Historical Society.

glitter and rags, elaborate layers and nudity, all in a single pose. Following Jack Smith's lead, they blurred lines between male and female, and between everyday living and theatrical performance.[87] Renowned "Pope of Trash" filmmaker John Waters described them as "hippie acid freak drag queens, which was new at the time. . . . You couldn't tell if it was men, or women. It was straight people, too. It was complete sexual anarchy, which is always a wonderful thing."[88]

Hibiscus, the founder of the Cockettes and Rosenthal's sometimes acolyte, combined the anticommercial aesthetic of New York City with Diggers-style principled anarchic anticapitalism and a San Francisco psychedelic sensibility. He lived in Rosenthal's Sutter/Scott Street Commune, better known simply as Kaliflower after the group's intercommunal free newsletter. Rosenthal intended Kaliflower to be a "publishing commune," as he wrote to Allen Ginsberg—a completely free, self-supporting publishing house not reigned in by any of the profit motives that drove Rosenthal to quit as editor of *Chicago Review*.[89] Several of the members of the Cockettes came from Kaliflower and brought with them the commune's defining anticapitalist, anticommercial ideology, principles other Cockettes did not fully embrace.[90] Hibiscus publicly claimed that the troupe's aim was to "perform unrelated to buying and selling and the man," a sentiment reflective of his inflexibly anticommercial principles.⁹¹ Discord over whether or not to charge money for their performances was central to the rupture of the group a year later, when Hibiscus left to start San Francisco's Angels of Light Theater—a strictly free-theater production.

The group's diversity inspired fans but also led to a quick dissolution. Overall, the thirteen or so original Cockettes had little in common aside from a love of drag. Drag referred to any elaborate accouterment, regardless of the wearer's gender or sexual predilections. A tricked-out, embroidered, and sequin-laden Victorian velvet skirt was drag whether worn by a man or "a biological girl." Clothes were central to the identities of the performers. Almost everything was secondhand. Acquisition was so important to the group that Fayette called shopping their "job." John Waters (who lived with Cockettes member Rumi Missabu) reported that for the group, "going to thrift shops was a ritual. People practically chanted when they did it." Glitter—the promiscuous use of which Jack Smith is often given credit, and which he and Hibiscus purportedly sometimes made from crushed Christmas tree ornaments—was one of the only "new" things the group ever bought.⁹²

Most of the Cockettes did not have an income but subsisted on some form of government aid—many were adjudged mentally disabled and awarded Aid to the Totally Disabled (ATD).⁹³ The Diggers free store and cheap thrift shops accounted for much of their raw material, though Hibiscus, fellow Cockette Bambi Lake recounted, would "use his SSI check to buy ten bags of glitter and two expensive beaded vintage gowns at secondhand stores and then rip the gowns to shreds."⁹⁴ Hibiscus described this sort of destructive transformation of materials in terms similar to those of Jack Smith, Charles Ludlam, and indeed, the founders of the Salvation Army and Goodwill Industries, but made it strictly personal. Hibiscus took advantage of the "waste of a culture" to craft a new identity, one that did not rely on standard interpretations of gender or sexuality.⁹⁵

The "waste" Cockettes found determined details of their performances—which, in the first year, were all in San Francisco and mostly at the Palace. In 1970, MGM studios had a giant auction at their Los Angeles studio, selling artifacts such as Judy Garland's *Wizard of Oz* ruby slippers.⁹⁶ While the Cockettes could not have afforded the A-list clothing, such as the iconic green "Curtain Dress" worn by Vivian Leigh as Scarlett O'Hara, they were invited to a solo shopping spree at a San Francisco warehouse stocked with B-movie and chorus clothing from 1920s–1950s Hollywood—perfect fodder for a trash aesthetic. Fayette credits the MGM sale with the elevation of the Cockettes' performances, calling it "the magic potion." In fact, she laughingly swore the sale was "the most significant thing to happen to the hippie culture."[97] The warehouse sale coincided with the rise of the Cockettes' popularity, and the members were dazzled by the possibilities arrayed there. As Fayette put it, "It's like having a crush on someone when you're twelve and then getting to have sex with them when you're grown up."[98]

According to Fayette, the MGM sale affected everything from the Cockettes' stage aesthetic to the content of the plays. Because most of the costumes were made for black and white film, all the shades were soft and tonal—reminiscent, in fact, of the colors favored by turn-of-the-century artistic dressers, whose antiquated apparel was clearly in demand. The colors and designs of costumes both softened and grew more elaborate after the sale, inspired by the theming, quality, and quantity of the Hollywood material. While never abandoning the glittering glitz of Smith's "flittering Technicolor trash," the Cockettes layered on the lace and muted shades of early Hollywood films. The items allowed members to play out preexisting "fantasies" centered on old movies and stars. Even before his incarnation as Hibiscus, George Harris Jr., decorated his room with images of 1940s movie icons torn from library books; he adapted these fantasies according to his material provisions.[99]

The thing about secondhand cloth products that historically made some consumers squeamish was an assumption about transference, whether tangible or not, from the clothing's previous wearer. In this case, that transference was positive: glamour, stardom, beauty. Slipping into Hollywood clothing allowed the performers "to *be* the fantasies."[100] As one 1971 profiler of the group agreed (though with a less than approving tone), "[e]ach [of the Cockettes] is the embodiment of a myth, a dream, a fantasy."[101] The lyrics and action of Cockettes' shows were sometimes written around a single fabulous costume (much like Ludlam's *Galas*), or an array of newly gleaned outfits.[102] For example, the Cockettes shared a stage at the Palace Theater with the Peking Opera, who came a few times a year to perform. In November of 1970, the opera left behind a huge steamer trunk packed with costumes, which subsequently disappeared. Its contents soon reappeared on various Cockettes. Rumi was given a "gorgeous tangerine colored taffeta with beautiful orange sequins all over it with a headdress and everything."[103] The costume was so strongly associated with its Peking Opera character that Rumi was identified as that character while wearing it, echoing Jack Smith's motto that the costume was the character and the actor only a vessel.[104] The very next Cockettes performance was "Pearls Over Shanghai," one of their more famous numbers (renditions of which are repeated to this day). With the Kabuki makeup, Geisha wigs, and raunchy songs, many lyrics of which were an idea

FIGURE 6.5 Sylvester James, circa 1970. Photograph by Clay Geerdes. Courtesy of David Miller.

of broken Chinese-English, "Pearls Over Shanghai" was a tableau of Orientalist mockery, a culturally insensitive parody of the source of their costumes.[105]

Of course, the Cockettes could not rely on opera costume trunks and movie studio divestments for all their wares. Expert clothing acquisition skills earned the respect and loyalty of Cockettes members, and even secured membership to the group. Before heterosexual married couple Marshall and Diane joined, their shop, the Third-Hand Store, furnished the group with much of their elaborate garb. Sweet Pam, an original Cockette, worked at the Third-Hand Store to have first shot at the "vintage" goods. Sylvester James (who would go on to become one of the most famous Cockettes as Sylvester, "Queen of Disco") first attracted the attention of Reggie, another "chocolate Cockette"—as the few African American participants called themselves—because of his beautifully androgynous appearance. They bonded by wandering the thrift stores of Haight-Ashbury, where Sylvester found everything he needed—a woman's suit, silk stockings, women's shoes, a woman's jacket, and a feathered hat—"and put it right on and just wore it in the street, brazen." Reggie thought, "*That bitch can shop.*"[106] Sylvester's raiment, exampled in figure 6.5, quickly impressed the other Cockettes immediately, too—almost as much his undeniable musical and performance talent. Sylvester proved to be the biggest star in the Cockettes, if never quite the biggest star *of* the Cockettes, at least not as long as Hibiscus was on stage.[107] At the end of 1970, after Hibiscus left to form The Angels of Light, the Cockettes' much-anticipated New York City debut mostly tanked, but it did initiate Sylvester's successful career.[108] Several years later, Sylvester's 1978 disco hit "You Make Me Feel (Mighty Real)" earned him distinction as the first openly gay top-selling artist.

The original Cockettes disbanded within a year after the New York debacle, but their aesthetic contributions did not end there. In addition to Sylvester's success, many members influenced 1970s and 1980s popular culture from a number of positions. A later Cockettes' member, Divine, became John Waters' acclaimed muse, starring in a string of aptly named "trash films" that very nearly took Ridiculous theater mainstream, including *Hairspray* (1988), which grossed $8 million domestically.[109] Other Cockettes continued to work with clothing for a living, becoming stylists and designers. After impersonating her, Rumi Missabu styled Tina Turner for a year and a half, and Fayette Hauser dressed her friend Bette Midler when Midler began her Vegas show.[110] Bill Bowers dressed members of the New York Dolls, the Rolling Stones, Led Zeppelin, Alice Cooper, and Aerosmith. He also designed his own glam rock wearables—his designs were featured in a 1971 issue of Italian *Vogue*, when his creations still relied on secondhand materials.[111]

In the brief eighteen months or so of their original run, from the start of 1970 until the middle of 1971, the Cockettes' use of thrift-store goods and their trash-glamour aesthetic rooted in anticapitalist sentiments profoundly shaped American glam style. Hibiscus's one-time lover Allen Ginsberg claimed the Cockettes "affected the entire suburban culture" of the 1970s. "Kids who wanted some way to express difference from the homogenized television culture adopted the plumage" of the Cockettes.[112] Members of the Cockettes helped commercialize a trash aesthetic forged by those with anticapitalist motivations, such as Hibiscus and Jack Smith. Despite the apparent forfeiture of anticommercialsm, there was at least a retrospectively principled justification for the popular dissemination of a gender-transgressive trash aesthetic. As Ginsberg suggests, "The Cockettes were part of a large-scale spiritual liberation movement and reclamation of self from the homogenization of the military state. They were expressing themselves as actual people with their own natures and tendencies, rather than being ashamed—and doing it with humor."[113]

Political meaning was easy to attribute to the Cockettes, especially postmortem. As Cockette John Rothermel said, "Since we were so open to interpretation, we were used by radical factions and distorted well beyond what our statement really was—that we were simply having a party."[114] Members of the Cockettes disagreed about whether they were a political group. Fayette said that for her it was about aesthetic development, not political claims. "Of course, it was political," fellow member Martin Worman argued, "but no one among us verbalized it."[115] The politics Worman references is not anticapitalist, Diggers-style hippie rhetoric, nor simply about sexual freedom. Rather, according to Worman, the bricolage aesthetic was about disrupting the postwar era's manipulation of prewar nostalgia. "Nostalgia became an insidious tool used by mass marketers to cover up shortages of spirit, imagination and raw material," Worman claimed. "But in our wake, old clothes and old songs, became ends in themselves."[116] While regional malls and department stores categorized and segmented fashion by brand, sex, style, and cost, secondhand clothing lacked those barriers, opening their use up to playful and deviant style interpretations that only superficially—and often ironically—acknowledged the materials' original contextualization, upending the conservative reverence underlying most nostalgic attachments to secondhand objects.

By the time of the Cockettes' New York debut, Hibiscus had formed a new free theater troupe, the Angels of Light. He held fast to his ideology of free, but steadfastly refused to be drafted into overtly political causes, especially equality movements. In response to a question about what he thinks of "women's liberation," Hibiscus simply reported an incident about a women's group "attacking" a show with the Angels of Light—the details were fuzzy, as Hibiscus admitted to having been very drunk. Similarly, when asked about gay liberation, Hibiscus responded vaguely that everybody should love each other. "As for Gay Liberation, I wouldn't be thinking of pure gay."[117] On the one hand, this message might sound progressive, coming decades before twenty-first-century pop star Miley Cyrus's characterization of herself as "pansexual," but Hibiscus was mostly evasive when it came to questions of gender or sexual equality. When pressed on such issues, he insisted his only nonaesthetic concern—practically his sole occupational focus—was that "there is no admission. We're just going to perform in our free cabaret."

Hibiscus masculinized drag; he openly wanted to be a man who could borrow from the mythical glamour of Hollywood starlets' appearances in order not to dampen but actually to emphasize aggressive masculinity. He scoffed when asked if he wanted to be a woman, and pointed to the florid dress of men in Bali as being representative of the height of masculinity.[118] Technically, men or women could participate in the transgressive practice of genderfuck, but almost invariably, examples were of men—"glitter boys" with sparkling beards, hairy legs under miniskirts, or gowns torn to artfully frame penises. However, the gender radicality of the Cockettes themselves was not that they were a gay performance troop, as they are too often recalled, but that its members included straight and bisexual men, women, and children. Indeed, the inclusion of women—who appeared on stage in elaborate gowns or tuxedoes—determined the group's genderfuck identity as much as any individual example of male appearance. Female Cockettes most often dressed as female characters, but as Dusty Dawn said, "If I want to be Hamlet onstage, why should someone tell me I can't be just because I don't have a joint hanging out?"[119] But despite the group's heterogeneous makeup, the flamboyant men were the undisputed stars and the leaders; they were the characters most admired and most reviled.

The Boyfriend Look

Conversely, the public reception and descriptions of women wearing men's clothing connoted far less sexual transgression than that of their male counterparts. In the 1970s, after department stores abandoned a brief flourish of unisex clothing sections, the fashion industry dubbed the persistent practice of women wearing male clothing items "the boyfriend look," a term that still periodically recirculates.[120] The label "boyfriend look" recalled the 1950s fashion of wearing a boy's varsity jacket as a signal of intimacy, a public declaration of "going steady."[121] In 1977, Diane Keaton appeared as Woody Allen's title star in *Annie Hall*, providing a popular image of a sweet, nervous, gaminely attractive woman quirkily dressed in outdated men's clothing. Much of Keaton's clothing in the film, from ties to slacks to bowler hats, and shoes, is men's clothing—yet no one perceived the presentation as transgressive enough to qualify as genderfuck.[122] The outsized clothes and floppy ties and hats emphasized Keaton's petiteness, underlining her femininity in converse correlation to how Hibiscus's torn gowns showcased masculine attributes. Whereas Hibiscus often looked as though his feminine apparel was unable to contain his male body's strength, Keaton's Chaplinesque wardrobe sometimes threatens to overwhelm and eliminate the appearance of her body, which is encased as thoroughly as Jack Smith's photographic Eve. Keaton's dress is hyper-modest (as befits her character's sexual anxieties), while Hibiscus revels in lascivious display.

But before *Annie Hall* won four Oscars and made Woody Allen even more of a household name, there were other, less submissive examples of female genderfuck using secondhand clothes. Poet, songwriter, "Godmother of punk," and fashion icon Patti Smith is frequently credited with establishing a vein of modern female androgynous style—a kind of postwar, thrift-store Marlene Dietrich, fashionably fey and carelessly stylish. Smith straddles ambiguous territory regarding her appropriation of conventionally male garments.[123] One fashion historian appropriately refers to her as "a rangy, disheveled gamine channeling Rimbaud and Baudelaire."[124] Smith was also often claimed by feminists, who read her rough-hewn music and adaptation of thrift-store men's clothing as a proclamation of feminine liberation, despite Smith's repeated denouncements—like Hibiscus's—of movement affiliation. In a 1976 interview with Penthouse, Smith vigorously denied a role in women's liberation, saying "Whenever I'm linked to a movement, it pisses me off." Smith continued, "A word like Ms is really bullshit . . . these assholes take the only fuckin' vowel out of the word *Miss*. So what do they have left? *Ms*. It sounds like a sick bumblebee, it sounds frigid. I mean, who the hell would ever want to stick his hand up the dress of somebody calling herself something like Ms.?"[125] With her sexually blunt language, casual posturing, and masculine style, Smith's persona was that of "one of the guys," rather than an empowered woman.

For Jack Smith, Maria Montez was his sole stylistic inspiration, his icon of performance perfection. In comparison, Patti Smith had a whole legion of male influences, men she admitted to fantasizing about. Her famous, instantly androgynizing hair cut was inspired by Keith Richards, and she copied much of her attitude, persona, and even walk from Bob Dylan, about whom she thought of so much at one point that, in her words, "It was as if he had been my boyfriend."[126] In figure 6.6, Smith passes as Dylan simply by placing a magazine cut-out of his face in front of her own. As she often did with her intellectual "crushes," Smith had no trouble seeing herself as becoming her own object of desire.

Consistently, Smith's admiration and emulation of male artists was underscored by a kind of self-reflexive sexual desire. She repeatedly said of her teenaged obsession with the poet Arthur Rimbaud that (like Dylan), "he was like my boyfriend," but her affection for him morphs into a fantasy of absorption. Smith's ode to him, "dream of rimbaud" is rife with violently sexual language. Her desire is aggressive; she is the initial seducer: "he who hesitates is mine. we're on the bed. I have a knife to his throat."[127] The narrator then drops the knife and gives in to the affair. The last line, "total surrender," applies to both Rimbaud and Smith, as they become one entity, intellectual desire melding with physical.[128]

Clothing's proximity to the wearer's flesh gives used clothes excellent potential as "precipitates of desire," as Breton called special found objects.[129] Smith, when investing in secondhand men's clothing, imagined an intimate

FIGURE 6.6 Patti Smith as Bob Dylan, 1970. © Judy Linn.

sartorial transference of masculine power—an erotic exchange. Smith imagined contiguity to masculine style as key to a membership to a sort of all-boys' creative genius club in the male Romantic tradition. Following this, her rejection of female apparel often seemed cerebral. In her 1967 poem "Female," Smith expressed her discomfort with femininity and a related "phallic identity," ultimately expressed in clothing choice: *"female. feel male. Ever since I felt the need to / choose I'd choose male. I felt boy rhythms when I / was in knee pants. So I stayed in pants."*[130]

During her college days, Smith "searched for greatcoats in thrift stores like those worn by Oscar Wilde and Baudelaire."[131] Just like Zane, the autobiographical feminist in Alix Kates Shulman's *Burning Questions*, a teenaged Patti Smith held Joan of Arc to be a role model—Joan of Arc, an icon of feminine strength and beauty fortified by a guise of masculinity. In May 1967, Smith traveled to Philadelphia to visit the Joan of Arc statue near the Museum of Art. To the baby she had just surrendered to more capable care and to the maiden warrior, Smith vowed to make something of herself. Smith recalls, in the same rhetorical breath as that vow, buying a long gray raincoat at a Goodwill store in Camden, New Jersey, on her way home.[132] The purchase, a manifestation of her vow and a symbolic masculine cloak of creative authority, marked a turning point for Smith. The coat traveled with her to New York City, where she used it as a blanket sleeping in the park. When Smith wondered why a homeless man helped her find food and rest, she concluded that it was because they both wore "long coats in July, the brotherhood of *La Bohème.*" By echoing Champfleury's 1855 assessment of the impoverished affects of painters—and by running to New York City—Smith joined a century's worth of aspiring bohemians.

Smith slept on the coat at the bookstore where she got her first New York City job, and she wore it when she first met the future famed photographer Robert Mapplethorpe, whose camaraderie became iconic. Mapplethorpe's and Smith's relationship was mutually enacted genderfuck. Aesthetically they became each other, eliding and erasing markers of clear femininity or masculinity. They were exactly the same age and had similar backgrounds; Mapplethorpe's biographer agrees that he found in Smith "a doppelganger."[133] Smith and Mapplethorpe bonded and expanded their creative outlook scouring the same Bowery thrift shops and the same flea markets that inspired Breton, Cornell, and Ernst in decades prior. They swapped styles—with Mapplethorpe often advising Smith—and shared secondhand clothing.[134]

Mapplethorpe captured what was perhaps the most famous image of Patti Smith, which appeared on the cover of her 1975 debut album *Horses*. As often happened to Smith, people appropriated the image as an icon of feminism. Camille Paglia said of the picture, it "immediately went up on my wall, as if it were a holy icon. It symbolized for me not only women's new liberation but the fusion of high art and popular culture."[135] And as usual, Smith disputed such interpretations, pleading ignorance and poverty were responsible for the accidentally dissident picture. "I wasn't thinking I was going to break any boundaries. I just like dressing like Baudelaire," she said, once again portraying her impulses as purely artistic, unsullied by political inclination and inspired, if anything by a lustful, imagined camaraderie with male idols.[136]

Precociously postfeminist, the readily available photo is a map of Smith's many and often sexually charged, masculine influences. While Paglia acknowledges this "homage to her major male progenitors," she overlooks the nature of those relationships broadcast through Smith's stance, her glance, and definitely, elements of her outfit. Patti Smith's androgyny communicated heterosexual desire. Sometimes her style attracted men, who like Mapplethorpe, desired masculine beauty (Allen Ginsberg once mistook her for a "very pretty boy"), but this should not be misread as nonheterosexual, or even, as Paglia asserts, as defying the "rules of femininity."[137] Smith's attraction to masculine style was at root narcissistic and self-referential, like much of her aesthetic relationship with Mapplethorpe. She imagined herself as male, so she was attracted to men (or perhaps, since she was attracted to men, she imagined herself as male). Instead of dressing to attract a mate, she dressed to attract herself.

Mapplethorpe took the *Horses* photo. Smith confesses she never sees just herself in this photo, but the both of them—another instance of mirroring or absorbing a male interest, like in her Rimbaud poem. Her attraction to Mapplethorpe resonates in her expression's familiarity and tenderness. In an account of the photo session, Mapplethorpe's biographer Patricia Morrisroe writes that Smith "had a mental image of the portrait, in which she would blend together Rimbaud, Baudelaire, Frank Sinatra, and Jean-Luc Godard to create a French Symbolist-Las Vegas-*Nouvelle Vague* persona—but she knew better than to explain any of this to Mapplethorpe."[138] Even as subject, Smith directs the photographer, and so elides their roles.

When preparing for this shot, Mapplethorpe requested she doff her coat, exposing the stark whiteness of her man's button-up shirt. Smith agreed, flinging the coat over her shoulder in an intentionally Frank Sinatra-ish way. A plain white shirt was already a signature element of Smith's wardrobe, whether a button-up or a plain T-shirt. This particular men's white dress shirt Smith recalls having bought at the Salvation Army on the Bowery, one among a stack purchased. She chose to wear the one she did for the photo because it reminded her of "a Brassaï shot of Jean Genet." The cut sleeves even mirrored the length of Genet's rolled sleeves in figure 6.7. By envisioning her shirt as part of this photo, Smith transposes her relationship with Mapplethorpe onto the dynamic between the famous Hungarian photographer, Brassaï, and his friend Genet, wherein she becomes the thief turned author. Brassaï's portraits of Genet show a naked vulnerability on the author's face, as seen in figure 6.7, despite his relaxed, hands-in-pockets posture. Brassaï, as a friend and fellow artist, reportedly disallowed for Genet's habitual affectations, which may account for the striking simplicity of the shot.[139] Smith, in her imitation, is affecting disaffection, while also paralleling the photographer/subject relationship. Smith's admiration for Genet as a writer extended beyond his

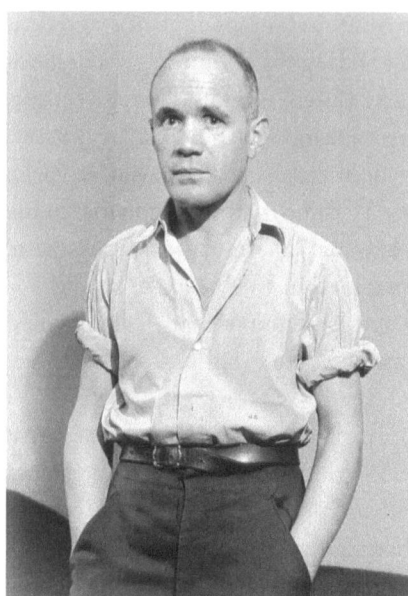

FIGURE 6.7 Jean Genet, 1948. Photograph by Brassaï. © Estate Brassaï-Réunion des musées nationaux-Grand Palais/Art Resource, N.Y.

work, to the person, to the fact that, as Dick Hebdige puts it in his seminal cultural studies text *Subculture: The Meaning of Style*, "he more than most has explored in both his life and his art the subversive implications of style."[140]

The monogram on the shirt, RV, perfected it for Smith, who imagined it was once worn by Roger Vadim, director of *Barbarella*, a 1968 futuristic flick about a scantily clad, hypersexual woman tasked with saving the world—played by Vadim's then-wife Jane Fonda.[141] Feminist film critic Molly Haskell called Vadim a "Svengali," attributing Fonda's carnality in the film to his portrayal.[142] In this permutation, Smith takes the directorial seat, underlining the narcissism of her androgyny, and the fact that, as Morrisroe points out, Smith plotted the photo while seeming to take direction from Mapplethorpe.[143] At the same time, she is also the hyper-carnal subject, Barbarella.

While the punk aesthetic and lifestyle provided women with a powerfully antiestablishment aesthetic concurrent with second-wave feminism, the descriptive term that emerged in the 1970s to describe female cross-dressing, "the boyfriend look," had a commercial resonance that defused its potential defiance. Calling the style "the boyfriend look" reassured an anxious public that the cross-dressing female was unquestionably heterosexual. Power gained through association with masculine abilities or talents was part of a long-established sexual economy. In this way, Smith was like a goy Yentl, dressing in her father's clothes to get a desired education, from a tale based on a short story by Isaac Bashevis Singer which United Artists made into a hit musical film in 1983, starring Barbra Streisand (who also played Second Hand Rose chanteuse Fanny Brice in the 1968 musical comedy *Funny Girl*). Patti Smith did not seek to repudiate that assumption, but rather sought to play all the parts—to take the role of her own seducer and her own inspiration, as well as the submissive acolyte. Her complicated array of cultural identifications demanded the cultivation of an appearance that balanced heightened sensuality and self-regard, heterosexuality, and a catalogue of male intellectual influences. Using secondhand materials, Smith was able to accommodate her wardrobe demands and financial limitations to set a new, oblique standard for female genderfuck.

By the 1960s, America's firsthand commercial zones were categorized and organized for greater consumer ease and convenience. These systems, however expedient, acted as style directives, separating male and female, young and adult, rich and poor. At the same time, various types of secondhand outlets multiplied rapidly, and while chain thrift stores also tried to facilitate consumer convenience by segmenting apparel, used goods commerce remained comparatively unlabeled and enormously accessible. In offering a greater variety of goods at usually lower prices, alternative consumer outlets such as flea markets, junk shops, thrift stores, and garage sales attracted a growing minority of excluded shoppers who did not wish to conform their style to the designated department store sections.

The postwar rise of secondhand consumerism coincided with the political intensification of drag, the public presentation of queer identities, and the disruption of definitions of gender. Secondhand materials, including discarded abstract ideas, theatrical characters, literary themes, and clothing and other physical goods, were intrinsic to camp sensibilities crafted as critiques of novelty and corporate capitalism. The liminal state of discarded items, materials ostensibly freed or "disappointed" of their intended use and apparently disconnected from capitalist streams of exchange—what André Breton called the *désenchaînement* of pre-owned goods—invited artistic experimentation. Queer presentations of style, like those of Jack Smith and Patti Smith, depicted identities not necessarily linked to easily definable sexualities. During the 1970s, an affinity between androgynous appearances and certain categories of celebrity grew, and a queer, trash aesthetic became part of mass culture's panoply of images—especially for musicians.

CHAPTER SEVEN

Connoisseurs of Trash in a World Full of It

Grunge is nothing more than the way we dress when we have no money.
—Jean-Paul Gaultier

In 1976, DC Comics launched *Ragman*, a short-lived series featuring Rory Regan, the son of a well-meaning but unsuccessful junk man. In the first issue, Rory's father saw a chance to fulfill his promise to provide for his son, a struggling Vietnam veteran, when a mattress stuffed with $2 million came into the shop. Crooks soon came around to reclaim the cash—loot from an armored car heist—and found the junk man and his friends drunk and unyielding. The criminals tortured Rory's father and his friends with live electrical wires; amazingly, they held out for Rory's sake, to leave him with the fortune. Rory returned to the shop to find his father and friends in the final moments of their travails. A last massive shock from the wires knocked Rory unconscious and killed his father. Coming to, Rory vowed revenge. While pacing the junk shop angrily, he found a rather psychedelic outfit of rags his father bought for him to wear to a costume party. Donning it, Rory became "the Tatterdemalion of Justice," a social crusader of the Batman sort.[1]

In the original series, only five issues long, the Ragman, of barely mentioned Irish descent, had no magical powers, just improbably bulging muscles. He fought run-of-the-mill hoods and gangsters, not supervillains.[2] In 1991, three comic creators who recalled Ragman from their youth brought him back. When artist-writer Keith Giffen, writer Robert Loren Fleming, and artist Pat Broderick resurrected *Ragman* for an eight-issue series, they wrote in significant character changes. Ragman's new ethnicity, Jewish, was central to the plot and action, acknowledging the historic role of Jews in the junk industry. The Ragman's rebirth coincided with attempts to overhaul the junk industry's negative image and the "rise of the tough Jew," as exemplified in efforts to recast Jewish men in American history in more "muscular" roles befitting a current notion of masculinity. Those roles ranged from gun-toting gangsters to physically powerful manual laborers—and, if you count the Ragman, junk-shop superheroes.[3]

In the 1990s *Ragman*, the patched-together rag costume had a much more central role in the making of the hero. In the original *Ragman*, the suit of rags held no enchanted powers; Ragman was strong in a regular bulked-up gym rat kind of way, and fought his battles through improbable but still-human feats of strength. But "Post-Crisis," when many D.C. Comic characters' histories were revised, the Ragman suit bore supernatural gifts, affording its wearer insurmountable strength, speed, and acuity. Constructed by the same Prague rabbi who built the Golem, each patch of the rags housed the soul of a conquered evildoer, whose abilities the Ragman accessed, in amplified form, by wearing it.[4] When the suit's powers threatened to overwhelm Rory, he apprenticed himself to a rabbi to learn to control the evil soulishness embedded in the secondhand clothes.

By investing the old material with supernatural powers able to be transferred but difficult to control, *Ragman's* re-creators joined a long line of writers articulating the perennial belief in used clothing as vector, including Charles Dickens, Henry James, Guido Bruno, the *Tales of Manhattan* screenwriters, and poet Gary Snyder. Although Ragman never did make the canonical comic hero ranks, the timing of the series' re-release was propitious: in the early 1990s, the popularity of secondhand commerce and dress resurged, spiking mainstream interest as never before. Popular ideas about secondhand clothing were repurposed and strengthened to suit a new generation of secondhand dressers. At nearly the same moment that a supernaturally powerful and ethnically proud Ragman hit the shelves, a Seattle-based music and fashion movement was infusing secondhand clothing with distinctive and powerful cultural capital. Voluntary secondhand dress on the part of mostly middle-class youth maintained its appearance of dissidence, but grunge and its affiliates leaned heavily on world-weary sartorial irony, adapted in part from the pop-kitsch styles of the 1980s and containing an awareness of the contradictions inherent in anticonsumer consumerism. Examining the phenomenon with an understanding of the political, economic, and cultural history of secondhand styles—such a central part of the collective performance—helps to place the grunge movement beyond its popular role as emblematic of generational ennui and apathy.

Nineties "grunge" began in the eighties, but vaulted into national renown in 1991 with the release of Nirvana's second album *Nevermind*. The term "grunge" first applied to the Pacific Northwest garage rock of the late 1950s and 1960s; the word itself, like much of the clothing, was apparently recycled. Examples of the postwar genre include the Wailers, the Sonics, and the Kingsmen, whose 1963 skrunky, distorted version of African American blues performer Richard Berry's "Louie, Louie" is probably the best-known song from this category.[5] The region's musical past—including cross-racial appropriation—informed mid-1980s Seattle grunge, but so did a vast array of other musical varieties, such as "Stooges-style punk, Black Sabbath metal, and arena rock à la Aerosmith."[6] For a few years, grunge grew as a local sound, essentially ignored by the rest of the country, with bands playing small venues and cribbing each other's sounds and styles in relative isolation. Then, in 1988, the Seattle band Mudhoney formed out of the remnants of Green River (often honored as the "first" grunge band). Mudhoney's 1988 debut EP, *Superfuzz Bigmuff* and their single, "Touch Me I'm Sick," released on the consummate grunge label, Sub Pop, enjoyed moderate national success. Mudhoney introduced many Americans to grunge and elevated Sub Pop's reputation.[7] The following year, Nirvana released their first album, *Bleach*, on Sub Pop—which also got some chatter, though it failed to chart until its 1992 re-release. *Nevermind* (put out on the major label DGC Records in 1991) turned the tide. The album crossed genres to rise up multiple charts, and grunge became the sound track to thousands of adolescent lives.

Like many popular musical trends at least since punk (but certainly traceable to 1920s styles and sounds), as Dick Hebdige's much-considered thesis on subcultures asserts, the grunge phenomenon was as much about fashion as it was about the songs.[8] A correlating personal appearance peppered high school hallways with plaid flannel shirts, ripped baby doll dresses, laddered tights, and rainbow-hued DIY hairstyles. Nirvana's leading man, Kurt Cobain, exerted the most powerful influence over the popular interpretation of grunge dress. As part of his look, Cobain performed a jaded variation on the Cockettes' thrift store–styled genderfuck, sometimes donning vintage floral dresses with unwashed hair and old Converses or dirty hiking boots, adding a distinctly working-class edge to the by-then established pop habit of drag. Cobain appeared in music videos and, as seen in figure 7.1, posed for magazine covers in this jaded variation of drag.

Cobain—along with other grunge affiliates, including Pearl Jam's Eddie Vedder and Riot Grrrl feminists such as Kathleen Hanna from Bikini Kill—helped define a youth-culture look once again reliant on visibly secondhand materials. The December 1992 issue of *Vogue* magazine declared grunge the year's hottest fashion trend. The popularity of the grunge look led to a spike in the sale of a variety of clothing, including flannel shirts from L.L. Bean—not long before a firmly Ivy League brand—punk accessories, and a broad array of fashionably unfashionable thrift-store duds (things too new to be vintage and too old to be mistaken for new), many carefully unclean-seeming.[9] "Distressed" clothing joined department store racks, inspiring confusion in some shoppers as to why something made to look old and damaged should be more expensive than its intact counterpart. In *Vogue*'s "Grunge & Glory" spread,

FIGURE 7.1 Kurt Cobain on the cover of *Request* magazine, November 1993.

established designers upped the ante, with Ralph Lauren and Calvin Klein offering pieces in fine fabrics featuring poor-dress accents, such as runs, rips, and unfinished hems and edges. A "grunge" cashmere Ralph Lauren Classic sweater retailed at $1,400. For those of more modest means, Donna Karan's ready-to-wear line DKNY offered a "humble" plaid shirt for just $155.[10] Within the next couple of years, adaptations of the "street-born" grunge look helped elevate novitiate fashion designers such as Marc Jacobs and Anna Sui to international success. Jacobs shocked his senior affiliates at Perry Ellis with a runway display of sand-washed silk and cashmere versions of the faded flannel plaid shirt, and crocheted skullcaps.[11] Sui's 1994 line featured a series of filmy, floral, ankle-length and babydoll-short dresses—similar to Depression-era tea dresses or "granny frocks," which designers such as Laura Ashley and Miss Selfridge mimicked in the 1970s.[12] The originals became premier flea market items in France and England in the late-1980s, and various 1990s versions served as cornerstone items in American grunge closets, ideally offset by secondhand military boots.[13] So, while similar original designs had long served as models for retro or as vintage items, the grunge accents of intentional disrepair and disjunctive accessorizing proved far more controversial than less contextualized iterations.

The successful adaptation of grunge to high fashion rankled both young thrift-store devotees and some high-end designers. One *Vogue* reader demanded the magazine "[l]eave us and our culture alone," suggesting the style relied on internally defined codes of subcultural authenticity not available to nationally recognized designers and fashion magazines. Meanwhile, designer Jean-Paul Gaultier's dismissive statement that "grunge is nothing more than the way we dress when we have no money" deeply misunderstood the motivations of thousands of middle-class, mostly white youth—as well as those who, though older, found it increasingly harder to find ways to be fashionable outside of various youth cultures' influences.[14] His statement also ignored the fact that these trends had long been skulking the corridors of high fashion, not just lurking beneath Seattle's bridges on homeless teens. For example, Japanese designer Rei Kawakubo opened a premier New York City boutique in 1975, astonishing wealthy patrons with clothes described as "as threadbare and disheveled as Salvation Army rejects," "post-atomic," and "unwearable"—as if "fashion . . . [were] having a nervous breakdown." Certainly Kawakubo had crafted her signature tattered seconds look by the early 1980s, and well-off Americans were already buying.[15] Gaultier could not very well blame Kurt Cobain for that.

Grunge successfully consolidated preexisting trends in music and in secondhand dress. Certain bands' meteoric success stemmed in part from an ability to interpret "alternative" music styles—a category rapidly becoming ironic in its mainstreaming—in terms of pop conventions. But in keeping with the shredded edges and imperfect hemlines characterizing the clothing, the stylistic melds were rarely seamless. In sight and sound, grunge emphatically showed its stitches. The (re)creators of the heroic junkman's son, the Ragman, wrought a similar aesthetic change in the superhero's wardrobe. In 1976, the rag suit swirled in a blend of melded colors, impressionistic in its patchwork and more resembling a psychedelic pattern than distinctly different fabrics, thus giving the effect of a tie-dyed catsuit. Fifteen years later, Ragman's suit gained visual clarity, in keeping with the mysticalized properties of individual pieces of cloth. Each patch could be distinguished and the stitches were keenly visible, large, and emphasized. Similarly, understanding the irony of grunge dress required some clarity as to the chronological and associational origins of individual components. Disjunctions—between old and new, masculine and feminine, bright and dingy—defined grunge appearances. Dismissing these attributes as merely sloppy and disinterested underestimates such design details' roots in the bricolage effects of 1980s postmodern art and style, which in turn adopted symbols and methods from previous decades.

Debates surrounding the dissident potential of secondhand dress dotted popular discourse in the early 1990s, coinciding with national concerns about the apparent apathy and cynicism of Generation X, the direction of rock music, and the cultural role of fashion. Many blamed "the grunge phenomenon" on a mass reaction to the extravagances of the socially conservative and fiscally profligate Reagan years.[16] The dismissive idea of fashion in any form as strictly reactionary limits its role as a historically meaningful cultural device. Like descriptions of "hippie style," grunge style was often facilely understood as another youthful generational snub, when in reality the music and fashion sustained at least as many central elements as it disrupted. Attributing secondhand styles to a simple backlash against the conservative vibes of the foregoing decade preserves the false understanding of voluntary thrifting as a socially and politically liberal response and ignores the long history of secondhand style's restrained nostalgia and antiprogressivism. Viewing grunge as wholly reactive indicates a general tendency to summarize rebellions as halves of simplified dichotomies, ignoring the inevitable ambiguities and inconsistencies; often, real political or social meanings are lost in such impressionistic condensations. Sociologist Adrian Franklin argues that by the 1980s and 1990s, "retro" styles—whether actually secondhand or reproductions—not only retained their nostalgic value for older consumers who recalled the original trends but held a new kind of nostalgic allure for youth familiar with older designs from romanticized depictions in television, music, and film.[17] So while secondhand goods were still desirable to people who saw acquiring discarded commodities as a radical act, the rising popularity of retro styles also reflected an increasing degree of mass-media engagement, and arguably represented a disavowal of generational belonging, one that ironically resulted in relative cohesiveness.

Couture for Culture Wars

As Betty Luther Hillman points out in her recent book *Dressing for the Culture Wars*, the clothes associated with youth-culture rebellion in the 1960s and into the 1970s became symbolic of the major divide in American politics and society eventually dubbed the "culture wars."[18] While the term only entered political vocabularies in 1991 (that year again), the political conflict over secular culture defined the Reagan years, when religious right-wing groups such as Jerry Falwell's Moral Majority wielded considerable power.[19] Reflecting the widespread discord in political opinions, the 1980s saw little to no national consensus about fashion—but plenty of loud and raucous contestations. By the start of that decade, prominent trends already confounded the design predictors of the 1970s, some of whom had envisioned a unisex mélange of creaseless, collarless softness and body-molded plasticity. The economic insecurity of the 1970s, along with rising political conservatism, bore some of the responsibility for a partial retreat to conventional dress as more Americans prioritized lucrative employment over personal expression. In 1975, John T. Molloy's best-selling guide to appropriate workplace appearance, *Dress for Success*, reestablished the once-anathema gray flannel suit and its middle-class counterparts as de rigueur for most business places, and frowned upon the floral remnants of the peacock revolution. Two years later, Molloy's *The Woman's Dress for Success* similarly cautioned women against the "imitation man look," offering instead specific instructions on feminized versions of classic business wear.[20]

Still, the unisex influence persisted. Long after department stores removed their experimental unisex departments, men's and women's styles retained a certain measure of flexibility—particularly regarding hem lengths, suit cuts, color palates, and hairstyles.[21] While power suits and yuppie tweed flooded the market, elements of glam also persisted, running through the Spandexed designs of the new fitness culture, and in the hairsprayed heights of both men's and women's bangs. Similarly, amidst the output of new synthetic fabrics, garish neon dyes, and faddish Hypercolor technology, secondhand styles retained a generalized allure. The voluntary consumption of secondhand clothing expanded attendant not only to 1970s trends such as punk and glam but also to a broader acceptance of the casual inclusion of secondhand items alongside mainstream fashions. Also, after the craze for Victorian and Art Nouveau styles among designers of the late 1960s, stylists continued to mine passé trends for annexation in their new productions.

The same year Molloy published *Dress for Success*, another sort of how-to-dress guidebook, *Cheap Chic*, gained a loyal albeit smaller following than Molloy's; its authors recommended numerous secondhand sources for the "chic" and thrifty dresser.[22] Also in 1975, *New Yorker* fashion critic Kennedy Fraser observed an ironic "flea marketry" among a youth starved for nostalgic reflection. By the early 1980s, "vintage" had reemerged as a term and claimed the category of especially desirable, older used clothes—eventually defined by many as items older than thirty years but younger than one hundred, the latter being deemed antique. Dress compendiums cataloguing vintage items emerged in 1982, and accelerated in popularity.[23] Much of the first literature formally tagging "vintage clothing" was structured as identification manuals, mimicking guides for antique objects by including illustrations, descriptions, and price indexes.²⁴ The mid-1980s saw publications on care and storage, and photograph-heavy accounts of personal collections, in addition to the continuing parade of price guides.²⁵ A quarter of a century after the Greenwich Village Salzmans helped Lord & Taylor sell "vintage raccoon coats" to Ivy League students, the term finally stuck. Clothing was officially collectible.

A distinction that was visible and available to those attentive to an ideal of authenticity reliant on secondhand acquisition emerged between vintage lovers, flea-market hunters, and thrift shoppers on the one hand, and buyers of new, retro-style clothing on the other. Elizabeth E. Guffey writes that "retro" gradually crept into the English-language vocabulary in the last quarter of the twentieth century, after the storm of late 1960s' trends featuring Victorian and Art Nouveau details, both old and new. By the late 1970s, the term "retro" in relation to fashion had formally entered the English vocabulary—around the same time vintage stuck. Initially, retro was a broad term including both secondhand wares and newly made reproductions or reinterpretations of older styles. The term had negative connotations, representing an exploitative or offensive reflection of the past, as when punk rock star Sid Vicious wore a red swastika T-shirt while driving through Jewish neighborhoods in Paris, or when Yves Saint Laurent clothing runway models wore outfits like those worn by wartime prostitutes.²⁶ Postmodern theorists derided the phenomenon. In 1981, Jean Baudrillard described the "death pangs of the real and of the rational," and, in examining the retro impulse in contemporary cinema, concluded that retro reflections of historical aesthetics were essentially hollow and meaningless.²⁷

By the 1990s, retro more often meant newly made reproductions or incorporations of older styles, in clothing as well as film and other cultural productions, and the negative connotations faded toward amorality. In *Theatres of Memory*, British historian Raphael Samuel treated retro much more generously than foregoing theorists, viewing it as part of a populist enthusiasm for the past: "after its own fashion . . . a way of constructing knowledge." According to Samuel, these flea-market historical composites rely on the flickering gaslights of human memory. Clearly not accurate re-creations of the past, retro transposes the problems and concerns of the present on the perceptions of the past. Samuel's assessment breaks with the idea that retro reflections were just recycled junk piles devoid of meaning or historical context, proposing instead a hybrid blend of reflections on the past and contemporary concerns.²⁸

Of course, the practice of re-evoking past styles was not new to the late twentieth century. The late-nineteenth-century aesthetic dress movement discussed in chapter 1 of this book transparently mimicked elements of pre-Raphaelite dress, such as empire waists and muted fabric tones. Back-to-school fashions in the late 1940s cast at least a wistful side eye at flapper cheekiness and 1920s gender disruption. After the rush of revivalism in the late 1960s, though, the periodic evocation of older styles became increasingly standard, and recently outdated modernities—not echoes of antiquity—were the models.[29] Beginning in the early 1970s, designers borrowed cast-off styles for a variety of motives. For example, Welsh designer Laura Ashley diverged sharply from the revealing 1960s silhouettes when she featured long, gathered skirts, lacey, decorous necklines, and delicate cotton prints. The first of the so-called lifestyle designers, Laura Ashley appealed to middle-class dressers weary of the persistent aesthetic of sexiness and invoked instead the innocence and wholesome energy of scenes from Edwardian storybooks, such as *Rebecca of Sunnybrook Farms*. In the 1980s, Laura Ashley would reproduce versions of 1930s and 1940s tea dresses based on similar sentiments of nostalgic modesty.[30]

By the 1980s, the styles of elective poverty were also integrated into new fashion production. "Pope of trash" John Waters had a long-standing affiliation with secondhand culture and clothes. Waters himself rarely had enough money to buy new clothes until the late 1980s, when his success escalated with *Hairspray* (1988) and *Crybaby* (1990), trash theater gone big time—each grossed over $8 million. *Hairspray* and *Crybaby* highlighted a rising popularity of "trash art," occupying a similar cultural space as would the performative vulnerabilities of Kurt Cobain in combat boots and a dress. But before mainstream audiences discovered Waters in the late 1980s, he found the self-taught Japanese fashion designer Rei Kawakubo, whose clothing would eventually lure him away from his vaunted Baltimore thrift stores. According to Waters, Kawakubo in 1983—at which time she had already been designing for eight years—"specialized in clothes that are torn, crooked, permanently wrinkled, ill-fitting, and expensive. What used to be called 'seconds' (clothes that were on sale in bargain basements of department stores because of accidental irregularities) was now called 'couture.'" When Waters first checked out Kawakubo's New York City boutique, Comme des Garçons, he couldn't afford the clothing—which looked to him to be from the "sale bin at the Purple Heart thrift shop in Baltimore."[31] But after *Hairspray* made Waters an international kitsch sensation, Kawakubo became his go-to designer.

The same year Waters first coveted Kawakubo's designs, British fiction writer and social commentator Angela Carter observed the persistence of elective poverty, or in her words, "the aesthetics of poverty," in the face of rising unemployment in London, and its role in couture. Describing a high-end fashion advertisement, she mused at an extreme image of dandyism that, were it not labeled as the opposite, might be mistaken for "a paper-bag lady (or rather, person), in her asexually shapeless jacket, loose trousers, and sagging socks, with a scarf of dubiously soiled colour wrapped round her head, like a bandage beneath a hat jammed firmly down."[32] Carter viewed this style as a breakthrough in the gallery of poverty aesthetics—which she identified as thriving on the street level at least since the 1970s, most notably in the form of punk. Calling this "the recession style," Carter argued that one possible motivation for wealthy youth to masquerade as otherwise "may well be a self-protective measure." However, Carter observes the telltale sign emblematic of elective poverty, the trace element portraying voluntary participation; in this case, "the model's exquisitely painted face indicates that *her* get-up is intentional." Ironically, during the early 1980s, working-class girls in London crafted their impeccably tidy looks after Princess Diana, while rich girls "swan[ned] about in rancid long johns with ribbons in their hair," a description anticipating the mainstay thermals of grungewear.[33] The latter observation echoes Wolfe's assessment of white middle-class activists in the late-1960s, whose schlumpy poor-dress—proto-grunge, too, with stiff wool plaid and ugly green socks—missed the mark, according to him, since black ghetto residents were gussying up, James-Brown style. Like the sixties activists, the wealthy students in dirty thermals likely were not trying to actually pass as working class, but were performing a by-then ritualistic ambivalence toward their own class position.

In the 1980s, throwback styles and elective poverty looks added diversity to the American wardrobe. Other dissident styles—many reliant on secondhand items—persisted; punk dress and music, for example, diffused but barely diminished in influence. Other boldly visible subcultures emerged, spawned partly from the dueling yet parallel genres of punk and glam, and were still associated with music. Like grunge would, many eighties genres paired punk and glam elements—which after all were not always posed as opposites. Punk was not merely what Hebdige called "an addendum designed to puncture glam rock's extravagantly ornate style."[34] Punk drew on elements of glam rock style (such as the use of makeup), punk bands remade glam anthems, and punk audiences celebrated "glam" rockers such as David Bowie, Marc Bolan, and Lou Reed.[35]

Hybrid eighties musical and style trends borrowing from glam/punk themes often relied on habits of secondhand use. For example, the sonically diverse English band Bauhaus helped popularize a dark and gloomy gothic sensibility that depended heartily on long-forgone historical references. "Goths" blended popular allusions to Gothic and Romantic literature and dress in feats of chronological slipstream. Bauhaus's 1979 debut single, "Bela Lugosi's Dead," exemplifies this multireferencing by tagging the twenty-three-year-old death of the Hungarian-American cult actor best known for his portrayal of Count Dracula in the original 1931 film based on Bram Stoker's 1897 Gothic novel *Dracula*. Fittingly, goth fashion relied on blends of old and new clothing, styles, and fabrics, and the visual quotation of fads, even of fads that themselves referenced fads—exampling Baudrillard's hyperreal simulacra, a copy of a copy of a copy.

The catch-all genre New Wave looked to specific versions of the past.[36] Iconizing the 1950s and 1960s in stiffly stylized formats, New Wave fashion in the United States reacted against the revealing clothing standards for 1970s rock stars (as did Laura Ashley, but to a much different effect). New Wave images cultivated comparatively modest, retrospective styles that nonetheless retained elements of punk. Cyndi Lauper paired 1950s prom dresses with brightly dyed hair and a Johnny Rotten sneer. British rockers such as members of The Jam featured the fast discordance of punk riffs but distinguished themselves as "Post-Punk" in part by replacing ripped clothing with the tailored suits and skinny ties of the 1960s—and incorporating, instead of rejecting, 1960s rock and R&B influences.[37]

Yesterdays' Tomorrows

New Wave style often presented images based on past notions of the future. The New Wave band Devo, formed in 1972 and most popular following their 1980 hit single "Whip It," toyed with retro science fiction themes, surrealist humor, and commentary on the apparent regression of society (the name is short for "Devolution"). The details of their style, from their bright orange hazmat suits and Star Trek glasses to the flicker buttons and 3D glasses sold through their fan club catalogue reflected a fixation on what Elizabeth Guffey called "yesterdays' tomorrows." Recently abandoned modernities fueled the ironic nostalgia of retro in the last quarter of the twentieth century. The B-52s, an Athens, Georgia, band formed in 1977, well exemplify this specific sort of retro stylization. In dress and sound, the B-52s consistently referenced the late 1950s and early 1960s, with its space race fixation and utopian ideals of suburbia. In addition to their rocket-high bouffant wigs, Kate Pierson and Cindy Wilson sported thigh-high white boots and super-short gold lamé minis reminiscent of André Courrèges's 1964 Moon Girl collection.[38]

After their first gig playing a Valentine's Day party in 1977, the newly named B-52s—which they claimed was slang for the early sixties bouffant hairstyles the female band members sported—were a local hit. After taking their "southern camp" on the road and making a splash on the New York City scene, their eponymous first album reached number 59 on the Billboard 200 and included several chart-topping singles. As central to their total image as their synthesizer-based sound was their "thrift-store detritus look."[39] Just as nearly every review of the Cockettes mentioned their thrift-store drag, early commentary revolved around the B-52s' predilection for recycled sounds and image. *Rolling Stone*'s review of the B-52s' second album, *Wild Planet* (1980), called the group "connoisseurs of trash in a world full of it."[40] Critics focused on the band's absurdist versions of 1950s and 1960s style and culture. Their sound used "B movie 'sci-fi' keyboard sounds and surf riffs," and live shows incorporated invented dance fads with evocatively old-school names like Aqua-Velva.[41] As Nirvana's drummer Dave Grohl would remark years later, they had "a real unified feel."[42] Even the keyboards Schneider and Pierson played were pawn shop finds, discontinued 1960s models, whose cheap, tinny reverberations joined the chorus of examples of why the band was labeled "camp," "kitsch," or "trash."

The three above designations usually apply to material (physical or intellectual) that recycles popular culture. Camp has closest ties to underground theater and gay subcultures; trash is similar, but with the suggestion of an even "lower" aesthetics, like the intentionally cheap-looking and hollow parodies that are John Waters's films, echoing the precepts of Jack Smith's *Flaming Creatures* (1963). In general, a trashy camp aesthetic was alive and well in late-1970s Athens, Georgia. Among a small but highly visible crowd of young University of Georgia students and local glam-inspired partiers, the lineage from both Jack Smith and the Cockettes was clear: "they took Alice Cooper as inspiration and the New York Dolls as fashion advisors. All the boys, straight or gay, had at least one dress in their closets; all the girls had their Charlie Chaplin look." They scoured area thrift shops—like Potter's House, a thrift store run by recovering alcoholics—looking for the right costume party clothes, bought gallons of Aqua Net, and danced all night.[43]

Compared with the two above designations, "kitsch" perhaps most directly critiques commodity culture and the planned obsolescence driving the postwar economy. Derived from the German word meaning "to cheapen" (*verkitschen*), kitsch was used to critically describe certain cultural outputs as early as the 1860s, when applied to inexpensive, marketable, and sentimental artwork sold in the streets of Munich.[44] In the 1930s, Theodor Adorno applied the term to critique certain kinds of popular music that relied on "hyper-romanticism."[45] Adorno referred to kitsch as "pre-established forms that have lost their content in history," that is, styles that borrow from the past without establishing the context of historical relevance, similar to the way postmodern theorists derided retro in the 1980s.[46] Sometimes also called "a specifically aesthetic form of lying," kitsch has as much of a relationship with the future as with the past, and often "evokes a future utopia but only by looking back at a past that is selectively (mis)remembered."[47]

With successions of products, technologies, and styles that idealized a space-age notion of the future, the aesthetics of the late 1950s and early 1960s were labeled "kitsch" in their own context. The re-evocation of utopic suburban kitsch style twenty years after the original aesthetic invited even more layers. The B-52s' interest in cheaply made and fleetingly iconic cultural ephemera originating in a time just out of their childhood memories' reach was comparable to Jack Smith's referencing of 1940s B movies. But by the late 1970s, the quantity of physical materials available was massive, with much of the briefly fashionable styles and commodities of the postwar era now abandoned to flea markets and thrift shops, and quickly becoming the province of the culturally curious.[48]

Despite the B-52s' clear affinity with labels such as "camp," "kitsch," and "trash," members of the group disavowed such descriptions, especially their connotations of parody and mockery, insisting they evoked past styles and sounds out of genuine enjoyment of them—Jack Smith said the same thing about his inspiration from B movies starring Maria Montez. However, the B-52s had multiple possible reasons for refusing such labels. Musically, they sought to avoid the limitations of such pigeonholing, not wishing to stay trapped by a "party band" or "trash art" label. Second, aspects of the image reflected the actual backgrounds of the musicians; not only was the band labeled "trash"—around the time that John Waters's trash films were gaining creeping attention—but often their fashion sense was associated with *southern white* trash. Critics assumed Cindy Wilson's and Kate Pierson's costumes to be working-class mockery when they described the women as "waitresses" or "manicurists." Yet these stylizations were not wholly the product of cultural slumming, as band members actually did eek out livings waiting tables and had backgrounds more closely linked to the area's working class than its transient college population.[49] Finally, by the late 1970s, camp, trash, and kitsch were all firmly associated with gay male subcultures. Three of the B-52s musicians were homosexual men unwilling to reveal their sexual preference at a time when the AIDS epidemic was polarizing the nation on subject, and at a time when performers could become creatively immobilized by their sexual identities. Band members instead kept their homosexuality private until 1985, when guitarist Ricky Wilson died of AIDS-related causes.[50]

The band's desire not to be pegged as "queer camp" may have informed their adherence to established gendered appearances—male members wore Hawaiian shirts and suburban slacks while the women combined go-go dancer with fifties housewife. But in the 1980s, many other pop musicians extended kitsch conventions to gender presentation: if it was kitsch in the first place for a housewife to vacuum wearing an apron, high heels, and even higher hair, it was even kitschier for a man to borrow those elements in an incomplete masquerade that disrupted culturally ascribed categories of gender and sexuality. Genderfuck became shorthand for musical pop. When another Athens scenester-turned-rocker, R.E.M.'s singer Michael Stipe, wore a dress at a 1989 Syracuse, New York, performance, the implications of male rock stars in women's clothing on stage had almost two decades of examples to follow. According to a writer for the *Observer*, "the dress has a particular significance: it marks R.E.M.'s passing from their cult rock band status to the blurred, warping world of pop stardom."[51] By the late 1980s, boys in bands in thrift-store dresses signaled high-energy rock, following in the sparkling footsteps of glam.

Genderfuck and Grunge

By 1991, the idea that gender was performative was part of celebrity life—even for those without the edifying benefit of critical theorist Judith Butler's pivotal work on the subject.[52] Gender-bending displays used clothing to enhance audience perceptions of music, theater, and film. Individuals adapted styles to project a culturally valuable eccentricity. The "retro-rock" stylings of the B-52s and the tongue-in-cheek gritty prettiness of Kurt Cobain were just a few examples of how bodies and appearances were by then necessary parts of popular musical performances, especially after the spread of music videos. Clothing—often secondhand or retro—became part of the materials by which to recreate and simulate the "sudden parallels" that Breton sought at flea markets and junk shops. A reliance on the disjuncture of older styles attended this simulation.

Like the B-52s' style, the irony of Cobain's grunge posing was multifaceted, reflecting in part genuine class and regional affiliation. For Cobain, claims of an "authentic" poverty were valid. Cobain and his original band mates spent their high school days in the rural town of Aberdeen, Washington, where thrift stores and leisure time were plentiful, and money was not.[53] Homeless at times, Cobain slept on friends' couches and, purportedly, even under a bridge. Still, grunge clothing was not just a practical default, but a crafted style, developed alongside musical ambitions, and colored by glam, metal, and pop influences. Cobain, like Nirvana's future drummer, Dave Grohl, who was across the continent in a middle-class home in Virginia, knew he wanted to be a rock star before puberty, and he crafted his personal style accordingly, with fewer financial (but possibly more cultural) resources than Grohl. What Cobain and Grohl shared was not a class identity but a musical aesthetic, an aesthetic that coincided and diverged in the right degrees required to create the conflicted tonalities characteristic of the generational anthems produced by Nirvana.

Although the cynical sartorial tone and overall grittiness of grunge musicians was recognizably different from the poppier trends of the 1980s, the heterogeneous musical diet on which they were weaned included the New Wave bands of the late 1970s and 1980s, whose architects were in turn influenced by glam rockers. Members of Nirvana grew up admiring not only Black Sabbath and KISS but also second-generation glitter boys and girls like those in R.E.M. and the B-52s. Cobain first caught sight of the B-52s on *Saturday Night Live* when he was twelve years old. The band's televised performance reportedly kick-started Cobain's love of New Wave music and style—and inspired him to paint black and white squares on his sneakers in imitation of vocalist Fred Schneider's checkerboard Vans.[54] In Virginia, an adolescent Grohl was similarly enamored; unlike Cobain, however, Grohl had the means to buy a "proper" pair of checkerboard Vans. The totality of the B-52s' image still impressed Grohl years later: "The women looked like they were from outer space, and everything was linked in—the [record] sleeves, the sound, the clothes, the iconography, the logo, everything."[55]

As some described it, grunge was a "sartorial representation of nihilism that had been evolving around members of the college rock and hardcore underground for more than a decade."[56] This "nihilism" was rooted in part in playful New Wave nostalgia and glam rock, elements of which remained apparent in grunge style, especially through male cross-dressing. Much as Jack Smith forged the way for the Cockettes, Andy Warhol, and the New York Dolls, the dress-donning, retro-style elements of grunge hailed from exposure to 1980s "alternative" pop bands, themselves inheritors of Ridiculous Theater aesthetics.[57] According to Cobain's remarks to the *Los Angeles Times*, wearing women's clothes revealed a cynical awareness of culturally ascribed gender ideology as well as a nonchalance about sexuality. "Wearing a dress shows I can be as feminine as I want," Cobain remarked, adding, "I'm a heterosexual... big deal. But if I was a homosexual, it wouldn't matter either."[58] Beyond gender ambiguity, Cobain's dresses were a knowing nod to his savvy about the trappings of pop music. Paired with white socks, undershirts, and dirty boots, his total style was obviously not just the result of slim-pickings at the Aberdeen Goodwill, but a self-conscious elaboration on an established pop uniform.

While grunge evolved musically most directly from punk and heavy metal, the liberal sublayer of glitter rock and pop influences helped make bands like Nirvana internationally renowned. Cobain himself seemed to most desire to cultivate folk and blues influences, intending to elevate the band to canonical status. Sartorially, the style was equally bricolage—but leaned heavily on cultivated Pacific Northwest working-class cues, such as thick flannels, ear-warming stocking caps, and sturdy, worn footwear. Juxtaposed, the deviations in standardized gender dress materialized the glam undertones of the music. Cobain used dress cues to refute categorization—to avoid the kind of pigeonholing that inspired the B-52s to reject the label "camp." After just wading into stardom in with the release of *Nevermind*, in November 1991 Cobain showed up at Headbangers Ball in a bright yellow full-length taffeta gown, complete with a puffy, banana-colored Queen Victoria neck ruff, a proudly tacky ensemble that screamed cheap thrift-store find. To many in the heavy metal community, his appearance at the lackluster interview was a rebuff to his inclusion in the heavy metal genre.[59] A man in a dress, in and of itself, is not outside the imagery of heavy metal. As former member of the New York Dolls, Buster Poindexter, points out in the beginning of his 1987 music video for "Hot, Hot, Hot," while flipping through the covers of old New York Dolls albums featuring vamped-up band members: "You know, these heavy metal bands in L.A. don't have the market cornered on wearing their mother's clothes." Poindexter, wearing a tux with a trim New Wave bouffant, perched in front of a New York City cityscape, brandishes his former self to both acknowledge his musical credentials and to distance himself stylistically from the past, to announce his musical makeover. In case the viewer did not yet understand that what he wears is tantamount to how he sounds, Poindexter tosses aside the old albums, straightens his bowtie, and explains that he is "into a really refined and dignified kind of a situation.... I'm playing music that's so soft and sweet, I mean, you can sit next to the fireplace and listen to it, you can have a little glass of wine, maybe. You can even have dinner with this music."[60] Clothing firmly signified musical direction.

It was not that Cobain wore a dress; it was the *way* he wore it that distanced him from heavy metal and announced his band's reluctance to be classified. The ball gown certainly brushed up against visual tropes borrowed by metal rockers from the "extravagantly ornate style" of glam, but Cobain intentionally got it wrong.[61] The dress was obviously too much, a terrible color, cheap material, presumably secondhand, and perhaps most important, unaccessorized. By throwing the dress on over pants and slippers, paired with his standard choppy bob, dime-store sunglasses, uncrossed legs, and slumped posture, Cobain mocked the gender-bending thing at least as much as he performed it. He plucked certain sartorial elements from certain genres to portray a complex musical vision. Cobain wore women's clothing ironically, divorced from the glam/metal accouterments of big hair and/or glittery makeup: the result was grunge genderfuck.

Perhaps increasing doses of irony were unavoidable when the subgenre dubbed "alternative" by MTV shows like *120 Minutes* migrated to the mainstream. Growing up at a time when rebellion was the popular thing to do made rebelling enormously frustrating—but no less compelling. Quickly, the less cool something seemed, the cooler it became, and not only because of the quickening pace of corporate co-optation and youth-catering commercial interests dying to stay relevant. Cynicism was the tenor and tone of the so-called Generation X; in fact, cynicism was the single most cohesive element, according to those eager to dissect "kids these days." The term "generation X" was coined the same year Nirvana released their record-breaking album *Nevermind*. Even though generation categorizing is a notoriously flawed sociological tool, the practice persisted, and at least reflected popular perception. Commentators profiled the youth growing up behind baby boomers even before Douglas Coupland's 1991 novel *Generation X; Tales for an Accelerated Culture* named them. In 1990, *Time* magazine described a subset of young Americans as "lacking in ambition," "indecisive," and obsessed with blaming their parents' generation for economic and political disarray.[62]

Secondhand and DIY clothing choices were tailor-made for ironic posturing, serving as a self-deprecating sneer at the futility of rebellion and offering acknowledgment of what many baby boomers had failed to recognize—the contradictions inherent in using consumption to oppose consumption. Images such as Kurt Cobain wearing a T-shirt hand-penned with the words "corporate magazines still suck" on the cover of *Rolling Stone* magazine in 1992 shruggingly gave up on the possibility of operating "outside the system." After all, the economy, politics, the environment—it all "sucked." These young people grew up learning that they had missed the last best chance at rebellion, the only time when rock 'n' roll and social protest mattered.[63] Yet the nineties did echo the rebellion of the sixties, and perhaps repetition was unavoidable. In both eras, youth cultures expressed disillusionment and resentment toward the foregoing generation; the difference for nineties kids was that not only had their parents ruined the environment, relationships, politics, and the global economy, but they had even ruined rebellion.

Still, ascribing Gen-X idolatry of cynicism-induced irony to a unique epoch, to another reaction to the follies of elders, forgets the necessity of irony in making kitsch and camp effective. Certainly, the New York Dolls' gender-bending posturing in the seventies could not be taken wholly at face value. Rather than making personal authenticity claims, their aggressively glittery appearances highlighted the weirdness of culture.[64] New Wave bands, with their superimposition of the cultural flotsam of a particular recent past onto contemporary musical themes, relied on irony. According to theorist Linda Hutcheon, it is the "rubbing together" of disparate representations that "makes irony happen."[65]

Cobain's Cardigan

A used object implies a narrative, a past-lives story that sometimes supports ironic meaning—such as that imbedded in the banana-yellow belle-of-the-ball dress Cobain appeared in on Headbangers Ball—and sometimes underscores artistic mission. Like the Charlatans' Edwardian westernwear and the 1990s Ragman's magical suit, grunge dress manipulated assumptions that used clothing retained some of the characteristics of previous owners. Take, for example, the shapeless, pilled, fuzzy neutral-colored cardigans Cobain favored, appearing in them in photos, on MTV's *Unplugged* in 1994, and in band publicity photos. The cardigan, whether men's or women's (he wore both left-buttoned and right-buttoned versions), so exemplified Cobain's image that his avatar in Guitar Hero 5 wears a fuzzy beige one, like the one he appeared in on MTV's *Unplugged* in 1994.[66] By then, the cardigan bore well over a century of signifiers, starting from an association with British aristocracy—the Earl of Cardigan and his light brigade in the Crimean War (1853–56) wore short, close-fitting, collarless knitted jackets of Berlin wool or English worsted, lending the outerwear its name.[67] In the 1950s and early 1960s, the British prime minister, Harold Macmillan, took to wearing a knitted, baggy cardigan as part of his country gentleman's persona, and a well-worn cardigan became international shorthand for English comfort and dignified intellect. This and the cardigan's appearance on Rex Harrison in the film *My*

Fair Lady helped make an oversized cardigan (not of the perky twin-set variety) a smart item for young college women, lending it an androgynous, academic implication.[68] Perhaps most immediately accessible to the memory of Cobain's fans, a cardigan was integral to the image of children's television personality Mister Rogers of public television's *Mister Rogers' Neighborhood* (1968–2001), a gentle, avuncular figure whose ritualistic removal of dress shoes and sports coat in favor of a soft cardigan and blue sneakers evoked cross-generational nostalgia. The sweater, like Mister Rogers' pleasingly generic neighborhood, had an "honest," "familiar" feel to it: "simple and classic."[69] Whether or not the viewers of *Unplugged* consciously registered anything of the cardigan's richly storied past, the way in which Cobain often wore it, with his own dirty sneakers and over homemade, punk-band T-shirts, arguably made the cardigan an ironic statement. Just as arguably, however, the clothes-conscious Cobain wore the cardigan as part of his bid for musical respectability, as a way to seem familiar and iconic himself.

Cobain longed to take Nirvana beyond the label of grunge, which he saw as "as potent a term as New Wave," and even more difficult to supersede. He wanted something to launch him into the spectrum of other singers/songwriters able to morph and stay relevant, like Bob Dylan or David Bowie—or R.E.M., a band that, by Cobain's death, had risen well above the "college rock" label.[70] Nirvana's entire 1994 *Unplugged* performance has been read as an attempt to reframe the band—an attempt spearheaded by Cobain, and to many, a failed attempt. His personal appearance on *Unplugged*, along with their song choices, suggests a bid for "authenticity," an assertion of a claim for a natural seat among the musical pantheon. Wearing greasy hair, stained jeans, dirty Converses, a feminist punk band tee, a wrinkled pastel-striped button-up shirt, and signature cardigan, Cobain performed covers not only of the glam master of reinvention and bisexual theatrics, David Bowie, but also Lead Belly, an African American, Texas-born ex-convict blues singer famously recorded for Alan Lomax's New Deal–sponsored collection of folk music.[71] In his music, Cobain followed in a long tradition of white rock stars leaning on the established marginality of black Americans to claim their own authenticity. In his dress, he also relied on references and reminders to craft his public persona.

Vintage and Retro Economies

While highly exemplary, Cobain was not the only sartorial role model for emulative young fans. In the 1990s, for both males and females, dressing from thrift shops was a rite of passage and a mode of personal identity transformation intimately tied to musical pursuits. Allison Wolfe was lead vocalist for Bratmobile, an all-female, feminist band that, along with Bikini Kill, challenged the male-dominated grunge era with their "Riot Grrrl" style and sound. In an interview, Wolfe described what she did immediately after "something clicked" during a violent altercation with her high school jock boyfriend, inspiring her to change her lifestyle: "I chopped off one side of my hair, and started wearing crosses, eyeliner, thrift store clothes.... I got really more into music."[72] Incorporating an alternative style and unconventional musical pursuits required unorthodox forms of consumption and dress. Like Michael Stipe wearing a dress, Wolfe's adolescent thriftshopping indicated a significant change. When the Riot Grrrl movement quickly stalled and sputtered, Wolfe attributed its demise to the co-optation of their style by mainstream consumer outlets such as Urban Outfitters—which, though it had existed since the 1970s, gained even more widespread popularity in the 1990s. Wolfe said, "You know, you'd go to Urban Outfitters and the fake riot grrrl bands playing over the loudspeakers, all these clothes that were just like what we would wear . . . we ended up just kind of abandoning it, because it became so trendy, and it wasn't our fault," Wolfe claimed, protesting accusations of "selling out."[73]

In 1993, Urban Outfitters was the "clearinghouse of the young and now." The stores' stock looked "as if it came from a design house run by the Salvation Army."[74] In fact, some of it did. Outfitters took a page from Lord & Taylor's 1957 playbook and sold clothing that was actually pre-owned, calling it, of course, vintage: "For those who wouldn't deign to go to an actual thrift store, Outfitters has its own line of vintage apparel: Urban Renewal," grumbled the *Washington Post* writer of the keenly titled article "Not-So-Radical Chic."[75] Major city branches of the store also displayed found objects as art, indicating a surrealist link. Urban Outfitters replicated what was cool and hip about secondhand outlets but minimized the discomfort or inconvenience of wading through undesirable wares and bearing with the glaring fluorescence and cheap, cracked tiling of thrift stores. The catch, of course, was the upsell; the same ten-year-old jeans that would have gone for a buck at Goodwill cost twenty times that at Urban Outfitters.

Urban Outfitters served as a tangible example of Baudrillard's hyperreal—"a place that is a map without a history," offering place-oriented immersive kitsch with glimpses at uncontextualized past styles.[76] But however apparently unhinged the Urban Outfitters style may have been from chronology, the business itself and the borrowed ideas do have a history. In 1970, Dick

Hayne opened a head shop/thrift store named Free People's Store. Despite the name and at least hinted-at appropriation of the Digger's modus operandi, Hayne's pursuits were firmly capitalist. The original 400-square-feet worth of "used clothes, T-shirts, housewares, dope paraphernalia, and ethnic jewelry" were sold from the start, and Hayne pursued expansion and adapted to his target audience with great marketing savvy, combining the Free Store notion with the profit-making acumen of those late sixties London boutiques, complete with accents of Moroccan exoticism and Native American design. In other words, Hayne combined the political aesthetics of elective poverty with vintage exhibitionism for the purpose of making money. Utilizing his degree in anthropology, he crafted a commercial environment just outlandish enough to appeal to aspiring young hipsters without well-articulated ideals or motivations to help shape their visual ambitions.

By 1976, the original venue name, Free Peoples Store, had worn out its hippie appeal, and the chain was rechristened Urban Outfitters, expressing the postindustrialist cachet of the struggling American city.[77] In 1992, Hayne launched a new "lifestyle" brand, Anthropologie, which was higher end than Urban Outfitters, appealing to an older crowd with reproductions of various vintage styles (cheaply made and unable to withstand many washings, despite their price). By 1993, Urban Outfitters' own vintage line was rapidly shrinking. Mostly, Urban Outfitters sold newly produced retro-style clothes, introducing kids only barely too young to remember them to brands like Hang Ten and Stussy, labels whose brief, original moment had ended about half a generation ago. These were clothes that, for the diligent shopper, would be hip, surrealist "sudden parallels" when found amidst the racks of medical scrubs and Dress Barn shifts at the local thrift store. Stores like Urban Outfitters removed the necessity of hunting, mostly by recreating looks in combinations just hip enough to excite youth into spending their still-increasing disposable incomes, but not daring enough to limit their target audience—a sales associate admitted that the store tended to be "on the safer side of cutting edge."[78]

Throughout the twentieth century, secondhand clothing served numerous practical, economic, and cultural purposes—purposes that periodically diverged, intersected, and merged to form a bewildering hodgepodge of socioeconomic display. Among consumers, there were those who thrift-shopped covertly, seeking apparel they hoped might "pass" as new, which would visually boost their apparent economic status. Then there was the growing segment of thrift shoppers who sought to disaffiliate with the middle class by dressing either up or down, in vintage exhibits or displays of elective poverty. On the heels of grunge's mass influence, another consumer of the secondhand aesthetic resurged, the sort who patronized the higher-priced faux-thrift designers such as Anna Sui and Todd Oldham, who themselves scouted flea markets and thrift stores to hone the details of their nineties' lines—participants in an even costlier version of what the San Francisco Diggers dubbed "hip capitalism" in 1967, and what Thomas Frank argued grew alongside or was the precursor of similar street styles. In the nineties, these shoppers wanted the nostalgic, eclectic styles patched together from remnant piles, but they balked at the creative effort required, or the negative associations of dirtiness and cheapness that actual secondhand things still maintained. In a 1996 *Los Angeles Times* article about the latest Oldham collection, Mimi Avins opined that Oldham's secondhand-seeming apparel was aesthetically on point with the vintage fads, but saved consumers' time and promised higher quality. And perhaps most important, the clothing was not cursed with someone else's past: "The sort of Treasures you'd have to scour many vintage stores to bag not only smell fresh when provided by Oldham, but lack the sad mien of the discarded."[79] Urban Outfitters was the safe, affordable, middle-class version of Anna Sui and Todd Oldham. In echoing elements of grunge style that themselves referenced older trends, Sui and Oldham created a specialized sort of "retro" clothing.

While the look of secondhand style could be appropriated—a term not intended to express simply unwillingness on the part of a monolithic subculture to sell out their "brand" to high bidders, but a complex negotiated process of consumer distribution—the use of genuinely pre-owned clothing was harder to co-opt, economically. Undoubtedly, though, in the last quarter of the twentieth century, the economic and social meaning of secondhand trade changed, too, with many venues taking on more profit-oriented, corporatized models. During the postwar years, consignment shops emerged as a popular cooperative take on for-profit thrift stores. Consignment—where participants offered unwanted items for sale with the promise of a percentage of the sales profit or store credit—had long been an option for collectors of valuable objects, a way of profiting from fine objects no longer desired, perhaps when a collector's fancy shifted. The rise of consignment clothing shops, beginning as early as the 1950s, showed the increased valuation of secondhand clothing during this era. The idea gained added appeal in its affinity with cooperative consumer models in the late 1960s. Before long, for-profit chains of consignment stores geared toward young consumers flourished. Buffalo Exchange began in 1974, and Crossroads Exchange in 1991. Appealing to an even younger, "teenybopper" crowd, Plato's Closet joined the game in 1998.

Consignment models did not overtake thrift stores, which maintained a monopoly on ease and convenience (and tax deductibility) for consumers looking to guiltlessly discard unused wares. The for-profit chain Savers, Inc., expanded its locations and profits throughout the 1970s and 1980s, but at the same time, philanthropic thrift stores continued to multiply and diversify, reflecting current social priorities. In 1981, the discovery of the human immunodeficiency virus (HIV) and acquired immunodeficiency syndrome (AIDS), led to a great many changes in LGBT communities, especially among gay men.[80] In 1987, activists, including Michael Weinstein, formed the AIDS Hospice Foundation to offer specialized palliative care to those suffering from AIDS, which at the time was assumed terminal in most cases. As medical possibilities for handling HIV became more accessible, the organization changed its mission from providing dignified hospice care to HIV/AIDS patients to a focus on quality of life with the disease. Weinstein's Hospice Foundation became the AIDS Healthcare Foundation (AHF) in the mid-1990s, relying in part on federal and local governmental support and providing AIDS care services not only in the United States but also in Africa and Mexico.[81]

In 1990, Weinstein opened a Los Angeles thrift store, Out of the Closet, the proceeds from which went to support AHF. In the mold of the 1960s homophile organization SIR's own thrift store, the SIRporium, Out of the Closet not only sold clothing and accessories but also offered services for gay men and women. Instead of giving away conservative interview outfits, however, Out of the Closet offered free rapid STD and HIV testing. Weinstein continued to expand through the 1990s, adding new stores in Los Angeles, San Francisco, and south Florida. Weinstein used the profit from the sale of secondhand clothing not only to help prevent the spread of AIDS through testing and education but to legally fight pharmaceutical companies for triple-drug-therapy price cuts—especially for low-income HIV sufferers in developing nations.[82]

Despite the diversification in the used goods trade in the United States, by 1990, the American secondhand market was not nearly large enough to accommodate the thousands of tons of clothing discarded annually. As Karen Tranberg Hansen records in her pivotal book about "salaula" (a Bemba term meaning "to rummage through a pile") much of this clothing was sold in bulk to developing countries such as Zambia. By the 1990s, international goods recycling companies with modest midcentury beginnings were hugely profitable, and not without their share of scandals. For example, the Domsey Trading Corporation, a secondhand clothing export company started by

German-Jewish immigrants in New York City just after World War II grossed an estimated $40 million in 1996. That decade, the wealthy corporation faced intensely negative publicity, workers strikes, and several lawsuits for labor violations, including *International Ladies' Garment Workers' Union vs. Domsey Trading Corporation*, a 1990 case that stemmed from the illegal firing of unionizing workers—mostly Haitian immigrants—and the harassment of striking workers.[83]

In 1988, Todd Gitlin frowningly wrote that the aesthetics of postmodernity disregarded continuity, preferring instead "copies, repetition, and the recombination of hand-me-down scraps." But by the 1980s, the practice of gleaning historical data and physical materials was already a well-established means of new cultural expression, one certainly indulged by Gitlin's most studied and personal demographic, young baby boomers. Rather, long-standing academic disregard for the growth of secondhand economies and styles across the twentieth century have blinded many scholars to historical processes relying on pre-owned materials—both imaginary and physical. According to historian Daniel T. Rodgers, avant-garde artists (like those from at least Duchamp's time forward) in the 1980s approached the past as a "big, open warehouse of reusable styles." "History was not a process to be advanced or resisted. History was a great consignment shop of reusable fashions."[84] While Rodgers was far from alone in assigning the 1980s chief responsibility—for better or worse—for the avant-garde habits of salvaging, his commentary sounds remarkably like a rephrasing of Jack Smith's quote from the 1960s: "Art is one big thrift shop." To say that grunge style was a spontaneous reaction to the conservatism and affluence of the 1980s ignores the economic growth and cultural resonance of secondhand commerce and style throughout the postwar decades.

Grunge was not simply, as Jean-Paul Gaultier put it, "the way we dress when we have no money," nor was it an original, creative rebellion spontaneously orchestrated by youthful misanthropes. Grunge connected to major economic and cultural developments spanning the twentieth century. It relied on globalizing, highly orchestrated secondhand economies. It built on the innovations of dada dresser Baroness Elsa von Freytag-Loringhoven; Vaudeville acts such as Fanny Brice's "Second Hand Rose"; the adolescent posing of 1950s Ivy League football fans in musty 1920s raccoon coats; the aristocratic stylings of jet-setting London nobility in the 1960s; the lipsticked, hair sprayed, latexed New York Dolls of the 1970s; the dark camp of 1980s John Waters's films; and even the prim retrospection of Laura Ashley's floral dresses. Though ironic, the energy invested in full-fledged grunge style was full of ambition and cultural knowledge, despite occasional dismissals of the trend—and its adherents—as lazy and apathetic.

The global secondhand market and the adaptations of poor dress by high fashion I critique here did develop alongside the imaginative use of secondhand goods to break down restrictive formulas of gender, sexuality, and class, to create aesthetically and politically groundbreaking art, and to provide incomes for small entrepreneurs or to support pressing social issues. From before the Salvation Army sold used bronze heels to dancing girls and made children's coats from discarded automobile upholstery, secondhand commerce was an incorporated part of the broader cultural economy, reacting to, encouraging, establishing, and resisting major consumer trends. Understanding the ways in which alternative and mainstream economies interacted allows for a more fully educated and enabled consumer body, one that can take responsibility for the harms of a consumer-based culture—and maybe still indulge in the pleasures it affords.

Epilogue
Popping Tags in the Twenty-First Century

By the end of the twentieth century, voluntarily buying and wearing visibly secondhand clothing had become a rite of passage for rebellious youth. As ever, the meanings embedded in the performances of dress remained malleable and sometimes obscure. As this book has shown, no single political, social, or economic group popularized the buying of used goods and clothing or maintained its status. Eager secondhand patrons appeared from nearly all directions, encouraged by the monumental economic expansion turning the United States into a consumer society. While motives, methods, and meanings varied widely, an enduring belief in the almost mystical transformative and transitive properties of pre-owned clothing remained at the heart of voluntary secondhand styles. From Henry James's 1868 short story "The Romance of Certain Old Clothes" to the 1990s creators of the comic book *Ragman*, American mass culture perpetuated the idea that wearers imbue their clothing with personal attributes and leave wardrobes with traces of their own faults and virtues.[1]

Another myth about secondhand sales persisted. Shoppers continued to view secondhand venues as exceptions to the social and economic critiques of dominant capitalisms. Throughout the twentieth century, used goods economies codified and expanded, branching out into million-dollar industries. First, the Salvation Army and Goodwill Industries forged a new kind of philanthropic capitalism, buttressed in part by Progressive reform sentiments related to rising anxieties about urbanization and immigration. New urban laws curtailing the activities of informal street economies supported the growth of static storefronts selling secondhand, while Christianizing companies targeted the same groups marginalized by those regulations. However, the act of shopping, and of dressing, remained heavily negotiated terrain, with no decisive actor wholly determining the popularity or use of consumer goods.

From at least 1902 on, when the *New York Times* reported on the Navy Street dancer searching for a flashy pair of shoes at the Brooklyn Salvation Army, some thrift-store clients thwarted formal expectations by using the venues creatively, as other than as a means to better assimilate to white, middle-class expectations or to pursue established models of upward mobility.[2] After

World War I ended, the baroness Elsa von Freytag-Loringhoven's performative dada dress linked sartorial artistry with a rising avant-garde penchant for discarded materials. A growing disdain for mass production and capitalist growth grew alongside a conservative nostalgia for older American-made items and the related expansion of antique markets. Self-designated flea markets capitalized on these trends while taking practical advantage of the vacuum left in both rural and public markets by agricultural crises and the advent of chain grocery stores such as the A&P, strengthening the role of secondhand commerce in the United States.

After World War II, garage sales, markedly suburban innovations, linked civic responsibility and political activism to the United States' growing affluence by creating new ways to responsibly discard older material goods to make room for new purchases. In the 1950s and 1960s, the desire for personal distinction—for visible exception from the buying crowds—marked consumer rationales for voluntary secondhand fashions, fueling the strength of secondhand economies. The postwar decades marked the definitive arrival of trends in voluntary secondhand dress and the rapid expansion, domestically and globally, of used clothing markets. Bohemian writers, political agitators, radical lesbians, and groundbreaking environmentalists assumed that systems of goods recirculation somehow circumvented, and even undermined, global capitalist patterns. While secondhand clothing did, in various ways, enable increasing acceptance of non-normative personal appearances, many advocates ignored the corporatization of used goods trade—and its complicity in the growing global labor controversies surrounding firsthand fashion.

The examples given and the paths traced in this book are by no means the only ones that chart the trajectory of all secondhand commerce in the twentieth century. Nor did vintage exhibitionism and elective poverty pass from popular view with the end of grunge. Arguably, the two veins of voluntary secondhand dress merged even more decisively at the end of the millennium. After habitual heroin user Kurt Cobain took his own life with a shotgun in 1994, styles straight-facedly called "shabby chic," "heroin chic," or "poor chic" enjoyed greater cultural currency than ever before.[3] These productions of style represented the sardonic popularity of intentional "bad taste."[4] "Fashionizing" poverty, as the House of Dior did with its 2000 line of "hobo chic," obscured the real costs of poverty and homelessness for those entrenched in it, while still leaning on the performative history of artistic and social commentary chronicled in this book.

Dior designer John Galliano's 2000 hobo chic haute couture collection bore a mocking similarity to the rogue dada dress of Baroness Elsa von Freytag-Loringhoven. While the baroness paraded the post–World War I Greenwich Village streets with gleaned tomato cans covering her breasts and borrowed bicycle taillights adorning her rear, Galliano's emaciated models walked an elite Paris runway with "tin cups dangling from the derriere bottle caps, plastic clothes-pins and safety pins."[5] Amidst the requisite compliments and castigations, Galliano said he was inspired by the French homeless and the mentally ill, and that his designs evoked the array of tattered gowns famed designer Charles Frederick Worth made for French socialites to wear to popular 1930s' Rag Balls.[6] Ben Stiller's parodic film *Zoolander* (2001) included a scathing imitation of Dior's "hobo chic." The movie, which mocked and exposed many negative aspects and stereotypes of the fashion industry, showcased a premier couture line called "Derelicte," whose fictional designer mocked Galliano by describing the tattered garb as "a fashion, a way of life inspired by the very homeless, the vagrants, the crack whores that make this wonderful city so unique."[7] Reflecting accusations of another gilded age, some commentators reacted much as the masses did when Marie Antoinette dressed as a shepherdess: with a "glint of the guillotine."[8]

Designers such as Galliano creating "a poor-girl look that only a rich one could afford"—some of his hobo chic dresses retailed for $25,000—risked trivializing the plight of those whose rags are not affect, whose denim is unavoidably distressed.[9] In 2002, sociologist Karen Bettez Halnon proposed a thesis complementary to Michael Harrington's 1962 argument that the well-dressed poor (clad in cast-off clothing) help mask the true disadvantages of poverty. According to Halnon, expensive, poor chic consumption reproduces inequality through cross-class performativity.[10] Halnon suggests that this interpretation runs counter to optimistic assertions that Veblenian practices of conspicuous consumption and "work abstention" had ceased to indicate upper-class status. Instead, theorists proposed "lifestyle consumption" as a more fluid and individualized class and status project. In the instance of hobo chic, however, "lifestyle consumption" presents itself as an elaboration on or cooptation of vintage exhibitionism, one that thoroughly incorporates elective poverty with little political intent.

By the time such trends in poor chic made it to haute couture, the materials used were not secondhand. They were inspired by and hyped through the popularity of secondhand style, but retained few of secondhand commerce's sometimes-professed economic radicality or cross-class sympathies. The popularity of genuinely secondhand acquisitions continued alongside these trends, however. In the still-flourishing world of voluntary secondhand dress, prices varied along a spectrum from thrift stores to vintage shops, with the requisite privilege still being the time and knowledge necessary to get the cross-class, cross-generational stylings "right." The accumulation, sourcing, distribution, repackaging, and profit making of secondhand clothing itself also continued to accelerate as more and cheaper firsthand clothing increased the volume—and also often decreased the quality—of used offerings.[11]

At the start of the twenty-first century, "fast fashion," the rapid-fire production of slightly new styles and cuts priced to sell, directly encouraged a complementarily rapid discarding of barely worn clothing. Patrons most readily associated "fast fashion" with clearly mainstream companies such as Zara and Forever 21, but hip businesses once linked to secondhand commerce and firmly wedded to retro—Urban Outfitters again—also conformed to a corporate model relying on farmed-out labor and cheap construction. By the aughts, any ostensible connection to potentially radical uses of secondhand items were more than belied by "Made in" labels indicating countries— China, Sri Lanka, India, and Turkey—whose factory conditions and worker wages were far below American legal standards. Yet by aligning themselves with trendy Indie bands and music festivals, Urban Outfitters sought to keep up their "alternative" appeal.[12] Critiques of this alliance echoed 1960s' underground newspapers scathing dismissal of the Woodstock scene, a clear influence on popular contemporary festivals.

Despite these and other critiques of the "authenticity" of secondhand styles and commerce, used goods exchange continued to grow and diversify— and to be justified by anticapitalism and claims of originality. In the digital age, access to unwanted wares has once again grown. Begun in 1997, eBay (along with other Internet auctioning sites) represents the latest major innovation in secondhand markets. As a social space, the interactive dynamics are every bit as specific and unique as garage sales and thrift stores. Legally, eBay has faced some of the same questions of taxation as garage sales, similar concerns about counterfeiting as flea markets, and even trickier questions about international trade than any venue to date.[13] eBay's digital design, regulatory ambiguities, and social spectrums offer fertile ground for much more extensive scholarly analysis than exists currently.

Despite the definitive changes in the process and products of secondhand commerce, secondhand styles have not gone away. The recent success of independent rapper Macklemore—born and raised in the hometown of grunge, Seattle—attests to the continuing relevance of secondhand style to popular culture. In 2013, his song, "Thrift Shop," featuring Wanz and Ryan Lewis, became the first single since 1994 to reach number 1 on the U.S. Billboard Hot 100 chart without the support of a major record label. Its success, which resulted primarily from online exposure, showed—as has eBay—how the digital sphere has become another arena in which the popularity of secondhand goods is celebrated. Macklemore's "Thrift Shop" highlights the cultural and political capital of reuse and signifies the enduring association of creative output with secondhand commerce. Performing amidst a global economic recession, Macklemore uses thrift as a personal boast by deriding Gucci prices: "Fifty dollars for a t-shirt, that's just some ignorant bitch shit / I call that getting swindled and pimped, shit / I call that getting tricked by a business." Instead, with only twenty dollars, he goes "poppin' tags" at Goodwill. Macklemore goes on to make a claim for originality, calling having the same shirt as someone else a "hella don't."[14]

Whatever the continuing or resurgent stigmas and social critiques of secondhand products may be, many creative dressers agree with Macklemore on the sartorial potential of secondhand style: "This is fucking awesome." Voluntary secondhand dress persists precisely because it suggests both cultural and economic distinction. It satisfies a desire to be seen as different than the average consumer dupe—as willing to invest time in the cultivation of originality supposedly without utilizing class and wealth privilege. The commercial reality and the class subscripts portrayed here, however, paint a much more complicated portrait of secondhand economies and styles, one bound to get even more convoluted in the years ahead.

Notes

Introduction

1. For more on Salvation Army dress, see Jennifer Le Zotte, "'Be Odd': The Contradictory Use of Dress in the Gilded Age Salvation Army," *Winterthur Portfolio* 47, no. 4 (2012): 245–66. Diane Winston describes Evangeline Booth's attraction to and romanticization of poverty and her use of what I call cross-class dressing, as well as her important role in the Salvation Army in the United States and her reshaping of the group's public image. See Diane Winston, *Red-Hot and Righteous: The Urban Religion of the Salvation Army* (Cambridge, MA: Harvard University Press, 1999), 143–90.

2. The musical was named "The Commander in Rags" in reference to Booth. See "Miss Booth's Slum Tales Thrill Crowd," *New York Times*, 29 January 1906, 9.

3. Booth's parents once feared she would leave the mission for a life "on stage." P. W. Wilson describes Booth's dramatic inclinations in Wilson, *General Evangeline Booth of the Salvation Army* (New York: Charles Scribner's Sons, 1948), 63–65. For more on Evangeline Booth's life, see Margaret Troutt, *The General Was a Lady: The Story of Evangeline Booth* (Nashville: A.J. Holman, 1980). Evangeline Booth's views are also reflected in her own writing. See Evangeline Booth, *The Harp and the Sword: Published and Unpublished Writings and Speeches of Evangeline Cory Booth* (West Nyack, NY: Salvation Army, Literary Dept., USA Eastern Territory, 1992); Evangeline Booth and Grace Livingston Hill, *The War Romance of the Salvation Army* (Philadelphia: J. B. Lippincott, 1919).

4. See Lt.-Colonel Edith MacLachlan, "The Salvation Army Uniform" (The Salvation Army National Archives [TSANA], uncatalogued, 1977), 5. For more on how religious groups have historically used clothing as "symbolic boundary markers," see Linda B. Arthur, *Religion, Dress and the Body* (Oxford: Berg, 1999). See also, Le Zotte, "'Be Odd.'"

5. See Edward H. McKinley, *Somebody's Brother: A History of the Salvation Army Men's Social Service Department* (Lewiston, NY: Edwin Mellon Press, 1986), 158.

6. Frightwig, an all-female, feminist punk band, was suddenly popular after MTV aired the episode of *Unplugged* in December 1993. See David A. Ensminger, *Visual Vitriol: The Street Art and Subculture of the Punk and Hardcore Generation* (Jackson: University Press of Mississippi, 2011), 188.

7. This description is based on the author's viewing of the *MTV Unplugged* episode from which the live album and DVD were recorded. See Beth McCarthy-Miller, director, *Nirvana: MTV Unplugged* (New York: Geffen Records, 2007).

8. The term "grunge" was reportedly coined by Mudhoney front man Mark Arm to describe his band's sound, which leaned on heavy metal but was more stripped down and vocals-forward, but according to Mark Mazullo, the term was applied to Pacific

Northwest garage rock in the late 1950s and early 1960s. See Mazullo, "The Man Whom the World Sold: Kurt Cobain, Rock's Progressive Aesthetic, and the Challenges of Authenticity," *Musical Quarterly* 84, no. 4 (2000): 713–49. The music genre would become firmly associated with the angst-ridden, apathetic lyrical minimalism of Nirvana, and the fashion, with Cobain. See Kurt St. Thomas, *Nirvana: The Chosen Rejects* (New York: St. Martin's Press, 2004), 30. See also Kyle Anderson, *Accidental Revolution: The Story of Grunge* (New York: St. Martin's Press, 2007).

9. The publicity efforts to link grunge and the Salvation Army were local ones—specifically, four stores in Jacksonville, Florida, ran a small campaign touting themselves as "grunge headquarters." The national Salvation Army spokesman responded ambivalently, saying, "I'm not so sure the grunge headquarters is what we'd recommend, but if it works. . . ." (from an undated article, "Stores Try to Cash in on Grunge" [TSANA]).

10. *Singles*, directed by Cameron Crowe (Burbank, CA: Warner Bros., 1992), DVD.

11. James Truman, editor-in-chief of the men's fashion magazine *Details*, said that grunge "is not about making a statement, which is why it is crazy for it to become a fashion statement." See Rick Marin, "Grunge: A Success Story," *New York Times*, 15 November 1992, V1.

12. In 2001, Goodwill Industries reportedly brought in over $2 billion in revenues. Florida flea-market lobbyist Ed Collins reported that the Port Richey, FL, USA Flea Market sold for $10 million in the early 2000s. Ed Collins (Florida flea-market lobbyist), interview with the author, 4 November 2006.

13. See Thorstein Veblen, *The Theory of the Leisure Class: An Economic Study of Institutions* (New York: Macmillan, [1899] 1953), 60–80. For more on Veblen and his economist cohort's analysis of consumerism, see Daniel Horowitz, "Consumption and Its Discontents: Simon N. Patten, Thorstein Veblen, and George Gunton," *Journal of American History* 67 (1980): 301–17.

14. Consumer studies expanded into a wide-ranging field, of which an exhaustive representation is impossible here. During the mid-1950s, concern over the changing "character" of the American people as part of the shift from a producer society to a consumer society generated an array of sociological studies, including those by David Reisman, Reuel Denny, and Nathan Glazer Reisman, *The Lonely Crowd: A Study of the Changing American Character* (New Haven, CT: Yale University Press, 1950), and David Potter, *People of Plenty: Economic Abundance and the American Character* (Chicago: University of Chicago Press, 1954). Other important (and increasingly pessimistic) sociological works included those by Herbert Marcuse, *One-Dimensional Man* (Boston: Beacon Press, 1964), and Daniel Bell, *The Cultural Contradictions of Capitalism* (New York: Basic Books, 1976). For assessments of the role of advertising, see Stuart Ewen, *Captains of Consciousness: Advertising and the Social Roots of the Consumer Culture* (New York: McGraw-Hill, 1976); Roland Marchand, *Advertising the American Dream: Making Way for Modernity, 1920–1940* (Berkeley: University of California Press, 1985); William Leach, *Land of Desire: Merchants, Power, and the Rise of a New American Culture* (New York: Pantheon, 1993); and T. J. Jackson Lears, *Fables of Abundance: A Cultural History of Advertising in America* (New York: Basic Books, 1994). Lizabeth Cohen's *A*

Consumers' Republic: The Politics of Mass Consumption (New York: Knopf, 2003) examines politics through the lens of consumer culture, while several of Kathy Peiss's books examine consumers and consider the influence of less affluent buyers on commodities. See especially *Hope in a Jar: The Making of America's Beauty Culture* (New York: Metropolitan Books, 1998), and *Cheap Amusements: Working Women and Leisure in Turn-of-the-Century New York* (Philadelphia: Temple University Press, 1986).

15. Work addressing the recirculation of goods is (unlike its subject matter) new, but it builds on earlier studies of material value, waste, and consumerism, such as Michael Thompson's seminal theory of "rubbish" and the creation of value. See Thompson, *Rubbish Theory* (London: Oxford University Press, 1979). Other important theoretical works include Pierre Bourdieu, *Distinction: A Social Critique of the Judgment of Taste* (Oxon: Routledge, 1984), and Arjun Appadurai, ed., *The Social Life of Things: Commodities in Cultural Perspective* (New York: Cambridge University Press, 1986). Susan Strasser tracks the changing relationship between material objects and their owners, emphasizing the ways industrialization affected notions of individual stewardship. See Strasser, *Waste and Want: A Social History of Trash* (New York: Henry Holt, 1999). Alison Isenberg's forthcoming book uses antique and secondhand trades as a lens for understanding the relationships between the racial reconfiguring of nineteenth- and twentieth-century cities and the politics and economy of preserving and redistributing objects of American heritage. Alison Isenberg, "Second-hand Cities: Unsettling Racialized Hierarchies" (paper presented at the 2013 American Historical Association conference, New Orleans January). In Addition, Briann Greenfield's history of the "invention" of antiques in the United States explores the high end of secondhand goods value. See Greenfield, *Out of the Attic: Inventing Antiques in Twentieth-Century New England* (Amherst: University of Massachusetts Press, 2009). Scholars interested in secondhand markets in the British context are slightly more prevalent. Beverly Lemire, for example, notes the importance of considering the "second tier" of clothing consumption in gauging consumer demand in preindustrial and early-industrial England. See Lemire, "Consumerism in Preindustrial and Early Industrial England: The Trade in Secondhand Clothes," *Journal of Business Studies* 27 (1988): 1–24, and "Shifting Currency: The Culture and Economy of the Second Hand Trade in England, c. 1600–1850," in *Old Clothes, New Looks: Second Hand Fashion*, ed. Alexandra Palmer and Hazel Clark (New York: Berg, 2005). See also Louise Crewe and Nicky Gregson, *Second-hand Cultures* (Oxford: Oxford International, 2003).

16. For an example of this declension narrative of thrift, see David M. Tucker, *The Decline of Thrift in America: Our Cultural Shift from Saving to Spending* (New York: Praeger, 1991). In a compilation of essays on thrift, several historians, including T. J. Jackson-Lears, Jennifer Scanlon, Olivier Zunz, and Lawrence Glickman acknowledge the altered but persistent role for thrift in modern consumer society. See Joshua J. Yates and James Davison Hunter, eds., *Thrift and Thriving in America: Capitalism and Moral Order from the Puritans to the Present* (New York: Oxford University Press, 2011). Alison Humes offers an account (framed by personal experience), describing the selfish pleasures of thrift that buying used items affords. See Humes, "A Hundred Years of

Thrift Shops," in *Franklin's Thrift: The Lost History of an American Virtue*, ed. David Blankenhorn, Barbara Dafoe Whitehead, and Sorcha Brophy-Warren (West Conshohocken, PA: Templeton Press, 2009), 98–126.

17. These ideas are attributed to Stephen Mihm and Julia Ott, respectively, in "Interchange: History of Capitalism," *Journal of American History* 101, no. 2, (September 2014): 504 and 506.

18. By looking at the success of the world's largest corporation, Wal-Mart, Bethany Moreton describes how a Christian service ethos fueled domestic and global capitalism. See Moreton, *To Serve God and Wal-Mart: The Making of Christian Free Enterprise* (Boston: Harvard University Press, 2010). Jonathan Levy focuses on the changes in both the business world and society at large that encouraged the development of economic futures and the role of "risk" in capitalist endeavors. See Levy, *Freaks of Fortune: The Emerging World of Capitalism and Risk in America* (Boston: Harvard University Press, 2012). Sven Beckert's *Monied Metropolis: New York City and the Consolidation of the American Bourgeoisie, 1850–1896* entwines the roles of capital and culture in creating "class" and economic growth, and his recent global exploration of cotton and its relationship to violence, politics, and capitalism expands his purview internationally. See Beckart, *Monied Metropolis: New York City and the Consolidation of the American Bourgeoisie, 1850–1896* (Cambridge: Cambridge University Press, 2001), and *Empire of Cotton: A Global History* (New York: Knopf Doubleday, 2014).

19. Michael Harrington's book *The Other America* argues that increasingly invisible poverty plagued the supposedly affluent United States, affecting more than 25 percent of its overall population. One cause of that invisibility, according to Harrington, was the comparatively high quality of clothing to which the poor had access. See Harrington, *The Other America: Poverty in the United States* (New York: Touchstone Books, 1962).

20. Elizabeth Cline examines the huge profit-making industries that arose to accommodate the increasing tonnage of cast-off clothing in the past few decades, and relates the expectation of ever cheaper new clothing to the changes in secondhand clothing trade and recycling. See Elizabeth L. Cline, *Overdressed: The Shockingly High Cost of Cheap Fashion* (New York: Penguin Group, 2012), 119–37. Karen Tranberg Hansen offers one study of such export practices in *Salaula: The World of Secondhand Clothing and Zambia* (Chicago: University of Chicago Press, 2000).

21. See Cline, *Overdressed*, 119–37.

22. For an examination of secondhand exportation to Zambia, see Hansen, *Salaula*.

23. Quoted in Earl Christmas, *House of Goodwill: A Story of Morgan Memorial* (Boston: Morgan Memorial Press, 1924), 55.

24. See Wilson, *Adorned in Dreams: Fashion and Modernity* (Berkeley: University of California Press, 1985), 9.

25. Janice Susan Gore uses *Tales of Manhattan* in her dissertation to illustrate Michael Thompson's fluctuating valuation of objects. See Thompson, *Rubbish Theory: The Creation and Destruction of Value* (Oxford: Oxford University Press, 1979). See Janice Susan Gore, "Used Value: Thrift Shopping and Bohemia Incorporated" (PhD diss., University of Southern California, 1999), 46–49.

26. Chauncey relied on a vast array of primary sources to demonstrate that gay society openly thrived in pre-World War II New York City. See Chauncey, *Gay New York: Gender, Urban Culture, and the Making of the Gay Male World, 1890–1940* (New York: Basic Books, 1994). I apply the methodological approaches from a range of academic disciplines and find inspiration in the works of a diverse group of scholars, including historians and fashion theorists such as Kathy Peiss, George Chauncey, Nan Enstad, Daniel Horowitz, Grace Hale, Deirdre Clemente, and Anne Hollander; sociologists and cultural theorists, including George Simmel, Angela McRobbie, Wini Breines, Elizabeth Wilson, and Diana Crane; material culture experts such as Alexandra Palmer and Hazel Clark; and historical geographers such as Nicky Gregson and Louise Crewe. The materials and analytical approaches represented by this group of scholars introduced me to ways of exploring the relationship between mass culture and quotidian life, methods I have applied to secondhand commerce and style in the context of broader economics and culture.

27. Tanya Clement, "The Baroness in Little Magazine History," *Jacket2* (5 May 2011), accessed 19 May 2015, http://jacket2.org/article/baroness-little-magazine-history. See also Jane Heap, "Dada," *The Little Review* 6, no. 6 (1919): 46, and references to the Baroness in Margaret Anderson's *My Thirty Years War* (New York: Horizon, 1969), 181–82.

28. This quote is from the *New Yorker*'s review on the back of the book. See Vance Packard, *The Hidden Persuaders* (Brooklyn, N.Y.: Ig, 2007; first published in 1957).

29. Thomas Frank, *The Conquest of Cool: Business Culture, Counterculture, and the Rise of Hip Capitalism* (Chicago: University of Chicago Press, 1997).

30. See Claude Lévi-Strauss, *The Savage Mind* (Chicago: University of Chicago Press, 1966), esp. pp. 21–23.

31. Jean Baudrillard, *Simulacra and Simulation*, trans. Sheila Fraser Glaser (Ann Arbor: University of Michigan Press, 1994), 43.

32. Raphael Samuel, *Theatres of Memory: Past and Present in Contemporary Culture* (London: Verso, 2012), 95.

33. Grace Elizabeth Hale describes how notions of "authenticity"—along with "rebellion"—are particularly in flux during the postwar decades, as white, middle-class Americans identify with and redefine themselves as cultural outsiders. This book argues for the significance of variable, sometimes conflicting, sartorial expressions of those identifications. See Hale, *A Nation of Outsiders: How the White Middle Class Fell in Love with Rebellion in Postwar America* (Oxford: Oxford University Press, 2011).

34. Reflections on secondhand economies often include them in the broader category of informal economies and assess them solely as resources for the underprivileged and marginal (many of these theories derived from studying the Latin American context). For examples of work on informal economies, see Alejandro Portes, Manuel Castells, and Lauren A. Benton, eds., *The Informal Economy: Studies in Advanced and Less Developed Countries* (Baltimore: Johns Hopkins University Press, 1989); Portes, Alejandro, "The Informal Sector: Definition, Controversy, and Relation to National Development," *Review* 7, no. 1 (1983): 151–74; Alejandro Portes and Saskia Sassen-Koob, "Making It Underground: Comparative Material on the Informal Sector in Western Market Economies," *American Journal of Sociology* 93, no. 1 (1987).

Chapter One

1. Percy Herbert, "The Blue Silk," *Saturday Evening Post*, 3 May 1884, 63, 42.

2. Rev. James Porter, *Operative's Friend and Defence; or, Hints to Young Ladies Who Are Dependent on Their Own Exertion* (Boston: Charles H. Pierce, 1850), 123. Karen Halttunen examines the role of etiquette manuals in the uneasy relationship between fashion and the growing middle class in mid-eighteenth-century U.S. cities. See Halttunen, *Confidence Men and Painted Women: A Study of Middle-Class Culture in America* (New Haven, CT: Yale University Press, 1986), especially chap. 4.

3. Elizabeth Wilson uses this story to illustrate the perceived autonomy of clothing whose owners have died. See Wilson, *Adorned in Dreams: Fashion and Modernity* (Berkeley: University of California Press, 1985), 2; Charles Dickens, *The Works of Charles Dickens: Sketches by Boz* (New York: P.F. Collier & Sons, 1911), 70–76.

4. Henry James, "The Romance of Certain Old Clothes," *Atlantic Monthly* 21, no. 124 (1868): 209–25.

5. I apply my term philanthropic capitalism rather than broader terms such as "scientific giving" to better underscore the profits desired and attained by thrift-store owners. See Judith Sealander, "Curing Evils at Their Source: The Arrival of Scientific Giving," in *Charity, Philanthropy, and Civility in American History*, ed. Lawrence J. Friedman and Mark D. McGarvie (New York: Cambridge University Press, 2003), 222. For more on the origins and history of nonprofit organizations, see David C. Hammock, ed., *Making the Nonprofit Sector in the United States: A Reader* (Bloomington: Indiana University Press, 1998).

6. Chain stores must have at least ten units and a central headquarters. The only chain store established before the Salvation Army that still exists today is the Great Atlantic & Pacific Tea Company, or A&P, a supermarket and liquor store chain. A&P filed for bankruptcy in 2010 and became a private company in 2012. For more on A&P, see Mark Levinson, *The Great A&P and the Struggle for Small Business in America* (New York: Hill and Wang, 2011). Despite these central positions in business history, the importance of secondhand stores in Americans' commercial and social lives has gone unrecognized, even by scholars addressing the institutions responsible for the creation of thrift stores. Many studies closely assess the history of the Salvation Army as an evangelical mission group with eccentric paramilitary uniforms, raucous parades and marching bands, and somewhat progressive gender politics. Studies of the Salvation Army range from the hagiographic to the critical. See, for example, Norman Murdoch, *Origins of the Salvation Army* (Knoxville: University of Tennessee Press, 1996), and Diane Winston, *Red-Hot and Righteous: The Urban Religion of the Salvation Army* (Cambridge, MA: Harvard University Press, 1999). Lillian Taiz and Andrew Mark Eason both argue that women in the organization were extraordinary in how they appeared to the American public. See Lillian Taiz, *Hallelujah Lads and Lasses: Remaking the Salvation Army in America, 1880–1930* (Chapel Hill: University of North Carolina Press, 2001), and Andrew Mark Eason, *Women in God's Army: Gender and Equality in the Early Salvation Army* (Waterloo: Wilfred Laurier University Press, 2003). In addition to his *Somebody's Brother: A History of the Salvation Army Men's*

Social Service Department (Lewiston, NY: Edwin Mellon Press, 1986), which discusses the Army's Men's Social Service Department (which ran the first thrift stores), Edward H. McKinley has written *Marching to Glory: The History of the Salvation Army in the United States of America, 1880–1980* (San Francisco: Harper and Row, 1980). I focus on the Salvation Army and Goodwill Industries as the earliest and fastest-expanding examples of chain thrift stores. By midcentury, however, Catholic counterparts followed much the same trajectory and applied many of the same business tactics in sales and employment. For an anecdotal account of St. Vincent de Paul's thrift-store work, see Jane Knuth, *Thrift Store Saints: Meeting Jesus 25 Cents at a Time* (Chicago: Loyola Press, 2010). Deseret Industries was a post–World War II expansion of the Church of Jesus Christ of Latter-Day Saints' welfare aid. See Leonard J. Arrington and Davis Bitton, *The Mormon Experience: A History of the Latter-day Saints* (New York: Alfred A. Knopf, 1979), 272–74.

7. Daniel Horowitz's study of consumer attitudes shows that even without immigrants receiving condescending Progressive-Era guides geared toward instructing them on the role of frugality and hard work in success, foreign-born workers highly valued thrift and "moral" expenditures. See Horowitz, *The Morality of Spending: Attitudes toward the Consumer Society in America, 1875–1940* (Baltimore: Johns Hopkins University Press, 1985).

8. Colonial auctions and hybrid used and new sales events called *vendues* were widely regarded as unhealthy modes of sale. In *The Way to Wealth* (New York: New York Association for Improving the Condition of the Poor, [1758] 1848), Benjamin Franklin warned that the hucksters plying their trade at such venues stirred consumers' emotions to effect a ready sale (8). See also Joanna Cohen, "'The Right to Purchase Is as Free as the Right to Sell': Defining Consumers as Citizens in the Auction-House Conflicts of the Early Republic," *Journal of the Early Republic* 20, no. 1 (2010): 25–62, and T. H. Breen, *The Marketplace of Revolution: How Consumer Politics Shaped American Independence* (New York: Oxford University Press, 2004), 140–41.

9. Emily Fogg Mead, "The Place of Advertising in Modern Business," *Journal of Political Economy* 9, no. 2 (1901): 227.

10. John D'Emilio and Estelle B. Freedman, *Intimate Matters: A History of Sexuality in America* (New York: Harper and Row, 1988), 278.

11. Quoted in Earl Christmas, *House of Goodwill: A Story of Morgan Memorial* (Boston: Morgan Memorial Press, 1924), 55.

12. See McKinley, *Somebody's Brother*, 86.

13. See Frederick C. Moore, *The Golden Threads of Destiny* (Boston: Morgan Memorial Goodwill Press, 1952), 68. Rev. Helms had direct experience with cooperative models through running the Boston Settlement House and visiting cooperatives in the United States and England—including the original Rochdale Cooperative. Helms only selectively applied cooperative principles, however. Some principles, such as democratic member control, were never followed by the Goodwill Industries. The alliance with the cooperative movement seemed mostly rhetorical. For more on cooperatives in the United States, see Florence E. Parker, "Consumers' Cooperation in the United

States," *Annals of the American Academy of Political and Social Science* 191 (May 1937): 91–102; Ellen Furlough and Carl Strikwerda, "Economics, Consumer Culture, and Gender: An Introduction to the Politics of Consumer Cooperation," in *Consumers against Capitalism? Consumer Cooperation in Europe, North America, and Japan, 1840–1990*, (Lanham, MD: Rowman & Littlefield, 1999), 5–9; and Kathleen Donahue, *Freedom from Want: American Liberalism and the Idea of the Consumer* (Baltimore: Johns Hopkins University Press, 2003).

14. Anne Hollander outlines these and other vital aspects of the modernization of fashion, but because of the common scholarly disconnect between cultural histories of, for example, design and style, and histories of business and capitalism, their relevance to urban identity in modernizing the United States has been underdeveloped. See Hollander, "The Modernization of Fashion," *Design Quarterly*, no. 154 (1992): 27–33.

15. According to urban sociologist Richard Sennett, late-nineteenth-century appearances were "no longer at a distance from the self, but rather clues to private feeling." See Sennett, *The Fall of the Public Man* (Cambridge: Cambridge University Press, 1974), 153. Fashion theorist Joanne Entwhistle supports Sennett's earlier proposal in *Fashioned Bodies*, where she writes, "the anonymity of the city opens up new possibilities for creating oneself, giving one the freedom to experiment with appearance in a way that would have been unthinkable in a traditional rural community." See Entwhistle, *The Fashioned Body: Fashion, Dress and Modern Social Theory* (New York: Wiley, 2000), 138.

16. See Thorstein Veblen, *The Theory of the Leisure Class: An Economic Study of Institutions* (New York: Macmillan, [1899] 1953), 60–80. For more on Veblen and his economist cohort's analysis of consumerism, see Daniel Horowitz, "Consumption and Its Discontents: Simon N. Patten, Thorstein Veblen, and George Gunton," *Journal of American History* 67 (1980): 301–17.

17. See Kathy Peiss, *Cheap Amusements: Working Women and Leisure in Turn-of-the-Century New York* (Philadelphia: Temple University Press, 1986).

18. Nan Enstad, *Ladies of Labor, Girls of Adventure: Working Women, Popular Culture, and Labor Politics at the Turn of the Twentieth Century* (New York: Columbia University Press, 1999).

19. See "New York's Cheapest Department Store," *New York Times*, 4 May 1902, C1.

20. Ibid.

21. Marlis Schweitzer details the collisions and collusions between Broadway, fashion, and department stores at the beginning of the twentieth century. See Schweitzer, *When Broadway Was the Runway: Theater, Fashion, and American Culture* (Philadelphia: University of Pennsylvania Press, 2009).

22. "New York's Cheapest Department Store," C1.

23. Clara Bow would be born in a Brooklyn tenement apartment three years later. See David Stenn, *Clara Bow: Runnin' Wild* (New York: Cooper Square Press, 1988), 8. *It*, directed by Clarence Badger (1927; Hollywood, CA: Famous Player Film Company or Paramount Pictures, 2004), DVD.

24. That Bow's character cannot afford the clothing she helps sell is made clear just before she turned her scissors on her own unsatisfactory apparel, when she sighs wistfully over a newspaper ad for the store's new dresses.

25. A dozen years later, fourteen-year-old Al Capone would form the Navy Street Gang, apparently to halt the harassment of Italian girls and women by Irish neighbors. See Laurence Bergreen, *Capone: The Man and the Era* (New York: Simon and Schuster Paperbacks, 1994), 35–37.

26. Nancy L. Green, "Sweatshop Migrations: The Garment Industry between Home and Shop," in *The Landscape of Modernity, New York City, 1900–1940*, ed. David Ward and Olivier Zunz (Baltimore: Johns Hopkins University Press, 1997), 214. See also Nancy L. Green, *Ready-to-Wear, Ready to Work: A Century of Industry and Immigrants in Paris and New York* (Durham: Duke University Press, 1997), and Kathy Peiss's descriptions of young ethnic working women's predilection for dances in "Dance Madness," in *Cheap Amusements*, chap. 4.

27. Green, "Sweatshop Migrations," 214.

28. Enstad, *Ladies of Labor, Girls of Adventure*, 65.

29. See Winston, *Red-Hot and Righteous*, 118–119; for more detail, see Murdoch, *Origins of the Salvation Army*, 146–168.

30. For more on the secondhand trade in England, see especially Beverly Lemire, "Consumerism in Preindustrial and Early Industrial England: The Trade in Secondhand Clothes," *Journal of Business Studies* 27 (1988), 1–24, and "Shift in Currency: The Culture and Economy of Second Hand Trade in England, c. 1600–1850," in *Old Clothes, New Looks: Second Hand Fashion*, ed. Alexandra Palmer and Hazel Clark (New York: Berg, 2005).

31. Winston, *Red-Hot and Righteous*, 92. For more on the role of clothing and dress in the Gilded Age Salvation Army, see my article on the topic, "'Be Odd': The Contradictory Use of Dress in the Gilded Age Salvation Army," *Winterthur Portfolio* 47, no. 4 (2013): 245–65.

32. William Kostlevy, *Holy Jumpers: Evangelicals and Radicals in Progressive Era America* (Oxford: Oxford University Press, 2010), 12; Salvationists published their views on dress and public appearance in pamphlet and institutional documents. See J. B. Vance, "Why We Wear the Uniform?" *AWC*, September 1887, 214.

33. Lt.-Colonel Edith MacLachlan, "The Salvation Army Uniform" (The Salvation Army National Archives [TSANA], uncatalogued, 1977), 5.

34. Inducements to wear the uniform regularly appeared in the official Salvation Army publication. See, for example, *AWC*, 15 July 1882, 2, and Winston, *Red-Hot and Righteous*, 90. For more on the symbolic meaning of particular elements of the established uniform and its concessions to fashion's whim over time, see Le Zotte, "'Be Odd,'" 249–58.

35. "The Salvationists," *New York Times*, 2 February 1892, 4; Taiz, *Hallelujah Lads and Lasses*, 15.

36. Maud Ballington Booth wrote this sometime while she was commander of the American Salvation Army from 1886 to 1896; see Booth, "Women's Dress: Mrs. Ballington Booth's Letter to Salvation Women" (TSANA, catalogued letters, n.d.), 2; Winston, *Red-Hot and Righteous*, 84.

37. "Hampered by Ignorance," *New York Times*, 22 February 1886, 2. Scholars debate the unusual role of women in the Army at the time, especially considering the question of the fulfillment of institutional promises of equal opportunities. Founder William Booth claimed that women were given equal opportunity to progress in rank in the organization; some scholars indicate that only certain women were able to attain positions of authority, and this was often as a husband's adjutant. Maud Ballington Booth, upon marriage to the founder's son, was one such woman. Andrew Mark Eason evaluates the ways in which the formal dicta of gender equality were and were not adhered to for first- and second-generation Salvationists. See Eason, *Women in God's Army*.

38. "From Religion to Junk," *Washington Post*, 23 August 1909, 12.

39. David M. Tucker, *The Decline of Thrift in America: Our Cultural Shift from Saving to Spending* (New York: Praeger, 1991), 20.

40. Historian Wendy Woloson recounts the anti-Semitism that influenced American public reaction to pawnshops in the industrializing United States, as well as the shops' often-obscured economic importance. See Woloson, *In Hock: Pawning in America from Independence through the Great Depression* (Chicago: University of Chicago Press, 2009), 5–6.

41. Woloson, *In Hock*, 5–9. Christine Stansell describes how pawning was a common housewives' financial stopgap, used as a lending agency to make rent during tight months. See Stansell, *City of Women: Sex and Class in New York, 1789–1860* (Chicago: University of Illinois Press, 1987), 51.

42. Susan Strasser shows that the social practices of reuse and disposal altered drastically during this period. See Strasser, *Waste and Want: A Social History of Trash* (New York: Henry Holt, 1999), 13. Some Progressive-Era federal policies, such as the establishment of the Public Lands Commission during President Theodore Roosevelt's administration, demonstrate this shift from private to public responsibility. See Samuel P. Hays, *Conservation and the Gospel of Efficiency: The Progressive Conservation Movement, 1890–1920* (Pittsburgh: University of Pittsburgh Press, [1959] 1999). Various waste management industries also emerged at this time. See Carl Zimring, *Cash for Your Trash: Scrap Recycling in America* (New Brunswick, NJ: Rutgers University Press, 2000), 18–19, and "Dirty Work: How Hygiene and Xenophobia Marginalized the American Waste Trades, 1870–1930," *Environmental History* 9, no. 1 (2004): 80–101.

43. See Nancy Tomes, *The Gospel of Germs: Men, Women, and the Microbe in American Life* (Cambridge, MA: Harvard University Press, 1998), 56–57, and Zimring, *Cash for Your Trash*, 40. For more on popular ideas on cleanliness, see Suellen Hoy, *Chasing Dirt: The American Pursuit of Cleanliness* (New York: Oxford University Press, 1995), and Richard L. Bushman and Claudia L. Bushman, "The Early History of Cleanliness in America," *Journal of American History* 74, no. 4 (1988): 1213–38.

44. The germ theory was largely but not fully accepted in the scientific community around 1880. The public did not embrace the precepts until early in the twentieth century. See Phyllis Allen Richmond, "American Attitudes toward the Germ Theory of Disease (1860–1880)," *Journal of the History of Medicine* 9 (1954): 428–54.

45. J. P. Alexander, "Sales of Materials," *Electric Railway Journal* 23 (January 1915): 192–93; Harry H. Grigg and George E. Haynes, *Junk Dealing and Juvenile Delinquency*, text by Albert E. Webster (Chicago: Juvenile Protective Association, [1919?]), 50. Carl Zimring describes eastern European immigrants' involvement in the U.S. waste trades, noting "Scrap and garbage are linked to identifiable ethnic and criminal identities" ("Dirty Work," 80–101). See also Carl Zimring, *Cash for Your Trash*. Louis Harap covers literary depictions of Jews in America in *The Image of the Jew in American Literature: From Early Republic to Mass Immigration* (New York: Syracuse University Press, 2003).

46. According to Adam D. Mendelsohn, Chatham Street became so firmly associated with old clothing trade areas that similar zones as far away as China were called "the Chatham Street" of the city. See Mendelsohn, "'It's the Economy, Shmendrick': A New Turn in Jewish Studies?" *AJS Perspectives*, Fall 2009, 14–17. For a more in-depth, transatlantic exploration of Jews' relationship to clothing, textiles, and trade, see Mendelsohn, *The Rag Race: How Jews Sewed Their Way to Success in America and the British Empire* (New York: New York University Press, 2015). For more on Europe's second-hand trade, see Madeleine Ginsburg, "Rags to Riches: the Second Hand Clothes Trade, 1700–1978," *Costume: The Journal of the Costume Society* (London) 14 (1980): 125, and Woloson, *In Hock*, 16–17. On the economic history of Jews in modern Europe, see Derek Jonathan Penslar and Anthony W. Lee, *Shylock's Children: Economics and Jewish Identity in Modern Europe* (Berkeley: University of California Press, 2001), 16, 20.

47. Niles Carpenter, *Immigrants and Their Children* (Washington, DC: Government Printing Office, 1927), and David M. Reimers, "Immigrants and Thrift," in *Thrift and Thriving in America: Capitalism and Moral Order from the Puritans to the Present*, ed. Joshua J. Yates and James Davison Hunter (New York: Oxford University Press, 2011), 350.

48. The survey identified more than 2,440 peddlers. See Daniel Bluestone, "The Pushcart Evil," in *Landscapes of Modernity: New York, 1900–1940*, ed. David Ward and Olivier Zunz (Baltimore: Johns Hopkins University Press, 1992), 292–93.

49. Zimring, "Dirty Work," 80–101. See also Zimring, *Cash for Your Trash*, 5, 46–50, and Woloson, *In Hock*, 21–54. For more on the history, use, and misuse of nuisance laws, see William J. Novak, *The People's Welfare: Law and Regulation in Nineteenth-Century America* (Chapel Hill: University of North Carolina Press, 2000).

50. In *Garbage in the Cities: Refuse, Reform, and the Environment*, rev. ed. (Pittsburgh: University of Pittsburgh Press, 2004), Martin V. Melosi offers a history of urban environmental issues and waste management in a broad, world context with illustrative case studies, including chap. 2, "'The Apostle of Cleanliness' and the Origins of Refuse Management," esp. pp. 41–42. For the American industrial context, see also Strasser, *Waste and Want*, 125.

51. A similar program, a Salvation Army "workshop" attached to a shelter called the San Francisco Lighthouse, was launched in that city as early as 1893. Men collected makeshift materials from restaurants, saloons, and even dumps. A "Curiosity Shop" featuring used clothing provided goods and employment. See McKinley, *Somebody's Brother*, 24–25, and Strasser, *Waste and Want*, 141–53, 156–59.

52. See, for example, "The Evolution of an Idea and a Pushcart: The Story of an Industry Which Remakes Men and Materials" (TSANA, uncatalogued).

53. McKinley, *Somebody's Brother*, 34.

54. For more on Americanization projects in different contexts, see the essays in George E. Pozzetta, *Americanization, Social Control, and Philanthropy* (New York: Taylor & Francis, 1991). For variants of Americanization, ranging from "liberal" efforts that supported native languages and some cultural customs to the more aggressive, "100 percent Americanism" during the World War I era, see Otis L. Graham Jr. and Elizabeth Koed, "Americanizing the Immigrant, Past and Future: History and Implications of a Social Movement," *Public Historian* 15 (Fall 1992): 41.

55. See Eva V. Carlin, "A Salvage Bureau," *Overland Monthly*, September 1900, 247.

56. See Horowitz, *The Morality of Spending*.

57. See Carlin, "A Salvage Bureau," 247, and Marta Gutman, "Inside the Institution: The Art and Craft of Settlement Work at the Oakland New Century Club, 1895–1923," *Perspectives in Vernacular Architecture* 8 (2000): 248–79.

58. Ibid., 256.

59. Ibid., 248.

60. Quoted in Gutman, "Settlement Work at the Oakland New Century Club," 261.

61. Little attention has been devoted to "thrift clubs" specifically, but they usually functioned in coordination with charitable organizations' other Americanization efforts. See Kenneth Kusmer, "The Functions of Organized Charity in the Progressive Era: Chicago as a Case Study," *Journal of American History* 60, no. 3 (1973): 665.

62. Subcommittee on Memorial History, *Fifty Years of Boston: A Memorial Volume Issued in Commemoration of the Tercentenary of 1930* (Boston: Tercentenary Committee, 1932), 600.

63. Robert Rollin Huddleston, "The Relatedness of Goodwill Industries and the Christian Church" (PhD diss., Iliff School of Theology, 1959), 154.

64. Huddleston, "Goodwill Industries and the Christian Church," 173–74.

65. The name given to the charter granted the umbrella company in 1905, "The Morgan Memorial Cooperative Industries and Stores, Inc.," reflected Helms's interest in the contemporary trend of consumer cooperatives. Even more strikingly, beginning in the 1920s, and especially during the Great Depression, Goodwill Industries adopted distinctly Marxist rhetoric. Helms himself professed his desire to aid a "class exploited by the capitalists and despised by organized labor" (quoted in Ross Warren Sanderson, *The Church Serves the Changing City* [New York: Harper Books, 1955], 75). Reinhold Niebuhr considered such social gospel claims fakery, masking profit intent. See Niebuhr, *Moral Man and Immoral Society: A Study in Ethics and Policy* (Louisville, KY: Westminster John Knox Press, 2013; first published in 1932).

66. Christmas, *House of Goodwill*, 45–47, and Moore, *The Golden Threads of Destiny*, 69.

67. See Herbert G. Gutman, "Work, Culture, and Society in Industrializing America, 1815–1919," *American Historical Review* 78, no. 3 (1973): 531–88.

68. Christmas, *House of Goodwill*, 58.

69. See Eva V. Carlin, "A Salvage Bureau," *Overland Monthly*, September 1900, 246–57.

70. For more on the social gospel movement of the Progressive Era, see Gary Scott Smith, *The Search for Social Salvation: Social Christianity and America, 1880–1925* (Columbus, OH: Roman & Littlefield, 2000). In discussing widespread notions of national rebirth, Jackson Lears covers "social Christianity." See Lears, *Rebirth of a Nation: The Making of Modern America, 1877–1920* (New York: HarperCollins, 2009). For a focus on gender, see also Wendy J. Deichmann Edwards and Carolyn De Swarte Gifford, eds., *Gender and the Social Gospel* (Chicago: University of Illinois Press, 2003).

71. Christmas, *House of Goodwill*, 143.

72. Edgar J. Helms, *Pioneering in Modern City Missions* (Boston: Morgan Memorial Printing Dept., 1944), 71–72.

73. Quoted in McKinley, *Somebody's Brother*, 58.

74. For more on scientific giving, see Sealander, "Curing Evils at Their Source," 218–220.

75. Charles W. Calhoun, ed., *The Gilded Age: Perspectives on the Origins of Modern America*, 2nd ed. (Lanham, MD: Rowman & Littlefield, 2007), 102; Sealander, "Curing Evils at Their Source," 218.

76. See Sealander, "Curing Evils at Their Source," 218–20.

77. John D. Rockefeller, *Random Reminiscences of Men and Events* (New York: Doubleday, Page, 1909), 141–42, 145–47. Andrew Carnegie, "Wealth," *North American Review*, June 1889, 653–54, and "The Best Fields of Philanthropy," *North American Review*, December 1889, 682–98; quoted in Robert H. Bremner, *Giving: Charity and Philanthropy in Giving* (New Brunswick, NJ: Transaction Publishers, 1994), 159. For more on Carnegie's writings, see his *"The Gospel of Wealth" and Other Timely Essays* (New York: New York Century, 1901); see also Sealander, "Curing Evils at Their Source," 228–37. For more on changes in the structure of philanthropy in America, see Robert H. Bremner, *American Philanthropy*, 2nd ed. (Chicago: University of Chicago Press, 1988), and David Wagner, *What's Love Got to Do with It? A Critical Look at American Charity* (New York: New Press, 2001).

78. Peatrice Plumb, *Edgar James Helms, The Goodwill Man* (Minneapolis: T.S. Denison and Company, 1965) 199.

79. For more details on the persistent ideals of thrift supporting the renaming choice, see Jennifer Le Zotte, " 'Not Charity, but a Chance': Philanthropic Capitalism and the Rise of American Thrift Stores, 1894–1930," *New England Quarterly* 86, no. 2 (2013): 184–86.

80. "The Spectator," *Outlook*, 1 December 1900, anthologized in Alfred Emanuel Smith, ed., *New Outlook*, vol. 66 (New York: Outlook, 1900), 781.

81. Female African American activists used turn-of-the-century rummage sales to gain attention for their causes as well as to raise money. See Linda Gordon, "Black and White Visions of Welfare: Women's Welfare Activism, 1890–1945," *Journal of American History* 78, no. 2 (September 1991): 559–90.

82. See Beverly Gordon, *Bazaars and Fair Ladies: The History of the American Fundraising Fair* (Knoxville: University of Tennessee Press, 1998), 11–12. See also

F. K. Prochaska, "Charity Bazaars in Nineteenth-Century England," *Journal of British Studies* 16, no. 2 (1977): 62–84. Though Prochaska's study focuses on England, similar patterns emerged a little later in the United States, as Beverly Gordon verifies.

83. Robert J. Gamble, "The Promiscuous Economy," in *Capitalism by Gaslight: Illustrating the Economy of Nineteenth-Century America*, ed. Brian P. Luskey and Wendy Woloson (Philadelphia: University of Pennsylvania Press, 2015), 50.

84. The phrase "cult of domesticity" is often invoked to explain prevailing ideas about women's circumscribed role in American society, as Aileen S. Kraditor applies it in the introduction to *Up from the Pedestal: Selected Writings in the History of American Feminism* (Chicago: Quadrangle Books, 1968). See also Mary P. Ryan, "American Society and the Cult of Domesticity, 1830–1860" (PhD diss., University of California, Santa Barbara, 1971).

85. Elizabeth Stillinger, *The Antiquers: The Lives and Careers, the Deals, the Finds, the Collections of the Men and Women Who Were Responsible for Changing Taste in American Antiques, 1850–1930* (New York: Alfred A. Knopf, 1980), xi–xii. For more on fund-raising fairs, see Gordon, *Bazaars and Fair Ladies*. For more on the development of collecting as a hobby, see Steven Gelber, *Hobbies: Leisure and the Culture of Work in America* (New York: Columbia University Press, 1999), esp. pp. 60–152.

86. See Green, *Ready-to-Wear, Ready to Work*, 46.

87. Figures rounded off from the United States Immigration Commission, *Reports of the Immigration Commission*, 42 vols. (Washington, D. C.: Government Printing Office, 1911), 11:259. Quoted in Green, *Ready-to-Wear, Ready to Work*, 46.

88. Christine Bayles Kortsch, *Dress Culture in Late Victorian Women's Fiction: Literacy* (Burlington, VT: Ashgate, 2009), 80–90. For the movement in the United States, see Patricia A. Cunningham, *Reforming Women's Fashion, 1850–1920: Politics Health and Art* (Kent, OH: Kent State University Press), chap. 5, and Mary Warner Blanchard, *Oscar Wilde's America: Counterculture in the Gilded Age* (New Haven, CT: Yale University Press, 1998).

89. Kortsch, *Dress Culture in Late Victorian Women's Fiction*, 81–82.

90. T. J. Jackson Lears writes about the antimodernist implications of the Arts and Crafts movement in the United States; see Lears, *No Place of Grace: Antimodernism and the Transformation of American Culture, 1880–1920* (Chicago: University of Chicago Press, 1981).

91. Kortsch, *Dress Culture in Late Victorian Women's Fiction*, 81.

92. As historian of dress Mary Warner Blanchard points out, the novelist William Dean Howells titled his 1893 book lauding the value of artistic dress *The Coast of Bohemia*. See Blanchard, *Oscar Wilde's America*, 139–40.

93. Blanchard, *Oscar Wilde's America*, 138–40; Joyce Johnson, *Minor Characters: A Beat Memoir* (New York: Penguin Press, 1981), 210.

94. The Salvation Army uniform adapted to consumer demand over the years, adding variety and adjusting elements of the uniform according to changes in mainstream style. See Le Zotte, " 'Be Odd,' " 256–58.

95. In 1899, economist Veblen coined "conspicuous consumption" to describe how the richest members of society expressed status through buying. See Thorstein Ve-

blen, *The Theory of the Leisure Class: An Economic Study of Institutions* (New York: Macmillan, [1899] 1953), 60–80.

96. Jill Rappaport, *Giving Women: Alliance and Exchange in Victorian Culture* (New York: Oxford University Press, 2012), 111. For more on the slum sisters, see also Norris and Beverley Magnuson, *Salvation in the Slums: Evangelical Social Work, 1865–1920* (Eugene, OR: Wipf and Stock, 1977); *Secrets of Success in Slumland*, and *Slums, and Slum Sisters* (TSANA, undated pamphlet); Edwin Gifford Lamb, "The Social Work of the Salvation Army" (PhD diss., Columbia University, 1909); Eason, *Women in God's Army*, 138; Winston, *Red-Hot and Righteous*; and Taiz, *Hallelujah Lads and Lasses*.

97. For more about instances of male Salvationist leaders dressing down to explore dangerous or impoverished realms, as well as an elaboration on the slum sisters, see Le Zotte, "'Be Odd,'" 258–63.

98. Nathan Joseph uses "total metaphor" to describe the sartorial adaptations of espionage workers; see *Uniforms and Nonuniforms: Communication through Clothing* (New York: Greenwood, 1986), 17.

99. Magnuson, *Salvation in the Slums*, 32–34.

100. Jacob Riis, *How the Other Half Lives: Studies among the Tenements of New York* (New York: Charles Scribner's Sons, 1890). G. A. Davis, "Under the Blood-Red Banner—IV," *Frank Leslie's Weekly*, 21 December 1893, 331.

101. Slum sister stories were also often printed in the *AWC*; see, for example, *AWC*, 1 March 1890, 1, and 22 February 1890, 8. See also Winston, *Red-Hot and Righteous*, 69–73, and John Michael Giggie and Diane H. Winston, eds., *Faith in the Market: Religion and the Rise of Urban Commercial Culture* (Pisctaway, NJ: Rutgers University Press, 2002), 27–30.

102. Quoted in David W. Dayton, *Rediscovering an Evangelical Heritage: A History and Trajectory of Integrating Piety and Justice* (Grand Rapids, MI: Baker Academic, 2014), 88; Kostlevy, *Holy Jumpers*, 12.

103. This exhortation was from a letter Wesley wrote in 1769. See Luke Tyerman, *The Life and Times of the Rev. John Wesley, Founder of the Methodists* (London: Hodder & Stoughton, 1876), 344.

104. According to fashion theorist James Laver, whether performed in intimate settings or formalized on stage, disguise of any sort is innately immodest in its imitative ambitions. See James Laver, "The Immodesty of Disguise," in *Modesty in Dress: An Inquiry into the Fundamentals of Fashion* (Boston: Houghton Mifflin, 1969), 84–95.

105. Arthur T. Vanderbilt, *Fortune's Children: The Fall of the House of Vanderbilt* (New York: Harper Collins, 1991), 102–20.

106. Rappaport, *Giving Women*, 114.

107. There are several popular accounts of Evangeline Booth's life. See P. W. Wilson, *General Evangeline Booth of the Salvation Army* (New York: Scribner's, 1948), and Margaret Troutt, *The General Was a Lady: The Story of Evangeline Booth* (Nashville: Holman, 1980). Winston writes of Evangeline Booth's importance to the Army in America and her reshaping of its public image in Diane Winston, "The Commander in Rags," in *Red-Hot and Righteous*, 144–90. Evangeline Booth's views are also reflected in her own

writing. See Booth, *The Harp and the Sword: Published and Unpublished Writings and Speeches of Evangeline Cory Booth* (New York: Salvation Army Literary Department, USA Eastern Territory, 1992), and Evangeline Booth and Grace Livingston Hill, *The War Romance of the Salvation Army* (Philadelphia: Lippincott, 1919).

108. See Wilson, *General Evangeline Booth of the Salvation Army*, 63–65.

109. Ibid., 63–65. As "The Little Match Girl" story was published in 1845 and was a Victorian favorite, it is likely that Evangeline, who was well read and educated, was familiar with the tale.

110. Evangeline Booth, *The World's Greatest Romance*, in Evangeline Booth bibliographic files, TSANA.

111. Winston, *Red-Hot and Righteous*, 143–45.

112. The musical was named "The Commander in Rags" in reference to Booth. See "Miss Booth's Slum Tales Thrill Crowd," *New York Times*, 29 January 1906, 9.

113. Winston, *Red-Hot and Righteous*, 148. See also Diane Winston, "All the World's a Stage: The Performed Religion of the Salvation Army, 1880–1920," in *Practicing Religion in the Age of the Media: Explorations in Media, Religion, and Culture*, ed. Stewart M. Hoover and Lynn Schofield Clark (New York: Columbia University Press, 2002), 113–32.

114. Photos are housed at TSANA.

115. William R. Leach, "Transformation in a Culture of Consumption: Women and Department Stores, 1890–1925," *Journal of American History* 71, no. 2 (1984): 319–20.

116. Theodore Dreiser, *Sister Carrie* (Philadelphia: University of Pennsylvania Press, 1981; first published in 1900).

117. Nan Enstad reads the gendered, consumer meaning of this short film excellently. See Enstad, *Ladies of Labor, Girls of Adventure*, 10–12.

118. Yates and Hunter, introduction to *Thrift and Thriving in America*, 5–10, 13.

119. Adam Smith, *An Inquiry into the Nature and Causes of the Wealth of Nations* (1776), ed. Edwin Cannan (Chicago: University of Chicago Press, 1976), 359.

120. T. N. Carver, "Thrift and the Standard of Living," *Journal of Political Economy* 28 (November 1920): 284–325.

121. Horowitz, *The Morality of Spending*, xvii–xviii.

122. *The Goodwill Industries: A Manual, A History of the Movement, Departmental Methods of Work, Religious and Cultural Activities, Administration and Organization* (Boston: Morgan Memorial Goodwill Press, 1935), dedication.

123. For more about the relationship between mass philanthropy and thrift-store success, see Le Zotte, " 'Not Charity, but a Chance,' " 169–95.

124. Mary Antin, *At School in the Promised Land* (New York: Houghton-Mifflin, 1912), 30. For more about how Jewish women immigrants responded to American dress, see Barbara A. Schreier, *Becoming American Women: Clothing and the Jewish Immigrant Experience, 1880–1920* (Chicago: Chicago Historical Society, 1994).

125. Kathy Peiss assesses working women's relationship to ready-made clothing in turn-of-the-century New York City in *Cheap Amusements*, 56–87.

126. Anzia Yezierska, "Wings" (1920), reprinted in *How I Found America: Collected Stories of Anzia Yezierska* (New York: Persea Books, 1991), 3–16. See also Katherine

Stubbs, "Reading Material: Contextualizing Clothing in the Work of Anzia Yezierska," *MELUS* 23, no. 2 (Summer 1998): 157–72.

127. Shreier, *Becoming American Women*, 57.

128. Yezierska, "Wings," 9–11.

129. Katherine Stubbs clearly analyzes Yezierska's relationship to shopping and dress. See Stubbs, "Reading Material," 159. The secondhand shops as "banners of poverty" comes from Anzia Yezierska, *Salome of the Tenements* (Chicago: University of Illinois Press, 1923), 5. Yezierska's factory-working character responds with doubt at the suggestion of becoming a designer. "Waists" refers to waistshirts. See Yezierska, "Mostly about Myself," in *Children of Loneliness* (New York: Funk and Wagnalls, 1923), 30.

130. Stubbs, "Reading Material," 159.

131. See Winston, *The Urban Religion of the Salvation Army*, 220. For more on the influence of Wanamaker and his department stores on American consumerism, see T. J. Jackson Lears, *Fables of Abundance: A Cultural History of Advertising in America* (New York: Basic Books, 1994), 32. On the rise of chain stores, see Tracey Deutsch, *Building a Housewife's Paradise: Gender, Politics, and American Grocery Stores in the Twentieth Century* (Chapel Hill: University of North Carolina Press, 2010), 43–72.

132. *What the Camera Finds in a Salvation Army Industrial Home and Store* (TSANA, pamphlet, uncatalogued, undated).

133. Strasser, *Waste and Want*, 143.

134. Quoted in McKinley, *Somebody's Brother*, 87.

135. Woloson, *In Hock*, 154–58.

136. See, for example, Stuart Ewen, *Captains of Consciousness: Advertising and the Social Roots of Consumer Culture* (New York: McGraw-Hill, 1976); Lears, *Fables of Abundance*; and Roland Marchand, *Advertising the American Dream: Making Way for Modernity, 1920–1940* (Berkeley: University of California Press, 1985).

137. Mead, "The Place of Advertising in Modern Business," 227.

Chapter Two

1. Hope Ridings Miller, "Bettina Belmont Is Set to Open 'Flea Market': Hunt Leaders Expected to Visit Display of Boots, Saddles, Linen, Glassware at Middleburg; Project Patterned after European Idea," *Washington Post*, 31 September 1937, 16.

2. Miller, "Bettina Belmont Is Set to Open 'Flea Market,'" 16. For more about fundraising sales in general, see Beverly Gordon, *Bazaars and Fair Ladies: The History of the American Fundraising Fair* (Knoxville: University of Tennessee Press, 1998).

3. Daniel Bluestone, "The Pushcart Evil," in *The Landscape of Modernity: New York City, 1900–1940*, ed. David Ward and Olivier Zunz (Baltimore: Johns Hopkins University, 1992), 308–9.

4. Some struggling to define flea markets write simply that "you know it when you see it." See Albert LaFarge, *U.S. Flea Market Directory, 3rd Edition: A Guide to the Best Flea Markets in All 50 States* (New York: St. Martin's Press, 2000), ix.

5. Flea markets did not gain a central organization until 1997, when flea market owner Jerry Stokes formed the National Flea Market Association (NFMA). Information on the formation of the NFMA from NFMA founder Jerry Stokes, interview with the author, 25 November 2006.

6. In his study on the rise and fall of the American public market, James Mayo concludes that while the public markets became economically unviable for both municipalities and private interests by midcentury, they were perceived "as a viable cultural function." See Mayo, "The American Public Market," *Journal of Architectural Education* 45, no. 1 (1991): 41. For a history of the development of grocery stores, see Tracey Deutsch, *Building a Housewife's Paradise: Gender, Politics, and American Grocery Stores in the Twentieth Century* (Chapel Hill: University of North Carolina Press, 2010), and for more on the dispute over chain stores in the 1920s and 1930s and oppositional consumerism activism during the Great Depression, see Daniel Scroop, "The Anti-Chain Store Movement and the Politics of Consumption," *American Quarterly* 60, no. 4 (2008): 925–49.

7. See Pyle, "Farmers' Markets in the United States: Functional Anachronisms," *American Geographical Society* 61, no. 2 (1971): 167–197. In 2001, Allison Brown was more specific in her designation of the markets and more optimistic about their future. I argue that their resurgence is of a piece with the sale of secondhand items. See Brown, "Counting Farmers Markets," *Geographical Review* 91, no. 4 (2001): 655–74.

8. I am taking some liberties with the meaning of "public," as many flea markets ceased being municipal entities early in the century but retained attributes of older government-run and essentially socialized institutions. See Mayo, "The American Public Market," 42. Many "public" markets were funded by, owned by, and provided a profit for private interest as early as the mid-nineteenth century. A distinction is occasionally made between "municipal" or "quasi-public," in which case the land was city-owned, but the market structures were built by private companies, which managed them and collected revenues for a determined time, usually twenty-five years. See Robert A. Sauder, "The Origin and Spread of the Public Market System in New Orleans," *Louisiana, History: The Journal of the Louisiana Historical Association* 22, no. 3 (1981): 282.

9. John F. Sherry Jr., refers to flea markets as a "ritual and ceremonial venue for the experience of disorder"; see "A Sociocultural Analysis of a Midwestern American Flea Market," *Journal of Consumer Research* 17, no. 1 (1990): 28. "Libidinous" comes from Les Abrams, "Urban Marketplaces and Mobile Vendors: The Flea Market in the Metropolitan Economy. A Case Study of Two Flea Markets—Aqueduct and Roosevelt Raceway Flea Markets" (PhD diss., City University of New York, 2007), 4.

10. Surrealist André Breton extolled the virtues of flea markets for generating "chance encounters" with surreal disjunction. See André Breton, *Nadja*, trans. Richard Howard (New York: Grove Press, 1960), 53.

11. Margaret Cohen, *Profane Illumination: Walter Benjamin and the Paris of Surrealist Revolution* (Berkeley: University of California Press, 1993), 109; Breton, *Nadja*, 53.

12. Sontag was writing specifically about surrealist photography, but the principle extends to other media. See Sontag, *On Photography* (New York: Farrar, Straus and Giroux, 1973), 53–56.

13. Many scholars have highlighted the contrasts of the 1920s. For a broad view of the pluralism of American culture in that decade attendant to changes in national government, technology, and the economy, see Lynn Dumenil, *The Modern Temper: American Culture and Society in the 1920s* (New York: Hill and Wang, 1995). Paul V. Murphy traces the emerging inventions and trends through the eyes of experimental intellectuals. See Murphy, *The New Era: American Thought and Culture in the 1920s* (Lanham, MD: Rowman & Littlefield, 2012).

14. Thomas R. Pegram details the 1920s resurgence of the Ku Klux Klan and the expansion of their racist project to include xenophobia and anti-Catholicism. See Pegram, *One Hundred Percent American: The Rebirth and Decline of the Ku Klux Klan in the 1920s* (Lanham, MD: Ivan R. Dee, 2011).

15. Scholars periodize the Great Migration variously, with some extending it from World War I through the 1930s, and others through the 1970s. Others break the voluntary evacuation of black Americans form the South into two time periods. For example, Milton C. Sernett writes about African American religion during the first wave of southern black migration. See Sernett, *Bound for the Promise Land: African American Religion and the Promised Land* (Durham, NC: Duke University Press, 1997). Isabel Wilkerson's narrative, in-depth account of three different individuals' journeys North extends from 1915 to 1970. See Wilkerson, *The Warmth of Other Suns: The Epic Story of America's Great Migration* (New York: Random House, 2010).

16. In *Satisfaction Guaranteed*, Susan Strasser offers a sweeping history of the first decades of mass marketing, with an emphasis on branding and department store marketing from after the Civil War through the 1920s. See Strasser, *Satisfaction Guaranteed: The Making of the American Mass Market* (Washington, DC: Smithsonian, 2014; first published in 1989). Despite the overall increase in buying, consumption habits still varied widely across classes. Lizabeth Cohen writes about working-class consumption of mass culture in Cohen, "Encountering Mass Culture at the Grassroots: The Experience of Chicago Workers in the 1920s," *American Quarterly* 41, no. 1 (1989): 6–33. Roland Marchand's classic consumer history focuses on the role of advertising in creating the new American consumer. See Marchand, *Advertising the American Dream: Making Way for Modernity, 1920–1940* (Berkeley: University of California Press, 1985). Jackson Lears's cultural history of advertising offers a view assigning consumers a more active role in the process. See Lears, *Fables of Abundance: A Cultural History of Advertising in America* (New York: Basic Books, 1994).

17. According to dress historian Anne Hollander, "camera vision" had insurmountable influence over fashion and style, as it demanded a lean body, exacting cosmetics, and contextualized dress. See Hollander, *Seeing through Clothes* (Berkeley: University of California Press, 1993), 328–29.

18. See Dickstein, *Dancing in the Dark: A Cultural History of the Great Depression* (New York: W.W. Norton, 2009), 420–49.

19. Deborah Saville argues that Village dress beginning in 1910 influenced the mainstream look of flappers in the 1920s. See Saville, "Dress and Culture in Greenwich

Village," in *Twentieth-Century American Fashion*, ed. Linda Welters and Patricia A. Cunningham (New York: Berg, 2005), 34–35.

20. Marja Warehime, "Photography, Time, and the Surrealist Sensibility," in *Photo-Textualities: Reading Photographs and Literature*, ed. Marsha Bryan (Cranbury, NJ: Associated University Presses, 1996), 55.

21. Dalia Judovitz, *Drawing on Art: Duchamp and Company* (Minneapolis: University of Minnesota, 2010), 122.

22. *Nadja*, 19, 52–53; Margaret Cohen, *Profane Illumination: Walter Benjamin and the Paris of Surrealist Revolution* (Berkeley: University of California Press, 1993), 109.

23. Marcel Duchamp with Michel Sanouillet and Elmer Peterson, eds., *The Writings of Marcel Duchamp* (Boston: Da Capo Press, 1973), 32.

24. See Rudy Ernst, *The Story of Dada: And How to Activate Your Dada-Gene* (New York: QCC Art Gallery, City University of New York, 2009), 79.

25. See Ruth Brandon, *Surreal Lives: The Surrealists, 1917–1945* (New York: Grove Press, 1999), 449–50. The Menil Collection in Houston, Texas, includes display of objects collected by surrealists in a room titled "Witnesses to a Surrealist Vision." The room demonstrates an array of objects conceived of as surreal, including primitive masks and accessories, proto-photographic equipment including a camera obscura, a flip book, a stereoscope, a zoetrope, and arrays of "mythic" images and visual puns. Many of these were acquired secondhand.

26. M. E. Walick, *Max Ernst and Alchemy: A Magician in Search of Myth* (Austin: University of Texas, 2001), 158–60. See also Brandon, *Surreal Lives*.

27. Diane Waldman, *Joseph Cornell: Master of Dreams* (New York: Abrams, 2002), 11, 17. See also Charles Simic, *Dime-Store Alchemy: The Art of Joseph Cornell* (New York: New York Review Books, 1992).

28. André Breton, *Mad Love [L'Amour Fou]*, trans. Mary Ann Caws (Lincoln: University of Nebraska Press, 1987), 41.

29. In this Guido Bruno short story, the "hour of the pawns" is the very last hour of 1919, at a Park Row pawnshop. See Bruno, "Midnight in a Pawn Shop," in *Sentimental Studies: Stories of Life and Love* (New York: published by author, 1920), 8–15.

30. Susan Glaspell was a feminist playwright living in Greenwich Village in the 1920s. See Glaspell, *Chains of Dew*, unpublished play (Washington, DC: Library of Congress, 21 February 1920).

31. For example, the German Dada Kurt Schwitters used fashion to represent the persistence of "traditional" gender arrangements and feminine stereotypes amidst increasing social and political equality. To underscore a major paradox in modern society, Schwitters related fashion, consumption, and modernity, but also used fashion plate images in such a way that reinforced a male-dominated power structure. See Dorothea Dietrich, "Love as Commodity," in *Women in Dada: Essays on Sex, Gender, and Identity*, ed. Naomi Sawelson-Gorse (Boston: MIT Press, 1998), 233.

32. Ghislaine Wood outlines the role of the mannequin in defining the surrealist conception of the body. See Wood, *The Surreal Body: Fetish and Fashion* (London: Victoria and Albert Museum, 2007), 26–31.

33. Salvador Dali's interest in fashion continued, and he created a series of surrealist jewelry in the 1940s and 1950s, including jewel-encrusted telephone ear clips and brooches resembling lips and starfish. See Wood, *The Surreal Body*, 35–37.

34. Avedon quoted in Vicki Goldberg, "Photography: The Fashionable Man Ray, 'Breaking the Stranglehold of Reality' in 'Bazaar' Years," *New York Magazine*, 10 September 1990, 98; claim about Avedon's effect on the public's acceptance of bohemianism in Janice Susan Gore, "Used Value: Thrift Shopping and Bohemia Incorporated" (PhD diss., University of Southern California, Department of Philosophy, 1999), 81–83.

35. See Albert Parry, "The Trilby Craze: Bohemia for All," in *In Bohemia: The Code of the Self-Exiled*, eds. César Graña and Marigay Graña (New Brunswick, NJ: Transaction, 1990), 286–289. See also Gore, "Used Value," 72–73. Ideas of bohemian lives and styles were transmitted even earlier by Henri Murger's 1851 *Scènes de la vie de Bohème*, discussed further in chapter 4.

36. See Irene Gammel, *Baroness Elsa, Gender, Dada, and Everyday Modernity* (Boston: Massachusetts Institute of Technology, 2003), 64–67. Gammel cites Linda Mizejewski's study on the Ziegfeld Girl to describe the Zentral Theater chorus girl. See Mizejewski, *Ziegfeld Girl: Image and Icon in Culture and Cinema* (Durham, NC: Duke University Press, 1999), 68–69. For more on containing the transgressive image of female sexuality, see also Robert C. Allen, *Horrible Prettiness: Burlesque and American Culture* (Chapel Hill: University of North Carolina Press, 1991), 96.

37. "She Wore Men's Clothes," *New York Times*, 17 September 1910, 6. The baroness arrived in the United States to meet her second husband, novelist Frederick Philip Greve, who left her a year later, at which time she left for New York City, where she would meet her third and final husband, and acquire her most fitting and lasting name.

38. Gammel, *Baroness Elsa*, 150–59.

39. See Elizabeth Wilson, *Bohemians The Glamorous Outcasts* (London and New York: I. B. Tauris, 2003), 41. See also Christine Stansell, *American Moderns: Bohemian New York and the Creation of a New Century* (New York: Henry Holt, 2000).

40. For an examination of the baroness's hand in making *Fountain*, see Gammel, *Baroness Elsa*, 222–26.

41. See Marlis Schweitzer, *When Broadway Was the Runway: Theater, Fashion, and American Culture* (Philadelphia: University of Pennsylvania Press, 2009). In his recent book, *The Practice of Misuse: Rugged Consumerism in Contemporary American Culture*, literary scholar Raymond Malewitz points to Duchamp's *Fountain* (side by side with William Carlos Williams's poem "Between Walls") to illustrate this cohort's innovation of recycled objects as a setting for art. However, the masculinism of Malewitz's "rugged consumerism" leaves sparse space for the realm of dress, historically assigned to femininity. See Malewitz, *The Practice of Misuse*.

42. Gammel uses the apt term "corporeal art" to describe the baroness's personal appearance. See Gammel, *Baroness Elsa*, 5.

43. While few illustrative photos exist, descriptions of the baroness's sartorial performances come from numerous sources. Amelia Jones drew from descriptions in

Robert Reiss's memoir, "'My Baroness': Elsa von Freytag-Loringhoven," in *New York Dada*, ed. Rudolf E. Kuenzli (New York: Willis Locker & Owens, 1986), 81, in Jones, "Eros, That's Life, or the Baroness' Penis," in *Making Mischief: Dada Invades New York*, ed. Francis M. Naumann and Beth Venn (New York: Whitney Museum of American Art, 1996). Gammel quotes from various sources, including George Biddel and Djuna Barnes's unpublished autobiography of the baroness. See Gammell, *Baroness Elsa*, as well as Ross Wetzsteon, *Republic of Dreams: Greenwich Village: The American Bohemia, 1910–1960* (New York: Simon & Schuster, 2002), 318–19. For more on artists living in the Village during and after World War I, see Steven Watson, *Strange Bedfellows: The First American Avant-Garde* (New York: Abbeville Press, 1991).

44. Mizejewski, *Ziegfeld Girl*, 22.

45. George Biddle, *An American Artist's Story* (Boston: Little, Brown, 1939), 137, quoted in Gammel, *Baroness Elsa*, 202.

46. Gammel notes that the tomato-can bra came just five years after the invention of the bra in New York, which signified a liberation of the female body from the restraints of the corset. See Gammel, *Baroness Elsa*, 202.

47. Mary Flanagan, *Critical Play: Radical Game Design* (Boston: MIT Press, 2009), 132.

48. Amelia Jones, *Irrational Modernism: A Neurasthenic History of New York Dada* (Boston: M.I.T. Press, 2004), 4.

49. Heap, and *The Little Review*'s copublisher Margaret Anderson, had no difficulty facing down controversy; the baroness's poem "Holy Skirts," which addresses sexuality in terms of the Catholic Church, appeared alongside and alluded to the last episode of James Joyce's *Ulysses* before Heap and Anderson were taken to court and sued over the excerpts. See Tanya Clement, "The Baroness in Little Magazine History," *Jacket 2* (5 May 2011), accessed 19 May 2015, http://jacket2.org/article/baroness-little-magazine-history. See also Jane Heap, "Dada," *The Little Review* 6, no. 6 (1919): 46, and references to the baroness in Anderson's *My Thirty Years War* (New York: Horizon, 1969), 181–82.

50. Jones, *Irrational Modernism*, 3. Wallace Stevens and William Carlos Williams were among the many other modernists who revered the baroness's artistic mission—even when her sexually driven intensity terrified and repelled them personally. William Carlos Williams confessed, "Elsa von Freytag Loringhoven came to me as sunlight. . . . But she revolted me, frightened me" (quoted in Tanya E. Clement, "The Makings of Digital Modernism: Rereading Gertrude Stein's *The Making of Americans* and Poetry by Elsa Von Freytag-Loringhoven" [PhD diss., University of Michigan, Ann Arbor, 2009], 160). Ernest Hemingway risked his role as subeditor of the *transatlantic review* in 1924 to publish the baroness's work, with its generous use of sexual description and original portmanteaus, such as kissambushed and spinsterlollipop, her neologism for dildo. See Gammel, *Baroness Elsa*, 5.

51. Quoted in Irene Gammel and Suzanne Zelazo, eds., introduction to *Body Sweats: The Uncensored Writings of Elsa von Freytag Loringhoven* (Cambridge: Massachusetts Institute of Technology, 2011).

52. Irene Gammel serves as the baroness's most comprehensive biographer, with *Baroness Elsa: Gender, Dada, and Everyday Modernity* (Cambridge, MA: MIT Press, 2002). In 2011, more than a decade after her arrival in the United States, Gammel and Suzanne Zelazo edited a complete collection of the baroness's poetry. Gammel and Zelazo, eds., *Body Sweats*. See also Robert Reiss, "'My Baroness': Elsa von Freytag-Loringhoven," *Dada surrealism* 14 (1985): 81–101, and Amelia Jones *Irrational Modernism: A Neurasthenic History of New York Dada* (Cambridge, MA: MIT Press, 2004).

53. Gammel, *Baroness Elsa*, 203.

54. Saville, "Dress and Culture in Greenwich Village," 33–56.

55. Ibid., 44.

56. Robert Edwards, *Bob Edwards' Guide to Greenwich Village and all through Life with Map History Directory Music Verse Pictures Advice & Formyla for Art, Love, Etc...* (New York: The Quill, 1919), 27.

57. See Sontag, *On Photography*, 53–56.

58. Ibid, 54. In her comments on Sontag's critique, Marja Warehime argues that Sontag elided "a whole range of surrealist "found image" practices they used to create otherworldly visions. See Warehime, "Photography, Time, and the Surrealist Sensibility," 55.

59. The concept of flea market–style exchanges are as old as commerce. Arguably, in the Middle Ages, Middle Eastern *bazaars* and Arabic *souks* were some of the earliest examples. See Anneli Rufus and Kristan Lawson, *The Scavengers' Manifesto* (New York: Penguin, 2009), 156–57.

60. For example, some say the term originated because looking for coveted goods at such a market is akin to looking for fleas on a dog. See Leavitt F. Morris, "Travel Editor's Diary," *Christian Science Monitor*, 7 June 1957, 10.

61. Similarly, United States thrift stores' success relied in part on the new philanthropic ideals of Progressive-Era politics, as well as the growth in discarded firsthand goods stemming from increased large-scale production at the end of the nineteenth century. See Jennifer Le Zotte, "'Not Charity, But a Chance': Philanthropic Capitalism and the Rise of American Thrift Stores," *New England Quarterly* 86, no. 2 (2013): 169–95.

62. While the name "flea market" almost certainly derived from Paris, older examples of "old things" markets exist, such as the Brussels' Marché Place du Jeu de Balle, which was founded in 1873 and has roots in a similar market dating back to 1640, strictly for old and used wares, held Tuesdays and Thursdays. Even as early as the sixteenth century, sources document an "Oude Merckt." See Paul F. State, *Historical Dictionary of Brussels* (Lanham, MD: Scarecrow Press, 2004), 192, and Rufus and Lawson, *The Scavengers' Manifesto*, 157. Current assessments of Marché aux Puces do not thoroughly consider the social, legal, and economic machinations that complicated the market's growth. For brief histories, see Pamela Hough and Stuart Hough, *Bit by the Fleas: An Insider's Guide to the Paris Flea Market* (Paris: Vilo, 2002); Sebak, "A Flea Market Documentary" (Pittsburgh, PA: WQED PBS Documentary, 2001); Pamela Klaffke, *Spree: A Cultural History of Shopping* (Vancouver: Arsenal Pulp Press, 2003), 112–14; and

Maureen Stanton, *Killer Stuff and Tons of Money: Seeking History and Hidden Gems in Flea-Market America* (New York: Penguin Press, 2011), 7–8.

63. See Richard Sennett, *The Fall of the Public Man* (New York: Knopf, 1974), and Michael B. Miller, *The Bon Marché: Bourgeois Culture and the Department Store, 1869–1920* (Princeton, NJ: Princeton University Press, 1981), 2–11. For more on department stores and the effect of advertising and display on American consumers' desires around the turn of the century, see, for example, William Leach, *Land of Desire: Merchants, Power, and the Rise of a New American Culture* (New York: Vintage Books, 1993).

64. Stanton, *Killer Stuff and Tons of Money*, 7–8. See also Sandy Price, *Exploring the Flea Markets of France* (New York: Three Rivers Press, 1999), and Jerry Stokes, "A Flea Market by Any Other Name Is a Flea Market," in *Antique and Flea Markets of London and Paris*, ed. Rupert Thomas and Eglé Salvy (London: Thames & Hudson, 1999).

65. Of course, standards barring commercial participation were not new in France; previously, guilds had regulated entry to trades and governed craftsmanship and competition. This period represents a transition to different types of commercial limitations, not a departure from an entirely open system. These changes required adaptation on the part of participants at all levels of commerce. See Miller, *The Bon Marché*, 21–22.

66. The municipal garbage cans retain the name *poubelle*, after the Paris prefect M. Poubelle, who advocated for the ordinance. See David Bouchier, *The Cats and the Water Bottles, and Other Mysteries of French Village Life* (New York and London: ASJA Press, 2002), 37–38.

67. A 1923 article boasted of "the prestige afforded by a flea market." See "Real Flea Market Will Open in Paris," *Washington Post*, 26 August 1923, 33. In 1930, the Paris market was a place to which "[n]early every tourist who visits France plans to make at least one visit," according to "The Flea Market," *New York Times*, 22 October 1930, 23.

68. Hough and Hough, *Bit by the Fleas*, 18.

69. Paris faced some of the urbanization challenges earlier than the United States, and responded as well with race- and class-based prejudice. Paris's immigrant population doubled between 1800 and 1840, compromising the city's economic structure and political stability. As Jerrold Seigal writes, "the image of the working classes merged with the specter of *les classes dangereuses*, the dangerous classes." See Seigal, *Bohemian Paris: Culture, Politics, and the Boundaries of Bourgeois Life, 1830–1930* (New York: Penguin, 1986), 22–23.

70. As mentioned in chapter 1, street peddling was a trade that Jewish immigrants historically favored. In New York City as early as 1855, before the major influx of eastern European immigrants, the number of Jewish peddlers in the United States began to overtake that of Irish ones. An estimated minimum of 4 to 5 percent of all gainfully employed Jews in New York City were peddlers in the mid-nineteenth century. See Robert Ernst, *Immigrant Life in New York City, 1825–1863* (Syracuse, NY: Syracuse University Press, 1994), 84.

71. "War on the Cart Venders: An Even Dozen Rounded Up and Fined in the Police Court," *Washington Post*, 14 August 1894, 8.

72. See Mendelsohn, " 'It's the Economy, Shmendrick': A New Turn in Jewish Studies?" *AJS Perspectives*, Fall 2009, 14–17. For more on Europe's secondhand trade, see Madeleine Ginsburg, "Rags to Riches: the Second Hand Clothes Trade, 1700–1978," *Costume: The Journal of the Costume Society* (London) 14 (1980): 125. On the economic history of Jews in modern Europe, see Derek Jonathan Penslar and Anthony W. Lee, *Shylock's Children: Economics and Jewish Identity in Modern Europe* (Berkeley: University of California Press, 2001), 16, 20. Wendy Woloson links immigrant Jews' secondhand sales experiences to the establishment of pawnshops in the United States. See Woloson, *In Hock: Pawning in America from Independence through the Great Depression* (Chicago: University of Chicago Press, 2009), 16–17. See also, Le Zotte, " 'Not Charity, But a Chance,' " 173.

73. Alison Isenberg's forthcoming book discusses the roles African Americans played in the home furnishings and second-hand industries, including black antique dealers who established the Americana trade in the nineteenth century. Isenberg, "Second-hand Cities: Race and Region in the Antique Americana Trade, from the Civil War to Urban Renewal" (unpublished manuscript, 2 August 2016), Microsoft Word file.

74. Documentarian Phil Ranstrom outlines the battle to keep Maxwell Street Market in place in *"Cheat You Fair": The Story of Maxwell Street* (Ranstrom, 2012), documentary DVD.

75. Carolyn Eastwood, *Near West Side Stories: Struggles for Community in Chicago's Maxwell Street Neighborhood* (Chicago: Lake Claremont Press, 2002), 19–21.

76. Eastwood, *Near West Side Stories*, 21.

77. "Buy Much for a Penny: Commercial Side of One of Chicago's Oldest Neighborhoods," *Chicago Daily Tribune*, 20 September 1896, 34.

78. To many native-born Americans, immigrants' seemingly irresponsible procreation signaled a willingness to live in the substandard conditions endemic to urban tenement housing in the United States. While many reformists attributed the unsanitary industrial-era housing condition to their inhabitants, others sought to encourage municipal responsibility, in part through comparison with other industrialized countries' housing provisions for workers. For example, Angela M. Blake recounts a tenement housing exhibition held on Fifth Avenue in New York City in 1900 whose purpose was to show the insufficiency of tenements in New York and the United States in general compared with other countries. See Blake, *How New York Became American, 1890–1924* (Baltimore, MD: Johns Hopkins University Press, 2006), 39–48.

79. "Shylock" refers to the vengeful Jewish moneylender in Shakespeare's *Merchant of Venice*. See "Buy Much for a Penny," 34.

80. Ibid., 34.

81. Eastwood, *Near West Side Stories*, 21.

82. For more on the legislation of peddlers' noise in Chicago's near west side, see Derek Valliant, "Peddling Noise: Contesting the Civic Soundscape of Chicago, 1890–1913," *Journal of the Illinois State Historical Society* 96, no. 3 (2003): 257–87.

83. Amendment quoted in *Chicago Record Herald*, 2 July 1913; reference in Carolyn Eastwood, *Chicago's Jewish Street Peddlers* (Chicago: Chicago Jewish Historical Society, 1991), 29.

84. A long series of articles chronicled the ongoing struggles between the Maxwell Street vendors and allegedly corrupt market masters. See, for example, "Peddlers Accuse Market Master Say A. J. Goldstein of Maxwell Street Collects Too Many Dime Fees," *Chicago Daily Tribune*, 1 June 1913, 3, and "Riots Near at Market Hearing," *Chicago Daily Tribune*, 12 June 1913, 5. Similar charges continued with future market masters. See "Fick Charges 'Big Money' Paid for Market Favors," *Chicago Daily Tribune*, 15 July 1921, 15.

85. For more on the transformation of Maxwell Street Market, see Ira Berkow, *Survival in a Bazaar* (New York: Doubleday, 1977); Mike Shea, *And This Is Free*; and Shuli Eshel, *Maxwell Street: A Living Memory* (Kartemquin Films, 2008).

86. Lori Grove and Laura Kamedulski offer images and brief accounts of the blues influence on Maxwell Street after the 1920s, including Daddy Stovepipe, in *Chicago's Maxwell Street* (Chicago: Arcadia, 2002), 81. Brief histories of Daddy Stovepipe, born Johnny Watson, appear in several blues histories, such as Robert Springer, ed., *Nobody Knows Where the Blues Come From: Lyrics and History* (Jackson: University of Mississippi Press, 2006), 41–42.

87. "Giving the Pushcart Men a Place of Business," *New York Times*, 3 July 1904, SM3.

88. East Side Peddlers' Association to Mayor George B. McClellan, 14 November 1906, MGB-117; Bluestone, "The Pushcart Evil," 293–94.

89. "The Romance of the Picturesque Pushcart," *New York Times*, 14 June 1912, SM9.

90. Bluestone, "The Pushcart Evil," 301.

91. In "Pushcart Question Reduced to Politics: Those Who Profit by Lack of Regulation Expected to Oppose Reform," *New York Times*, 7 July 1912, 12.

92. See, for example, "Pushcart Peddlers Menace to Health," *New York Times*, 6 July 1912, 16; "Pushcart Question Reduced to Politics," *New York Times*, 7 July 1912, 12.

93. See, for example, "The Push-Cart Peddlers," *New York Times*, 4 June 1907, 6; "Peddlers Fight $1 Fee," *New York Times*, 27 June 1922, 18.

94. *Proceedings of the City Council* (6 July 1899), 987; Valliant, "Peddling Noise," 266; Deutsch, *Building a Housewife's Paradise*, 30–31.

95. For a specific study of these advantages as Chicago housewives perceived them, see Deutsch, *Building a Housewife's Paradise*, 31–32, and "Merchants Sue for Push Cart Competition: Say Peddlers Parked at Door Boost Trade," *New York Times*, 30 July 1925, 21.

96. This comment appeared one year after the Triangle Shirtwaist Factory fire of 1911. See "The Romance of the Picturesque Pushcart," *New York Times*, 14 June 1912, SM9.

97. For a description of municipally constructed nineteenth-century U.S. public markets and their role in the public sphere, see Helen Tangires, *Public Markets and Civic Culture in Nineteenth-Century America* (Baltimore, MD: Johns Hopkins University Press, 2003). For a broader examination of public markets, including their relationship with the City Beautiful Movement, see Tangires, *Public Markets* (New York: W & W

Norton, 2008), and Robert J. Shepherd, *When Culture Goes to Market: Space, Place and Identity in an Urban Marketplace* (New York: Peter Lang, 2008), 25–32. Tracey Deutsch details the changes in food distribution in *Building a Housewife's Paradise*. See also Marc Levinson, *The Great A & P and the Struggle for Small Businesses in America* (New York: Farrar, Straus, and Giroux, 2011).

98. While many recent books advocate buying local and recount the environmental, civic, and personal benefits of the local foods movement (or, of being a "locavore"), few historical accounts of its rise exist. Britta Ann-Christin Solan offers a case study of the local foods movement in Iowa City in *The Culture of Local Food: A Life History Study of Farmers' Market Customers in a Midwest City* (Iowa City: University of Iowa Press, 2002).

99. Allan Kulikoff, "Households and Markets: Toward a New Synthesis of American Agrarian History," *William and Mary Quarterly*, 3d ser., 1, no. 1 (1993): 342–55. For a brief history of First Mondays, see David Nelson Wren, *Every First Monday: A History of Canton, Texas* (Wichita Falls, TX: Nortex Offset, 1973). Town squares were frequent sites of political speeches and the headquarters for travelers' amusements and accommodations. They often housed the public well or cistern and hosted auctions. Nineteenth-century observers commented on the particular economic significance of town squares across Texas. See, for example, Fort Worth's *Daily Gazette*, 16 January 1879, in which it was remarked that any obstruction to the square would be protested by a myriad of business interests; quoted in Willard B. Robinson, "The Public Square as a Determinant of Courthouse Form in Texas," *Southwestern Historical Quarterly* 75, no. 3 (1972): 339–72. Despite the fact that histories of First Monday love to recount the popularity of hangings, there were only two formally recorded ones in Van Zandt County, home of Canton's First Mondays market. See David Nelson Wren, *Every First Monday*, 8.

100. Canton was also home to the first woman to be sentenced to life in prison in Texas and to a very active homegrown version of the Klu Klux Klan. See Wren, *Every First Monday*, 8–9.

101. Gerald Lynch, *Roughnecks, Drillers, and Tool Pushers* (Austin: University of Texas Press, 1987), 53.

102. Wren, *Every First Monday*, 28.

103. Webster's Westside Market claims to be Florida's largest and oldest flea market. See Bruce Hunt, "Webster," in *Visiting Small-Town Florida*, 3rd ed. (Sarasota, FL: Pineapple Press, 2011), 131–35; Terry Goodson (Webster Westside Market vendor), interview with the author, 9 September 2005. See also websterwestside.com.

104. Blue laws, or Sunday-closing laws, which were part of U.S. policy for several hundred years, were still enacted until after World War II in many places. David N. Laband and Deborah Hendry Heinbuch describe what sustained and eventually reversed these sales prohibitions. See Laband and Heinbuch, *Blue Laws: The History, Economics, and Poltics of Sunday-Closing Laws* (Lanham, MD: Lexington Books, 1987).

105. Hunt, "Webster," 132–33.

106. The Arts and Crafts movement in America de-emphasized the smoothness of mass production in favor of a more "primitive" and "natural" style. For the implications

of this for American thought and culture, see T. J. Jackson Lears, *No Place of Grace: Antimodernism and the Transformation of American Culture, 1880–1920* (New York: Pantheon Books, 1981).

107. See Le Zotte, "'Not Charity, But a Chance,'" 194; Peter F. Buckley, "The Old Curiosity Shop and the New Antique Store: A Note on the Vanishing Curio in New York City," *Common-place* 4, no. 2 (2004), accessed 17 May 2013, http://www.common-place.org/vol-04/no-02/buckley/; and Briann Greenfield, *Out of the Attic: Inventing Antiques in Twentieth-Century New England* (Amherst: University of Massachusetts Press, 2009), 9.

108. For more on the museum exhibits at the beginning of the century, see Elizabeth Stillinger, *The Antiquers* (New York: Alfred A. Knopf, 1980), xiii–xv, and Greenfield, *Out of the Attic*, 2–3.

109. Ford said many seemingly disparaging things about history, such as "History is myth" and "History is more or less bunk." The concise quotation usually cited, "History is bunk," was recorded in the *New York Times* in 1921. See "History Is Bunk, Says Henry Ford," *New York Times*, 28 October 1921. He also clarified that "history you can see is of great value." Ford, quoted in Steven Conn, *Museums and American Intellectual Life, 1876–1926* (Chicago: University of Chicago Press, 1998), 156.

110. J. G. de Roulhac Hamilton, "The Ford Museum," *American Historical Review* 36, no. 4 (1931): 772–75.

111. Ford, quoted in Hamilton, "The Ford Museum," 773. For more on Ford's motivation and the role of businessmen in transforming the genre of history museums, see Michael Wallace, "Visiting the Past: History Museums in the United States," in *Presenting the Past: Essays on History and the Public*, ed. Susan Porter Benson, Stephen Brier, and Roy Rosenzweig (Philadelphia: Temple University Press, 1986), 137–61.

112. Michael Kammen, *Mystic Chords of Memory: The Transformation of Tradition in American Culture* (New York: Random House, 1993), 352.

113. For more on the decline of family farms in the Midwest and South, see, for example, Mary Neth, *Preserving the Family Farm: Women, Community, and the Foundations of Agribusiness in the Midwest, 1900–1940* (Baltimore, MD: Johns Hopkins University Press, 1998), and Jack Temple Kirby, *Rural Worlds Lost: The American South, 1920–1960* (Baton Rouge: Louisiana State University Press, 1987).

114. Greenfield, *Out of the Attic*, 77–79.

115. Walter Dyer, *The Lure of the Antique* (New York: Century, 1910), 13; quoted in Greenfield, *Out of the Attic*, 79.

116. See Isenberg, *Second-hand Cities*.

117. Greenfield, *Out of the Attic*, 53.

118. Stillinger, *The Antiquers*, 252; see also Kate Sayen Kirkland, *The Hogg Family and Houston* (Houston: University of Texas Press, 2009), 244.

119. Greenfield, *Out of the Attic*, 13.

120. Ibid., 57–89.

121. For more on the rise of outdoor and "cross-class" vacationing in the 1910s and 1920s, see Cindy Aron, *Working at Play: A History of Vacations in the United States* (Oxford: Oxford University Press, 1999).

122. Mabel Herbert Urner, "Their Married Life: Helen and Warren Go on an Auto Tour and Spend the Night at a Farmhouse," *Washington Post*, 24 July 1916, 5. Helen Sheumaker writes about Mabel Urner Harper's fans and their investment in Harper's married-life collecting narratives. From Sheumaker, "'I Hope You Won't Mind My Writing You': Mabel Urner Harper and her antique-collecting fans," unpublished paper presented at the American Historical Association annual conference, New Orleans, LA January 2013.

123. Mabel Herbert Urner, "Their Married Life: A Remote Farmhouse Offers Dubious Shelter on a Stormy Night," *Washington Post*, 26 August 1928, SM5.

124. Willard Wesley Cochrane, *The Development of American Agriculture: A Historical Analysis* (Minneapolis: University of Minnesota Press, 1993), 100–104.

125. Book collector William Dana Orcutt noted the increase in rare book prices "even during periods when the country is suffering from industrial depression and Wall Street prices are steadily declining." See Orcutt, *The Magic of the Book: The Story of Collecting* (London: Herbert Jenkins, 1924), 13, quoted in Steven M. Gelber, *Hobbies: Leisure and the Culture of Work in America* (New York: Columbia University Press, 1999), 109.

126. Eve Cousin, "Planning for Autumn Activities in Society," *Chicago Daily Tribune*, 16 August 1931, D1.

127. Mabel Herbert Urner, "The Married Life of Helen and Warren," *Los Angeles Times*, 28 March 1937, 118.

128. See Rosalind Shaffer, "Bodyguard Is Accepted Rule in Hollywood," *Chicago Daily Tribune*, 17 July 1932, F5. For another example of a shop calling itself a flea market, see Ed Sullivan, "Broadway: 42nd Street," *Washington Post*, 16 July 1936, 18.

129. Many scholars explore Poiret's appropriation of non-Western styles. See, for example, Adam Geczy, *Fashion and Orientalism: Dress, Textiles and Culture from the 17th to the 21st Century* (London: Bloomsbury Academic, 2013), esp. pp. 137–152. Reina Lewis, *Rethinking Orientalism: Women, Travel, and the Ottoman Harem* (London: Tauris, 2004), 216, 243–46.

130. In *When Broadway Was the Runway*, Marlis Schweitzer highlights actress's performances of fashion as a homogenizing force, but also points out that actresses presented women who might not have otherwise been instructed in the art of sartorial expression with ideas. See Schweitzer, *When Broadway Was the Runway*.

131. Ibid., 9–10. Schweitzer's chap. 1, "The Octopus and the Matinee Girl" highlights the effects female attendance and attention to clothing had on theater, from advertising gimmicks to choice of plays. See ibid., 18–49.

132. For more on how race and eugenic ideals interacted with performance personas particularly in crafting the Ziegfeld Girl, see Mizejewski, *Ziegfeld Girl*, 103–8. For more on how racial, cultural, and sexual drag can be co-opted by dominant powers as controlling devices, see Marjorie Garber, *Vested Interests: Cross-Dressing and Cultural Anxiety* (New York: HarperPerennial, 1993), 227.

133. Mizejewski, *Ziegfeld Girl*, 3.

134. Ibid., 96–97.

135. Schweitzer, *When Broadway Was the Runway*, 69–70.

136. Ibid., 71.

137. See the costume sketches CS.07.03.07 (Homer Conant), Costume Designs—Photos—Schubert Archives, quoted in ibid., 71–74.

138. Timothy R. White, *Blue-Collar Broadway: The Craft and Industry of American Theater* (Philadelphia: University of Pennsylvania Press, 2014).

139. Fanny Brice (as told to Palma Wayne), "Fannie of the Follies," *Cosmopolitan*, March 1936, 106. Quoted in Schweitzer, *When Broadway Was the Runway*, 113–14.

140. Quoted in Schweitzer, *When Broadway Was the Runway*, 114.

141. See "Fanny Brice's Nose to Be Scaled Down," *New York Times*, 15 August 1923, 10; "Fanny Brice under Knife," *New York Times*, 16 August 1923, 2.

142. John Higham gave an early comprehensive account of nativists' complex and evolving racism. See Higham, *Strangers in the Land: Patterns of American Nativism, 1860–1925* (New Brunswick, NJ: Rutgers University Press, 1955), 131–57.

143. Mizejewski, *Ziegfeld Girl*, 131–32.

144. For more on the ghetto in Gold and Roth, see Dickstein, *Dancing in the Dark*, 19–49.

145. Barbara W. Grossman, *Funny Woman: The Life and Times of Fanny Brice* (Bloomington: Indiana University Press, 1992), 118–19.

146. Ballard MacDonald and James F. Hanley, "Rose of Washington Square" (New York: Shapiro, Bernstein, 1920), MCNY; Emily Kies Folpe, *It Happened in Washington Square* (Baltimore: Johns Hopkins University Press, 2002), 9.

147. Quoted in Bradley Bailey, "Rrose of Washington Square: Marcel Duchamp, Fanny Brice, and the Jewish Origins of Rrose Sélavy," *Notes in the History of Art* 27, no. 1 (2007): 42.

148. Grant Clarke and James F. Hanley, "Second Hand Rose" (New York: Shapiro, Bernstein, 1921), MCNY.

149. Ted Merwin contextualizes Fanny Brice's performance as Second Hand Rose alongside the shifting role of Jews in commerce and as producers of fashion. See Merwin, "Unbuttoned: Clothing as a Theme in American Jewish Comedy," in Leonard Greenspoon, *Fashioning Jews: Clothing, Culture and Commerce: Studies in Jewish Civilization* (West Lafayette, IN: Purdue University Press, 2013), 24:137–67.

150. E. H. McKinley, *Somebody's Brother: A History of the Salvation Army Men's Social Service Department* (Lewiston: Edwin Mellon Press, 1986), 97.

151. See James Stuart Olson, *Historical Dictionary of the Great Depression, 1929–1940* (Westport, CT: Greenwood, 2001), 97–98.

152. Robert T. Grimm Jr., "Working with Handicaps, Americans with Disabilities, Goodwill Industries and Employment, 1920s–1970s" (PhD diss., Indiana University, 2002), 13–15.

153. See, for example, Freeman Cleaves, "The Junk Man: Collecting Scrap for Industry Has Become a $2 Billion Business," *Wall Street Journal*, 17 March 1944, 1.

154. Grimm, "Working with Handicaps," 54–58; Strasser, *Waste and Want: A Social History of Trash* (New York: Henry Holt, 1999), 226, 240.

155. See "Old-Clothes Market," *New York Times*, 6 May 1945, SM17.
156. "Old-Clothes Market," *New York Times*, SM17.

Chapter Three

1. "The Garage Sale: Finally, a Reason to Clean Out the Attic," *Life* 73, no. 7 (1972): 82–84.
2. Ibid., 83.
3. Galbraith wrote much of the text the summer of 1956. *The Affluent Society* was first published in 1958, with subsequent revised editions appearing in 1969, 1976, and 1984. See John Kenneth Galbraith, *The Affluent Society* (Boston: Houghton Mifflin, 1984).
4. These are some of the names given in 1950s and early 1960s advertisements. Tag sales, household liquidation sales, and estate sales differ somewhat because they offer many or most of a household's contents. Garage sale was the preferred appellation by the end of the 1960s, according to Ellen M. Prohaska, "The Garage Sale: A Quasi-Economic Institution" (MA thesis, Northern Illinois University, 1974), 1, and Jean Young and Jim Young, *The Garage Sale Manual: Alternate Economics for the People* (New York: Praeger, 1973), 1. For examples of early advertisements, see Classifieds, "Person-to Person," *Orlando Sentinel*, 23 June 1956, and Classifieds, *Orlando Sentinel*, 7 April 1958.
5. Marian Markham, "Garage Sale," *Chicago Tribune*, 14 May 1967, E10.
6. Susan Matt's book about envy in consumer culture from 1890 to 1930 typifies the argument for class competition and accords with a Veblenian discourse of trickle-down consumer culture with the lower classes following the lead of the wealthy. Examining secondhand economies is instructive of the gaps in such arguments—or even just finessing the argument to include less tangible values, such as originality and obscurity. See Matt, *Keeping Up with the Joneses: Envy in American Consumer Society, 1890–1930* (Philadelphia: University of Pennsylvania Press, 2003).
7. John F. Sherry quotes "suburban subversiveness" from Roger Abrahams's undated working paper, "On Garage Sales and Other Madnesses," Department of Folklore and Folklife, University of Pennsylvania. Quoted in John F. Sherry Jr., "A Sociocultural Analysis of a Midwestern American Flea Market," *Journal of Consumer Research* 17, no. 1 (June 1990): 28.
8. As early as 1843, Engels was already reporting the end of bargaining as a component of trade, declaring, "[p]olitical economy came into being as a natural result of the expansion of trade, and with its appearance elementary, unscientific *Schacher* [haggling] was replaced by a developed system of licensed fraud, an even more offensive, 'scientific' one." See Friedrich Engels, "Outlines of a Critique of Political Economy," in *Karl Marx, Frederick Engels: Marx and Engels: 1843–1844*, ed. Jack Cohen et al. (New York: International Publishers, 1843–1844), 418; see also Richard Sennett, *The Fall of the Public Man* (Cambridge: Cambridge University Press, 1974).
9. *Father Knows Best* ran as a radio show from 1949 to 1954, and was a hit television sitcom lasting from 1954 to 1960. Like other sitcoms of the era, the show depicted the ideal nuclear family, with a responsible working father and an organized, reliable

housewife mother. For a critique on suburban sitcoms and the role of the 1950s homemaker, see Mary Beth Haralovich, "Sitcoms and Suburbs: Positioning the 1950s Homemaker," in *Critiquing the Sitcom: A Reader*, ed. Joanne Morreale (Syracuse, NY: Syracuse University Press, 2003), 69–86. For more on this and other television programs of the time, see James W. Roman, *From Daytime to Primetime: The History of American Television Programs* (Westport, CT: Greenwood Press, 2005).

10. For more on existing scholarship on garage sales, see Stephen M. Soiffer and Gretchen Herrmann, "For Fun and Profit: An Analysis of the American Garage Sale," *Urban Life* 12 (1984): 397–421. See also Ruth H. Landman, "Washington's Yard Sales: Women's Work, but Not for the Money," *City and Society* 1, no. 2 (1987): 148–61; Gretchen M. Herrmann, "Gift or Commodity: What Changes Hands in the U.S. Garage Sale?," *American Ethnologist* 24, no. 4 (1997): 910–30; Gretchen M. Herrmann, "Women's Exchange in the U.S. Garage Sale: Giving Gifts and Creating Community," *Gender and Society* 10, no. 6 (December 1996): 703–28; Gretchen M. Herrmann, "Negotiating Culture: Conflict and Consensus in U.S. Garage-Sale Bargaining," *Ethnology* 42, no. 3 (Summer 2003): 237–52; Gretchen M. Herrmann, "Haggling Spoken Here: Gender, Class, and Style in US Garage-Sale Bargaining," *Journal of Popular Culture* 38, no. 1 (2004): 55–81; and Nurit Bird-David and Asaf Darr, "Commodity, Gift, and Mass-Gift: On Gift-Commodity Hybrids in Advanced Mass Consumption Cultures," *Economy and Society* 38, no. 2 (2009): 304–25. John Lastovicka and Karen V. Fernandez also discuss the social and individual meaning of resale in contemporary culture in "Three Paths to Disposition: The Movement of Meaningful Possessions to Strangers," *Journal of Consumer Research* 31, no. 4 (2005): 813–23. See also Margaret Crawford, "The Garage Sale as Informal Economy and Transformative Urbanism," in *The Informal American City: Beyond Taco Trucks and Day Labor*, ed. Vinit Mukhija and Anastasia Loukaitou-Sideris (Cambridge, MA: MIT Press, 2014), 21–38.

11. The garage in U.S. history dates back to the very beginning of the twentieth century, when rare residences of city-dwellers included "automobile houses," which ranged in type from the ramshackle to the elaborate. However, these structures were unusual and often impermanent and disconnected from the home. See Leslie G. Goat, "Housing the Horseless Carriage: America's Early Private Garages," *Perspectives in Vernacular Architecture* 3 (1989): 62. Developers began to include garages that were integral to homes, especially in ranch-style houses, during the early 1950s. See Herbert Gottfried and Jan Jennings, *American Vernacular Buildings and Interiors, 1870–1960* (New York: W. W. Norton, 2009), 207–8.

12. For more on the development of car culture in the United States, see David L. Lewis and Laurence Goldstein, eds., *The Automobile and American Culture* (Ann Arbor: University of Michigan Press, 1980), and John Heitmann, *The Automobile and American Life* (Jefferson, NC: McFarland, 2009).

13. For more on Sloan's innovative strategies, see David Farber, *Sloan Rules: Alfred P. Sloan and the Triumph of General Motors* (Chicago: University of Chicago Press, 2002).

14. See James J. Fink, *The Automobile Age* (Cambridge, MA: MIT Press, 1988), 130–31. For more on reconversion, see Paul A. C. Koistinen, *Arsenal of World War II: The Politi-

cal Economy of American Warfare, 1940–1945 (Lawrence: University Press of Kansas, 1994), 445–498. For changing tactics of publicity campaigns during this period, see Cynthia Lee Henthorn, *From Submarines to Suburbs: Selling a Better America, 1939–1959* (Athens: Ohio University Press, 2006).

15. Robert Genat, *American Car Dealership* (St. Paul: Motorbooks International, 2004), 10–13.

16. Clifford Edward Clark Jr., *The American Family Home, 1900–1960* (Chapel Hill: University of North Carolina Press, 1986), 213; Kenneth T. Jackson, *Crabgrass Frontier: The Suburbanization of the United States* (New York: Oxford University Press, 1985), 249; Elaine Tyler May, *Homeward Bound: American Families in the Cold War Era* (New York: Basic Books, 1988), 151.

17. Jackson, *Crabgrass Frontier*, 195–209.

18. Ibid., 210–18.

19. Landon Y. Jones, *Great Expectations: America and the Baby Boom Generation* (New York: Coward, McCann and Geoghegan, 1980), 38; quoted in Leerom Medovoi, *Rebels: Youth and the Cold War Origins of Identity* (Durham, NC: Duke University Press, 2005), 17.

20. Quoted in Gordon H. Stedman, "The Rise of Shopping Centers," *Journal of Retailing*, Spring 1955, 11–26; 11.

21. In the postwar years leading up to 1950, the annual growth rate of consumer credit was more than 50 percent. In the decades that followed, this rate varied, leveling off in years of recession and expanding in years of economic stability and growth. See George Kozmetsky and Piyu Yue, *The Economic Transformation of the United States, 1950–2000: Focusing on the Technological Revolution, the Service Sector Expansion, and the Cultural, Ideological, and Demographic Changes* (West Lafayette, IN: Purdue University Press, 2005), 406. For an early history of consumer credit, see Lendol Calder, *Financing the American Dream: A Cultural History of Consumer Credit* (Princeton, NJ: Princeton University Press, 1999). For more on the postwar proliferation of credit cards and consumer credit spending, see also Lewis Mandell, *The Credit Card Industry: A History* (Boston: Twayne, 1990).

22. Amber Watts, "Remaking Consumer Culture," in *The Great American Makeover: Television, History, Nation*, ed. Dana Alice Heller (New York: Palgrave MacMillan, 2006), 151. See also Ann Satterthwaite, *Going Shopping: Consumer Choices and Community Consequences* (New Haven, CT: Yale University Press, 2001), 119.

23. "One of Six New Garage Designs with Extra Storage Space," *Popular Mechanics*, October 1952, 240.

24. William H. Whyte Jr., "Budgetism: Opiate of the Middle Class," *Fortune*, May 1956, 133–37, 164–67, 133, quoted in Elaine Tyler May, "The Commodity Gap: Consumerism and the Modern Home," in *Consumer Society in American History: A Reader* (Ithaca, NY: Cornell University Press, 1999), 298.

25. "The Garage Sale: Finally, a Reason to Clean Out the Attic," 83.

26. Helen Dallas, *How to Win on the Home Front*, Public Affairs Pamphlet No. 72 (New York: Public Affairs Committee, 1942), 1–3, quoted in Elaine Tyler May, *Homeward Bound*, 63–64.

27. Horace Warren Kimbell, *This Is Goodwill Industries: An Address at New York* (New York: The Newcomen Society in North America, 1962), 7–8.

28. Reynolds wrote and recorded "Little Boxes" as a protest song, but the song was made popular by Pete Seeger in 1963, reaching no. 70 on the Billboard Hot 100. See Oliver Gilham, *The Limitless City: A Primer on the Urban Sprawl Debate* (Washington, DC: Island Press, 2002), 47.

29. See Clifford Edward Clark, *The American Family Home, 1880–1960* (Chapel Hill: University of North Carolina Press, 1986), 217–220

30. See Lizabeth Cohen, "A Middle-Class Utopia? The Suburban Home in the 1950s," in *Making Choices: A New Perspective on the History of Domestic Life*, ed. Janice Tauer Wass (Springfield, IL: Illinois State Museum, 1995), 59–67.

31. Quoted in Clark, *The American Family Home*, 217.

32. Cohen, "A Middle-Class Utopia?, 62.

33. Much scholarship on the 1950s emphasizes the proliferation of new goods during that decade, including those based on plastics innovated for wartime technologies. See Jeffrey L. Meikle, *American Plastic: A Cultural History* (New Brunswick, NJ: Rutgers University Press, 1995), and William H. Young with Nancy K. Young, *The 1950s* (Westport, CT: Greenwood Press, 2004), 45. For more on planned obsolescence, see Giles Slade, *Made to Break: Technology and Obsolescence in America* (Boston: First Harvard University Press, 2007).

34. See *The Economic Report of the President, Transmitted to the Congress January 20, 1955* (Washington, DC: Government Printing Office), 23. Many influential economists, including Marx and Galbraith, emphasized the role of the military in business cycles. Marx's view, notably, includes the caveat that increased worker buying power inevitably leads to a later depression—which Marxians note as remarkably predictive of the 1920s and 1930s. Marx's views are summarized in Galbraith, *The Affluent Society*, 58.

35. Some early exceptions include Lakewood, California, whose profitable regional shopping mall was erected within walking distance of the subdivision housing. Looking ahead to area development, builders also included 10,580 parking spaces. See Dolores Hayden, "Building the American Way: Public Subsidy, Private Space," unpublished paper delivered at the International Planning History Society conference, Barcelona, Spain, 17 July 2004, reprinted in *The Suburb Reader*, ed. Becky M. Nicolaides and Andrew Weise (New York: Routledge, 2006), 278–79. See also Joel Garreau, *Edge City: Life on the New Frontier* (New York: Doubleday, 1991).

36. Lizabeth Cohen, "From Town Center to Shopping Center: The Reconfiguration of Community Marketplaces in Postwar America," *American Historical Review* 101, no. 4 (1996): 1075–77. For details on how issues of parking were sometimes dealt with in cities transformed by suburbanization, see Richard W. Longstreth, *City Center to Regional Mall: Architecture, the Automobile, and Retailing in Los Angeles, 1920–1950* (Boston: Massachusetts Institute of Technology, 1998), 3–18. Parking was often considered a prime reason for loss of city business to such facilities. See "Urgent Parking Need," *New York Times*, 17 July 1958, 26.

37. Cohen, "From Town Center to Shopping Center," 1060.

38. Growth began in earnest during the mid-1950s. See "Six Shopping Centers Will Open by 1957," *Chicago Daily Tribune*, 3 Mar 1956 B5, and Cohen, "From Town Center to Shopping Center," 1052. By the 1960s, many centers were planned with upward of one hundred retail stores. See "Shopping Marts Get Bigger in Suburbs," *New York Times*, 30 September 1956, R1, and "Vast Shopping Center with 100 Retail Units Planned by Store in the Suburbs of Detroit," *New York Times*, 4 June 1950, R1. See also Richard Longstreth, *The American Department Store Transformed, 1920–1960* (New Haven, CT: Yale University Press, 2010), 169–72, and Satterthwaite, *Going Shopping*. By the end of the twentieth century, shopping malls were joined by corporate headquarters and office and industrial parks to comprise what urbanist Joel Garreau calls "edge cities." See Garreau, *Edge City*.

39. See Cohen, "From Town Center to Shopping Center," and Longstreth, *The American Department Store Transformed*, 170. Some attempts at community integration were more successful than others. Following European models, Viennese architect Victor Gruen created imaginative shopping centers with community and cultural activities central to his plans. Gruen's ideals survive to some extent in especially well-designed centers. See also, Lizabeth Cohen, *A Consumers' Republic: The Politics of Mass Consumption* (New York: Knopf, 2003). See Satterthwaite, *Going Shopping*, 109–11.

40. Satterthwaite, *Going Shopping*, 100.

41. Hayden, "Building the American Way," 278–79.

42. This chapter was revised in some later editions, but maintains its major argument. See, for example, "The Myth of Consumer Sovereignty," in *The Essential Galbraith*, sel. and ed. Andrea D. Williams and John Kenneth Galbraith (Boston: Houghton Mifflin, 2001), 31–39.

43. Thomas Frank makes this point to illustrate that the seeds of 1960s rebellion were sown in impatience with banal cultural habits during the 1950s. See Frank, *The Conquest of Cool: Business Culture, Counterculture, and the Rise of Hip Capitalism* (Chicago: University of Chicago Press, 1997), 11.

44. Herbert Marcuse critiqued communism as well as capitalism, especially highlighting the heavy-handed bureaucracies characterizing Marxist nations. See Marcuse, *One-Dimensional Man: Studies in the Ideology of Advanced Industrial Society* (New York: Routledge Classics, 2001; first published in 1964). William H. Whyte's *The Organization Man* was a 1956 best-seller, and argued that as more average Americans were subject to corporate employment, they began to subscribe to a collectivist ethic that resulted in approving organizational decisions and not advancing original ideas. See Whyte, *The Organization Man* (New York: Simon and Schuster, 1956).

45. For an early example of viewing mass culture as both oppressive and liberating, see John Fiske's *Reading the Popular* (Boston: Unwin Hyman, 1989).

46. Markham, "Garage Sale," E10.

47. Prohaska, "The Garage Sale," 30; May, *Homeward Bound*, 75–76.

48. Agnes E. Meyer, "Women Aren't Men," *Atlantic Monthly* 186 (August 1950): 32.

49. L. Clinton Oaks, *Managing Suburban Branches of Department Stores* (Stanford, CA: Graduate School of Business, Stanford University 1957), 73; Cohen, "From Town Center to Shopping Center," 1075–77.

50. See Alice Kessler-Harris, *Out to Work: A History of Wage-Earning Women in the United States* (New York: Oxford Publishing Press, 1982), 203; Susan Hartmann, "Women's Employment and the Domestic Ideal in the War Years," in *Not June Cleaver: Women and Gender in Postwar America, 1945–1960*, ed. Joanne Meyerowitz (Philadelphia: Temple University Press, 1994), 86; Brian Greenberg, Linda S. Watts, and Richard A. Greenwald, *Social History of the United States: The 1900s* (Santa Barbara, CA: ABC-CLIO, 2009), 87.

51. The poll of employed wives is quoted in Peter Filene, *Him/Her/Self: Sex Roles in Modern America*, 2nd ed. (Baltimore, MD: Johns Hopkins University Press, 1986), 161–162.

52. Kathy Bates, *Tupperware!*, directed by Laurie Kahn-Leavitt (Crossroad Films, 2004). See also Alison Clarke, *Tupperware: The Promise of Plastic in 1950s America* (Washington, DC: Smithsonian Institution Press, 1999). For a critical exploration of the party-plan system in general, see L. Susan Williams and Michelle Bemiller, *Women at Work: Tupperware, Passion Parties, and Beyond* (Boulder, CO: Lynne Rienner, 2011).

53. Brownie Wise appeared on the cover of *Business Week* on 17 April 1954. Information on Tupperware party hostesses from Bates, *Tupperware!*, and Clarke, *Tupperware: The Promise of Plastic in 1950s America*, 84. Hostess parties were not only advantageous for wives and mothers but also for the companies hiring them. After more than sixty years of employing door-to-door saleswomen, Avon's most successful decade for growth was clearly the 1950s, when sales multiplied fivefold by relying solely on direct sales. In 1953, Avon Products, using only direct sales, garnered more than three times the profits than their major retail outlet competition, Helena Rubenstein. See Laura Klepacki, *Avon: Building the World's Premier Company for Women* (Hoboken, NJ: John Wiley, 2005), 24.

54. Clarke, *Tupperware: The Promise of Plastic in 1950s America*, 100.

55. *Tupperware: A Household Word in Homes Everywhere!*, product catalogue (Orlando, FL: Tupperware, Home Parties, 1957), 24; Clarke, *Tupperware: The Promise of Plastic in 1950s America*, 110–111.

56. William H. Whyte, "How the New Suburbia Socializes," in *The Essential William H. Whyte* (New York: Fordham University Press, 2000), 38.

57. Mary Kay Cosmetics was a latecomer to the direct-sales business, starting out in 1963. However, that a pink Cadillac is a prized award for top sellers exemplifies the way that these companies enabled housewives to stake claim to otherwise masculine territory. See Bemiller, *Women at Work*.

58. Prohaska, "The Garage Sale," 30.

59. Ibid., 22, 33; "Hearing Slated on Garage Sale Plan," *Los Angeles Times*, 16 February 1971, SF6; "Wrong Zoning: City Moves against Illegal Garage Sales," *Los Angeles Times*, 23 November 1970, SF6; "Garage Sale Laws Will Be Studied," *Los Angeles Times*, 9 March 1971, SF7. In 1973, *Kiplinger's Personal Finance* reported that Dallas, TX, and Joliet, IL, both limited sales to two a year, per person. See *Kiplinger's Personal Finance*, July 1972, 36, and Crawford, "The Garage Sale as Informal Economy and Transformative Urbanism," 22.

60. Cohen, "From Town Center to Shopping Center," 1064.

61. See Herrmann, "Gift or Commodity"; Herrmann, "Women's Exchange in the U.S. Garage Sale"; and Landman, "Washington's Yard Sales."

62. Prohaska, *The Garage Sale*, 37.

63. See William Whyte, *The Organization Man*, 287, 300, 380; Herbert Gans, *The Levittowners: Ways of Life and Politics in a New Suburban Community* (New York: Pantheon Books, 1967); Robert D. Putnam, *Bowling Alone: The Collapse and Revival of American Community* (New York: Simon and Schuster Paperbacks, 2000), 209; May, *Homeward Bound*, 20.

64. Some of these groups peaked early, like the General Federation of Women's Clubs, whose decline began in the mid-1950s, while many others peaked in the early or mid-1960s. See Putnam, *Bowling Alone*, 55.

65. For more on American bazaars and fairs of various sorts, see Beverly Gordon, *Bazaars and Fair Ladies: The History of the American Fundraising Fair* (Knoxville: University of Tennessee Press, 1998).

66. "Two Ford Freedom," Ford Television Commercial (Prelinger Archives, 1956), accessed March 2012, http://archive.org/details/TwoFordFreed.

67. Putnam, *Bowling Alone*, 212.

68. Jackson, *Crabgrass Frontier*, 272.

69. May, *Homeward Bound*, esp. pp. 15–18.

70. Many books exist examining the effects of Senator Joseph McCarthy and McCarthyism in American life. See, for example, Brian Fitzgerald, *McCarthyism: The Red Scare* (Minneapolis: Compass Point Books, 2007). For more on the reporting of the political paranoia of the era, see Thomas Doherty, *Cold War, Cool Medium: Television, McCarthyism, and American Culture* (New York: Columbia University Press, 2003). David K. Johnson writes about the governmental persecution of homosexuals during the Cold War in *The Lavender Scare: The Cold War Persecution of Gays and Lesbians in the Federal Government* (Chicago: University of Chicago Press, 2004).

71. Jackson, *Crabgrass Frontier*, 272.

72. Gordon, *Bazaars and Fair Ladies*, 186.

73. If enough used goods donations were received, societies would feature white elephant sales with international themes (such as the Orient). See Gordon, *Bazaars and Fair Ladies*, 183–84.

74. Robert J. Grimm Jr., "Working with Handicaps, Americans with Disabilities, Goodwill Industries and Employment, 1920s–1970s" (PhD diss. Indiana University, 2002), 54–58.

75. Numerous postwar guides and resources for organizing bazaars were published. See Ruth H. Brent, "The Big Club Bazaar," *Good Housekeeping*, September 1956, 142; Janet Suzanne Benton, "A Modern Story of Loaves and Fishes," *American Home*, September 1954, 12, 14–15; Harriet Hawes and Eleanor Edelman, *McCall's Complete Book of Bazaars* (New York: Simon and Schuster, 1955); and Gordon, *Bazaars and Fair Ladies*, 186.

76. Gordon, *Bazaars and Fair Ladies*, 186.

77. Ibid., 192–95.

78. See *The Lyre of Alpha Chi Omega* 61, no. 4 (1958): 55; ibid., 67, no. 2 (1963), 1; and Gordon, *Bazaars and Fair Ladies*, 194–98.

79. See Lisa McGirr, *Suburban Warriors: The Origins of the New American Right* (Princeton, NJ: Princeton University Press, 2002), and Matthew D. Lassiter, *The Silent Majority: Suburban Politics in the Sunbelt South* (Princeton, NJ: Princeton University Press, 2006).

80. "GOP Garage Sale," *Los Angeles Times*, 22 October 1970, W59.

81. "Datebook: Garage Sale Set," *Los Angeles Times*, 24 August 1967, W59.

82. Anecdotal exceptions involving entrepreneurial preteens exist but were reported as anomalous at the time. See Prohaska, "The Garage Sale," 26, 27.

83. "Students Backing McCarthy Bake, Sweep, Clean for Gene," *Chicago Tribune*, 3 August 1968, 7.

84. "They Fight against Pollution," *Chicago Tribune*, 13 December 1970, G10.

85. T. J. Jackson Lears writes about the antimodernist implications of the Arts and Crafts movement in the United States at the turn of the twentieth century. See Lears, *No Place of Grace: Antimodernism and the Transformation of American Culture, 1880–1920* (Chicago: University of Chicago Press, 1981), and Steven Gelber, *Hobbies: Leisure and the Culture of Work in America* (New York: Columbia University Press, 1999), 5.

86. Mark A. Swiencicki differentiates between "buying" and "consuming," and denotes many other ways that men participated in consumer culture during the decades around the turn of the last century. See Swiencicki, "Consuming Brotherhood: Men's Culture, Style and Recreation as Consumer Culture, 1880–1930," *Journal of Social History* 31, no. 4 (Summer 1998): 773–808.

87. *Kiplinger's Personal Finance: Changing Times*, July 1973, 36; Gelber, *Hobbies*, 268–294.

88. See Cohen, "A Middle-Class Utopia?," 63–65.

89. Frank L. Mott, *A History of American Magazines*, vol. 5, *1905–1930* (Boston: Harvard University Press, 2002), 45–46.

90. Gelber, *Hobbies*, 66.

91. Ibid., 66; Thomas Hine, *Populuxe* (New York: Alfred A. Knopf, 1986), 11.

92. *Better Homes and Gardens* 43, no. 8 (1965): 101.

93. Many scholars comment on the sometimes contradictory social ideals of postwar families. See, for example, May, *Homeward Bound*. Stephanie Koontz looks at some of the disparities between expectations and realities in Koontz, *The Way We Never Were: American Families and the Nostalgia Trap* (New York: Basic Books, 1992). For an examination of the rise in family therapy and expert involvement in personal relationships, see Deborah Weinstein, *The Pathological Family: Postwar America and the Rise of Family Therapy* (Ithaca, NY: Cornell University Press, 2013).

94. *Better Homes and Gardens* 43, no. 8 (1965): 101.

95. See Cohen, "A Middle-Class Utopia?," 60.

96. Elizabeth Dunn, "The Chippendale Chest," *Ladies' Home Journal*, October 1956, 128–33, 135. Italics in the original.

97. Horace Coon, *Hobbies for Pleasure and Profit: New Worlds of Fun and Relaxation for Everyone* (New York: New American Library, 1955), 9–11, 16; see also Gelber, *Hobbies*.

98. David George Surnam, *Century of the Leisured Masses: Entertainment and the Transformation of Twentieth-Century America* (Oxford: Oxford University Press, 2015), 81.

99. Steven M. Gelber, "Do-It-Yourself: Constructing, Repairing and Maintaining Domestic Masculinity," *American Quarterly* 49, no. 1 (1997): 66–67. For more on the various social and economic influences on the rise of "masculine domesticity," see also Gelber, *Hobbies*.

100. "Personal Business," *Business Week*, 2 April 1955, 131.

101. Gelber, *Hobbies*, 278.

102. See Philip Wylie, *A Generation of Vipers* (New York: Pocket Books, 1942). Criminologist Albert K. Cohen argued that men were too busy working to offer boys opportunities to identify with them, resulting in anticonformist behavior. See Cohen, *Delinquent Boys: The Culture of the Gang* (Glencoe, IL: The Free Press, 1955), 165–66. For more about delinquency and rebellion, its appeal to postwar youth, and representations of it in media, see Leerom Medovoi, *Rebel: Youth and the Cold War Origins of Identity* (Durham: Duke University Press, 2005), and Grace Elizabeth Hale, *A Nation of Outsiders: How the White Middle Class Fell in Love with Rebellion in Postwar America* (Oxford: Oxford University Press, 2011). See also Ninca Mackert, "'But Recall the Kind of Parents We Have to Deal With': Juvenile Delinquency, Interdependent Masculinity and the Government of Families in the Postwar U.S.," in *Inventing the Modern American Family: Family Values and Social Change in 20th-Century United States*, ed. Isabel Heinemann (Frankfurt-on-Main, Germany: Campus Verlag, GmbH, 2012), and May, *Homeward Bound*.

103. Philip Wylie, "Mom's to Blame," *LOOK* 14, no. 24 (1950): 115–16; Bruno Bettelheim, "Fathers Shouldn't Try to Be Mothers," *Parents Magazine* 31, no. 10 (1956): 40, 126.

104. Robert W. Berry, "Father and Son Build a Sports Car," *Popular Mechanics*, October 1956, 125–27.

105. "Three Father-Son Projects for the Weekend," *Popular Mechanics*, April 1965, 182–188.

106. *Leave It to Beaver*, Episode 37, first broadcast on 25 June 1958 by ABC. Directed by Norman Tokar and written by Joe Connelly and Bob Mosher.

107. *Better Homes and Gardens* 45, no. 8 (1967): 50; ibid., 51, no. 2 (1973): 1–6.

108. Ibid., 44, no. 7 (1966): 56.

109. As Kenneth T. Jackson writes, "American suburbs come in every type, shape, and size: rich and poor, industrial and residential, new and old." See Jackson, *Crabgrass Frontier*, 5.

110. Clarke, *Tupperware: The Promise of Plastic in 1950s America*, 3.

111. See Cohen, "A Middle-Class Utopia?," 63.

112. Gordon, *Bazaars and Fair Ladies*, 203.

113. John Maynard Keynes, "Economic Possibilities for Our Grandchildren," originally published in *Nation and Athenaeum*, 11 and 18 October 1930.

114. Ken Kesey, *Kesey's Garage Sale* (New York: Viking Press, 1973).

115. Rachel Wolf, "The Other Museum Shop," *New York Guides*, 18 August 2012, accessed 27 May 2015, http://nymag.com/guides/fallpreview/2012/martha-rosler-2012-8/.

116. Martha Rosler, "Traveling Garage Sale," in *Martha Rosler: Positions in the Life World*, ed. Catherine de Zegher (Cambridge, MA: MIT Press, 1999); Crawford, "The Garage Sale as Informal Economy and Transformative Urbanism," 27–28.

117. Michael Thompson pointed this out in his seminal 1979 book on secondhand value, *Rubbish Theory*. See Thompson, *Rubbish Theory* (London: Oxford University Press, 1979); Crawford, "The Garage Sale as Informal Economy and Transformative Urbanism," 30.

118. Raymond Carver first submitted the story to *Esquire* in 1977, but it never appeared in print until the following year in *Quarterly West*. See Carver, "Why Don't You Dance," in *What We Talk about When We Talk about Love* (New York: Vintage Books, 1989).

Chapter Four

1. "The Twenties Kick," *New Yorker*, 17 August 1957, 20.

2. Additional information about the raccoon coat trend comes from Nan Robertson, "Fad Creates Big Tycoons in Raccoons," *New York Times*, 15 August 1957, 15; "Undergraduate Elegance," *Gentry*, Fall 1956, 100; and "Raccoon Swoon in New Flurry," *Life*, 9 September 1957, 82–84.

3. Valerie Mendes and Amy de la Haye, *20th Century Fashion* (London: Thames and Hudson, 1999), 10.

4. This phenomenon has other names, usually denoting broader practices of appropriation. I prefer a term that references the appropriated condition—poverty. In addition to Wolfe's "radical chic," Dean McCannell calls wearing clothing that mimics poverty or the working class "staged authenticity." See Tom Wolfe, *Radical Chic and Mau-Mauing the Flak Catchers* (New York: Noonday Press, 1994; first published in 1970). See also McCannell, *The Tourist: A New Theory of the Leisure Class* (New York: Shocken, 1976), 100.

5. Grace Hale, *A Nation of Outsiders: How the White Middle Class Fell in Love with Rebellion in Postwar America* (Oxford: Oxford University Press, 2011), 5–10.

6. See Alice Echols, *Shaky Ground: The Sixties and Its Aftershocks* (New York: Columbia University Press, 2002), 9.

7. Thomas Frank, *The Conquest of Cool: Business Culture, Counterculture, and the Rise of Hip Capitalism* (Chicago: University of Chicago Press, 1997), 11.

8. Quoted in Earl Christmas, *House of Goodwill: A Story of Morgan Memorial* (Boston: Morgan Memorial Press, 1924), 55.

9. For a comprehensive history and analysis of the zoot suit, see Kathy Peiss, *Zoot Suit: The Enigmatic Career of an Extreme Style* (Philadelphia: University of Pennsylvania Press, 2011); details about its possible secondhand origins on pp. 31–32.

10. Scholars debate the extent to which the zoot suit has overtly political meaning. Peiss contends that the politics of the style has been overstated in Peiss, *Zoot Suit*. For views claiming political implications, see Robin D. G. Kelley, "The Riddle of the Zoot: Malcolm Little and Black Cultural Politics During World War II," in *Race Rebels: Cul-*

ture, Politics, and the Black Working Class (New York: Free Press, 1994), 161–182, and Stuart Cosgrove, "The Zoot-Suit and Style Warfare," *History Workshop Journal* 18 (1984): 77–91.

11. For more on the influence of collegians on casual dress, see Deirdre Clemente, *Dress Casual: How College Students Redefined American Style* (Chapel Hill: University of North Carolina Press, 2014).

12. Much appreciation to Diane Maglio for her assessment of Salzman's "duck pants." The duck hunting outfits were prominently featured in the 1940s L.L. Bean catalogues. See William David Barry, *L.L. Bean, Inc.: A Company Scrapbook* (Freeport, ME: L.L. Bean, 1987).

13. Stanley Salzman's background information comes from his obituary. See Joan Cook, "Stanley Salzman, Architect-Teacher at Pratt, Dies at 67," *New York Times*, 17 July 1991, accessed 16 September 2015, http://www.nytimes.com/1991/07/17/obituaries/stanley-salzman-architect-teacher-at-pratt-dies-at-67.html.

14. "The Twenties Kick," 20–21; Robertson, "Fad Creates Big Tycoons in Raccoons," 15; and "Raccoon Swoon in New Flurry," 83.

15. The fad is mentioned in the same breath as flappers, the Charleston, "Tin Lizzies," Hoover's "normalcy," and hip flasks. See, for example, Kathleen Morgan Drowne and Patrick Huber's introduction to their work, *The 1920's* (Westport, CT: Greenwood Press, 2004), xiv; Ellen Wartella, "The Commercialization of Youth: Channel One in Context," *The Phi Delta Kappan* 76, no. 6 (February 1995): 448–51.

16. George Olsen, "Doin' the Raccoon" (Victor 21701).

17. "What the Young Man Will Wear," *Daily Princetonian*, 21 January 1924, 2; cited in Clemente, *Dress Casual*, 21.

18. "Twenties Kick," 21.

19. *Time* publisher Henry Luce coined the "American Century" in 1941 to describe the global role of the United States during the twentieth century and to urge the end of American political isolationism. See Luce, "The American Century," *Life*, 17 February 1941.

20. Apparently Stanley Salzman was more of a silent partner in the venture. See "The Twenties Kick," 20–21.

21. "Raccoon Swoon in New Flurry," 83; "Twenties Kick," 21.

22. See "Raccoon Swoon in New Flurry," 83.

23. Ibid., 83.

24. "The Twenties Kick," 22.

25. Robertson, "Fad Creates Big Tycoons," 15.

26. "College Fashions: They Stem from Past Eras and Strange Sources," *Life*, 29 August 1949, 66–73.

27. Hale draws from the large body of theoretical and philosophical literature on the meaning of authenticity, beginning with Lionel Trilling, *Sincerity and Authenticity* (Cambridge, MA: Harvard University Press, 1972).

28. Quote is from the *New Yorker*'s review on the back of the book. See Vance Packard, *The Hidden Persuaders* (Brooklyn, NY: Ig, 2007; first published in 1957).

29. Pluckett quote from *Time*, 3 July 1950, 72, cited in Douglas T. Miller and Marion Nowak, *The Fifties: The Way We Really Were* (Garden City, NY: Doubleday, 1977), 120. See also Lizabeth Cohen's *A Consumers' Republic: The Politics of Mass Consumption* (New York: Knopf, 2003), 293.

30. Clair Brown, *American Standards of Living: 1918–1988* (Cambridge, MA: Basil Blackwell, 1994), 277. For a longer scope on the rise in casual and sportswear, see Deirdre Clemente, "Made in Miami: The Development of the Sportswear Industry in South Florida, 1900–1960," *Journal of Social History* 41, no. 1 (2007): 127–48, and Clemente, *Dress Casual*. See also Elizabeth Ewing, *History of Twentieth Century Fashion* (Totowa, NJ: Barnes and Noble), 1986.

31. Rebecca Arnold details the process of American designers gaining recognition in the 1930s and 1940s in Arnold, *The American Look: Fashion and the Image of Women in 1930s and 1940s New York* (London: I.B. Tauris, 2008).

32. See Clemente, *Dress Casual*.

33. Lawrence B. Glickman examines the silk boycott movement of the late 1930s, as American sentiment turned against the Japanese after news of bellicose actions toward China emerged. See Lawrence B. Glickman, "'Make Lisle the Style': The Politics of Fashion in the Japanese Silk Boycott, 1937–1940," *Journal of Social History* 38, no. 3 (2005): 573–608. The wartime yearning for nylons was such that a popular song included the chorus, "I'll be happy when the nylons bloom again, cotton is monotonous to men." Within days of Japan's surrender, DuPont announced that eager civilians would have, "Nylons by Christmas!" See Susannah Handley, *Nylon: The Story of a Fashion Revolution* (Baltimore, MD: Johns Hopkins University Press, 1999), 48.

34. Handley, *Nylon*, 8. For more on DuPont's approach to selling synthetic-based fashions, see Regina Lee Blaszczyk, "Styling Synthetics: DuPont's Marketing of Fabrics and Fashions in Postwar America," *Business History Review* 80, no. 3 (2006): 485–528.

35. For more on the emergence of the American Look and its affiliated American designers, see Arnold, *The American Look*.

36. Handley, *Nylon*, 112–15; William H. Young and Nancy K. Young, *The 1950s* (Westport, CT: Greenwood Press, 2004), 81. For more on the history of plastic and its production, uses, and marketing, see Jeffrey L. Meikle, *American Plastic: A Cultural History* (New Brunswick, NJ: Rutgers University Press, 1995). People had been investing a greater percentage of their income in clothing since 1935. The greatest increase in real clothing expenditure per capita in all recorded periods was between 1935 and 1950. The technological innovations and the rise in many incomes halted the increase in percentage of expenditures while continuing to increase the amount of clothing acquired. See Brown, *American Standards of Living*, 202.

37. Jacques Barzun, *God's Country and Mine: A Declaration of Love Spiced with a Few Harsh Words* (Boston: Little, Brown, 1954), 38.

38. Wolfe, *Radical Chic*, 41.

39. Gordon, *Bazaars and Fair Ladies*, 176–77; Strasser, *Waste and Want: A Social History of Trash* (New York: Henry Holt, 1999), 279–80.

40. For more on the Deseret Industries, see Leonard J. Arrington and Davis Bitton, *The Mormon Experience: A History of the Latter-day Saints* (New York: Alfred A. Knopf, 1979), 272–74.

41. Patrick Dunne, Robert Lusch, and James Carver, *Retailing*, 7th ed. (Mason, OH: Cengage Learning, 2008), 138–40.

42. See Marilyn Hoffman, "Flea Market: Big Business in U.S.," *Christian Science Monitor*, 10 September 1976, 2.

43. For more details about the fight against daylight savings time on the part of theater owners, see Kerry Segrave, *Drive-in Theaters: A History from Their Inception in 1933* (North Carolina: McFarland, 1992), 126–30; Paul Lukas, "The Last Picture Shows," *Money* 30, no. 8 (2001): 90–96.

44. For example, in the 1970s, three drive-in theaters in Florida began using their lots for flea-market space during the day: Delray Lost Drive-In Swap Shop (1970), Naples Drive-In Theatre Flea Market (1974), and Ocala Drive-In Swap Shop (1979). NFMA director Gail Barron confirmed the relationship between the rise in flea markets and the decline of drive-ins. According to Barron, many theater owners simply converted the same undeveloped property they had been using for viewing space into a flea market. As Barron pointed out, these were businesspeople, eager to change the use of their land to something profitable with minimal expense. Barron, interview with the author, October 2006. Most early California swap meets seemed to be integrated with drive-in theaters. See, for example, Jack Schermerhorn, "Drive-in Traders Buy, Sell, Swap Everything from Bullets to Bikes," *Los Angeles Times*, 30 May 1965, CS10; Bart, "The Price of Parakeet? A Rolling Pin," *New York Times*, 8 November 1965, 37.

45. Segrave, *Drive-in Theaters*, 196.

46. Bart, "Price of Parakeet?" 37.

47. See, for example, Robert A. Wright, "See What They Did to the Garage Sale," *New York Times*, 15 July 1971, 26; Marilyn Hoffman, "Flea Market: Big Business in U.S.," *Christian Science Monitor*, 10 September 1976, 2; John Leonard, "Handcraft Swapping at Drive-Ins: A Bit of California Dreaming," *New York Times*, 17 January 1976, 44; and Sebak, "A Flea Market Documentary."

48. See, for example, Judith Cass, "Benefit Sales Offer Widely Varied Items," *Chicago Daily Tribune*, 15 April 1947; "Aids in Two Charity Benefits of the Near Future," *Chicago Daily Tribune*, 5 May 1947, 25.

49. For a history of "vintage wines," see P. T. H. Unwin, *Wine and the Vine* (New York: Routledge, 1996), 13.

50. The *Oxford English Dictionary* online indicates a 1928 mention of a "vintage Buick" as the first such usage. s.v., "vintage," *OED Online*, accessed 18 May 2013, http://www.oed.com/view/Entry/223593?isAdvanced=false&result=1&rskey=zOg4Z2&#contentWrapper.

51. See Judith Cass, "Fashion and Fancy," *Chicago Daily Tribune*, 30 September 1945, E1; Peggy Preston, "Congressional Club Members Delve in Old Trunks for Frocks," *Washington Post*, 19 February 1948, B7.

52. "Batavia Group to Wear Town, Suburb Styles," *Chicago Daily Tribune*, 10 October 1954, W7.

53. Louise Hutchinson, "First Ladies Feted; View Fashion Show," *Chicago Daily Tribune*, 11 August 1955, C6.

54. Gloria Emerson, "Second-hand Shop Helps Women in Capital Whirl," *New York Times*, 6 October 1958, 41.

55. Alistair O'Neill, *London: After a Fashion* (London: Reaktion Books, 2007), 91–93. See also Simon Reynolds, *Retromania: Pop Culture's Addiction to Its Own Past* (New York: Faber and Faber, 2011), 184–90.

56. Raphael Samuel, *Theatres of Memory: Past and Present in Contemporary Culture* (London: Verso, 2012), 194.

57. For a closer look at the "peacock revolution," see Geoffrey Aquilana Ross, *Day of the Peacock: Style for Men, 1963–1973* (London: Harry N. Abrams, 2011), and Jo Paoletti, *Sex and Unisex: Fashion, Feminism, and the Sexual Revolution* (Bloomington: Indiana University Press, 2015), 58–91.

58. Reynolds, *Retromania*, 186.

59. Cally Blackman, "Clothing the Cosmic Counterculture," in *Summer of Love: Psychedelic Art, Social Crisis and Counterculture in the 1960s*, ed. Christoph Grunenberg and Jonathan Harris (Liverpool: Liverpool University Press, 2005), 215; Anneli Rufus and Kristan Lawson, *The Scavengers' Manifesto* (New York: Penguin, 2009), 127.

60. See Dick Hebdige, "The Meaning of Mod," in *Resistance through Rituals: Youth Subcultures in Post-War Britain*, ed. Stuart Hall and Tony Jefferson (London: Routledge, 1993); Simon Frith, *Sound Effects: Youth, Leisure, and the Politics of Rock 'n' Roll* (New York: Pantheon, 1981), 220; Christine Jacqueline Feldman built on subcultural studies like Hebdige's and traces the international influences of the youth subculture. See Feldman, *"We Are the Mods": A Transnational History of a Youth Subculture* (New York: Peter Lang, 2009).

61. Quoted in Shawn Levy, *Ready, Steady, Go! Swinging London and the Invention of Cool* (London: Fourth Estate, 2003), 7.

62. Joel Lobenthal, *Radical Rags: Fashions of the Sixties* (New York: Abbeville Press, 1990), 27–30; Reynolds, *Retromania*, 187–88.

63. Reynolds, *Retromania*, 187.

64. Lobenthal, *Radical Rags*, 31–32.

65. Blackman, "Clothing the Cosmic Counterculture," 213–14.

66. Paul Gorman, *The Look: Adventures in Pop and Rock Fashion* (London: Sanctuary, 2001), 47.

67. Quoted in ibid., 47.

68. Ibid., 46.

69. For more on the boutique culture of London in this era, see Richard Lester, *Boutique London: A History: King's Road to Carnaby Street* (Woodbridge: ACC Additions, 2010).

70. A push for more colorful, cheerful men's dress in Britain was not entirely new to the postwar years. In fact, urged by the 1930 work of psychologist J. S. Flugel, interwar

England boasted a political party devoted to the cause, the Men's Dress Reform Party. See Barbara Burman, "Better and Brighter Clothes: The Men's Dress Reform Party, 1929–1940," in *The Men's Fashion Reader*, ed. Peter McNeil and Vicki Karaminas (Oxford: Berg, 2009), 130–43. In 1930, the psychologist J. S. Flugel popularized "the great male renunciation," the theory that men's attire had recently shifted radically, from elaborate and colorful to somber and drab, in response to shifts in class and gender—including those stemming from the French Revolution. See J. S. Flugel, *The Psychology of Clothes* (New York: International Universities Press, 1971; first published in 1930).

71. See Paoletti, *Sex and Unisex*, 59–62. For a case study of the relationship between gay male dress and Carnaby boutiques, see Clare Lomas, "'Men Don't Wear Velvet You Know!' Fashionable Gay Masculinity and the Shopping Experience, London, 1950–Early 1970s," in McNeil and Karaminas, *Men's Fashion Reader*, 168–78. Fashion historians debate the importance of the so-called peacock revolution and its influence on male style. For a skeptical analysis, see Fred Davis, *Fashion, Culture, and Identity* (Chicago: University of Chicago, 1992), 34–35. See also, Frank, *The Conquest of Cool*, 183–95.

72. Rob Young, *Electric Eden: Unearthing Britain's Visionary Music* (New York: Faber and Faber, 2010), 295–96; Blackman, "Clothing the Cosmic Counterculture," 215.

73. See Rufus and Lawson, *The Scavengers' Manifesto*, 125–27. For more on Ormsby-Gore and her fashion influence, see also Young, *Electric Eden*, 296–307.

74. Christopher Gibbs, "Jane Ormsby-Gore: Fashion Original," *Vogue*, U.K., January 1966.

75. In December 1966, *Life* noted "English youth is deserting Carnaby Street in favor of Portobello Road." See "In London, Old Clothes are the Latest Noise," *Life*, 2 December 1966, 85.

76. Gibbs, "Jane Ormsby-Gore."

77. For more on Paul Poiret, see Alice Mackrell, *Paul Poiret* (New York: Holmes and Meier, 1990). For more on the influence of Islamic Orientalism in Poiret's and others' designs, see Valerie Steele, *The Berg Companion to Fashion* (New York: Berg, 2010), 196.

78. I Was Lord Kitchener's Valet (IWLKV) was reportedly not very busy until 1966, when rock stars began to frequent it. In 1966, Mick Jagger appeared on television wearing a "red Grenadier guardsman dummer's jacket" purchased at IWLKV, and the store was swarmed. See Rufus and Lawson, *The Scavengers' Manifesto*, 125–27, and interviews with Jane Ormsby-Gore, conducted for the Victoria & Albert Museum, accessed 20 June 2013, http://www.vam.ac.uk/content/articles/i/jane-ormsby-gore/.

79. See Richard Lester, *Boutique London*, 70.

80. Lobenthal, *Radical Rags*, 39. For more on Poiret's aesthetic influences, including the Ballet Russes, see Mary E. Davis, *Classic Chic: Music, Fashion, and Modernism* (Berkeley: University of California Press, 2006), 22–47; Mendes and de la Haye, *20th Century Fashion*, 32–33.

81. Angela McRobbie, "Second-hand Dresses and the Ragmarket," in *Zoot Suits and Second-hand Dresses: An Anthology of Fashion and Music*, ed. Angela McRobbie (Boston: Unwin Hyman, 1988), 23–49.

82. McRobbie refers to Pierre Bourdieu's idea of cultural capital in specifying that students and young "bohemians" can afford to look poor and ruffled while their black and working-class counterparts follow a version of the politics of respectability, dressing up to counter assumptions of lowliness. See McRobbie, "Second-hand Dresses and the Ragmarket," 27.

83. Ibid., 29.

84. Reynolds, *Retromania*, 185–87.

85. See Barry Miles, *The British Invasion: The Music, the Times, the Era* (New York: Sterling, 2009).

86. Lobenthal, *Radical Rags*, 109.

87. For more on Hunter and the Charlatans, see Carol Brightman, *Sweet Chaos: The Grateful Dead's American Adventure* (New York: Pocket Books, 1998), 92–94; Barry Miles, *Hippie* (New York: Sterling, 2005), 28–30.

88. Ellis Amburn, *Pearl: The Obsessions and Passions of Janis Joplin* (New York: Warner Books, 1992), 50; Alice Echols, *Sweet Scars of Paradise: The Life and Times of Janis Joplin* (New York: Macmillan, 2000), 171.

89. John Bevus Reid and Ronal Michael James, eds., *Uncovering Nevada's Past: A Primary Source History of the Silver State* (Reno: University of Nevada Press, 2004), 201.

90. Hunter turned down Janis Joplin for the band, saying she did not look the part, and later remarked, "I still feel really stupid for having been so oblivious"; from an interview with Alice Echols, quoted in Echols, *Scars of Sweet Paradise*, 84. The Red Dog Saloon was central to the development of San Francisco's music scene in numerous ways, giving several psychedelic bands their early gigs and attracting luminaries of the countercultural scene. See Reid and James, *Uncovering Nevada's Past*, 200–202. See also Miles, *Hippie*, 30.

91. The best account of the Merry Pranksters remains that by Tom Wolfe, *The Electric Kool-Aid Acid Test* (New York: Farrar, Straus and Giroux, 1967). For more on the genesis of psychedelic concerts and the "symbiosis between music and art," see Sally Tomlinson, "Psychedelic Rock Poster: History, Ideas, and Art," in *The Portable Sixties Reader*, ed. Ann Charters (New York: Penguin Books, 2003), 291–305.

92. See Dayton Lummis, *Clippings from the Vine: Selections from the Public Works of Dayton Lummis* (Bloomington, IN: iUniverse, 2009), 162–63; Brightman, *Sweet Chaos*, 92–94.

93. See Elizabeth Guffey, *Retro: The Culture of Revival* (London: Reaktion Books, 2006), 8.

94. As David Hamilton Murdoch asserts, "[n]o other nation has taken a time and place from its past and produced a construct of the imagination equal to America's creation of the West." See Murdoch, *The American West: The Invention of a Myth* (Reno: University of Nevada Press, 2001), vii. The Wild West was a trope of popular cultural forms since the 1860s. Christine Bold writes about popular Western fiction in *Selling the Wild West: Popular Western Fiction, 1860 to 1960* (Bloomington: Indiana University Press, 1987). Michael L. Johnson discusses the extension of the idea of the

West—including clothing—into contemporary American culture in *The Westers: The West in Contemporary American Culture* (Lawrence: University of Kansas Press, 1996).

95. Echols, *Scars of Sweet Paradise*, 70–73; Lobenthal, *Radical Rags*, 111.

96. Lobenthal, *Radical Rags*, 112–14.

97. Los Angeles designer Holly Harp, a Radcliffe dropout from upstate New York, disagreed: "I was a junk-store-aholic. I couldn't drive by one without a snake charmer coming up and grabbing me. I would just buy every hand-me-down that they had." See Lobenthal, *Radical Rags*, 125.

98. For accounts of the event, see Charles Perry, *The Haight-Ashbury: A History* (New York: Random House, 1984), 28–29; Chris Carlsson and Lisa Ruth Elliot, eds., *Ten Years That Shook the City: San Francisco, 1968–1978* (San Francisco: City Lights Books, 2011), 320–22; and Echols, *Scars of Sweet Paradise*, 117–18.

99. Thorstein Veblen, *The Theory of the Leisure Class: An Economic Study of Institutions* (New York: Macmillan, 1921; first published in 1899), 171.

100. Gravenites, quoted in Lobenthal, *Radical Rags*, 114; Echols, *Sweet Scars of Paradise*, 188–90.

101. Lobenthal, *Radical Rags*, 34–35.

Chapter Five

1. Harrington described this as "well-meaning ignorance." See Michael Harrington, *The Other America: Poverty in the United States* (New York: Touchstone Books, 1962), 4–5.

2. Harrington, *The Other America*, 5. See also Jacques Barzun, *God's Country and Mine: A Declaration of Love Spiced with a Few Harsh Words* (Boston: Little, Brown, 1954), 38.

3. For an in-depth analysis of the War on Poverty, see David Zarefsky, *President Johnson's War on Poverty: Rhetoric and History* (Tuscaloosa: University of Alabama Press, 2005).

4. Eric Lott describes a continuing vein of blackface minstrelsy in American culture that illuminates and effects not only racial but class and gender difference throughout the nineteenth and twentieth century. See Lott, *Love and Theft: Blackface Minstrelsy and the American Working Class* (New York: Oxford University Press, 1993).

5. See Tom Wolfe, *Radical Chic and Mau-Mauing the Flak Catchers* (New York: Noonday Press, 1994; first published in 1970), 80–81.

6. Tom Wolfe, *Radical Chic*, 32.

7. In Virginia Nicholson, *Among the Bohemians: Experiments in Living, 1900–1939* (London: Penguin, 2002), 3.

8. Nicholson, *Among the Bohemians*, 3.

9. Jerrold Seigal, *Bohemian Paris: Culture, Politics, and the Boundaries of Bourgeois Life, 1830–1930* (New York: Penguin, 1986), 11.

10. Champfleury, *Les Excentriques* (Paris: Michel Levy, 1855), 230; quoted in Wilson, *Bohemians: The Glamorous Outcasts* (London: I.C. Tauris, 2003), 163–64.

11. César Graña, "The Ideological Significance of Bohemian Life," in, *On Bohemia: The Code od the Self-Exiled*, eds., César Graña and Marigay Graña (New Brunswick, NJ: Transaction Publishers, 1990), 13–41; Janice Susan Gore, "Used Value: Thrift Shopping and Bohemia Incorporated" (PhD diss., University of Southern California, Department of Philosophy, 1999), 105.

12. Wolfe uses Regency youth as an example of *nostalgie de la boue*. See Wolfe, *Radical Chic*, 27.

13. Morris Dickstein points out how the documentary tradition of the 1930s supported a romanticization of poverty as a way of assuaging the guilt of the well-off during the Depression. See Dickstein, *Dancing in the Dark: A Cultural History of the Great Depression* (New York: W. W. Norton, 2009), 91–124; see also Erskine Caldwell and Margaret Bourke-White, *You Have Seen Their Faces* (Athens, GA: University of Georgia Press, 1995; first published in 1937).

14. James Agee and Walker Evans, *Let Us Now Praise Famous Men: Three Tenant Families* (Boston: Houghton Mifflin, 1960; first published in 1939).

15. Morris Dickstein writes about Agee's paradoxical urge for "authentic" material portrayal and his fear of uncensored fragments being misinterpreted. See Dickstein, *Dancing in the Dark*, 107–9.

16. Walker Evans, "James Agee in 1936," in *Remembering James Agee*, ed. David Madden and Jeffrey J. Folk (Athens: University of Georgia Press, 1997), 98.

17. James Agee and Walker Evans, *Let Us Now Praise Famous Men: Three Tenant Families* (Boston: Houghton Mifflin, 2001), 274.

18. Tanisha Ford, "SNCC Women, Denim, and the Politics of Dress," *Journal of Southern History* 79, no. 3 (2013): 625–58.

19. Historian Evelyn Brooks Higginbotham first articulated the phrase "politics of respectability" in Higginbotham, *Righteous Discontent: The Women's Movement in the Black Baptist Church, 1880–1920* (Cambridge, MA: Harvard University Press, 1993), 14–15. See also Marisa Chappell, Jenny Hutchinson, and Brian Ward, "'Dress Modestly, Neatly . . . As If You Were Going to Church': Respectability, Class and Gender in the Montgomery Bus Boycott and the Early Civil Rights Movement," in *Gender and the Civil Rights Movement*, ed. Peter J. Ling and Sharon Monteith (New Brunswick, NJ: Rutgers University Press, 2004), 69–100; Danielle L. McGuire, *At the Dark End of the Street: Black Women, Rape, and Resistance—A New History of the Civil Rights Movement from Rosa Parks to the Rise of Black Power* (New York: Vintage, 2011), 76–77.

20. Ossie Davis, "The Significance of Lorraine Hansberry (1965)," in *African American Literary Criticism, 1773 to 2000*, ed. Hazel Arnett Ervin (New York: Twayne, 1999), 118.

21. Amiri Baraka, "War/Philly Blues/Deeper Bop," from *John Coltrane: Where Does Art Come From*, reprinted in *Selected Plays and Prose of Amiri Baraka/Leroi Jones* (New York: William Morrow, 1979), 229.

22. Alix Kates Shulman, *Burning Questions* (New York: Alfred A. Knopf, 1978).

23. Ibid., 27–28.

24. Ibid., 29.

25. Ibid., 31–32.

26. Ibid., 26.

27. New York City was not alone; in fact, several other cities felt this drain more acutely. Many historians have explored the context and effects of white flight in the decades after World War II. See, for example, Kevin Michael Kruse, *White Flight: Atlanta and the Making of Modern Conservatism* (Princeton, NJ: Princeton University Press, 2005), and Thomas J. Sugrue, *The Origins of the Urban Crisis: Race and Inequality in Postwar Detroit* (Princeton, NJ: Princeton University Press, 1996).

28. Many intellectuals of the time criticized postwar mass culture; notably, members of what would become known as the Frankfurt School, such as Theodor Adorno and Max Horkheimer, argued that the immersive qualities of radio and television precluded "imagination or reflection on the part of the audience." See Adorno and Horkheimer, "The Culture Industry: Enlightenment as Mass Deception," in *Dialectics of Enlightenment* (New York: Verso, 1997), 126. For more on a postwar shift to privileging individualism, see Grace Elizabeth Hale, *A Nation of Outsiders: How the White Middle Class Fell in Love with Rebellion in Postwar America* (Oxford: Oxford University Press, 2011), 36–43.

29. See John Clellon Holmes, "This Is the Beat Generation," in *The Rolling Stone Book of the Beats: The Beat Generation and American Culture*, ed. Holly George-Warren (New York: Hyperion, 1999), 6–7; first published in *The New York Times Magazine*, 16 November 1952. See also William Lawler, *Beat Culture: Lifestyles, Icons, and Impact* (Santa Barbara, CA: ABC-CLIO, 2005), 13.

30. Shulman, *Burning Questions*, 75.

31. Normal Mailer raged that beatnik was "a word coined by an idiot columnist in San Francisco." Quoted in William Lawler, *Beat Culture: Lifestyles, Icons, and Impact* (Santa Barbara: ABC-CLIO, 2005), 45.

The term "beatnik" is usually attributed to Herbert Caen, from a 1958 *San Francisco Chronicle* article printed soon after the launch of the Russian satellite Sputnik. See Lawler, *Beat Culture*, 45; Reilly, *The 1960s*, 145; Tom Dalzell, *Flappers 2 Rappers: American Youth Slang* (Springfield, MA: Merriam-Webster, 1996), 91–94. Recent claims have been made that African American Beat writer Bob Kaufman, cofounder, with Ginsberg, of the journal *Beatitude*, coined the term. See Mona Lisa Saloy, "Black Beats and Black Issues," in *Beat Culture and the New America, 1950–1965*, ed. Lisa Phillips (New York: Whitney Museum of Art, 1996), 163. Alice Echols uses "Beat" and "beatnik" interchangeably, arguing that to many, they were the same. See Alice Echols, "Hope and Hype in Sixties Haight-Ashbury," In *Shaky Ground: The Sixties and Its Aftershocks* (New York: Columbia University Press, 2002), footnote, 224, and *Scars of Sweet Paradise: The Life and Times of Janis Joplin* (New York: Macmillan, 2000), 70.

32. For a discussion of the major Beats and their influences, see Steven Watson, *The Birth of the Beat Generation: Visionaries, Rebels, and Hipsters, 1944–1960* (New York: Pantheon Books, 1995). Several studies exist on the influence of Beat culture in the 1950s and after, including Lisa Phillips, ed., *Beat Culture and the New American, 1950–1965*. For a look at Beats in Greenwich Village, see Fred W. McDarrah and Gloria S. McDarrah, *Beat Generation: Glory Days in Greenwich Village* (New York: Schirmer Books, 1996). Lawrence

Lipton offers a contemporary fictional account of the Venice Beach Beat scene. See Lipton, *The Holy Barbarians* (New York: Julian Messner, 1959); see also John Arthur Maynard, *Venice West: The Beat Generation in Southern California* (New Brunswick, NJ: Rutgers University Press, 1991).

33. Allan Ginsberg, "A Definition of the Beat Generation," in *Deliberate Prose: Selected Essays, 1952–1995*, ed. Bill Morgan (New York: HarperCollins, 2000), 239; quoted in Susan B. A. Somers-Willett, *Cultural Politics of Slam Poetry: Race, Identity and the Performance of Popular Verse in America* (Ann Arbor: University of Michigan, 2009), 56.

34. Jack Kerouac, *Visions of Cody* (New York: McGraw-Hill, 1973), 33. Many scholars relate Kerouac's repeatedly asserted asceticism to various spiritual inclinations, including his persistent Catholicism and dabblings in Buddhism. See, for example, James Terrence Fisher, *The Catholic Counterculture in America, 1933–1962* (Chapel Hill: University of North Carolina Press, 1989), 220–35. Paul Giles describes Kerouac's mission thus: "[to] sanctify the world." See Giles, *American Catholic Arts and Fiction: Culture, Ideology, Aesthetics* (New York: Cambridge University Press, 1992), 411–412. See also Benedict Giamo, *Kerouac, the Word and the Way: Prose Artist as Spiritual Quester* (Carbondale: Southern Illinois University, 2000), 46–47.

35. Lew Welch, "In Answer to a Question from P.W.," in *Ring of Bone: Collected Poems* (San Francisco: City Lights Bookstore, 2013), 56. Originally written between 1950 and 1960.

36. See Jack Kerouac, "The Beginning of Bop," in *Escapade* 3 (April 1959): 9.

37. "The Beginning of Bop," in *The Portable Jack Kerouac*, ed. Ann Charters (New York: Viking Penguin, 1995), 557.

38. Werner Sollors, *Amiri Baraka/LeRoi Jones: The Quest for a "Populist Modernism"* (New York: Columbia University Press, 1978), 27.

39. See Welters, "The Beat Generation," in *Twentieth-Century American Fashion*, ed. Linda Welters and Patricia A. Cunningham (New York: Berg, 2005), 153–54.

40. Beginning in 1958, several national magazine articles forwarded an idea of beatniks that covered everything from dress style to sexual proclivities, which shaped much of the public's impressions of Beats. See, for example, "Squaresville U.S.A. vs. Beatsville," *Life*, 21 September 1959, 31–37, and P. O'Neil, "The Only Rebellion Around," *Life*, 30 November 1959, 114–31. An August 1959 article, "Real Gone Garb for Fall, Beat but Neat," illustrated the mainstream adaptations of the media's beatnik image. See *Life*, 3 August 1959, 48–49.

41. See Linda Welters, "The Beat Generation," 164.

42. Multiple sources describe Rexroth at this event as wearing secondhand items, indicating that the provenance of Beat outfits was a topic of discourse. See, for example, Michael McClure, "Painting Beats by Numbers," in George-Warren, *The Rolling Stone Book of the Beats*, 35, and Barry Miles, *Ginsberg: A Biography* (New York: Harper Perennial, 1990), 195. Another account has Rexroth "[b]ow-tied and wearing a secondhand cutaway coat." See Roy Kotynek and John Cohassey, *American Cultural Rebels: Avant-Garde and Bohemian Artists, Writers and Musicians from the 1850s through the 1960s* (Jefferson, NC: McFarland, 2008), 171.

43. Jack Kerouac, *Dharma Bums* (New York: Penguin Books, 1976; first published in 1958), 11; Welters, "The Beat Generation," 156.

44. Kerouac, *Dharma Bums*, 11.

45. Kotynek and Cohassey, *American Cultural Rebels*, 171.

46. Rexroth's suit was also described as a "spiffy gangster-pinstripe suit." See Dennis McNally, *Desolate Angel: Jack Kerouac, the Beat Generation, and America* (New York: Random House, 1979), 203.

47. See, for example, Ann Douglas, "The City Where the Beats Were Moved to Howl," in George-Warren, *The Rolling Stones Book of the Beats*, 3–4.

48. Christopher Lasch, *The New Radicalism in America, 1889–1963: The Intellectual as a Social Type* (New York: Knopf, 1965), xv; quoted in Robert Allen Skotheim, introduction to Hutchins Hapgood, *A Victorian in the Modern World* (Seattle: University of Washington Press, 1972), xix.

49. See Neal Cassady, "The First Third," excerpt in ed. Anne Waldman, *The Beat Book: Writings from the Beat Generation* (Boston: Shambhala, 2007), 68, 71.

50. In a 17 April 1948 journal entry, Kerouac complained that he cannot be himself or accomplish the things he wants while being friends with his current "circle" (including Ginsberg and Burroughs), and ended the entry, "Because I want to live, work, and have a family." See Douglas Brinkley, ed., *Windblown World: The Journals of Jack Kerouac, 1947–1954* (New York: Viking, 2004), 69.

51. For more on Kerouac's life, see Ellis Amburn, *Subterranean Kerouac: The Hidden Life of Jack Kerouac* (New York: St. Martin's Press, 1998).

52. Jack Kerouac, *Desolation Angels* (New York: Riverhead Books, 1995; first published in 1965), 373.

53. Ibid., 373–74.

54. See Jack Kerouac, *On the Road* (New York: Penguin Books, 1991; first published in 1957).

55. Descriptions of bedraggled clothing appear throughout the book. See ibid., 6, 188, 199, 218, 249, 294.

56. Ibid., 9.

57. Ibid., 97.

58. Ibid., 11.

59. Shulman, *Burning Questions*, 280.

60. Kerouac, *Dharma Bums*, 18.

61. Gary Snyder, "Anarchist Buddhism," accessed on 7 September 2015, http://the anarchistlibrary.org/library/gary-snyder-buddhist-anarchism.pdf. "Buddhist Anarchism" was originally published by City Lights Books in *Journal for the Protection of All Beings* 1 (1961).

62. Petr Kopecký, "Nature Writing in American Literature: Inspirations, Interrelations, and Impacts of California Authors on the Deep Ecology Movement," *The Trumpeter* 22, no. 2 (2006). Snyder is often referred to as the "poet laureate of deep ecology." See for example, Victor Ferkiss, *Nature, Technology, and Society: Cultural Roots of the Current Environmental Crisis* (New York: New York University Press, 1994), 197.

63. *Silent Spring* exposed the harmful effects of pesticides on the environment, particularly the avian population, and is often cited as the starting point of the contemporary environmental movement. See Rachel Carson, *Silent Spring* (New York: Houghton Mifflin, 2002; first published in the *New Yorker*, 1962).

64. Gary Snyder, "Bubbs Creek Haircut," *Mountains and Rivers without End* (Berkeley, CA: Counterpoint, 2008), 33–38.

65. Guido Bruno, "Midnight in a Pawn Shop," in *Sentimental Studies: Stories of Life and Love* (New York: published by author, 1920), 8–15.

66. Snyder, "Bubbs Creek Haircut," 35.

67. Ibid., 36. For a total analysis of this "mirror" poem and the role of the past in personal revelations, see Patrick D. Murphy, *Understanding Gary Snyder* (Columbia: University of South Carolina Press, 1992), 67–70.

68. Joyce Johnson, *Minor Characters: A Beat Memoir* (New York: Penguin Press, 1981), 187–88.

69. Ibid., 210.

70. In the United States, the New Left can be defined as "a loosely organized, mostly white student movement that advocated for democracy, civil rights and various types of university reforms and protested against the Vietnam War." See John McMillian and Paul Buhle, eds., *The New Left Revisited* (Philadelphia: Temple University Press, 2003), 5. Sociologist C. Wright Mills, who popularized the term, vied for ideology that correlated to values of the counterculture. New revolutionary change, Wright claimed, would not come from the proletariat but from internationally connected young intellectuals. C. Wright Mills, "Letter to the New Left," in *"Takin' It to the Streets": A Sixties Reader*, ed. Alexander Bloom and Wini Breines (New York: Oxford University Press, 1995), 79.

71. According to SDS, these quotes are taken from the original draft, as distributed by Alan Haber at the SDS Northeast Regional Conference, 23 April 2006, accessed 6 May 2013, http://www.sds-1960s.org/PortHuronStatement-draft.htm.

72. Students for a Democratic Society, *The Port Huron Statement* (Chicago: C. H. Kerr, 1990), 28, 31, 63.

73. Robert C. Fuller, *Stairways to Heaven: Drugs in American Religious History* (Boulder, CO: Westview Press, 2000), 80.

74. For an example of an early popular use, see "Take a Hippie to Lunch Today," *San Francisco Chronicle*, 20 January 1967, 37. Peter Coyote accused *Time* magazine of coining "hippie" to trivialize "those seeking alternatives to *Time*'s official reality. See Coyote, *Sleeping Where I Fall: A Chronicle* (Washington, DC: Counterpoint, 1998), 76. See also Mark Matthews, *Droppers: America's First Hippie Commune, Drop City* (Norman: University of Oklahoma Press, 2010), 77–78.

75. See Malcolm X and Alex Haley, *The Autobiography of Malcolm X* (New York: Ballantine Books, 1999), 97; quoted in Scott Saul, *Freedom Is, Freedom Ain't: Jazz and the Making of the Sixties* (Cambridge, MA: Harvard University Press, 2005), 86. For more examples of early uses of the word "hippie," see George Mandel, *Flee the Angry Strangers* (New York: Thunder's Mouth Press, 1952), 385, and Bradford Morrow, ed., *World*

Outside the Window: The Collected Essays of Kenneth Rexroth (New York: New Directions Books, 1987; first published, 1961), 191–96.

76. Todd Gitlin, among others, catalogues the degradations of Haight-Ashbury, quoting a group of leafleteers calling themselves the "Communication Company," who declared "Rape is as common as bullshit on Haight Street. Kids are starving on The Street." See Gitlin, *The Sixties: Years of Hope, Days of Rage* (New York: Bantam Books, 1993), 219.

77. Joan Didion's *Slouching towards Bethlehem* (New York: Dell, 1968) offers one of the most affecting accounts of the situation of young hippies in 1967. See also Tom Wolfe, *The Electric Kool Aid Acid Test* (New York: Bantam, 1969).

78. Wolfe, *Radical Chic*, 126–27.

79. Among others, Jo B. Paoletti, in her book on the brief flourishing of unisex fashions in the 1960s and 1970s, makes the point that the baby boomers were not alone in protests, sartorial and otherwise, of dominant culture. See Paoletti, *Sex and Unisex: Fashion, Feminism, and the Sexual Revolution* (Bloomington: Indiana University Press, 2015), 17.

80. Tom Dalzell, *Damn the Man! Slang of the Oppressed in America* (New York: Dover, 2010), 178. Peter Coyote details the Diggers conflict with "hip capitalists," including the Haight Independent Proprietors (H.I.P.). See Coyote, *Sleeping Where I Fall*, 74–77.

81. See Echols, "Hope and Hype in Sixties Haight-Ashbury," 46; Issitt, *Hippies: A Guide to an American Subculture* (Santa Barbara, CA: Greenwood Press, 2009), 10.

82. Issitt, *Hippies*, 7. For more on the Diggers, see Dominick Cavallo, "'It's Free Because It's Yours': The Diggers and the San Francisco Scene, 1964–1968," in *A Fiction of the Past: Sixties in American History* (New York: Palgrave, 1999), 97–144, and Bradford D. Martin, *The Theater in the Street: Politics and Public Performance in Sixties America* (Amherst: University of Massachusetts Press, 2004), 86–124.

83. Coyote, *Sleeping Where I Fall*, 35.

84. *The Trip without a Ticket*, pamphlet, originally published by the Diggers, ca. winter, 1966–67. Reprinted by the Communication Company SF, 2nd ed., 28 June 1967. Included in The Digger Papers, August 1968, University of Virginia Special Collections.

85. Ralph Gleason, the music critic for the *San Francisco Chronicle*, coined the phrase "hip Salvation Army." According to Alice Echols's account, Peter Coyote felt that the more mild account of the free items' provenance covered up the group's true radicalism; one Digger thought Gleason was trying to create a cleaner image for the Diggers. See Echols, *Scars of Sweet Paradise*, 98. Grogan's claims about stolen goods appear in his autobiography, *Ringolevio: A Life Played for Keeps* (New York: New York Review of Books, 1972), 249.

86. For more on radical street theater and the Yippies, see Susanne Elizabeth Shawyer, "Radical Street Theatre and the Yippie Legacy: A Performance History of the Youth International Party, 1967–1968" (PhD, diss., University of Texas at Austin, 2008). For a contemporary perspective on the success of the Yippies' humorous approach to

political action, see Shana Alexander, "The Loony Humor of the Yippies," *Time*, 25 October 1968, 26b.

87. In 1967, Hoffman turned Liberty House over to the black community. See Hoffman, "Liberty House/Poor People's Corporation," *Liberation*, April 1967, 20. See also David Farber, *Chicago '68* (Chicago: University of Chicago Press, 1988), 7–9. For a biography of Hoffman covering his political life before and after this period, see Marty Jezer, *Abbie Hoffman: American Rebel* (New Brunswick, NJ: Rutgers University Press, 1992). See also Hoffman's autobiography, *Soon to Be a Major Motion Picture* (New York: Perigee Books, 1980).

88. See Patricia Peterson, "The Flapper Frugs," *New York Times*, 18 September 1965, SM104; Joel Lobenthal, *Radical Rags: Fashions of the Sixties* (New York: Abbeville Press, 1990), 96–97.

89. Jezer, *Abbie Hoffman*, 117. For more on the conflicts and alliances between the counterculture and antiwar activists, see David Farber, "The Counterculture and the Antiwar Movement," in *Give Peace a Chance: Exploring the Vietnam Antiwar Movement*, ed. Melvin Small and William D. Hoover (Syracuse, NY: Syracuse University Press, 1992). At the end of that year, Hoffman, his new wife Anita, Jerry Rubin, Nancy Kurshan, and Parl Krassner would come up with the idea of "Yippies" as a protest scheme for the Democratic National Convention in Chicago. To satisfy press questions about what "Yippie" meant, Yippie became the Youth International Party, and spearheaded the 1968 Chicago protest that ended in riots and arrests. See Neil A. Hamilton, *Rebels and Renegades: A Chronology of Social and Political Dissent in the United States* (New York: Routledge, 2002), 262–63. For more on the events surrounding the Chicago protest, see Frank Kusch, *Battleground Chicago: The Police and the 1968 Democratic National Convention* (Chicago: University of Chicago Press, 2008).

90. See Matthew Israel, *Kill for Peace: American Artists against the Vietnam War* (Austin: University of Texas Press, 2013), 77–78.

91. Norman Mailer, *Armies of the Night: History as a Novel, the Novel as History* (New York: Penguin Books, 1968).

92. Jezer, *Abbie Hoffman*, 88.

93. Ibid., 89–90. For a synopsis of the problems with Hoffman's Free Store, see also Anneli Rufus and Kristan Lawson, *The Scavengers' Manifesto* (New York: Penguin, 2009), 123.

94. Jezer, *Abbie Hoffman*, 88, and Hoffman, *Soon to Be a Major Motion Picture*, 97.

95. "Fighting to Save the Earth from Man," *Time* 95, no. 5 (1970): 60.

96. *The Trip without a Ticket*.

97. See Bob Ostertag, *People's Movement, People's Press: The Journalism of Social Justice Movements* (Boston: Beacon Press, 2006), 120. John McMillan writes comprehensively about the content of and motivation for underground press reporting, as well as the papers' role in galvanizing various movements of the era. See *Smoking Typewriters: The Sixties Underground Press and the Rise of Alternative Media in America* (Oxford: Oxford University Press, 2011).

98. Abe Peck was both involved with the underground press and produced the first monograph about the phenomenon. Upon later reflection, Peck, even while emphasizing the underground press's self-indulgence and poor organization, claimed the papers' acceptance of dissent and argument succeeded in breaking through "class, race, and national boundaries." See Peck, *Uncovering the Sixties: The Life and Times of the Underground Press* (New York: Citadel Press, 1991), xv, xvi.

99. Susan Brenner, "Corruption," *The Great Speckled Bird*, 24 February 1969, 14.

100. Italics in the original. For the assessment of appropriation from "poor white music," see Mark Kramer, "Woodstock—3 Days of Peace?," *The Great Speckled Bird*, 28 July 1969, 7 and 17.

101. Kramer, "Woodstock—3 Days of Peace?," 17.

102. Bobi, "STP," *The Great Speckled Bird*, 10 August 1970, 14.

103. Ibid., 14.

104. Baron Wolman, "Letters," *Rags* 1 (June 1970): 1.

105. Mary Jean Haley, "What Gay Women Wear," *Rags* 10 (March 1971): 20.

106. Ibid., 20.

107. See Betty Luther Hillman, *Dressing for the Culture Wars: Style and the Politics of Self-Presentation in the 1960s and 1970s* (Lincoln: University of Nebraska Press, 2015); Hillman, "'The Clothes I Wear Help Me to Know My Own Power': The Politics of Gender Presentation in the Era of Women's Liberation," *Frontiers: A Journal of Women Studies* 34, no. 2 (2013): 155–85.

108. bell hooks, *Feminist Theory: From Margin to Center* (New York: Routledge, 2015), 60–61. hooks evinced a long-standing love of fashion and a personal reliance on secondhand venues in her memoir of undergraduate and graduate collegian life, hooks, *Wounds of Passion: A Writing Life*, (New York, Henry Holt and Company, 1997). For more on how fashion and feminism interact, see Astrid Henry, "Fashioning a Feminist Style, or How I Learned to Dress from Reading Feminist Theory," in *Fashion Talks: Undressing the Power of Style*, ed. Shira Tarrant and Marjorie Jolles (Albany: University of New York Press, 2012), 13–32.

109. In the 1970s, Kaja Silverman used retro to include both secondhand clothing and new reproductions. See Silverman, "Fragments of a Fashionable Discourse," in *Studies in Entertainment*, ed. Tania Modleski (Bloomington: Indiana University Press, 1986), 151.

110. "Truth and Soul," *Rags* 9 (February 1971): 8 (advertisement).

111. Hoffman acknowledges that Izak Haber did much of the research for the book. Haber accused Hoffman of ripping him off. See Izak Haber, "An Amerika Dream: A True Yippie's Sentimental Education or How Abbie Hoffman Won My Heart and Stole 'Steal This Book,'" *Rolling Stone*, 30 September 1971, 32–33.

112. Daniel Simon, ed., *The Best of Abbie Hoffman* (New York: Four Walls Eight Windows, 1989), 209–10.

113. Barbara L. Tischler, *Sights on the Sixties* (New Brunswick, NJ: Rutgers University Press, 1992), 115.

114. For a typical example, an encyclopedia of youth culture reports that "[a]mong the young the wearing of old clothes was intended as an anti-establishment comment, a reaction to the new throw-away attitude that came along with the explosion of mass-produced clothing in the 1960s." See Shirley Steinberg, Priya Parmar, and Birgit Richard, *Contemporary Youth Culture: An International Encyclopedia* (Westport, CT: Greenwood Press, 2006), 2:392–93; Edward G. Reilly, *The 1960s* (Westport, CT: Greenwood Press, 2003), 87; Claudia A. Mitchell and Jacqueline Reid-Walsh, eds., *Girl Culture: An Encyclopedia* (Westport, CT: Greenwood Press, 2007), 499.

115. Angela McRobbie proposes that shopping and fashion often remain excluded from conversations about radicality because scholars dismiss them as intrinsically frivolous and therefore regard mention of the association as potentially compromising to radical status. See McRobbie, "Second-Hand Dresses and the Ragmarket," in *Zoot Suits and Secondhand Dresses: An Anthology of Fashion and Music*, ed. Angela McRobbie (Boston: Unwin Hyman, 1988), 34.

116. See, for example, Thomas Frank, *The Conquest of Cool: Business Culture, Counterculture, and the Rise of Hip Capitalism* (Chicago: University of Chicago Press, 1997), and Leerom Medovoi, *Rebels: Youth and the Cold War Origins of Identity* (Durham, NC: Duke University Press, 2005).

117. Although most modes of secondhand exchange remained unquantifiable, media reports of the popularity of garage sales peaked in the 1970s, and according to the NFMA, the number of nationwide flea markets grew enormously in that decade. Of course, exact statistics on flea markets are untenable, since the definition and assessment of the venues have always been unstable. See "The Flea Market Industry: Economic and Legislative Impact Data," from the Papers of Ed Collins, National Flea Market Association, 2006.

118. Angela McRobbie's exploration of secondhand commerce in postwar Great Britain emphasizes the monetary, entrepreneurial advantages to secondhand market participation, as well as the "[p]attterns of taste and discrimination [that] shape the desires of second-hand shoppers." McRobbie concluded that secondhand London markets provided financial opportunities for those without entrée to mainstream retail. In the U.S. context, I argue that aesthetics and politics were primary motivations among new participants in used-goods exchange, in the context of a singularly robust economy. See McRobbie, "Second-Hand Dresses and the Ragmarket," quote from p. 29.

119. See Caterine Milinaire and Carol Troy, *Cheap Chic* (New York: Harmony Books, 1975), 37.

120. Quoted in "Suit of Rags," *Rags* 1 (June 1970): 2.

121. Sociologist Karen Bettez Halnon makes a similar point about "poor chic" later in the twentieth century, arguing that in "Poor Chic" "class status is distinguished through work abstention and conspicuous (wasteful) consumption." See Halnon, "Poor Chic: The Rational Consumption of Poverty," *Current Sociology*, July 2002, 501–16, 506.

122. "Paris," reprinted in Kennedy Fraser, *The Fashionable Mind: Reflections on Fashion, 1970–1982* (New York: Alfred A. Knopf, 1981).

Chapter Six

1. In one of those twists of cartoon creative license (such as the way anvils never really hurt anybody), slender Wilma's rejected clothes mutate into a fair fit for blocky Fred. Perhaps Wilma dieted severely before the series' start, or maybe the donated clothes were Stone-Age maternity designs. "Ladies' Day," directed by William Hanna and Joseph Barbera (23 November 1962; Los Angeles, CA: Hanna Barbera, 1962).

2. Jean Spain Wilson, "You Don't Need a Placard with the 'Unisex' Styles," *Washington Post*, 24 June 1968, C3.

3. *Time*, 1 December 1967, cover.

4. Quoted in Wilson, "You Don't Need a Placard," C3. For more on Gernreich, who is credited with pioneering the unisex style, see Peggy Moffitt and William Claxton, *The Rudi Gernreich Book* (Cologne, Germany: Taschen, 1999), and Valerie Steele, *Fifty Years of Fashion: From New Look to Now* (New Haven, CT: Yale University Press, 1997), 71.

5. Quoted in Wilson, "You Don't Need a Placard," C3.

6. National attention to gay rights accelerated after the June 1969 uprising in response to a series of police raids at the Stonewall Inn, a gay bar in Greenwich Village. For more on the Stonewall Uprising, see Betsy Kuhn, *Gay Power! The Stonewall Riots and the Gay Rights Movement, 1969* (Minneapolis: Twenty-First Century Books, 2011), and David Carter, *Stonewall: The Riots That Sparked the Day Revolution* (New York: St. Martin's Press, 2004).

7. Charles Ludlam, May 1970, quoted in Stefan Brecht, "Jack Smith, 1961–71: The Sheer Beauty of Junk," in *Queer Theatre: The Original Theatre of the City of New York. From the Mid-60s to the Mid-70s*, book 2 (New York: Methuen Drama, 1978), 12.

8. Jack Smith, quoted in Ronald Tavel, "Maria Montez: Anima of an Antediluvian World," in *Flaming Creature: Jack Smith, His Amazing Life and Times*, ed. Edward Leffingwell et al. (New York: Serpent's Tail, 1997), 99.

9. See Christopher Lonc, "Genderfuck and Its Delights," reprinted in *Gay Roots: Twenty Years of Gay Sunshine*, ed. Winston Leyland (San Francisco: Gay Sunshine Press, 1991), 223–336. For personal accounts from members of the Cockettes, see Pam Tent, *Midnight at the Palace: My Life as a Fabulous Cockette* (New York: Alyson Books, 2004), and Bambi Lake and Alvin Orloff, *The Unsinkable Bambi Lake: A Fairytale Containing the Dish of Cockettes, Punks, and Angels* (San Francisco: Manic D Press, 1996). See also Joshua Gamson, *The Fabulous Sylvester: The Legend, the Music, the Seventies in San Francisco* (New York: Henry Holt, 2005), and Bill Weber and David Weissman, *The Cockettes*, documentary, 2002. Available at http://www.cockettes.com/.

10. Laud Humphrey, *Out of the Closets: Sociology of Homosexual Liberation* (New York: Prentice Hall, 1972), 169.

11. The bulk of studies on secondhand style in the 1960s–1970s refer to the English context and emphasize punk styles. See, for example, Dick Hebdige, *Subculture* (London: Routledge, 1979); Angela McRobbie, "Secondhand Dresses and the Ragmarket," in *Zoot Suits and Secondhand Dresses: An Anthology of Fashion and Music* (Boston: Unwin

Hyman, 1988); and Louise Crewe and Nicky Gregson, *Secondhand Cultures* (Oxford: Oxford International, 2003).

12. In *Spree: A Cultural History of Shopping*, Pamela Klaffke calls Diane Keaton in Woody Allen's 1977 film *Annie Hall* "the first poster girl for thrift shop chic ... with no ties to youth movements or to poverty." Keaton's dress in *Annie Hall* advertised for "the boyfriend look" by relying on men's clothing to create a hip, gamine appearance. See Klaffke, *Spree: A Cultural History of Shopping* (Vancouver: Arsenal Pulp Press, 2003), 115–16. See also *Annie Hall*, directed by Woody Allen (Beverly Hills, CA: United Artist, 1977), DVD.

13. Ginsberg, quoted in Benjamin Shepard, "History, Narrative, and Sexual Identity: Gay Liberation and Postwar Movements for Sexual Freedom in the United States," in *The Story of Sexual Identity: Narrative Perspectives on the Gay and Lesbian Life Course*, ed. Phillip L. Hammack and Bertram J. Cohler (New York: Oxford University Press, 2009), 33. For more on the Lavender Scare, see David K. Johnson, *The Lavender Scare: The Cold War Persecution of Gays and Lesbians* (Chicago: University of Chicago Press, 2004).

14. For more on *Stoumen v. Reilly*, see William Eskridge Jr., *Gaylaw: Challenging the Apartheid of the Closet* (Boston: Harvard University Press, 2002), 93–95, and Josh Sides, *Erotic City: Sexual Revolutions and the Making of San Francisco* (Oxford: Oxford University Press, 2009), 38–41.

15. Eskridge, *Gaylaw*, 94.

16. For more on José Sarria's life, performances, and political activism, see Michael R. Gorman, *The Empress Is a Man: Stories from the Life of José Sarria* (New York: Haworth Press, 1998); Nan Alamilla Boyd, "Transgender and Gay Male Cultures from the 1890s through the 1960s," in *Wide-Open Town: A History of Queer San Francisco to 1965* (Berkeley: University of California Press, 2003); Manuel Castells, "Cultural Identity, Sexual Liberation, and Urban Structure: The Gay Community in San Francisco," in *The City and the Grassroots: A Cross-Cultural Theory of Urban Social Movements* (Berkeley: University of California Press, 1983); Mark Thompson, "Children of Paradise," in *Out in Culture: Gay, Lesbian, and Queer Essays on Popular Culture*, ed. Corey K. Creekmur and Alexander Doty (Durham, NC: Duke University Press, 1995).

17. For more on the legal repercussions for homosexuality, see Johnson, *The Lavender Scare*. For more on the history of mental health and homosexuality, see Henry L. Monton, *Departing from Deviance: A History of Homosexual Rights and Emancipatory Science* (Chicago: University of Chicago Press, 2002), and Ronald Bayer, *Homosexuality and American Psychiatry: The Politics of Diagnosis* (Princeton, NJ: Princeton University Press, 1987).

18. Jackie M. Blount, *Fit to Teach: Same-Sex Desire, Gender, and School Work in the Twentieth Century* (Albany: State University of New York Press, 2005), 99.

19. Harvey Milk was the first openly gay man to be elected to public office in California when he won a seat on the San Francisco Board of Supervisors in 1977. For more on Milk, see Randy Shilts, *The Mayor of Castro Street* (New York: St. Martin's Press, 1982), and Kari Krakow, *The Harvey Milk Story* (Ambler, PA: Two Lives, 2001).

20. Gorman, *The Empress Is a Man*, 162; David Talbot, *Season of the Witch: Enchantment, Terror, and Deliverance in the City of Love* (New York: Free Press, 2012), 102–3.

21. Shilts, *The Mayor of Castro Street*, 51.

22. Boyd, *Wide Open Town*, 22.

23. Based on receipts from José Sarria Papers (photo box 6, #1996-01), San Francisco GLBT Historical Society.

24. Sarria's papers did also include records of purchase from mainstream department stores, including dresses. Sarria Papers, #1996-01.

25. Bulletin, League for Civil Education, 15 April 1961, José Sarria Papers, LCE documents, GLBT Historical Society; Boyd, *Wide Open Town*, 222. For more on the Tavern Guild, see Susan Stryker and Jim Van Buskirk, *Gay by the Bay: A History of Queer Culture in the San Francisco Bay Area* (San Francisco: Chronicle Books, 1996), and Bob Peck, "San Francisco Has America's Most Successful Tavern Guild," *VR*, February 1971. For the Society for Individual Rights' statement of policy, see Robert B. Ridinger, ed., *Speaking for Our Lives: Historic Speeches and Rhetoric for Gay and Lesbian Rights (1892–2000)* (Binghamton, NY: Harrington Park Press, 2004), 115–116.

26. Boyd, *Wide Open Town*, 220.

27. William N. Eskridge and John Ferejohn, *A Republic of Statutes: The New American Constitution* (New Haven, CT: Yale University Press, 2010), 159.

28. Marc Stein, *Rethinking the Gay and Lesbian Movement* (New York: Routledge, 2012), 69.

29. For one description of Sarria's bid for office, see Thompson, "Children of Paradise," 450.

30. Boyd, *Wide Open Town*, 220.

31. Bonnie Zimmerman, ed., *Encyclopedia of Lesbian and Gay Histories and Cultures* (New York: Garland, 2000), 192.

32. Nancy May, "Speaking Out," *Vector* 1, no. 6 (1965): 3, from Sarria Papers, #1996-01.

33. Ibid., 3.

34. "Clothing Needed," *Vector* 1, no. 6 (1965): 3, Sarria Papers, #1996-01. Women picketers wore correspondingly conventional outfits. For more on the 1965 picket, see Johnson, *The Lavender Scare*, 202–5.

35. "The SIRporium a Success," *Vector* 1, no. 9 (1965): 10. See also "What's Happening at the SIRporium," *Vector* 2, no. 12 (1966): 4.

36. Gorman, *The Empress Is a Man*, 179.

37. Daughters of Bilitis, San Francisco Chapter, newsletter, from Sarria Papers, #1996-01, Box 7. See also, B. Plath, "T.G.S.F. Auction Series Is Another Success," *Vector* 3, no. 6 (1967): 12.

38. "Mattachine Auctions Scheduled in August for Three Locations," *Town Talk*, August 1964, 1. Martin Meeker argues that the conservative reputation of the Mattachine Society has been historically exaggerated, with its public mask taken as reality and behind-the-scenes efforts overlooked. *Town Talk*, quoted in Martin Meeker, "Behind the Mask of Respectability: Reconsidering the Mattachine Society and Male Homophile Practice, 1950s–1960s," *Journal of the History of Sexuality* 10, no. 1 (2001): 109.

39. Betty Luther Hillman also points out these position inconsistencies in *Vector* in Hillman, "'The most profound revolutionary act a homosexual can engage in': Drag and the Politics of Gender Presentation in the San Francisco Gay Liberation Movement, 1964–1972," *Journal of the History of Sexuality* 20, no. 1 (2011): 153–81.

40. W. E. Beardemphl, "Drag—Is It Drab, Despicable, Divine?" *Vector* 3, no. 6 (1967): 13.

41. Hauser, telephone interview with author, 22 November 2010.

42. Talbot, *Season of the Witch*, 35–41. For more about the Diggers, their performance style, and evolving anarchic principles, see Bradford D. Martin, *The Theatre Is in the Street* (Amherst: University of Massachusetts Press, 2004), 86–124.

43. John D'Emilio tracks the changes of the meaning of heterosexual relations and family life throughout the transition from the economic self-sufficiency of family units to a capitalist free labor society. See D'Emilio, "Capitalism and Gay Identity," *Powers of Desire: The Politics of Sexuality*, ed. Ann Snitow, Christine Stansell, and Sharon Thompson (New York: Monthly Review Press, 1983), 101–3.

44. Bonnie Marranca and Guatam Dasgupta, *Theatre of the Ridiculous* (New York: Performing Arts Journal Publications, 1979), 6. For more on Ridiculous theater, see Stephen J. Bottoms, *Playing Underground: A Critical History of the 1960s Off-Off-Broadway Movement* (Ann Arbor: University of Michigan Press, 2006), and David Kaufman, *Ridiculous! The Theatrical Life and Times of Charles Ludlam* (New York: Applause Theatre & Cinema Books, 2002). For critical analyses of the plays produced by Ludlam's company, see Rick Roemer, *Charles Ludlam and the Ridiculous Theatrical Company* (Jefferson, NC: McFarland, 1998).

45. Bonnie Marranca calls Smith the "father of the style" in the introduction to a compilation of Ridiculous screenplays and scripts. See Marranca, introduction to Marranca and Dasgupta, *Theatre of the Ridiculous*, 5.

46. Stefan Brecht, "Family of the f.p.: The Theatre of the Ridiculous, 1965–1968," in *Queer Theatre*, 28.

47. Kenneth Bernard, "Confronting the Ridiculous/A Theatrical Review with John Vaccaro," *Confrontations*, Spring/Summer 1976, quoted in Brecht, "Family of the f.p.," 28.

48. Richard Foreman founded Ontological-Hysteric Theater in 1968. For more on Smith's broad-spanning influence, see "The World According to Jack Smith," in C. Carr, *On Edge: Performance at the End of the Twentieth Century* (Middletown, CT: Wesleyan University Press, 1993), 325–28. For more about Smith's influence on and relationship to avant-garde art, see Jerry Tartaglia, "The Perfect Queer Appositeness of Jack Smith," in *Experimental Cinema: The Film Reader*, ed. Wheeler Winston Dixon and Gwendolyn Audrey Foster (London: Routledge, 2002), 163–72. Jack Sargeant includes Jack Smith in the category of "Beat Cinema" in his book *Naked Lens: Beat Cinema* (Berkeley: Soft Skull Press, 2008; first published in 1997), 101–10.

49. Leffingwell, "The Only Normal Man in Baghdad," in Leffingwell et al., *Flaming Creature*, 71, 78.

50. Brecht, quoted in Leffingwell, "The Only Normal Man in Baghdad," 78.

51. Michael Moon, "Flaming Closets," in *Small Boy and Others* (Durham, NC: Duke University Press, 1998), 90. See also Judith Jerome, *Creating the World Waiting to Be Created: Jack Smith and D. W. Winnicott* (PhD diss., New York University, Department of Performance Studies, May 2007), 322–25.

52. See Kenneth Goldsmith, ed., *I'll Be Your Mirror: The Selected Andy Warhol Interviews: 1962–1987* (New York: Carroll and Graf, 2004), 67; Leffingwell, "The Only Normal Man in Baghdad," 70.

53. Stefan Brecht, "The Sheer Beauty of Junk," in Leffingwell et al., *Flaming Creature*, 43. Originally published in *Queer Theater* (Frankfurt Germany: Suhrkamp, 1978).

54. Brecht, "The Sheer Beauty of Junk," 43.

55. Abbie Hoffman, *Soon to Be a Major Motion Picture* (New York: Perigee Books, 1980), 97.

56. Jack Smith, quoted in J. Hoberman, *On Jack Smith's "Flaming Creatures" (and Other Secret-Flix of Cinemaroc)* (New York: Granary Books, 2001), 17.

57. For more on the filming and reception of *Flaming Creatures*, see Hoberman, *On Jack Smith's "Flaming Creatures."* Maria Montez was dubbed the "Queen of Technicolor" in the trailer for *Arabian Nights*, but was not highly regarded as an actress. See Ernest Mathjis and Jamie Sexton, *Cult Cinema* (New York: John Wiley & Sons, 2012). According to Sheldon Renan's *The Underground Film*, Jack Smith discovered the transvestite star Mario Montez (or Dolores Flores) in a subway station. In addition to his theatrical performances, Montez went on to appear in numerous underground films, including many of Warhol's films, such as *Mario Banana* and *Harlot* (both 1964), *Camp* (1965), *The Most Beautiful Woman in the World* aka *The Shoplifter* (1965), and *The Chelsea Girls* (1966). See Renan, *The Underground Film: An Introduction to Its Development in America* (London: Studio Vista Books, 1967), 202.

58. For more on the film's censorship and legal punting, see J. Hoberman, "Sight and Sound: Everything Overexposed," *New York* 1, no. 9 (1992): 4. For more on the public controversy, including Susan Sontag's defense of it, see also Peter Decherney, *Hollywood and the Culture Elite: How the Movies Became American* (New York: Columbia University Press, 2005), 198–99.

59. Leffingwell, "The Only Normal Man in Baghdad," 78.

60. Brecht, *Queer Theatre*, 177n. Michael Moon notes that "erotic charges in a work like *Flaming Creatures*" move across "circuits of gender and sexual identity." See Moon, "Flaming Closets," 83.

61. Susan Sontag, "Jack Smith's *Flaming Creatures*," in *Against Interpretation and Other Essays* (New York: Farrar, Strauss & Giroux, 1964), 230.

62. Sonya L. Jones, *Gay and Lesbian Literature since World War II: History and Memory* (Philadelphia: Haworth Press, 1998), 18.

63. Leffingwell, "The Only Normal Man in Baghdad," 71.

64. Ibid., 78.

65. Despite its controversy, *Flaming Creatures* did not launch Smith into a successful career in subversion. As Michael Moon remarks, Susan Sontag, through her published defense of the film in *The Nation*, perhaps became more "famous" for *Flaming*

Creatures than did Smith: "For every person who actually saw Smith's film, perhaps a hundred know it only from Sontag's description of it." See Moon, *A Small Boy and Others*, 77–78.

66. Leffingwell, "The Only Normal Man in Baghdad," 70.

67. Hoberman, "Sight and Sound," 4.

68. Brecht, "The Sheer Beauty of Junk," 43. The alliance between "desire" and "longing" and discarded objects can be found in many sources. It is worthwhile to note that Susan Sontag, Smith's most famous contemporary defender, began her best-selling novel *The Volcano Lover* at the entrance of a flea market, where the narrator wishes to find something that speaks "[t]o my longings." After listing potential desiderata, the protagonist admits before entering, "Desire leads me." See Sontag, *The Volcano Lover: A Romance* (New York: Doubleday, 1992), 3–4.

69. Jack Smith, "The Perfect Filmic Appositeness of Maria Montez," in *Film Culture* 27 (Winter 1962–63), 28.

70. Susan Sontag outlines the seminal course on the sensibility of camp in "Notes on 'Camp,'" in Sontag, *Against Interpretation and Other Essays* (New York: Farrar, Straus, & Giroux, 1966; essay first published in 1964), 275–92.

71. Ibid., 277.

72. Steven Samuels, ed., *Ridiculous Theatre: Scourge of Human Folly: The Essays and Opinions of Charles Ludlam* (New York: Theatre Communications Group, 1992), 20.

73. Samuels, *Ridiculous Theatre*, 17.

74. Helms, *Pioneering in Modern City Missions* (Boston: Morgan Memorial Printing Dept., 1944), 71–72.

75. See Brecht, quoted in Samuels, *Ridiculous Theatre*, 20.

76. Kaufman, *Ridiculous!*, 66.

77. From Martin Gottfried, "Money Is Endangering the Ridiculous Theatrical Company," *Women's Daily Wear*, 10 April 1972, 16, quoted in Kaufman, *Ridiculous!*, 160.

78. Hoberman, *On Jack Smith's "Flaming Creatures*," 16.

79. Samuels, *Ridiculous Theatre*, 116. For more on Charles James, see Richard Martin, *Charles James* (New York: Assouline Press, 2006).

80. André Breton, *Nadja*, trans. Richard Howard (New York: Grove Press, 1960), 52–53; Margaret Cohen, *Profane Illumination: Walter Benjamin and the Paris of Surrealist Revolution* (Berkeley: University of California Press, 1993), 109; Rosalind Krauss, "The Photographic Conditions of Surrealism," *October* 19 (Winter 1981): 3–34.

81. From an unpublished interview with Lawrence Rinder, 22 June 1996, quoted in Lawrence Rinder, "Anywhere Out of the World," in Leffingwell et al., *Flaming Creature*, 143.

82. The genealogy of the Cockettes' first performance's dragwear is recounted in a few sources. See, for example, Benjamin Shepard, "Play as World-Making: From the Cockettes to the Germs, Gay Liberation to DIY Community Building," in *The Hidden 1970s: Histories of Radicalism*, ed. Dan Berger (New Brunswick, NJ: Rutgers University Press, 2010), 180. In a 1993 interview with Stephen Taylor, Allen Ginsberg traces his own "glam rock" persona back to Smith and Rosenthal, through his boy-

friend Hibiscus's clothing, purloined from Rosenthal. See Jerome, *Creating the World*, 197.

83. Shepard, "Play as World-Making, 180.

84. See ibid., 181, and Talbot, *Season of the Witch*, 98–102. Details of the first show were also related by Rumi Missabu, 14 October 2010, interview with the author, and in Julia Bryan-Wilson, "Grit and Glitter," *Octopus* 4 (Fall 2008): 19–30.

85. See Lipsitz, "Who'll Stop the Rain? Youth Culture, Rock 'n' Roll, and Social Crises," in *The Sixties: From Memory to History*, ed. David Farber (Chapel Hill: University of North Carolina Press, 1994), 18.

86. See, for example, Clay Geerdes, "The Cockettes," *Door*, 29 September–13 October 1971), 23–24; "Hibiscus and the Angels of Light," *Good Times* 4, no. 32 (1971): 6–7; John Weiner, "Cockettes," *Rags*, August 1970; Jon Stewart, "From the Cockettes with Love and Squalor," *Ramparts*, December 1971; and "Les Cockettes de San Francisco," *Rolling Stone*, 14 October 1971.

87. Richard Ekins and Dave King describe the Cockettes as presaging "'transcending' gender stories that came to fruition in the mid-late 1990s." See Ekins and King, *Transgender Phenomenon* (London: Sage, 2006), 191.

88. John Waters, quoted in Weber and Weissman, *The Cockettes*. For more about Waters's relationship with the Cockettes, see Waters, *Shock Value* (New York: Thunder Mouth Press, 1995), 68–74.

89. See Matthew Ross, "Coming Together: The Communal Option," in *Ten Years That Shook the City: San Francisco, 1968–1978*, ed. Chris Carlsson and Lisa Ruth Elliot (San Francisco: City Lights Books, 2011), 197–200.

90. Actually, many Cockettes members, including Jalala, Jet, Tahara, Ralph, and Hibiscus, were kicked out of the commune, which did not allow external affiliations. Rumi Missabu, interview with the author, September 2010.

91. Gregory Pickup, *Pickup's Tricks*, unreleased film, 1973. According to Pickup, Hibiscus blocked him from releasing this film, in keeping with his staunch anticommercial stance.

92. Hauser, 22 November 2010 interview with the author. Waters, quoted in Weber and Weissman, *The Cockettes*.

93. John Waters and Rumi Missabu were roommates at this time and were among the few who could not get ATD. Rumi did not have a proper ID. Waters was told he was insane, but not permanently. Rumi Missabu, 14 October 2010 interview with the author; John Waters, in *The Cockettes*.

94. Lake and Orloff, *The Unsinkable Bambi Lake*, 29.

95. Benjamin Shepard, "Play as World-Making," 180.

96. The auction was part of the studio changing hands, and in general, the decline of the Old Hollywood studio system and the beginning of new conglomerates such as Paramount. See Leonard Quart and Albert Auster, *American Film and Society since 1945* (Santa Barbara, CA: Praeger, 2011), 77–78.

97. Fayette Hauser, 22 November 2010 interview with the author; Missabu, 14 October 2010 interview with the author.

98. Hauser, 14 November 2010 interview with the author.

99. Hauser, 14 November 2010 interview with the author; Shepard, "Play as World-Making," 180.

100. Hauser, 14 November 2010 interview with the author. Fashion theorist Elizabeth Wilson argues that critiques of fashion as "one example of a mass outbreak of inauthenticity" were based on the "utopias both of right and left, which were themselves fantasies, [and] implied an end to fantasy in the perfect world of the future." In this regard, the Cockettes were realists who understood the need for utopian representations. See Wilson, "Feminism and Fashion," in *Adorned in Dreams: Fashion and Modernity* (Berkeley: University of California Press, 1985), 246–47.

101. Barbara Falconer, "The Cockettes of San Francisco," *Earth*, October 1971. For similar references and examples, see also Gamson, *The Fabulous Sylvester*, 54, and Clay Geerdes, "The Cockettes," 23–24.

102. Tent, *Midnight at the Palace*, 95.

103. Missabu, 10 October 2010 interview with the author.

104. Ibid.

105. As Sweet Pam recalled, public reception of "Shanghai" was not all enthusiastic, especially when they took the act to the streets. "Our forcing a drag-queen rendition of fake Oriental platitudes down throats of people trapped in their own apartments upset the locals, and they made their displeasure known." Tent, *Midnight at the Palace*, 100. Since Edward Said's seminal work on the topic, many scholars have critiqued Western appropriation and interpretation of images and cultural ideas of the Orient. See Edward Said, *Orientalism* (New York: Vintage Books, 1979). Sheng-Mei Ma explores the relationship between American Orientalism and Asian American identity, including sexual and gender stereotypes in *The Deathly Embrace: Orientalism and Asian American Identity* (Minneapolis: University of Minnesota Press, 2000). For a study contextualizing the Orientalist attitudes during the postwar years, see Christina Klein, *Cold War Orientalism: Asia in the Middlebrow Imagination, 1945–1961* (Berkeley: University of California Press, 2003).

106. Gamson, *The Fabulous Sylvester*, 44–45, 59. For more on Sylvester James's upbringing and career, see also Judith A. Peraino, *Listening to the Sirens: Musical Technologies of Queer Identity from Homer to "Hedwig"* (Berkeley: University of California Press, 2006), 187–94.

107. Joshua Gamson relates several clashes between Sylvester and Hibiscus, including an instance when Sylvester slapped Hibiscus for upstaging him in a performance. See Gamson, *The Fabulous Sylvester*, 74–75.

108. Though much media surrounding the New York City debut was negative, Maureen Orth produced a more measured account and description of the Cockettes' performances, pointing to the overlooked avant-garde qualities. See Maureen Orth, "History of a Hype Worm in Big Apple," *Village Voice*, 25 November 1971, 5, 68.

109. For more on John Waters's personal life and film career, see Robert L. Pela, *Filthy: The Weird World of John Waters* (New York: Alyson Books, 2002). James Egan

has collected some of the many interviews Waters has given in *John Waters: Interviews* (Jackson: University of Mississippi Press, 2011).

110. Missabu, 10 October 2010 interview with the author; Hauser, 14 November 2010 interview with the author.

111. See "New York: Ragazzi Che Vestono, Pop-Group," *Italian L-Uomo Vogue*, February–March 1973. See also Alexandra Jacopetti, *Native Funk and Flash: An Emerging Folk Art* (San Francisco: Scrimshaw Press, 1974); Missabu, 10 October 2010 interview with the author.

112. Ginsberg, quoted in Thompson, "Children of Paradise," 449. Ginsberg performed with Hibiscus in his troupe Angels of Light, chanting to Blake's Songs of Innocence. Hibiscus claimed it was the poet's "first time ... ever in drag." See "Hibiscus and the Angels of Light," *Good Times* 4, no. 32 (1971): 6.

113. Thompson, "Children of Paradise," 449.

114. Ibid.

115. Ibid.

116. Ibid.

117. "Hibiscus and the Angels of Light," 6.

118. See Lonc, "Genderfuck and Its Delights," 223–336. See also Bryan-Wilson, "Grit and Glitter," 19–30.

119. Clay Geerdes, "The Cockettes," 23.

120. According to James Sullivan, members of the jeans industry dubbed women wearing men's jeans "the boyfriend look" in the early 1970s. See Sullivan, *Jeans* (New York: Gotham Books, 2006), 67.

121. Although visible signs of "going steady" varied in the 1950s, the boy giving the girl something of his to wear—class ring, letter sweater, varsity jacket—was a common practice. For more on these and other commodity exchanges as part of dating rituals of the 1950s, see Beth L. Bailey, *From Front Porch to Back Seat: Courtship in Twentieth-Century America* (Baltimore: Johns Hopkins University Press, 1998), 48–55.

122. Allen, *Annie Hall*.

123. Patti Smith is often credited as a "fashion muse" for fans and designers. Avantgarde clothing designer Ann Dermeulemeester, for example, credits Smith as a major inspiration for her mostly black, goth-inflected designs. See Valerie Steele, *The Black Dress* (New York: HarperCollins, 2007).

124. See Alicia Kennedy and Emily Banis Stoehler, with Jay Calderin, *Fashion Design, Referenced: A Visual Guide to the History, Language and Practice of Fashion* (London: Rockport, 2013), 283.

125. Nick Tosches, "Patti Smith," *The Nick Tosches Reader* (New York: Da Capo Press Books, 2000), 70.

126. Ibid., 78.

127. Nick Johnstone, *Patti Smith: A Biography* (London: Omnibus Press, 1997), 29; Patti Smith, "dream of rimbaud," *Early Work, 1970–1979* (New York: W. W. Norton, 1994), 42–43.

128. Smith, "dream of rimbaud," 43.

129. Breton, *Nadja*, 24.

130. Philip Shaw offers a Lacanian reading of Smith's work and her expressions of "phallic identity." See Shaw, *Patti Smith's Horses* (New York: Continuum International, 2008). See also Patricia Morrisroe, *Mapplethorpe: A Biography* (New York: Random Books, 1995), 49–50.

131. Patti Smith, *Just Kids* (New York: HarperCollins, 2010), 20.

132. Ibid., 29.

133. See Morrisroe, *Mapplethorpe*, 48.

134. Smith, *Just Kids*, 225.

135. Camille Paglia, "What's in a Picture," *Civilizations*, December 1996/January 1997.

136. Michael Bracewell, "Woman as Warrior," *Guardian Weekend*, 22 June 1996; Dave Thompson, *Dancing Barefoot: The Patti Smith Story* (Chicago: Chicago Review Press, 2011), 121.

137. Paglia, "What's in a Picture?"

138. Morrisroe, *Mapplethorpe*, 159.

139. For more on the friendship between Jean Genet and Brassaï, see Jeremy Reed, *Jean Genet: Born to Lose* (London: Creation Books, 2005), esp. p. 138.

140. Dick Hebdige, *Subculture* (London: Routledge, 1979), 2.

141. Vadim persuaded Fonda to star in *Barbarella*. She reportedly disliked the character and saw the film as misogynistic. See Patricia Bosworth, *Jane Fonda: The Private Life of a Public Woman* (New York: Houghton Mifflin, 2011), 272.

142. Molly Haskell, quoted in Bosworth, *Jane Fonda*, 271. See also Marie Lathers, *Space Oddities: Women and Outer Space in Popular Film and Culture, 1960–2000* (New York: Continuum International, 2010).

143. Morrisroe, *Mapplethorpe: A Biography*, 159.

Chapter Seven

1. Arie Kaplan, *From Krakow to Krypton: Jews and Comic Books* (Philadelphia: The Jewish Publication Society, 2008), 124. Many thanks to Jonathan Z. S. Pollack, whose 2016 American Historical Association paper, "The Many Lives of the *Ragman*: Jews, Comics, and Secondhand Goods," clued me into the existence of the *Ragman*.

2. Kaplan, *From Krakow to Krypton*, 124.

3. Pollack identifies the "rise of the tough Jew" as a 1990s phenomenon in "The Many Lives of the *Ragman*." Leonard Tannenbaum's memoir, published in 1993, sought to redeem junking and served to link Jewish junkmen to a more "masculinized" ideal of Jewishness. See Tannenbaum, *Junk Is Not a Four Letter Word* (Cleveland: author, 1993). See also Carl Zimring, *Cash for Your Trash: Scrap Recycling in America* (New Brunswick, NJ: Rutgers University Press, 2000). The "tough Jew" discourse peaked in the late 1990s, with Rich Cohen's book about Jewish gangsters in the Prohibition era. For Cohen, acknowledging the delinquent past of Jewish gangsters was an effective way of

dealing with having been born post-1945, with "being someone who has always had the Holocaust at his back." See Cohen, *Tough Jews: Fathers, Sons, and Gangster Dreams* (New York: Simon and Schuster, 1998), 21.

4. Kaplan, *From Krakow to Krypton*, 125.

5. Mark Mazzulo notes that Pacific Northwest garage postwar bands were sometimes called grunge. See Mazzulo, "The Man Whom the World Sold: Kurt Cobain, Rock's Progressive Aesthetic, and the Challenges of Authenticity," *Musical Quarterly* 84, no. 4 (2000): 718. Peter Blecha writes about the "de-evolutionary process" at play with the song "Louie, Louie," a Northwest band favorite even before the Kingsmen got ahold of it. See Blecha, *Sonic Book: The History of Northwest Rock, from "Louie Louie" to "Smells Like Teen Spirit"* (New York: Backbeat Books, 2009), 109–16, and Justin Henderson, *Grunge Seattle* (Berkeley, CA: Roaring Forties Press, 2010), 12.

6. Henderson, *Grunge Seattle*, 23.

7. Michael Azerra, *Our Band Could Be Your Life: Scenes from the American Indie Underground, 1981–1991* (New York: Little, Brown, 2012), chap. 12.

8. The meld of musical and sartorial style is central to Hebdige's text. See Dick Hebdige, *Subculture* (London: Routledge, 1979).

9. Timberland's stock doubled in 1991. See Rick Marin, "Grunge: A Success Story," *New York Times*, 15 November 1992, V1. For more on grunge music and fashion, see Anderson, "Accidental Revolution; 'Turning Points: Grunge,'" *Voguepedia*, accessed 1 June 2013, http://www.vogue.com/voguepedia/Grunge#cite_note-9. See also Susan Orlean, "Breaking Away," *Vogue*, September 1992.

10. Jonathan Poneman and Seven Meisel, "Grunge and Glory," *Vogue*, December 1992, 254. See also Janice Susan Gore, "Used Value: Thrift Shopping and Bohemia Incorporated" (PhD diss., University of Southern California, Department of Philosophy, 1999), 1.

11. Marin, "Grunge: A Success Story," V1.

12. See Andrew Bolton, *Anna Sui* (San Francisco: Chronicle Books, 2010), 53.

13. Ibid., 53; Angela McRobbie, "Secondhand Dresses and the Ragmarket," in *Zoot Suits and Secondhand Dresses: An Anthology of Fashion and Music* (Boston: Unwin Hyman, 1988), 28. See also Wilson, *Adorned in Dreams: Fashion and Modernity* (Berkeley: University of California Press, 1985), 5.

14. Katherine Marin, "Runway Report," *Vogue*, July 1993.

15. John Waters first saw Kawakubo's New York boutique in 1983 and was taken with the appealing trashiness of the couture items. See John Waters, *Role Models* (New York: Farrar, Strauss, and Giroux, 2010), chap. 4.

16. Susan Janice Gore echoed a common assumption when claiming that the "'grunge phenomenon' arose in reaction to the excesses and ravagements of the Reagan years." Gore, "Used Value," 6.

17. Adrian Franklin, "Consuming Design, Consuming Retro," in *The Changing Consumer: Markets and Meanings*, ed. Steven Miles, Alison Anderson, and Kevin Meethan (London: Routledge, 2002), 90–103.

18. Betty Luther Hillman, *Dressing for the Culture Wars: Style and the Politics of Self-Presentation in the 1960s and 1970s* (Lincoln: University of Nebraska Press, 2015).

19. "Culture wars" entered popular discourse with the publication of James Davison Hunter's *Culture Wars: The Struggle to Define America: Making Sense of the Battles over Family, Art, Education, Law, and Politics* (New York: Basic Books, 1992).

20. John T. Molloy, *Dress for Success* (New York: Warner Books, 1975); Molloy, *The Woman's Dress for Success Book* (New York: Warner Books, 1977), 28–29.

21. Jo Paoletti, *Sex and Unisex: Fashion, Feminism, and the Sexual Revolution* (Bloomington: Indiana University Press, 2015), 90.

22. Caterine Millinaire and Carol Troy, *Cheap Chic* (New York: Harmony Books, 1975). Paoletti recalled the book as more influential to her own style than were *Vogue* or *Cosmopolitan*. See Paoletti, *Sex and Unisex*, 52.

23. *Harriet Love's Guide to Vintage Chic* ushered in a new genre of clothing guides. See Harriet Love, *Harriet Love's Guide to Vintage Chic* (New York: Holt, Rinehart, and Winston, 1982), followed by Frances Kennett, *The Collector's Book of Twentieth-Century Fashion* (London: Granada, 1983). For more on the collectability of clothing in the 1980s, see Valerie Burnham Oliver, *Fashion and Costume in American Popular Culture: A Reference Guide* (Westport, CT: Greenwood Press, 1996), 45:93–94.

24. Chief among these was Tina Irick-Nauer, *The First Price Guide to Antique and Vintage Clothes: Fashions for Women, 1840–1940* (New York: E. P. Dutton, 1983), and Maryanne Dolan, *Vintage Clothing, 1880–1960: Identification and Value Guide* (Florence, AL: Books Americana, 1984).

25. See, for example, Naomi E. A. Tarrant, *Collecting Costume: The Care and Display of Clothes and Accessories* (London: Allen & Unwin, 1983), and Terry McCormick, *A Consumer's Guide to Vintage Clothing* (New York: Dembner Books, 1987).

26. See Guffey, *Retro: The Culture of Revival* (London: Reaktion Books, 2006), 9, 14–15.

27. Jean Baudrillard outlines his notions of the hyperreal in *Simulacra and Simulation*, trans. Sheila Faria Glaser (Ann Arbor: University of Michigan Press, 1981), 43.

28. Raphael Samuel, *Theatres of Memory: Past and Present in Contemporary Culture* (London: Verso, 2012), x, 95.

29. Ibid., 194.

30. Deirdre Clancy, *Costume since 1945: Couture, Street Style, and Anti-Fashion* (New York: Drama Publishers, 1996), 120.

31. John Waters, *Role Models* (New York: Farrar, Straus, and Giroux, 2010), chap. 4.

32. Angela Carter, "The Recession Style," reprinted in *New Statesman and Society*, 21 February 1992, 22–23 (first published in *New Society*, January 1983).

33. Carter, "The Recession Style," 22.

34. Hebdige, *Subculture*, 63.

35. Gary Clarke, "Defending Ski-Jumpers: A Critique of Theories of Youth Subcultures," in *On Record: Rock-Pop and the Written Word*, ed. Simon Frith (New York: Routledge, 2005; first published in 1990), 74.

36. Theo Cateforis examines New Wave nostalgia in *Are We Not New Wave? Modern Pop at the Turn of the 1980s* (Ann Arbor: University of Michigan Press, 2011).

37. Jay Goldberg, *Collectible Seventies: A Price Guide to the Polyester Decade* (Iola, WI: Krause, 2001).

38. Elizabeth Guffey, *Retro: The Culture of Revival* (London: Reaktion Books, 2006), 133–159.

39. Brown, *Party Out of Bounds*, 36.

40. Frank Rose, "The B-52s' *Wild Planet*," album review," *Rolling Stone*, 30 October 1980, accessed 30 June 2013, http://web.archive.org/web/20080212150347/http://www.rollingstone.com/artists/theb52s/albums/album/259322/review/5943590.

41. Cateforis, *Are We Not New Wave?*, 95.

42. Jeff Apter, "The Family Way," in *The Dave Grohl Story* (London: Omnibus Press, 2006).

43. Brown, *Party Out of Bounds*, 16, 26.

44. See Matei Călinescu, *Five Faces of Modernity: Modernism, Avant-Garde, Decadence, Kitsch, Postmodernism* (Durham, NC: Duke University Press, 2003), 235–37.

45. For a commentary that focuses partly on kitsch's relationship to music specifically and culture generally, see Richard Leppert, "Commentary," in Theodor W. Adorno, *Essays on Music*, trans. Susan H. Gillespie (Berkeley: University of California Press, 2002), esp. pp. 327–72. Quoted from p. 363.

46. Ibid., 362–63.

47. Ibid., 363.

48. For more on the specific styles and objects used to create the kitsch image of the B-52s, see Cateforis, *Are We Not New Wave?*, chap. 4.

49. See ibid., 106–7.

50. See ibid., 98.

51. Jon Savage, "R.E.M.: Post-Yuppie Pop," *Observer*, 21 May 1989, reprinted in Jon Savage, *Time Travel: Pop, Media, and Sexuality, 1976–1996* (London: Chatto & Windus, 1996), 250–51.

52. Judith Butler's renowned critical study of gender, published in 1990, is credited with the notion of gender performativity. See Butler, *Gender Trouble: Feminism and the Subversion of Identity* (New York: Routledge, 1990).

53. For more on the history and influences surrounding grunge music and style, see Kyle Anderson, *Accidental Revolution: The Story of Grunge* (New York: St. Martin's Press, 2007). For more on Nirvana's rise to fame, see Michael Azerrad, *Come as You Are: The Story of Nirvana* (New York: Broadway Books, 2001). Numerous biographies exist on Kurt Cobain, including Charles R. Cross, *Heavier Than Heaven: A Biography of Kurt Cobain* (New York: Hyperion, 2001).

54. Ian Halperin and Max Wallace, *Who Killed Kurt Cobain? The Mysterious Death of an Icon* (New York: Citadel Books, 1999), 16.

55. Jeff Apter, "The Family Way."

56. Tim Blanks, "Grunge; Marc Jacobs Got Fired Over it and Hedi Slimane Praised," *A.G. Nauta Couture*, https://agnautacouture.com/2013/09/15/grunge-marc-jacobs-got-fired-over-it-hedi-slimane-praised/ accessed August 1, 2016.

57. For more on the B-52s, along with other Athens bands such as R.E.M. and Pylon, see Rodger Lyle Brown, *Party Out of Bounds: The B-52s, R.E.M., and the Kids Who Rocked Athens, Georgia* (Atlanta, GA: Everthemore Books, 2003; first published in 1991).

58. Quoted in Amy Wallace and Handsome Dick Manitoba, *The Official Punk Rock Book of Lists* (New York: Backbeat Books, 2007), 125.

59. Chuck Klosterman, *Fargo Rock City: A Heavy Metal Odyssey in Rural North Dakota* (New York: Scribner, 2001), chap. 2.

60. Music video by Buster Poindexter performing "Hot Hot Hot" (BMG Music, 1987), first 32 seconds.

61. Hebdige, *Subculture*, 63.

62. Analysts of the idea of generational politics have debated the usefulness of the very idea of distinct generational breaks. See, for example, Stephen Earl Bennett and Stephen C. Craig, with Eric W. Rademacher, "Generations and Change: Some Initial Observations," in *After the Boom: The Politics of Generation X*, ed. Stephen Earl Bennett and Stephen C. Craig (Lanhamd, MD: Rowman & Littlefield, 1997), 3–8; Douglas Coupland, *Generation X: Tales for an Accelerated Culture* (New York: St. Martin's Press, 1990); David Gross and Sophronia Scott, "Proceeding with Caution," *Time*, 16 July 1990, 56–62.

63. Gina Arnold, *Route 666: On the Road to Nirvana* (New York: St. Martin's, 1993), 3.

64. Cateforis, *Are We Not New Wave?*, 96.

65. See Hutcheon, *Irony's Edge: The Theory and Politics of Irony* (New York: Routledge, 1994), 19.

66. Cobain's inclusion in Guitar Hero 5 was much critiqued due to his avatar's uncharacteristic performances of songs like Bon Jovi's "You Give Love a Bad Name." See Steve Kandell, "Kurt Cobain in 'Guitar Hero 5' Horrifying," *Spin*, 2 September 2009, accessed 18 September 2015, http://www.spin.com/2009/09/kurt-cobain-guitar-hero-5-horrifying/.

67. Entry in *The Dictionary of Fashion History*, ed. Valerie Cummin, C. W. Cunnington, and P. E. Cunnington, s.v. "cardigan," 40.

68. See Wilson, *Adorned in Dreams*, 5.

69. Mary Rawson, "Other Viewers, Other Rooms," in *Mister Rogers' Neighborhood: Children, Television, and Fred Rogers*, ed. Mark Collins and Margaret Mary Kimmel (Pittsburgh: University of Pittsburgh Press, 1997).

70. See Kurt Cobain, interview by David Fricke, *Rolling Stone*, 27 January 1994, 35. See also, Mazullo, "The Man the World Sold: Kurt Cobain, Rock's Progressive Aesthetic, and the Challenges of Authenticity," *Musical Quarterly* 84, no. 4 (2000): 722.

71. Philip Auslander writes about David Bowie's mastery of a theatrical, performative stage presence, as opposed to the communitarian performing styles of many psychedelic performers. See Auslander, *Performing Glam Rock: Gender and Theatricality in Popular Music* (Ann Arbor: University of Michigan Press, 2006), 106–149. Much has

been written about Lead Belly (or Leadbelly), and about the American romance with folk music since the 1930s. See, for example, Benjamin Filene, *Romancing the Folk: Public Memory and American Roots Music* (Chapel Hill: University of North Carolina Press, 2000).

72. For more on Riot Grrrls, see Sara Marcus, *Girls to the Front: The True Story of the Riot Grrrl Revolution* (New York: HarperCollins, 2010), and Christa D'Angelica, "Beyond Bikini Kill: A History of Riot Grrrl, from Grrrls to Ladies" (master's thesis, Sarah Lawrence College, May 2009). Greg Prato, *Grunge Is Dead: The Oral History of Seattle Rock Music* (Toronto: ECW Press, 2009), 304.

73. Ibid., 304.

74. Peter Gilstrap, "Not-So-Radical Chic," *Washington Post*, 12 September 1993, 35.

75. Ibid., 35.

76. Baudrillard, *Simulacra and Simulation*. Raymond F. Betts correlates the hyperreal with Urban Outfitters in Betts with Liz Bly, *A History of Popular Culture: More of Everything, Faster and Brighter* (New York: Routledge, 2013), 148.

77. Gilstrap, "Not-So-Radical Chic," 35.

78. Ibid.

79. Mimi Avins, "Big Attractions *Plus* a Sideshow," *Los Angeles Times*, 1 April 1996, E1; quoted in Gore, "Used Value," 99–100.

80. Scholars have written about the effects of AIDS on gay communities, conservative public reactions, and the medical and political history surrounding the epidemic. On the early reactions in the Unites States to the growing epidemic, see Dennis Altman, *AIDS and the New Puritanism* (London: Pluto Press, 1987). Randy Shilts critiqued political reaction (and inaction) in the early days of the AIDS diagnoses and affected communities' attempts to gain public awareness. See Shilts, *And the Band Played On: Politics, People, and the AIDS Epidemic* (New York: St. Martin's Press, 1987). For collections of essays on cultural and political reactions to the epidemic, see Peter Aggleton, Peter Davies, and Graham Har, *AIDS: Individual, Cultural, and Policy Dimensions* (London: Falmer Press, 2013), and David P. Willis and Scott V. Parris, eds., *A Disease of Society: Cultural and Institutional Responses to AIDS* (Cambridge: Oxford University Press, 1991).

81. Lillian Faderman and Stuart Timmons, *Gay L.A.: A History of Sexual Outlaws, Power Politics, and Lipstick Lesbians* (New York: Basic Books, 2006), 317–21.

82. "Action and Devotion: World AIDS Day," *HIV Plus*, November–December 2009, 27.

83. Karen Tranberg Hansen, *Salaula: The World of Secondhand Clothing and Zambia* (Chicago: University of Chicago Press, 2000), 113. For more on Domsey's "blatant disregard for the law," see Richard W. Hurd and Joseph B. Ueblein, "Patterned Responses to Organizing: Case Studies of the Union-Busting Convention," in *Restoring the Promise of American Labor Law*, ed. Sheldon Freeman et al. (Ithaca, NY: Cornell University Press, 1994), 61–74.

84. Daniel T. Rodgers, *Age of Fracture* (Cambridge, MA: Harvard University Press, 2011), 230.

Epilogue

1. Henry James, "The Romance of Certain Old Clothes," *Atlantic Monthly* 21, no. 124 (1868): 209–25. For more on *Ragman*, see Arie Kaplan, *From Krakow to Krypton: Jews and Comic Books* (Philadelphia: The Jewish Publication Society, 2008), 124.

2. See "New York's Cheapest Department Store," *New York Times*, 4 May 1902, C1.

3. Sociologist Karen Bettez Halnon gives pages of examples, such as designer "street-person chic" attire, emaciation, Kid Rock, Prada bowling shoes, "shantytown chic" funk balls—to name only a small handful of cultural imitations of poverty from the late 1990s. See Halnon, "Poor Chic: The Rational Consumption of Poverty," *Current Sociology* 50, no. 4 (2002): 501–16.

4. Kitsch is often described as exhibiting and glamorizing "bad taste." See, for example, Gillo Dorfles, *Kitsch: The World of Bad Taste* (Ann Arbor: University of Michigan Press, 1969).

5. See Maureen Dowd, "Homeless Chic," *Denver Post* 24 (January 2000), B6.

6. Ibid.

7. *Zoolander*, director: Ben Stiller; writers: Drake Sather and Ben Stiller; producers: Scott Rudin, Ben Stiller, and John Hamburg (Paramount Pictures, 2001).

8. Dowd, "Homeless Chic," B6.

9. The quote refers to 1993 couture by Rei Kawakubo of the Japanese design label Comme des Garçons. See Trish Donnally, "Young Designer's Street-Person Chic/More Rags and Tatters from Paris, *San Francisco Chronicle*, 16 March 1993, B3.

10. Halnon, "Poor Chic," 506.

11. For more on the global growth of cheap clothing consumption, see Elizabeth L. Cline, *Overdressed: The Shockingly High Cost of Cheap Fashion* (New York: Penguin, 2012), 119–37.

12. Yet, as Kaya Oakes points out, Urban Outfitters sell themselves as hiply "Indie." See Oakes, *Slanted and Enchanted: The Evolution of Indie Culture* (New York: Henry Holt, 2009), 197–201.

13. See Justin Nicholas Redman, "Post Tiffany (NJ) Inc. v. eBay, Inc.: Establishing a Clear, Legal Standard for Online Auctions," *Jurimetrics* 49, no. 4 (2009), 467–90.

14. Macklemore and Ryan Lewis, "Thrift Shop," *The Heist*, on Macklemore LLC, 2013.

Index

The A & P (The Great Atlantic and Pacific Tea Company), 56, 76, 240
ABC (Alcohol Beverage Control), 186
Aberdeen, Washington, 227, 229
Admen, 13, 115, 181
Adorno, Theodor, 225–26
The Affluent Society (Galbraith), 93, 103
African Americans, 7, 37, 170, 204, 215; Beat Generation, 163; civil rights movement, 158–60; marginalization, 86, 97; performers, 74, 204, 215, 232; rummage sales, 36; secondhand sales, 70, 73–74. *See also* Black Panthers; Racial segregation
Agee, James, 157–58, 167
AHF (AIDS Healthcare Foundation), 236
Alice Cooper, 205, 225
Allen, Woody, 207
Americana, 55, 70, 78–80, 113–14
Angels of Light, 202, 205–6
Annie Hall (1977), 207
Anthropologie, 234
Anticapitalism, 124–25, 167–69, 177–81, 185, 191–206, 242
Antiques: clothing as, 144, 220; dealers of, 122, 140, 144, 148; rise in popularity of, 36, 69, 78–71, 91, 95, 113–15, 137; stores, 107, 144
Anti-Semitism: Broadway, 97–90; diaspora, 68; secondhand commerce, 8, 19, 29, 47, 75. *See also* Immigrants; Street peddling
Art Nouveau, 140, 149, 220–21
Ashley, Laura, 217, 222, 224
Assemblage art, 15, 59, 62, 64
ATD (Aid to the Totally Disabled), 202
Atlanta, Georgia, 172, 176, 293, 314

Auctions: eBay, 242; postwar suburbs, 114–16; queer politics and dress, 190–91, 202; rise of everyday collectibles, 77–79; vintage clothing, 147
Avedon, Richard, 60
Avon Products, 94–95, 106

B-52s, 224–29, 232
Balzac, Honoré de, 156
Baraka, Amiri (LeRoi Jones), 159, 162
Barbarella (1968), 212
Barnes, Djuna, 66
Bartering, 107, 138, 200
Barzun, Jacques, 135, 153
Baudelaire, Charles, 208–11
Baudrillard, Jean, 15, 221, 224, 233
Bauhaus, 223–24
Bazaars, 106, 108, 110–13, 118, 138
Beat Generation: African American influences on, 163; The Black Cat Café, 186; drug culture, 119; elective poverty, 93, 162–63, 165; environmentalism, 165–68, 176; gender, 162; general style and appearances of, 12, 39, 124–25, 158, 164; Greenwich Village, 126–27, 161; hippies, 149–50, 169–70, 174; middle-class backgrounds of, 152, 156, 159. *See also* Beatnik
Beatles, 142
Beatnik, 142, 151, 160–63, 167, 169–70, 199; origins of the word, 293n31
Bebop, 163
Beckert, Sven, 4
Bernard, Kenneth, 192
Better Homes and Gardens (magazine), 113–14, 117
Biba, 140, 143, 152

Biddle, George, 63
Bikini Kill, 216, 233
The Black Cat Café, 186–89, 191–92
Black Panthers, 154–55, 159, 171, 176
Blackface/minstrelsy, 73, 82, 86, 291n4
Blass, Bill, 144
Bohemians: Atlanta's Little Five Points, 176; cultural representations of, 66–67; East Village, 169–70, 174; fashion/dress, 38, 60, 85–89; Greenwich Village, 8, 57, 62, 82, 87, 126–27; identity, 7, 240; London, 140–47; origins of, 155–60; Patti Smith, 210; race, 163–65; San Francisco, 148, 171–73; vintage clothing, 123–25
Bon Marché, 68, 94
Booth, Evangeline, 1–2, 19, 42–44, 84, 92, 125
Booth, Maud Ballington, 26
Booth, William, 25, 31, 33
Booth-Tucker, Frederick, 34
Bourke-White, Margaret, 157
Bow, Clara, 23–24, 89
Bowers, Bill, 205
Bowery, 14, 91, 184, 210–11
Bown, Emma, 40–41
The boyfriend look, 13–14, 186, 207–13. *See also* Genderfuck; Smith, Patti
Brassaï, 211–12
Bratmobile, 233
Brecht, Stefan, 192–93, 196
Breitenbach, Josef, 60
Breton, André: elective poverty, 167; secondhand acquisition, 53–54, 67, 120, 167, 210, 227; secondhand objects, 10, 58–59, 92, 199, 208, 213
Brice, Fanny (Borach, Fania), 8, 57, 66, 84–89, 92, 125, 213, 237, 274
Bricolage: examples, 125, 155, 193, 206, 218, 229; origins of the term, 14–15. *See also* Levi-Strauss, Claude
Broadway, 1, 66, 81–86, 129, 143. *See also* Brice, Fanny (Borach, Fania)
Broderick, Pat, 214

Bruno, Guido, 52, 59, 168, 215
"Bubbs Creek Haircut" (Snyder), 168
Buddhism, 163, 166–67. *See also* Beat Generation
Burning Questions (Shulman), 160–62, 167–69, 209. *See also* Shulman, Alix Kates
Burroughs, William S., 162, 164–65
Butler, Judith, 227

Caldwell, Erskine, 157
California, 31, 119, 165, 167, 174, 186; and the Beat Generation, 162, 169; and the Cockettes, 200; and flea markets, 137–38; and hippies, 149, 171
Canton, Texas, 76–77, 79
Capitalism: and American work habits, 33; and the Cold War, 92–97; and consumerism, 103–5, 213; and immigrants, 51–52; and secondhand commerce, 4–8, 13, 15–16, 18–21, 239; and thrift/stewardship, 46, 49. *See also* Anticapitalism; Hip capitalism; Philanthropic capitalism
Cardigan, 2, 231–32
Cardin, Pierre, 144
Carnaby Street designers, 144, 147
Carnegie, Andrew, 34–35. *See also* Scientific giving
Carrington, Leonora, 59
Carson, Rachel, 167–68
Carter, Angela, 222–23. *See also* Elective poverty; Grunge
Carver, Raymond, 120
Cassady, Neal, 162, 165–66
Chain stores, 49, 56, 76, 102–5, 137; dress and fashion, 133, 178; thrift stores, 98–100, 136, 177, 213. *See also* The A & P (The Great Atlantic and Pacific Tea Company); Consignment: stores; Goodwill Industries; The Salvation Army
Champfleury, 156, 210, 291

Charity fairs, 36–37. *See also* Rummage sales
Charity shops, 141
The Charlatans, 149–50, 152, 231
Chatham Street market, 29, 37, 70, 81, 255n46
Chauncey, George, 9
Chicago: immigrant population, 29–30, 48; secondhand commerce, 30, 70–73, 75, 81, 159. *See also* Immigrants
Chicago Review, 199, 201
Chicago Seven, 176
Chippendale, 115, 132
Clapton, Eric, 142, 147
Clark, Alison, 118. *See also* Tupperware, Inc.
Clemente, Deirdre, 128
Cline, Elizabeth, 5, 248
Cobain, Kurt, 2, 15, 216–18, 222, 227–32, 240
The Cockettes: anticapitalism, 14, 185, 201–2; cultural influence of, 204–5, 216, 225, 228; gay liberation movement, 191, 206; genderfuck, 185–86, 207; New York City, 205; politics of, 205–6; secondhand clothing, 200–204, 225
Coco Chanel, 57, 60
Cohen, Lizabeth, 100
Cohen, Sheila, 141
Collegians, 12, 122–23, 127–28, 132, 169
Commander in Rags (1906), 43
Conant, Homer, 84
The Conquest of Cool (Frank), 13, 124
Consignment of clothing, 11, 18, 27, 29, 140, 235–37
Consignment stores: Buffalo Exchange, 2, 235; Crossroads Exchange, 235; Henri, 140; Plato's Closet, 235
Copland, Aaron, 57
Cornell, Joseph, 54, 59, 120, 210
Counterculture, 13, 124
Coupland, Douglas, 230
Courrèges, André, 224
Cry-Baby (1990), 222

Dada, 10, 81, 168, 174; fashion design, 60; secondhand objects/commerce, 54–55, 58, 67; von Freytag-Loringhoven, Baroness Elsa, 60–67, 237, 240–41
Daddy Stovepipe, 73
Dali, Salvador, 60
Davis, Ossie, 159
Democratic National Convention (1968), 176
Désenchaînement, 54, 167, 213
Deseret Industries, 136
Desolation Angels (Kerouac), 165
Devo, 224
Dharma Bums, The (Kerouac), 125, 166
Di Prima, Diane, 162
Dickstein, Morris, 57
Dietrich, Marlene, 208
The Diggers, 169, 172–76, 185, 192, 200–202, 206, 234–35
Disco, 200, 204–5
Divine, 191, 205
DIY (Do-It-Yourself), 113, 116–17, 216
DKNY(Donna Karan New York), 217
Domsey Trading Corporation, 236–37
Drag, 3, 8, 88; the Cockettes, 14, 185, 200–206; gay rights activism, 187–91, 213; national or cultural, 83; rock music and, 216, 225; Sarria, José, 187–88. *See also* Glam rock
Dreiser, Theodore, 45, 47
Drive-in movie theaters, 11, 137–38
Duchamp, Marcel, 10, 54, 58, 62, 64, 87–89, 237
Du Maurier, George, 60
Dylan, Bob, 208–9, 232

Earth Day, 175
East London Christian Mission, 25
eBay, 242–43
Echols, Alice, 124
Edwardian dress, 123, 141, 144–46, 148, 174, 222, 231
Eisenhower, Dwight D., 97, 101
Elective poverty, 123–24; Beat Generation, 124, 163–67; fashion design,

Elective poverty (cont.) 222–24, 234–35, 240–41; genderfuck, 185; hippies, 151–52, 168; London, 147, 151; middle-class rebellion, 12, 123, 154, 159–61, 171, 182; politics, 172–77, 182–83. *See also* Grunge

Ellison, William, 136

Emerson, Ralph Waldo, 163

Engels, Friedrich, 94

Enstad, Nan, 21–22, 47

Environmentalism: garage sales, 112, 120; Snyder, Gary, 167–70, 175–76; recycling, 5, 7, 12, 175, 240; secondhand dress, 125, 158–59

Ernst, Max, 54, 59, 210

Evans, Walker, 157–58

Fair Labor Standards Act of 1938, 90, 136

Fast fashion, 5, 242

Federal Aid Highway Act of 1956. *See* National Interstate and Defense Highways Act

Federal Housing Administration (FHA), 97

Feminism, 122, 158–60, 167, 216; dress, 178–79; genderfuck, 14, 186, 208–12, 232–33; performance, 59, 65, 119. *See also* Smith, Patti

Flaming Creatures (1963), 186, 194–97, 199, 225

Flea markets, 10–11; classification of, 53–54; farmer's markets and, 76–77; French origins of, 67–69; post-World War II, 137–38; surrealists, 54–55, 58; United States origins of, 55–56, 69–76

The Flintstones (1960–1966), 183–84

Ford, Henry, 10, 53, 78–82, 91, 96

Fortune (magazine), 98

Frank, Thomas, 13, 124, 235

Franklin, Adrian, 219

Fraser, Kennedy, 181–82

Free stores, 172–75, 179, 202. *See also* The Diggers

Frightwig, 2, 245

Futurism, 62

Galbraith, John Kenneth, 93, 103, 153

Galliano, John, and hobo chic, 241. *See also* Hobo chic

Gammel, Irene, 63, 65

Garage sales, 1, 3–4, 6, 9, 11, 242; and civic participation/politics, 108–12; and collecting as a hobby, 112–14; and culture, 119–21; and gender, 104–8, 116–18; growth of, 138, 179, 213; origins of, 91–92 physical space of, 96–99; in postwar America, 92–96; and thrift, 99–100

Gates, Frederick, 34. *See also* Scientific giving

Gaultier, Jean-Paul, 14–15, 214, 218, 237

Gay rights/liberation movement, 9, 124, 207–13; drag, 186–92, 200, 206–7; musicians/performers, 205, 225–26; reactions to *Flaming Creatures*, 196; secondhand commerce, 5, 14, 178, 184–86, 189–91, 236. *See also* Genderfuck

Genderfuck, 13–14, 200–204, 205–6; definition and origins of, 185; and gender, 206–13; and musical performances, 205, 216, 227–31; and politics, 205–7

Generation of Vipers (Wylie), 117

Generation X, 230–31

Genet, Jean, 196, 211–12

George Olsen and His Music, 128. *See also* Raccoon-skin coats

Gernreich, Rudi, 144, 183–84

Gibbs, Christopher, 122, 144–45, 152. *See also* Peacock revolution; Vintage clothing/dress

Gillespie, Dizzy, influence on Beat style, 163

Ginsberg, Allen: and the Beat Generation, 151, 162–65, 168; and the Cockettes, 186, 201, 205; and Patti Smith, 211

Gitlin, Todd, 237

Glam rock, 184–86, 200, 205, 220, 223, 225; influence of, 227–30, 232

Glaspell, Susan, 52, 59–60

Goodwill Industries, 1–4, 46, 78, 98, 153, 198; the Beat Generation, 164, 168; clothing, 6, 20, 125, 140, 151, 188, 210, 229; the Diggers, 173; disabilities, 90, 136; origins of and growth, 10–11, 18, 21, 27, 49; postwar economy, 98, 100–101, 108, 110; profits, 51, 76; religion, 31–35, 202; World War II, 91. *See also* Thrift: ideology of; Thrift stores; Philanthropic capitalism

Gore, Susan, 145–46, 151–52

Goth style, 223–24

Gravenites, Linda, 150–52, 291

The Great Speckled Bird, 176–177

Great Migration, 70, 73, 159. *See also* African Americans

Greenfield Village, 78–79. *See also* Ford, Henry

Greenwich Village, 8, 221, 241; after World War II, 82, 122, 126, 168–69, 174; interwar period, 10, 39, 57, 60, 62, 65–67, 85; literature, 87, 160–61. *See also* Beat Generation; "Second Hand Rose" (Brice); von Freytag-Loringhoven, Baroness Elsa

Grogan, Emmett, 172–73. *See also* The Diggers

Grohl, Dave, 225, 228

Grunge, 15, 214, 219, 242; fashion, 216–18, 223, 233–40; genderfuck, 227–30; nostalgia, 231–32; origins, 215–16. *See also* Cobain, Kurt; Nirvana

Guffey, Elizabeth E., 221. *See also* Retro

Haggling, 54, 68, 71, 94, 107. *See also* Engels, Friedrich

Haight-Ashbury, 125, 149–51, 169–74, 199, 204

Hairspray (1988), 205, 222

Hall, Stuart, 156

Hanna, Kathleen, 216

Hansberry, Lorraine, 159, 292

Hansen, Karen Tranberg, 236

Harlem, 128, 170

Harper, Mabel Urner, 80–81

Harrington, Michael, 5, 153–55, 169, 241

Harvard University, 46, 127, 144, 158. *See also* Collegians

Hauser, Fayette, 191, 205

Hayne, Dick, 234

Headbangers Ball (television program), 229, 231

Hebdige, Dick, 212, 216, 223

Helms, Rev. Edgar J., 6, 19–21, 32–34, 46, 198. *See also* Goodwill Industries

Hendrix, Jimi, 12, 142, 147–48

Hibiscus, 14, 184–85, 200–203, 205–8. *See also* Angels of Light; The Cockettes; Genderfuck

The Hidden Persuaders (Packard), 133

Hillman, Betty Luther, 219

Hine, Thomas, 114. *See also* Populuxe

Hip capitalism, 151–52, 172–74, 176–79, 181–82, 199

Hippie culture, 13, 234; community, 124, 149; dress, 39, 138, 140–41, 151, 164, 182, 191, 219; hip capitalism, 151–52, 171–77, 199; middle-class backgrounds of, 156–58, 171; politics, 168–71, 174–75, 206; secondhand clothing, 92, 148, 156, 175–77, 183, 186. *See also* The Cockettes; Elective poverty; The New Left; Underground media: newspapers

Hobo chic, 241. *See also* Galliano, John

Hoffman, Abbie, 152, 153, 173–76

Hogg, Ima, 76, 79

HOLC (Home Owners Loan Corporation), 97

Holiness movement, 25. *See also* The Salvation Army

Hollander, Anne, 57

Hollywood: avant-garde performers/artists, 194, 197; the Cockettes, 199, 202–3, 206; secondhand commerce, 81; vintage clothing, 149

Holmes, John Clellon, 161

Homosexual League of New York, 196

Horses (Smith), 210–11

Hostess parties/home sales, 94–95, 98, 104, 106. *See also* Avon Products; Tupperware, Inc.
Humphreys, Laud, 185
Hunter, George, 149

Immigrants, 3, 29, 65, 83, 97; assimilation of, 6, 19, 31–33; consumerism, 47–48, 51; flea markets, 55, 57, 71–74, 138; garment industry, 22, 24; informal/secondhand economies, 11, 17–18, 20, 22, 52–55, 57, 69–70, 237. *See also* Anti-Semitism; Yezierska, Anzia
Informal economies, 48, 53, 69–70, 91, 95, 118, 294n34
Isenberg, Alison, 3, 70
Italian: Americanization, 31–32; fashion, 48, 160, 167, 205; immigration, 29, 48; labor, 24. *See also* Schiaparelli, Elsa
IWLKV (I Was Lord Kitchener's Valet), 142, 147. *See also* London boutiques

Jackson, Kenneth T., 109–10
Jacobs, Marc, 217
Jagger, Mick, 142, 145, 147
James, Henry, 8, 17–18, 59, 120, 215, 239
James, Sylvester, 204–5
Jazz, 73, 142, 163
Jews, 59, 84–89, 125, 154, 161, 221; Chicago, 71–74; consumers, 19, 47–48; immigration, 7, 68, 70; New York City, 74–75; secondhand trades, 8, 17–18, 22, 25, 28–30, 66, 142, 159, 214, 237. *See also* Anti-Semitism; Brice, Fanny (Borach, Fania); *The Ragman* (comic)
Joans, Ted, 162. *See also* Beat Generation
Johnson, Joyce, 126, 162, 169. *See also* Beat Generation
Joplin, Janis, 12, 150–52, 171

Kawakubo, Rei, 218, 222
Keaton, Diane, 207
Keats, John, 100

Kennedy, John F., 119, 145, 154
Kerouac, Jack, 12, 125, 133, 152–53, 162–66, 186
Kesey, Ken, 119, 149
Keynes, John Maynard, 119
Keynesian economics, 92, 103, 105, 120
Kitsch, 14, 141, 192, 215, 222, 225–27, 231
Klein, Calvin, 217
Ku Klux Klan, 55

La Bohème (Murger), 155, 210
Ladies' Home Journal (magazine), 115, 132
LaGuardia, Fiorello, 52
Lake, Bambi, 202
Lauper, Cyndi, 224
Lauren, Ralph, 217
The Lavender Scare, 186
LCE (League for Civil Education), 188
Lead Belly, 232
Leave It to Beaver (1957–1963), 117
Lennon, John, 142, 147
Levi-Strauss, Claude, 14
Life (magazine), 132, 145, 164
Lipsitz, George, 200
Lomax, Alan, 232
London boutiques, 141–47, 173, 234
Lord & Taylor, 12, 122, 129, 131, 139, 140, 147, 233. *See also* Vintage clothing/dress
Ludlam, Charles, 185–86, 192, 197–99, 202–3, 301, 304–6

Macklemore, 242–43, 316
Macy's, 12, 24, 54, 102, 122, 129, 132, 188. *See also* Vintage clothing/dress
Mad Men, 13
Mailer, Norman, 163, 170, 174
Malcolm X, 119, 170
Manhattan: flea markets, 52–53, 57–59, 70, 74–75; Italian and Jewish communities, 24, 29. *See also* Greenwich Village
Mapplethorpe, Robert, 210–12
Marché aux Puces, 52, 58, 67–69, 81, 94, 139, 146. *See also* Paris, France
Marcuse, Herbert, 103
Marx, Karl, 103, 119

Mattachine Society, 191
Mau-Mauing the Flak Catchers (Wolfe), 284
Maxwell Street Market, 70–75, 81, 159. *See also* Jews: Chicago; Street peddling
McCarthy, Eugene, 112
McCarthyism, 109, 186
McClure, Michael, 164
McRobbie, Angela, 147–48
Mead, Emily Fogg, 19–20, 47
Methodists, 25, 27, 32, 41
Mexico, 163, 166, 236
MGM (Metro-Goldwyn-Mayer Studios, Inc), 202–3
Midler, Bette, 205
Miss Selfridge, 217
Missabu, Rumi, 191, 202, 205
Mister Rogers' Neighborhood (1968–2001), 232
Mod, 123, 140, 142–43
Molloy, John T., 220
Monk, Thelonious, 163
Montez, Maria, 194, 197–98, 208, 226
Montez, Mario, 194
Moreton, Bethany, 4
Morgan Memorial, 32–33
Moriarty, Dean, 166
Moroccan, 66, 125, 234
Morrisroe, Patricia, 211–12
MTV Unplugged (television program), 2, 231–32
Mudhoney, 216, 245
Murger, Henri, 155, 157
Museums, 78–79, 114, 119, 149

Nadja (Breton), 58, 262, 264, 306, 310
National Interstate and Defense Highways Act (or, Federal Aid Highway Act of 1956), 97
Nativism, 57, 86
Nevermind (1991), 215–16, 229–30
New Deal, 90, 232
The New Left, 124, 154, 168–73, 176, 296n70
New Wave, 224, 228, 229, 231

New York Dolls, 205, 225, 228–29, 231, 237
The New York Hat (1912), 45–47
Nightwood (Barnes), 66
Nirvana, 2–3, 215–16, 225, 228–30, 232
Nixon, Richard, 170, 175–76
Nostalgia: the Cockettes, 206; flea markets, 138; for preindustrial goods, 7, 35–36, 49, 55–56, 78, 81, 240; in the postwar era, 113, 116, 165, 166; retro, 219–20, 222, 224, 235; rock and roll styles, 228, 232; street peddling, 74; vintage clothing, 131, 140. *See also* *Nostalgie de la boue*
Nostalgie de la boue, 154–56

Obsolescence: fashion, 101, 120, 122, 133; postwar economy, 170, 225; second-hand shopping, 6, 15, 20, 51, 121
Oldham, Todd, 235. *See also* Grunge
O'Neill, Alistair, 141
Orientalism, 203–4
Ormsby-Gore, Jane, 143, 145–46, 151–52. *See also* Vintage clothing/dress
The Other America (Harrington), 153
Out of the Closet, 236
Out of the Closets: Sociology of Homosexual Liberation (Humphreys), 185

Packard, Vance, 12, 133, 170
Paglia, Camille, 210–11
Palace Theater, 200, 202–3
Paris, France: bohemianism, 155, 163; fashion, 82, 134, 144, 221, 241; flea markets, 52, 67–69, 91, 138–39, 146; surrealists, 58–60, 67; von Freytag-Loringhoven, Baroness Elsa, 66
Pawn shops/pawn broking, 35, 52, 59, 138, 168, 225; anti-Semitism, 6, 18, 21–22, 27, 71; consumers, 27–28, 48; Methodists, 27; rebranding of, 50. *See also* Bruno, Guido
Peacock revolution, 141, 144–45, 220
Peiss, Kathy, 21–22, 47
Philanthropic capitalism, 5–6, 18, 32–35, 48–51, 185, 239

Pickford, Mary, 45
Pierson, Kate, 224–26
Pittsburgh, Pennsylvania, 61, 71
Poindexter, Buster, 229
Poiret, Paul, 57, 82, 146–47
Popular Mechanic (magazine), 98, 117
Populuxe, 114, 118, 282
Port Huron Statement, 170
Portobello Road, London, 141–42, 145–46, 148, 151. *See also* Vintage clothing/dress
Postmodernity, 14–15, 148, 218, 221, 226, 237
Pound, Ezra, 65
Pre-Raphaelites, 38–39, 143, 169, 222
Psychedelicism, 200–201; the Cockettes, 14, 184–85, 191; dress/fashion, 148–52, 214, 218; drug culture, 119, 149, 200; music, 149–50
Punk, 207, 212; dress/fashion, 4, 232; music, 2, 8, 216, 225; secondhand clothing, 7–8, 14, 184, 186, 207, 220–21. *See also* Elective poverty; Smith, Patti
Purple Heart Thrift Store, 136, 188, 222
Pushcart pedddling. *See* Street peddling
Push-Cart Peddler's Trust, 74. *See also* Street peddling

Raccoon-skin coats, 86, 122–31, 142–47, 169, 221, 237. *See also* Collegians; Vintage clothing/dress
Racial segregation, 55, 97, 153. *See also* African Americans
Radical Chic (Wolfe), 135, 154, 171
The Ragman (comic), 214–15, 218, 231, 239
Rags (magazine), 177–80, 182
Rainey, Michael, 143
Ray, Man, 60, 65, 88
R.E.M., 227–28, 232
Retro, 15, 141, 148, 179, 217, 219–21
Rexroth, Kenneth, 164
Richards, Keith, 208
Ridiculous Theater, 185–86, 192–99, 205, 228

Riis, Jacob, 40
Rimbaud, Arthur, 199, 208, 211
Riot Grrrl, 216, 233
The Ritz, 23, 89
Rockefeller, John D., 34. *See also* Scientific giving
Rodgers, Daniel T., 237
Rosenthal, Irving, 199–201
Rosler, Martha, 92, 119
Roszak, Theodore, 124
Rothermel, John, 205
Rubin, Jerry, 173–74, 176. *See also* The Diggers
Rummage sales, 35–38, 49, 67, 94, 139, 160–61, 183; postwar suburbs, 101, 106–12. *See also* Charity fairs
Ryder, Japhy (character), 125, 166–67

Saint Laurent, Yves, 221
Saint-Ouen, France, 68
Salaula, 236
The Salvation Army: cleanliness, 30–31; early salvage programs, 19, 27, 30; elective poverty, 177–79, 182; gender, 26, 178; influence of, 33–34; Lower Still dress, 1, 2, 18, 39–42, 49–51, 84, 125, 158; postwar era, 98, 100, 108, 110; scientific giving, 34–35; thrift stores, 2, 9–10, 20–22, 49–51, 76, 78, 98, 136; uniforms, 24–26; voluntary consumers of, 127, 142, 168, 173, 188, 202, 211, 233, 238–39; World War II, 90–91. *See also* Evangeline Booth; Methodists; Philanthropic capitalism
Salvation Army Industrial Homes, 30, 34, 49
Salzman, Stanley and Sue, 126–29, 131–32
Samuel, Raphael, 15, 221
Sarria, José, 9, 14, 184, 186–88, 190, 192. *See also* Gay rights/liberation movement
Saturday Evening Post, (magazine), 17, 89, 128
Savers, Inc., 136, 236. *See also* Value Village
Schiaparelli, Elsa, 60, 63, 146
Schneider, Fred, 225, 228

Scientific giving, 20, 33–34
Seattle, 2, 215–16, 218, 242, 295, 311, 315
"Second Hand Rose" (Brice), 8, 57, 66, 81, 84–89, 142, 213, 237
Sélavy, Rrose (character), 97–99
Shubert, Jacob, Lee, and Sam, 83–84
Shulman, Alix Kates, 160, 209
Sinatra, Frank, 211
Singer, Isaac Bashevis, 213
SIRporium, 190, 236, 303
Six Gallery, 164, 195
Sloan, Alfred P., 96, 133
Smith, Jack, 14, 62, 184–86, 237; genderfuck, 201–3, 205, 208, 213, 225–26, 228; Ridiculous Theater, 192–200
Smith, Patti, 8, 14, 184, 186, 207–13. *See also* The boyfriend look; Genderfuck; Punk
SNCC (Student Non-Violent Coordinating Committee), 158–59, 174
Snyder, Gary, 164, 166–68, 175, 215
Society for Individual Rights (SIR), 188–90, 236
Sontag, Susan, 55, 67, 196–97
St. Vincent's Thrift Shop, 136, 168
Steal This Book (Hoffman), 179
Stipe, Michael, 227, 233
Stonewall Uprising, 187, 301n6
Stoumen, Sol, 186–87
Stoumen v. Reilly, 186–87
Strasser, Susan, 3
Street peddling, 107, 136; automobiles, 56; Chicago, 70–74; Jewish predominance in, 18, 29, 70, 268n70; Manhattan, New York City, 74–76. *See also* Immigrants; Informal economies; Jews
Streisand, Barbra, 213
Sub Pop (music label), 216
Sui, Anna, 235
Surrealism, 10, 53–55, 65; fashion, 60, 81, 146, 234; performance, 198–99, 224; secondhand objects, 57–59, 67, 164, 174, 194, 233. *See also* André Breton
Svengali, 61, 212
Swap meets. *See* Flea markets

Synthetic materials, 22, 38, 56, 143, 220; polyesters, 134–35

Tales of Manhattan (1942), 8–9, 215
Tavel, Ronald, 185, 192
Theater. *See* Broadway; Ridiculous Theater; Zentral Theater
Thoreau, Henry David, 163
Thrift: ideology of, 4; philanthropic capitalism, 19, 21, 31–33, 46–47; postwar suburbs, 98–100; voluntary secondhand dress, 131, 140, 155. *See also* Anticapitalism
"Thrift Shop" (Macklemore), 242–43
Thrift stores, 6, 78, 91–92, 96, 136–38; Americanization, 6, 10, 19, 27–32, 37, 51; avant-garde art, 58, 67, 184–85, 193, 215; Beat Generation, 164–69; gay right/liberation movement, 188, 190, 236; genderfuck, 200–206, 208–12; Great Depression, 80–81; postwar era, 100, 108, 110; scientific giving, 2, 10, 18–19, 27, 34–35; vintage clothing, 122, 129, 142, 149; World War II, 90–91. *See also* Anticapitalism; Charity shops; London boutiques; Philanthropic capitalism; *individual thrift store names*
Transvestism, 185–89, 192–94
Trilby (du Maurier), 60–61
Tupperware, Inc., 92, 94–95, 104–6, 118
Twiggy, 143

Underground media: art and cinema, 184–85, 192, 225; magazines, 177–78; newspapers, 172–74, 176–77, 242. *See also The Great Speckled Bird*; *Rags* (magazine); Ridiculous Theater; Smith, Jack
Unisex fashions, 144, 181, 184, 207, 220
United Citizens Peddlers' Association, 74. *See also* Street peddling
Urban Outfitters, 234–35, 242

Vaccaro, John, 185, 192, 197
Vadim, Roger, 212

Valentino, Rudolph, 128
Value Village, 136. *See also* Savers, Inc.
Van Der Zee, James, 128
Vanderbilt family, 41, 50
Vaudeville, 85, 89, 181, 183. *See also* Broadway
Veblen, Thorstein, 3, 12, 21, 39, 151
Vedder, Eddie, 216
Victorian clothing, 56; drag, 202; hippies, 140, 171, 174; London, 123, 125, 141–44; retro, 220–21, 229; San Francisco, 148–51. *See also* hippie culture Vintage clothing/dress
Victoriana, 59, 141–42, 149
Vietnam war, 12, 119, 147, 154, 170, 172, 174, 176, 214
Vintage clothing/dress, 5, 133, 135, 182, 240–42; consumers of, 15, 122–25, 143–44, 152, 235; dealers in, 122, 141, 146–47, 173, 233–34; genderfuck, 185, 202, 204; grunge, 216–17; guides/literature, 220–21; origins of the term, 12, 139–41; raccoon coats, 122, 129–31, 133. *See also* Collegians; Edwardian dress; London boutiques; Lord & Taylor; Macy's; Salzman, Stanley and Sue; Victorian clothing
Visions of Cody (Kerouac), 162
Vogue (magazine), 144–46, 172, 205, 216, 218
von Freytag-Loringhoven, Baron Leo, 177, 299
von Freytag-Loringhoven, Baroness Elsa, 10, 54, 71, 125, 193, 237, 240–41; as artist, 61–66; Berlin, 60–61; influence of, 82–84, 87–88. *See also* Dada

Wanamaker, John, 24, 49, 54, 63
Warhol, Andy, 62, 192–93, 197, 228
Waring, Jr., George E., 29–30
Waters, John, 192, 201–2, 205, 222, 225–26, 237
Webster's Westside Market, 77
Welch, Lew, 163
Welters, Linda, 163
Wesley, John, 25, 40
Whyte, William H., 98, 100, 103, 106, 132
Wilde, Oscar, 39, 209
Wilhelm, Mike, 150
Willard, Frances, 42
Wilson, Cindy, 224, 226
Wilson, Ricky, 227
Wise, Brownie, 104, 106
Wolfe, Allison, 233
Wolfe, Tom, 135, 154–56, 159, 171, 223
Wolman, Baron, 177–79
Woloson, Wendy, 3
Woodstock Festival, 151, 177, 242
World War II, 91–92, 99, 108–16
Worman, Martin, 206
Wylie, Philip, 116–17

Xenophobia, 9, 29, 31, 69, 83. *See also* Anti-Semitism; Immigrants

Yentl (character), 212
Yezierska, Anzia, 19, 47–48, 87, 260–61
Yippies, 173, 176, 185, 297–98

Zambia, 236
Zane (character), 160–61, 167, 209
Zentral Theater, 61, 83
Ziegfeld, Florenz, 57, 61, 83–86, 88, 185
Ziegfeld Follies, 57, 83, 85–86
Zoolander (2001), 241
Zoot suits, 126

www.ingramcontent.com/pod-product-compliance
Lightning Source LLC
Chambersburg PA
CBHW051207300426
44116CB00006B/465